The Adnominal Genitive
in the Pauline Corpus

Studies in Biblical Greek

D. A. Carson
General Editor

Vol. 19

The Studies in Biblical Greek series is part of the Peter Lang Humanities list.
Every volume is peer reviewed and meets
the highest quality standards for content and production.

PETER LANG
New York • Bern • Berlin
Brussels • Vienna • Oxford • Warsaw

Ghassan Elia Khalaf

The Adnominal Genitive in the Pauline Corpus

Edited by
J. William Johnston

PETER LANG
New York • Bern • Berlin
Brussels • Vienna • Oxford • Warsaw

Library of Congress Cataloging-in-Publication Data

Names: Khalaf, Ghassan Elia, author. | Johnston, J. William, editor.
Title: The adnominal genitive in the Pauline corpus / Ghassan Elia Khalaf;
edited by J. William Johnston.
Description: New York: Peter Lang, 2022.
Series: Studies in biblical Greek; vol. 19 | ISSN 0897-7828
Includes bibliographical references and index.
Identifiers: LCCN 2020021723 (print) | LCCN 2020021724 (ebook)
ISBN 978-1-4331-6886-4 (hardback)
ISBN 978-1-4331-6887-1 (ebook pdf) | ISBN 978-1-4331-6888-8 (epub)
Subjects: LCSH: Bible. Epistles of Paul—Language, style. | Greek language,
Biblical—Case grammar. | Greek language, Biblical—Syntax.
Classification: LCC BS2650.55 .K43 2022 (print) | LCC BS2650.55 (ebook) |
DDC 487/.4—dc23
LC record available at https://lccn.loc.gov/2020021723
LC ebook record available at https://lccn.loc.gov/2020021724
DOI 10.3726/b15568

Bibliographic information published by **Die Deutsche Nationalbibliothek.**
Die Deutsche Nationalbibliothek lists this publication in the "Deutsche
Nationalbibliografie"; detailed bibliographic data are available
on the Internet at http://dnb.d-nb.de/.

Table of Contents

Preface   xiii
Abbreviations   xv

Introduction   1
   The Adnominal Genitive   1
   Ongoing Debate   3
   A State of Dissatisfaction   4
   Defining the Goal   5
   Ablative and Genitive   6
   Basic Meaning   7
      Ablatival   7
      Possessive   8
      Restrictive   10
      Adjectival   10
      Definitional   12
   Nature of the Genitive   12
      Appurtenance   12
      Concatenation   13
      Adnominal Construction   13
      Propagation of Meanings   14

Ambiguity 14
Method 15
Basic Tools 16
Bibliography 17
Chapter One: The Pauline Corpus as a Model 19
Distinctive Style 20
Extensive Use of the Genitive 22
Frequent Genitive Clusters 23
Wide Range of Meanings 24
The Need for Careful Exegesis 24
Paul's Use of the Genitive Is Typical 25
Bibliography 25
Chapter Two: The Genitive in New Testament Grammars 27
G. B. Winer 28
A. Buttmann 30
S. G. Green 31
J. H. Moulton 32
A. T. Robertson 33
H. E. Dana and J. R. Mantey 35
F. Blass and A. Debrunner 36
M. Zerwick 37
C. F. D. Moule 38
Nigel Turner 39
J. A. Brooks and C. L. Winbery 40
S. E. Porter 42
R. A. Young 43
D. B. Wallace 44
Conclusion 46
Cumulative Outline of Usage 47
Principles for Interpretation 48
Bibliography 48
Chapter Three: The Semantics of Adnominal Genitives 51
Short History of Linguistic Theory 52
Rationalistic 53
Comparative-Historical 53
Structuralist 54
Transformational-Generative 55
From Dictionary to Meaning 55
Lexical 55

Grammatical 56
Syntactical 57
Semantic 57
The Genitive in the Era of Semantics 58
William L. Wonderly 59
Harold K. Moulton 60
Nida and Taber 60
Beekman and Callow 62
J. P. Louw 64
Conclusion 65
Bibliography 66
Chapter Four: Adnominal Two-Word Genitive Constructions 69
Introduction 69
Adnominal Genitive Meanings 71
Genitive of Definition 72
Possessive Genitive 72
Genitive of Relationship 75
Genitive of Identification 77
Genitive of Location 80
Genitive of Association 82
Genitive of Accordance 84
Ascription-Recipient Genitive (Ascribed-to Genitive) 85
Appositive (Epexegetic) Genitive 86
Adjectival Genitive 91
Descriptive Genitive 92
Qualitative Genitive 93
Hebrew Genitive 94
Attributed Genitive 101
Genitive of Manner 104
Objective Genitive 105
Pure (Accusative) Objective Genitive 105
Genitive of Advantage 106
Genitive of Destination 108
Genitive of Reference 110
Genitive of Derivation 112
Superlative Genitive 112
Subjective Genitive 114
Genitive of Source 115
Genitive of Origin 116

Genitive of Authorship 117
Genitive of Cause 118
Instrumental Genitive 119
Genitive of Resemblance 120
Ablatival Genitive 123
Genitive of Separation 124
The Partitive Genitive 126
Genitive of Comparison 127
Conclusion 128
Bibliography 129
Chapter Five: Adnominal Three-Word Genitive Constructions 135
The Grammatical Aspect 137
Structural Elements 137
Three-Word Genitives Connected by καί 140
The Semantic Aspect 142
Sentence Approach 142
Subject-Predicate Approach 142
Inter-relational Approach 143
Meanings of the Three-Word Genitive 144
Cumulative Genitive 144
Adjectival Genitive 146
Multivalent Functions of the Middle Word 151
Appendix: List of Three-Word Genitive Constructions 153
Bibliography 159
Chapter Six: Adnominal Four-Word Genitive Constructions 161
Structural Elements 161
Pure Nouns 161
Pronoun Involved 162
Four-Word Genitives Connected by καί 162
The OT Roots of Paul's Genitive Clusters 166
Meanings of the Four-Word Genitive 169
Cumulative Genitive 170
Epexegetical Genitive 171
Adjectival Genitive 172
Appendix: List of Four-, Five-, and Six-Word Genitives 175
List of Four-Word Genitives in Paul 176
List of Four-Word Genitives in the NT 176
Bibliography 177

Chapter Seven: Interpretive Principles 179
  Syntactical Aspects of the Genitive 179
    The Article 179
    Article as Substantive 180
  Emphatic Position of the *Nomen Rectum* 182
    Article + Article$_g$ + N$_g$ + N 183
    Article + N$_g$ + N 183
    Article + N$_g$ (Pronoun) + N 183
    N$_g$ (Pronoun) + Article + N 184
    N$_g$ + N 184
    N$_g$ (Pronoun) + N 184
    Article + N$_g$ + N 185
    Prepositions 185
  Conjunctions in Genitive Constructions 186
  Exegetical Principles for Genitive Interpretation 191
    Relationships Between Substantives 192
    Figures of Speech 193
    Verbal Head Nouns 195
    Immediate Context 197
    Wider Context 199
    Same Wording but Different Meanings 199
    Parallel Genitive Expressions 200
    Different Passages by the Same Author 201
    Genitive and Non-genitive Expressions 203
    Authorial Usage 204
    Beneath the Surface 205
    Septuagintal Influence 206
    Contemporary Texts 206
  Genitive in Concatenation 209
    History of Interpretation 209
    Interpretive Principles 211
    Syntactical Categories to Add 213
    Multivalence of the Middle Word 214
    The Four-Word Genitive 214
    Additional Categories for the Four-Word Genitive 215
  Conclusion 215
  Bibliography 216

Chapter Eight: Conclusion 219

    Summaries 219

        Problematic Genitive Interpretation 219

        Method 220

        Traditional Grammars 220

        Semantics and Structuralism 220

        Transformational Grammar 221

    Levels of Investigation 221

        Meaning 222

        Categorization 222

        Genitives in Concatenation 222

        Criteria for Genitive Interpretation 223

    Challenges and Contributions 224

        Confirmation of Existing Meanings 225

        Designation of New Meanings 227

        Concatenate Genitive Constructions 228

    Bibliography 229

Index 231

Preface

This volume in the Studies in Biblical Greek series is a revision of the Ghassan Khalaf's doctoral dissertation ("The Syntactical Meanings of the Adnominal Genitive Constructions in the Pauline Corpus") presented in 2001 to the Evangelical Theological Faculty of Heverlee (Leuven), Belgium. Regrettably, Ghassan Khalaf passed into the presence of the Lord Jesus before he could complete the manuscript.

Khalaf accomplished the work of identifying NT adnominal genitive constructions (and counting the words in each) using paper editions and some computer assistance. I have verified this work using Logos Bible Software. I have also worked through the data by hand in NA^{28}, following in his footsteps. I have a real sense of the lofty task Ghassan Khalaf set for himself in this enterprise.

But he is no stranger to heavy lifting. Khalaf produced an Arabic-Greek concordance during Lebanon's civil war without the aid of computers or typesetting software. He is known in the Arabic-speaking world for this landmark accomplishment, and for years of service to the world of theological education in Lebanon and beyond. He was actively engaged in producing a fresh NT translation into Arabic up until the day he departed this life. It is my hope that the wider world of scholarship will appreciate the work Ghassan Khalaf left behind, and that it will be a help to those who have struggled to take hold of the slippery genitive case.

My heartfelt thanks are due to several people. Those thanks begin with gratitude to Smyrna Khalaf, Ghassan's daughter, for entrusting me with this part of her father's legacy. It was an honor to meet Smyrna and her family in Beirut and to hear about Ghassan Khalaf's life and work. Thanks are also due to Daniel B. Wallace, my mentor and colleague, who put my name forward to Smyrna Khalaf to carry this project forward. I still have fond memories of a retreat I went on as a graduate student intern with Dr. Wallace and several fellow interns to discuss—of all things—the genitive case. I am also grateful for D. A. Carson's comments and correspondence with Khalaf and Wallace, which have proved very helpful in updating the manuscript.

It is a daunting task to undertake editing the work of another scholar when he is no longer available for consultation. I have endeavored throughout the work to retain Khalaf's voice as I worked to fill in the lacunae in the manuscript he had begun to expand. I updated the text by adding interactions with newer works in some cases and more recent editions in others. Unless otherwise indicated, translations are Ghassan Khalaf's or my own. Most often, these translations are simple functional equivalents given alongside an example to be discussed. It is truly an honor to have joined Ghassan Khalaf in this study. It is my profound hope that he would have been pleased to see the finished product.

J. William Johnston
17 June 2020

Abbreviations

For biblical and related primary source literature, consult the standard abbreviations of *The SBL Handbook of Style: For Biblical Studies and Related Disciplines,* ed. Billie Jean Collins, Bob Buller, and John F. Kutsko, 2nd ed. (Atlanta: SBL Press, 2014), §8.3 pp. 124–71.

AB	Anchor [Yale] Bible
AYBRL	Anchor Yale Bible Reference Library
BBR	*Bulletin of Biblical Research*
BDAG	Bauer, Walter. *A Greek-English Lexicon of the New Testament and Other Early Christian Literature*. 3rd ed., revised and edited by Frederick W. Danker. Chicago: University of Chicago Press, 2000.
BDF	Blass, Friedrich and Albert Debrunner. *A Greek Grammar of the New Testament and Other Early Christian Literature*. Translated by Robert Walter Funk. Chicago: University of Chicago Press, 1961.
BDR	Blass, Friedrich and Albert Debrunner. *Grammatik des neutestamentlichen Griechisch*. Edited by Friedrich Rehkopf. 18th ed. Göttingen: Vandenhoeck & Ruprecht, 2001.
Beekman-Callow	Beekman, John and John Callow. *Translating the Word of God*. Grand Rapids: Zondervan, 1974.

Brooks-Winbery	Brooks, James A. and Carlton L. Winbery. *Syntax of New Testament Greek.* Lanham, MD: University Press of America, 1979.
Buttmann, *Grammar*	Buttmann, Alexander. *A Grammar of the New Testament Greek.* Translated by J. H. Thayer. Andover: Draper, 1880.
BSac	*Bibliotheca Sacra*
CSB	Christian Standard Bible
Dana-Mantey	Dana, H. E. and Julius R. Mantey. *A Manual Grammar of the Greek New Testament.* New York: Macmillan, 1927. Reprint, 1957.
EEC	Evangelical Exegetical Commentary
ESV	English Standard Version
GNT	Good News Translation
GTJ	*Grace Theological Journal*
HALOT	*The Hebrew and Aramaic Lexicon of the Old Testament.* Ludwig Koehler, Walter Baumgartner, and Johann J. Stamm. Translated and edited under the supervision of Mervyn E. J. Richardson. 5 vols. Leiden: Brill, 1994–2000.
HCSB	Holman Christian Standard Bible
Herm. Mand.	Shepherd of Hermas, Mandates
HFT	Helps for Translators
Householder, *Apollonius*	Householder, Fred W. *The Syntax of Apollonius Dyscolus.* Amsterdam Studies in the Theory and History of Linguistic Science Series Studies in the History of Linguistics 3/23. Amsterdam: Benjamins, 1981.
ICC	International Critical Commentary
JBL	*Journal of Biblical Literature*
JGL	*Journal of Greek Linguistics*
JLL	*Journal of Latin Linguistics*
JLSM	Janua linguarum, Series minor
JSNT	*Journal for the Study of the New Testament*
JSNTSS	Journal for the Study of the New Testament Supplement Series

KJV	King James Version
LB	The Living Bible
LN	Louw, Johannes P. and Eugene Albert Nida. *Greek-English Lexicon of the New Testament: Based on Semantic Domains.* 2nd ed. New York: United Bible Societies, 1996.
LUT	*Die Bibel nach Martin Luthers Übersetzung.* Stuttgart: Deutsche Bibelgesellschaft, 2017.
LXX	Septuagint
MHT$_1$	Moulton, J. H. *A Grammar of New Testament Greek.* 4 vols. Edinburgh: T. & T. Clark, 1908–76. Vol. 1 (1908): *Prolegomena*, by J. H. Moulton.
MHT$_2$	Moulton, J. H. *A Grammar of New Testament Greek.* 4 vols. Edinburgh: T. & T. Clark, 1908–76. Vol. 2 (1929): *Accidence and Word Formation*, by W. F. Howard.
MHT$_3$	Moulton, J. H. *A Grammar of New Testament Greek.* 4 vols. Edinburgh: T. & T. Clark, 1908–76. Vol. 3 (1963): *Syntax*, by Nigel Turner.
MHT$_4$	Moulton, J. H. *A Grammar of New Testament Greek.* 4 vols. Edinburgh: T. & T. Clark, 1908–76. Vol. 4 (1976): *Style*, by Nigel Turner.
MNTC	Moffat New Testament Commentary
Moule, *Idiom Book*	Moule, C. F. D. *An Idiom Book of New Testament Greek.* 2nd ed. Cambridge: Cambridge University Press, 1959.
N	(head) Noun or *nomen regens*
NA^{28}	Aland, Barbara et al., eds. *Novum Testamentum Graece.* 28th rev. ed., ed. Holger Strutwolf. Stuttgart: Deutsche Bibelgesellschaft, 2012.
NAC	New American Commentary
NEB	New English Bible
NET	New English Translation
NETS	*New English Translation of the Septuagint.* Edited by Albert Pietersma and Benjamin G. Wright. Oxford: Oxford University Press, 2007.
N$_g$	Noun [in the] g[enitive], a dependent genitive or *nomen rectum*
NIGTC	New International Greek Testament Commentary
NIV	New International Version

NIV84	New International Version, 1984.
NJB	New Jerusalem Bible
NKJV	New King James Version
NRSV	New Revised Standard Version
NT	New Testament
NTS	New Testament Studies
OT	Old Testament
P$_g$	Pronoun (in the genitive case)
PNTC	Pillar New Testament Commentary
Porter, *Idioms*	Porter, Stanley E. *Idioms of the Greek New Testament.* 2nd ed. Biblical Languages—Greek 2. Sheffield: JSOT Press, 1994.
REB	Revised English Bible
Robertson, *Grammar*	Robertson, A. T. *A Grammar of the Greek New Testament in the Light of Historical Research.* 4th ed. New York: Hodder & Stoughton, 1923.
RSV	Revised Standard Version
SNTG	Studies in New Testament Greek
SNTSMS	Society for New Testament Studies Monograph Series
SPIB	Scripta Pontificii Instituti Biblici
TDNT	*Theological Dictionary of the New Testament.* Edited by G. Kittel and G. Friedrich. Translated by Geoffrey W. Bromiley. 10 vols. Grand Rapids: Eerdmans, 1964–76.
TEV	Today's English Version
TNK	*TANAKH: A New Translation of the Holy Scriptures according to the Traditional Hebrew Text.* Philadelphia: Jewish Publication Society, 1985
TNTC	Tyndale New Testament Commentaries
TOB	Traduction œcuménique de la Bible
TR	*Textus Receptus*
TrinJ	*Trinity Journal*
UBSHS	United Bible Society Handbook Series
Wallace, *ExSyn*	Wallace, Daniel B. *Greek Grammar Beyond the Basics: An Exegetical Syntax of the New Testament.* Grand Rapids: Zondervan, 1996.
Wallace, *Sharp's Canon*	Wallace, Daniel B. *Granville Sharp's Canon and Its Kin: Semantics and Significance.* Studies in Biblical Greek 14. New York: Lang, 2009.

WB	Barclay, William. *The New Testament: A New Translation*. London: Collins, 1969. Reprint, Louisville, KY: Westminster John Knox, 1999.
Winer, *Grammar*	Winer, Georg Benedikt. *A Treatise on the Grammar of New Testament New Testament Greek: Regarded as a Sure Basis for New Testament Exegesis*. Translated by W. F. Moulton. 3rd ed. Edinburgh: T&T Clark, 1882.
WPC	Westminster Pelican Commentaries
Zerwick, *Biblical Greek*	Zerwick, Maximillian. *Biblical Greek: Illustrated by Examples*. Translated by Joseph Smith. Scripta Pontificii Instituti Biblici 114. Rome: Pontifical Biblical Institute, 1963.

Introduction

The Adnominal Genitive

The present work will investigate what F. Blass and A. Debrunner call "the adnominal genitive,"[1] and A. T. Robertson calls "the genitive with substantives."[2] To qualify as an adnominal genitive, a construction must have a nominal related to other nominals via the genitive case. Thus, this study omits all other genitive case uses, such as constructions involving participles, infinitives, verbs, adverbs, and prepositions. The uses of the genitive case in this latter category of construction are much less difficult to construe. The adnominal genitive has been chosen because of the interpretive challenges this kind of genitive creates. The variety of nuances that may arise from linking two or more nouns in a genitive construction is immeasurable, especially when those nouns have symbolic or metaphorical reference.

The genitive case, as a whole, is an enormous and diversified subject for study. It involves a very long history. The genitive originated in the primitive periods of the formation of the Greek language, passing to the Greek language from Sanskrit. It was used in the classical and Hellenistic periods, and has survived into modern

---

1 BDF §§162–68 pp. 89–93. The term comes from §4.A. p. 89.
2 Robertson, *Grammar*, 495.

usage in Modern Greek. The dative case, in comparison, has disappeared from Modern Greek.[3]

The genitive is used extensively in the NT. A statistical study of the case forms in the New Testament reveals that in terms of frequency the genitive case's forms come after the nominative and the accusative. Grammarian Daniel B. Wallace informs us that the genitive case occurs 19,633 times in the New Testament—a quarter of the total number of the occurrences of all case forms: 7681 nouns, 4986 pronouns, 5028 articles, 743 participles, and 1195 adjectives.[4]

Understanding the adnominal genitive can be seen as a critical need for exegesis because the relationship between the "head" noun (*nomen regens*) and the noun in the genitive (*nomen rectum*)[5] often requires disambiguation. No detailed statistical survey has yet been done on adnominal genitive constructions in the NT. In preparation for this study, I [Ghassan Khalaf] surveyed the Pauline corpus and calculated approximately 1800 two-word adnominal genitive constructions and two hundred adnominal genitives in clusters. It is hoped this survey will lay the groundwork for the same kind of studies that will eventually cover the whole NT.

No comprehensive study of the adnominal genitive in the New Testament has been undertaken. Readers of the standard grammatical tools for the NT know these books' treatment consists of *introductory* analyses of the syntax of the genitive. Distinguished grammarians, such as G. B. Winer, J. H. Moulton, A. T. Robertson, F. Blass and A. Debrunner, M. Zerwick, C. F. D. Moule, N. Turner, S. E. Porter, and D. B. Wallace have each made their contribution. The works of those scholars form the basis of many other derivative Greek grammars, but all their analyses of the genitive case—as helpful and insightful as they are—remain limited in scope.[6]

Several decades passed during the twentieth century without any new major investigation of the genitive case in the NT. All that was available about the genitive had been contained in the traditional NT grammars. A new development, however, occurred in the 1960s. A renewed interest in the genitive arose, driven

---

3   Robertson, *Grammar*, 535. This was a trend already observable in Byzantine-era papyri (so Joanne Vera Stolk, "Dative by Genitive Replacement in the Greek Language of the Papyri: A Diachronic Account of Case Semantics," *JGL* 15.1 (2015): 91–121, doi:10.1163/15699846-01501001).

4   According to Wallace (*ExSyn*, 35, 37), the total number of all the cases' forms in the New Testament is 79,846. The nominative forms occur 24,618 times, that is 31% of the total number. The genitives are 19,633 (25%). The datives are 12,173 (15%). The accusatives are 23,105 (29%).

5   Wallace (*ExSyn*, 74–55) notes the traditional Latin terms (*nomen regens* = head noun; *nomen rectum* = dependent genitive) to describe the constituents as well as the abbreviated description N-N$_g$.

6   Since grammars treat all the parts of speech in limited space, it stands to reason that discussion of case usage cannot be comprehensive.

mainly by issues raised by modern linguistic theories and the need for the refinement of Bible translations.

It is difficult to find *sustained* discussions of adnominal genitive constructions. The works of Harold K. Moulton, Eugene A. Nida and Charles R. Taber, John Beekman and John Callow, Stanley E. Porter and Johannes P. Louw contain the only treatments of the adnominal genitive in the NT that have been done outside the standard grammars.[7]

One of the most important of the recent studies of the genitive case in the NT appears in the work of D. B. Wallace.[8] Wallace utilizes almost all the genitive studies that have been done before him to the date of the release of his grammar in 1996. Yet, due to the inherent limitations of the reference grammar format, his treatment of the adnominal genitive syntax (especially the genitive in concatenations) cannot be comprehensive.

The need for thorough study of all the uses and kinds of adnominal genitives still exists. There is still no treatment of the subject that can be described as comprehensive. This work hopes to begin the task by undertaking a discussion of the usage of the adnominal genitive in the Pauline corpus.

Ongoing Debate

Some genitive constructions still receive intense scrutiny. For example, many scholars continue to debate the meaning of the genitive expression πίστις Χριστοῦ used by Paul (e.g., Rom 3:22, 26; 5:1; Gal 2:16; 3:22; Phil 3:9). Investigations concerning πίστις Χριστοῦ continue to appear in print as further proof of the need of continual study in the field of the genitive case.[9]

---

7 Harold K. Moulton, "Of," *Bible Translator* 19.1 (1968): 18–25, doi:10.1177/000608446801900105; Eugene A. Nida and Charles R. Taber, *The Theory and Practice of Translation*, HFT 8 (Leiden: Brill, 1969; repr., 1982), 35–55; Johannes P. Louw, *Semantics of New Testament Greek* (Atlanta: Scholars Press, 1982), 77–89; Stanley E. Porter, "The Adjectival Attributive Genitive in the New Testament: A Grammatical Study," *TrinJ* 4.1 (1983): 3–17. Beekman-Callow, 249–66, 358–62.

8 Wallace, *ExSyn*, 72–136.

9 The vast array of secondary literature is certainly impossible to cover comprehensively. A recent collection of essays such as *The Faith of Jesus Christ: Exegetical, Biblical, and Theological Studies*, ed. Michael F. Bird and Preston M. Sprinkle (Peabody, MA: Hendrickson, 2010), or commentaries such as those by Joseph A. Fitzmyer, *Romans: A New Translation with Introduction and Commentary*, AB 33 (New York: Doubleday, 1993), 354–59; Robert Jewett, with the assistance of Roy David Kotansky, *Romans: A Commentary*, ed. Eldon Jay Epp, Hermeneia (Minneapolis: Fortress, 2007),

Heated debate also surrounds phrases such as τὰ ὑστερήματα τῶν θλίψεων τοῦ Χριστοῦ (*the things lacking of the afflictions of Christ* Col 1:24), which has bewildered commentators. What does Paul mean by τῶν θλίψεων τοῦ Χριστοῦ? Is it the afflictions *of* Christ (subjective genitive) or Paul's afflictions *for* Christ (genitive of advantage)?[10] Another example is found in Phil 1:27: τῇ πίστει τοῦ εὐαγγελίου *the faith of the Gospel*. Although the phrase is simple, debates continue about whether the genitive is descriptive, objective, subjective, or appositive.[11] Likewise, the phrase θανάτου δὲ σταυροῦ *death of the cross* in Phil 2:8. What does the genitive mean? Is it a genitive of location, or means, or manner, or identification? One other difficult adnominal genitive construction is ἀπὸ κυρίου πνεύματος (2 Cor 3:18). Margaret Thrall offers seven different possible meanings for this phrase.[12] All these examples implicitly argue that adnominal genitive constructions need a careful treatment in order to decode their meanings.

There is also an important feature of genitive usage grammarians have only touched on briefly—the use of the genitive in clusters. The concern of scholars has been mainly concentrated upon the two-word adnominal genitive constructions, so that no careful investigation has been done into the three-word and four-word genitive constructions. This area of genitive constructions deserves much attention and deeper investigation.

A State of Dissatisfaction

Comparing modern with traditional Greek grammars reveals no significant development in grammatical studies. Modern grammars have followed the traditional pattern of methods in both form and content, with only slight revision here or an improvement there. Some scholars have expressed dissatisfaction with the present state of grammatical studies of the genitive case and the science of grammar in general. D. A. Carson's observations—though made about a quarter-century ago—still ring true:

along with Fitzmyer's general bibliography, testify amply to the quantity of discussion devoted to this *crux interpretum*.

10   Wilhelm Michaelis (*TDNT* 5:933 s.v. πάθημα) sees the afflictions of Christ as the afflictions of Paul *for* Christ.

11   See Richard R. Melick, Jr., *Philippians, Colossians, Philemon*, NAC 32 (Nashville: Broadman, 1991), 90.

12   Margaret E. Thrall, *A Critical and Exegetical Commentary on the Second Epistle of the Corinthians*, 2 vols., ICC (London: T&T Clark, 1994), 1:287. See Chapter Seven under the heading *Wider Context* for a more complete discussion.

Many are the students who has looked up every instance of ἐκκλησία (*ekklēsia*) in the New Testament and drawn some questionable conclusions; but how many have looked up every instance of the genitive absolute in the New Testament, performed an inductive study, and drawn questionable conclusions? Until very recently, such a list could be compiled only by reading through the Greek New Testament and noting every instance; therefore *hundreds of common constructions have never been subjected to the inductive scrutiny* which words have undergone. Second, grammatical analysis has not been popular in the last few decades of biblical study. Far more time and energy have been devoted to lexical semantics than to grammar. *The result is a broad assumption that many grammatical questions are closed, when in fact they are not.*[13]

Classical philologist Lars Rydbeck complained in 1975 that, "research into post-classical Greek in general and NT Greek in particular has come almost to a stand-still."[14] Though today "standstill" would be an overstatement, there is still much room for expansion of research.

In particular, John Beekman and John Callow recognize the need for the systematic study of the genitive case and the development of a method for understanding its meaning.

Until a thorough and exhaustive study of the thousands of genitive constructions found in the New Testament is made available to the translator, it is obviously essential that he have available to him some systematic method …. This, it would seem, would be an appropriate subject for a dissertation, which could then be popularized and made available to translators, rendering them an invaluable service.[15]

This book is an answer to their challenge: a fresh and deeper investigation into the syntax and meaning of adnominal genitive constructions is still needed.

Defining the Goal

The first question that comes to mind when a reader of the NT encounters an adnominal genitive is, "What does it mean?" So, to answer the ultimate question, then, one must first ask "What principles of analysis will enable successful disambiguation of genitive constructions?" These two basic questions constitute the goal of the present work.

---

13   D. A. Carson, *Exegetical Fallacies*, 2nd ed. (Grand Rapids: Baker, 1996), 65–66. [emphasis added]
14   Lars Rydbeck, "What Happened to New Testament Greek Grammar after Albert Debrunner?," *NTS* 21.3 (1975): 424.
15   Beekman-Callow, 251.

The ambiguity of genitive case usage lies in its nature. The genitive case is basically "the specifying case ... the case of appurtenance."[16] It is a noun + noun case or a substantive added to another substantive.[17] Relating one noun to (an)other noun(s) without using a verb or a preposition generates ambiguity, hence the dilemma of the interpreters when they encounter genitive constructions.

Ablative and Genitive

It will be helpful to note that the starting perspective of the present work is the five-case system. The arguments for seeing the genitive as one of eight cases (Robertson) or as one of five cases (Wallace) have been sufficiently engaged in other works. As it relates to the present study, the question is (as Wallace puts it) whether case is a question of *function* or *form*.[18] For the five-case system the genitive has distinct case forms; for the eight-case system the ablative and genitive share the same forms. It is best to see the ablative *functions* as a subset of genitive case functions. Our study, then, will draw on the adnominal genitive forms.

Scholars disagree about the number of Greek cases that are used under the static five forms, or inflections. Some, such as A. T. Robertson, with their comparative-historical approach, consider the five basic forms have eight functions, and thus eight cases,[19] while some other grammarians like J. H. Moulton with their descriptive approach believe that the five forms have only five functions; other functions have disappeared.[20]

The eight case grammarians rely on syntactical categories rather than inflections, as noted by Porter:

> Their argument rests on two criteria. First is the supposition that Greek originally had ablative, locative and instrumental case forms. Second is their supposed ability to differentiate legitimate functions of these cases ... Semantic or functional criteria provide a dubious argument for eight cases, since by this standard one might well cite a far larger number of cases than eight .... *Formal synchronic criteria (i.e. treatment of the Greek language as used during the Hellenistic period, especially as it is found in the Greek of the NT) dictate that analysis begin with at most five cases.*[21]

---

16 Robertson, *Grammar*, 493.
17 Or, as Zerwick puts it, "the appurtenance of one notion to another" (Zerwick, *Biblical Greek* §39 p.14).
18 Wallace, *ExSyn*, 32.
19 See Robertson, *Grammar*, 446–49.
20 See MHT₁, 60–61.
21 Porter, *Idioms*, 81. [emphasis his]

Wesley Perschbacher observes a practical reason for adopting the five-case system. He says, "Of even greater practical significance is the fact that virtually all lexicons, concordances, and analytical helps follow the five-case system."[22] This work follows the descriptive approach. The five inflections express five cases. Accordingly, there is no separate consideration of an "ablative" case.

Basic Meaning

Determining the basic meaning of the genitive case is an important factor in understanding its functions in diverse applications. Some grammarians consider it to be ablatival. Some regard it as possessive. Others believe that it is adjectival. Still others say it is definitive and reduce the adjectival element.

Disagreements abound over what basic sense of the genitive case—if one indeed can be found—might be. This putative basic sense should be useful in explaining the origin of the other semantic values the genitive case covers. A wide range of suggestions for the genitive's basic meaning appear in the literature, but among these are: possessive,[23] ablatival,[24] adjectival,[25] and restrictive.[26] Even if some of these basic ground rules for genitive case usage can be settled, there still remains the task of describing and distinguishing the uses of the genitive using one or a combination of those starting points. Porter wryly observes, "The number of classificatory schemes of the genitive are almost as many as the various classifications themselves."[27]

Ablatival

Winer lists a variety of meanings for the genitive, but as for the basic meaning he says, "The genitive is unquestionably the *whence-case*, the case of *proceeding from* or

---

22 Wesley J. Perschbacher, *New Testament Greek Syntax: An Illustrated Manual* (Chicago: Moody Press, 1995), viii.

23 See Kiki Nikiforidou, "The Meanings of the Genitive: A Case Study in Semantic Structure and Semantic Change," *Cognitive Linguistics* 2.2 (1991): 149–205, https://www.degruyter.com/view/j/cogl.1991.2.issue-2/issue-files/cogl.1991.2.issue-2.xml. See below for a brief interaction with Nikiforidou. See also Wallace's comment (*ExSyn*, 75n6).

24 See Winer, *Grammar*, 230.

25 William Douglas Chamberlain, *An Exegetical Grammar of the Greek New Testament* (New York: Macmillan, 1941; repr., Grand Rapids: Baker, 1979), 29.

26 Porter, *Idioms*, 92.

27 Porter, *Idioms*, 92.

out of."[28] Green follows Winer's position and states that "The Genitive Case primarily signifies *motion from,* answering to the question, *whence?* From this general meaning arise many modifications."[29] By this definition of the genitive Winer and Green restrict its meaning to ablatival, which, as we will see (Chapter Two) is usually considered one of the rarer genitive usages.

Possessive

The possessive is a universally recognized function of the genitive case, but leading NT grammars do not consider the possessive as the basic meaning of the genitive. Kiki Nikiforidou, however, has defended the possessive as a unifying meaning of the genitive.[30]

Nikiforidou would likely take grammarians like Winer (see Chapter Two) to task for trying "to postulate an abstract, general function for the genitive, meant to cover all of the manifested uses,"[31] because the abstraction is difficult to sustain. On the other hand, she reacts to the method of Greek grammarians "to divide the meanings into sub-groupings, each containing meanings which in the author's view are more closely related to each other than to the other groups."[32] Instead, she points to *structured polysemy,* by which is meant that there is a "nonaccidental grouping of meanings,"[33] Nikiforidou examines genitive semantics in Greek, Latin, French, and English in diachronic fashion. Her diachronic approach explores "what kinds of meanings can develop regularly out of what kinds."[34] So, the reasonable starting point for Nikiforidou is the idea that there are natural and somewhat explainable paths for meanings to develop over time.

Though her argument is that the possessive sense of the genitive is the most general and pervasive sense of the case, she does not mean "possessive" in the strictest sense. "The general meaning," she says, "is not that of grammatical dependency but rather 'there exists a relationship' instruction .... the genitive can be used to express absolutely any relationship with respect to the modified head noun."[35] Domain mapping is a key part of her analytical approach, in which

---

28 Winer, *Grammar,* 230.
29 Samuel G. Green, *Handbook to the Grammar of the Greek Testament,* rev. and imp. ed. (New York: Revell, 1904), 207.
30 Nikiforidou, "Genitive," 149–205.
31 Nikiforidou, "Genitive," 156.
32 Nikiforidou, "Genitive," 155.
33 Nikiforidou, "Genitive," 150.
34 Nikiforidou, "Genitive," 152.
35 Nikiforidou, "Genitive," 157.

metaphor and extension of meaning are the basis for explaining the relationship between senses of the genitive case. The principle works independent of case (since we are talking about semantics). So, for instance, "She's GOT arms and legs—let her do it herself." The relationship of possessor/possessions maps to whole/parts, thus "parts are possessions."[36]

On the subjective genitive, Nikiforidou notes helpfully, "what is expressed by the genitive freely and productively is the experiencer, with the head noun denoting such things as feelings, moods, dispositions, etc."[37] This is traced from possession in the sense that "experiencers are possessors."[38] E.g., τὸν πόλεμον τῶν Πελοποννησίων καὶ Ἀθηναίων (Thucydides, *Peloponnesian War* 1.1), *the war of* [i.e., "fought by"] *the Peloponnesians and the Athenians*. So, the ideas of agent (subjective genitive) / patient, experiencer (objective genitive) are part and parcel of this possessive idea. Also of note here is the distinction between partitive genitive and "alienable and inalienable possession,"[39] which traditional NT grammars neglect in this connection. Wallace summarizes well when he says that Nikiforidou "points out how the various uses evolved into notions that ultimately were far removed from the thought of possession."[40]

The possessive meaning could be the basic meaning of the genitive on the grounds that human beings when they needed to identify their possessions such as house, horse and knife, originally used a genitive like "the house of mine, or the house of the chief." Similarly, when they wanted to identify a relationship they used a genitive like "the wife of mine, the child of the carpenter," or "the brother of them."[41] It is reasonable to conclude that identifying possession and relationship may have been the original meaning of the genitive and stood behind the development of the diversity of later genitive meanings. On the other hand, Moulton claims, from a sampling of a NT few chapters, that the examples of "clear" (without indication of what this means) possessive usage of the genitive are not very common in the NT and less so in the Pauline Epistles. This leads Moulton to say these data strike "an immediate blow at the assumption that the genitive is mainly possessive."[42] This is hardly an argument against the prominence of this sense, though. The *Lexham Syntactic Greek New Testament* database classifies

36 Nikiforidou, "Genitive," 170.
37 Nikiforidou, "Genitive," 177.
38 Nikiforidou, "Genitive," 177.
39 Nikiforidou, "Genitive," 160.
40 Wallace, *ExSyn*, 75n6; Something he regards as a "plausible argument" (77n15).
41 Robertson (Robertson, *Grammar*, 493) says that the genitive of relationship is really "the possessive genitive of a special application."
42 Moulton, "Of," 19.

2,679 forms in the NT as "possessive genitive," 605 of them in the Pauline epistles. By way of contrast, the number of "attributive genitive" forms in the NT is listed as 329.[43] Of course, scholars will argue over the classifications of individual forms—especially the genitive—but at least there is a quantifiable number available.

Restrictive

Some scholars consider the genitive's main function to be limitation or restriction. Brooks and Winbery briefly say that the genitive "limits the meaning and application of a substantive."[44] Porter expands Louw's formula that both the headword and its adjunct are restrictive by saying, "the item restricted might be that which is placed in the genitive case, or the item in the genitive case might restrict something else. In either instance *the essential semantic feature of the genitive case is restriction.*"[45]

Dana and Mantey note the restrictive idea of the genitive is like the accusative, "But the genitive limits as to kind, while the accusative limits as to extent."[46] Wallace helpfully clarifies the nature of this limitation: "another way to put this is that the genitive limits as to *quality* while the accusative limits as to *quantity*. The genitive is usually related to a noun while the accusative is usually related to a verb."[47]

In relation to verbs, Moule calls the relationship between the genitive and the accusative a "disputed territory" where distinction in some cases is impossible.[48] This accusative function of the genitive can be clearly seen in categories like subjective and objective genitive. In conclusion, then, one could say that limitation is the *technical* aspect of the genitive while definition is the *syntactical* aspect.

Adjectival

Robertson, however, defends the specifying element as the basic meaning of the genitive. He analyzes the genitive case's name etymologically:

---

43 *The Lexham Syntactic Greek New Testament* [software], ed. Albert L Lukaszewski and Mark Dubis (Bellingham, WA: Logos Bible Software, 2009). [Version 0.9]

44 Brooks-Winbery 7–8.

45 Porter, *Idioms*, 92.

46 Dana-Mantey, 73.

47 Wallace, *ExSyn*, 76.

48 Moule, *Idiom Book*, 36.

The genitive case has the wrong name. The Latin *genitivus* is a translation of γεννητική (more like the ablative in idea). It is ἡ γενική πτῶσις. The name γενική comes from γένος (*genus*), 'kind,' and corresponds to the Latin *generalis* .... It is a pity that one still has to call it "genitive."[49]

Robertson prefers to see the genitive case as "the specifying case ... and no other."[50]

Dana and Mantey make no effort to separate adjectival or definitional senses of the genitive. In one place they say the genitive is primarily adjectival.[51] In another passage they state, "the basal function of the genitive is to define."[52] Thus in the same text Dana and Mantey endorse the "adjectival function" and the "defining function" without any distinction.[53]

Blass and Debrunner do not attempt a discussion of the original meaning of the genitive, preferring instead to focus on usage: "The genitive with the function of an adjective is the commonest way in which the case is used."[54] Smyth endorses the adjectival function of the genitive by saying, "The genitive is akin in meaning to the adjective and may often be translated by an epithet .... But the use of the adjective is not everywhere parallel to that of the genitive."[55] Wallace follows the same line when he says the adjectival genitive as a category, "really touches the heart of the genitive. If the genitive is primarily descriptive, then it is largely similar to the adjective in functions."[56]

Moule commences his list of the functions of the genitive by the "genitive of definition" as if it is the basic idea of the genitive. In his treatment of the genitive as definitional he says, "The chief thing to remember is that the Genitive often practically does the duty of an adjective, distinguishing two otherwise similar things."[57] Moule here comes close to the identifying function of the genitive, which is synonymous with definition.

---

49 Robertson, *Grammar*, 492.
50 Robertson, *Grammar*, 493.
51 Dana-Mantey, 72.
52 Dana-Mantey, 73.
53 Brooks-Winbery (7) express a similar view: "The basic function of the genitive is to describe and to define."
54 BDF §4.A. p. 89.
55 Herbert Weir Smyth, *Greek Grammar*, rev. ed. by Gordon M. Messing (Cambridge: Harvard University Press, 1956), §1291 p. 313.
56 Wallace, *ExSyn*, 78.
57 Moule presents Ἰάκωβον τὸν τοῦ Ζεβεδαίου (Matt 4:21) as an example (Moule, *Idiom Book*, 38).

Definitional

Although the genitive has a considerable variety of adjectival applications it is not possible for the adjectival element to embrace all applications. The chief function of the genitive is that of definition. All other functions, such as descriptive, qualitative, attributive, and adjectival, are derivative from this basic idea. Smyth's reservation, "but the use of the adjective is not everywhere parallel to that of the genitive,"[58] is both precise and prudent. Robertson is open to preferring the adjectival function as the basic idea of the genitive when he says, "the function of the case is *largely* adjectival,"[59] although he states that "the adjective and the genitive are not exactly parallel,"[60] and that the genitive "is not adjectival in origin."[61] Chamberlain affirms that the "Hebraistic Genitive" (i.e., adjectival genitive) "is primarily a genitive of definition."[62] After a full investigation of the genitive in all its uses and nuances, one is inclined to conclude that *definition* is the most basic meaning of the genitive case.[63]

Nature of the Genitive

After discussing the basic meaning of the genitive in all its facets as scholars see it, we come to discuss the nature of the genitive as a linguistic phenomenon. Genitive constructions are characterized by appurtenance, concatenation, propagation of meaning, and ambiguity. These characteristics make interpretation of its uses a challenge.

Appurtenance

Appurtenance or addition is the primary factor in the constituency of the genitive case. It is a noun + noun case. The genitive as a grammatical structure is a noun or substantive that is added to another without using a verb or preposition or other means of connecting words together in a meaningful sentence.[64] Zerwick

---

58 Smyth, *Greek Grammar*, §1291 p. 313.
59 Robertson, *Grammar*, 493. [emphasis added]
60 Robertson, *Grammar*, 493.
61 Robertson, *Grammar*, 493.
62 Chamberlain, *Grammar*, 30.
63 As noted above, Dana and Mantey assert that "the basal function of the genitive is to define" (73). See also Porter, *Idioms*, 92.
64 For example, δικαιοσύνης τῆς πίστεως (Rom 4:11), τῶν ἀρχόντων τοῦ αἰῶνος (1 Cor 2:6), and ὀσμὴν εὐωδίας (Eph 5:2).

says the exact "nature and the extent of the relation involved in this appurtenance is to be grasped by a consideration not of grammatical usage but of the context."[65] Robertson calls the genitive "the case of appurtenance" (i.e., something added or attached to another).[66]

Concatenation

Since addition is in the very nature of the genitive, genitive additions may multiply. Grammarians call this phenomenon *accumulation, multiplicity, concatenation* or simply a *cluster* of genitives. The multiplicity of genitives may grow from one addition to four additions constituting respectively the two-word genitive (εὐαγγέλιον θεοῦ Rom 1:1), the three-word genitive (ὁ νόμος τοῦ πνεύματος τῆς ζωῆς Rom 8:2), the four-word genitive (φωτισμὸν τῆς γνώσεως τῆς δόξης τοῦ θεοῦ 2 Cor 4:6) and the five-word genitive (ὑμῶν τοῦ ἔργου τῆς πίστεως καὶ τοῦ κόπου τῆς ἀγάπης καὶ τῆς ὑπομονῆς τῆς ἐλπίδος τοῦ κυρίου ἡμῶν 1 Thess 1:3).[67]

Adnominal Construction

A genitive cannot be an adnominal genitive unless it is attached to another nominal. In this case, the genitive which is added to the headword is considered an integral part of the genitival construction. When a substantive is added to a noun or another substantive a genitival construction emerges. In the genitival construction the first noun, being a genitive or any other case, constitutes with the second (or successive) genitive noun one compound unit. The two nouns that constitute the genitival compound are "traditionally called *nomen regens-nomen rectum*."[68]

---

65 Zerwick, *Biblical Greek*, §39 p. 14.
66 Robertson, *Grammar*, 493.
67 These additions are treated extensively in Chapters Five to Six.
68 Wallace, *ExSyn*, 75n5. This situation is analogous to that of the Semitic languages. In Arabic, the constructional factor of the genitive is well presented in the grammatical names given to the genitive case's compound substantives in Arabic. The genitive case is called *halat al idhafa* (the case of addition). The head noun is called *mudhaf* [added (to what follows)] and the second noun the genitive is called *mudhaf ilayhi* [added to (what precedes)]. The genius of Arabic language relates the two nouns in one compound unit and both are given names related to adding (i.e. the genitive). This property of the genitive operates the way it does in Semitic languages. As Bruce Waltke and Michael O'Connor put it: "In the language antecedent to Biblical Hebrew … If a noun preceded a noun in the genitive, however, that noun often came to be marked; such a 'pregenitive' noun stands in the [genitive] *construct state*" (*An Introduction to Biblical Hebrew Syntax* [Winona Lake, IN: Eisenbrauns, 1990], 138).

Propagation of Meanings

Adding substantives to each other opens the possibility for propagating unlimited meanings and nuances depending on the purpose of the author, the words involved and the demands of the differing contexts.

Robertson also comments on what causes the variety of genitive meanings. For him, the genitive case retains its root meaning, but "the resultant idea will naturally vary greatly according as the root-conception of the case is applied to different words and different contexts."[69] Moule well expresses the propagating nature of the genitive when he describes it as "so immensely versatile."[70] Nida observes about the genitive:

> In translating from Greek or English, the most complex series of difficulties arise respectively from the genitive case form and the preposition *of*, for these are the forms in the corresponding languages which cover *the widest range of meaningful relationships between words*.[71]

Robertson is very much aware of Paul's diverse language: "The genitive is employed by Paul with every variety of application."[72]

Ambiguity

As a matter of fact, adding a substantive to another without any connecting means automatically produces ambiguity. The ambiguity increases as genitives are added to each other, as in the case of three-word or four-word genitives. This additive factor in genitive constructions is the core of the genitive's enigma.

A practical example of the ambiguity of the genitive is seen in the phrase ἡ κοινωνία τῆς πίστεώς σου *the fellowship of your faith* (Phlm 6). Translations render this phrase with a variety of expressions: (1) "The communication of thy faith" (KJV), (2) "The sharing of your faith" (RSV); (3) "Your fellowship with us in our common faith" (NEB), (4) "The faith you hold in fellowship with us" (REB), (5) "Your fellowship in faith" (NJB), and (6) "our fellowship with you as believers" (TEV).

Grammarians are well aware of the difficulty. "This is a large subject," says Nigel Turner, "as the genitive is *so hard worked* a case in Greek."[73] Of Paul's use of

---

69 Robertson, *Grammar*, 493.
70 Moule, *Idiom Book*, 37.
71 Eugene A. Nida, *Toward a Science of Translating: With Special Reference to Principles and Procedures Involved in Bible Translating* (Leiden: Brill, 1964), 207. [emphasis added]
72 Robertson, *Grammar*, 130.
73 MHT₃ 207. [emphasis added]

the genitive in particular, Turner adds that the piling up of genitives is, "character-istic of Paul and often ambiguous or obscure."[74]

To summarize the matter, there are several factors that make the genitive construction vague and difficult to understand. First, when genitives in concat-enation are added to each other "whereby an author, particularly Paul, occasion-ally produces *a quite cumbersome* accumulation of genitives."[75] Second, when "the same genitive construction may have opposite meanings in different contexts,"[76] for example, "the love of God." Third, when one or both of the nouns in the gen-itive construction is an abstract noun. In this case, there exists "a doubly complex problem—the function of the abstract noun(s) and the function of the genitival relationship"[77] for example, "the door of faith" (Acts 14:27).

Method

The method of investigation in order to reach the goal defined consists of two stages: historical and constructive. The first stage will discuss the value of the choice of the Pauline corpus for investigating adnominal genitive constructions. Then our investigation will turn to critical analysis of the genitive case's syntax as presented in NT Greek grammars. We will then survey the present state of semantic studies in relation to the genitive case from contemporary works on techniques of Bible translation and hermeneutics. Examining what has been done in the field of gen-itive syntax is essential for developing the science of syntax and for reaching ac-curate conclusions. The application of modern linguistic theories to NT Greek resulted in opening new recourses for solving genitive problems.

The constructive stage involves a thorough investigation of the relevant data. Thus, the adnominal genitive constructions are divided into three sections ac-cording to the number of nouns or substantives contained in each genitive construc-tion: the two-word genitive, the three-word genitive, and the four-word genitive. By *two-word genitive* is meant an adnominal genitive construction involving a head noun (ignoring the article–if present–for the counting) in any case with one dependent genitive (in Wallace's notation: N-N$_g$), such as τῷ θεῷ μου (Rom 1:8). The constructions are named simply by the number of *main* terms (head noun

---

74 MHT$_3$ 218.
75 BDF §168 p. 93 [emphasis added]; an observation Turner echoes. See MHT$_3$ 218.
76 Beekman and Callow explain, "One particular complication is the fact that the same genitive construction may have opposite meanings in different contexts. The phrase, 'the love of God,' … can mean either 'you love God' or 'God loves you'" (Beekman-Callow, 250).
77 Beekman-Callow, 250.

and dependent genitives) involved, not counting articles, adjectives, appositives, or other such modifiers. For instance, both τὸν λόγον τοῦ θεοῦ (Col 1:25) and λόγον θεοῦ (1 Thess 2:13) count as two-word constructions for this taxonomy. Likewise, the *three-word genitive* construction involves a head noun with two dependent genitives (N-N$_g$-N$_g$ e.g., Rom 1:9 ἐν τῷ εὐαγγελίῳ τοῦ υἱοῦ αὐτοῦ). Sometimes the third word is joined to the construction by a coordinating conjunction such as καί or δέ. In similar fashion, the *four-word genitive* construction involves three dependent genitives (N-N$_g$-N$_g$-N$_g$), sometimes involving conjunctions as well. Very few examples with more than three dependent genitives appear in the NT text; and at that, such examples can be analyzed differently.

Naturally, in construing the genitive clusters of the three- and four-word variety one must consider the boundaries of the cluster. This identification is made more difficult by appositives in the genitive case occur nearby. Genitives in simple apposition are not counted as part of the cluster in this kind of situation. For instance, in the cluster ὁ θεὸς τοῦ κυρίου ἡμῶν Ἰησοῦ Χριστοῦ (Eph 1:17), the proper name Ἰησοῦ Χριστοῦ stands in apposition to κυρίου. So, this cluster counts as a three-word genitive construction (θεὸς ... κυρίου ἡμῶν). Such appositional scenarios are frequent.

The aim of doing research in the two-word genitive is to survey the meanings of the genitive constructions and classify them under main categories. The crucial question to be asked concerning decoding two-word genitive constructions is "what is the relationship between the two substantives?" Accordingly, the answer should deal with the direction of the relationship between the two, the value of their word order, and which noun is added to the other.

Likewise, inquiry into the three- and four-word genitives, should follow the same procedure. Besides, there should be explanations about the relationship between the first noun and the third noun, or the second and the fourth, and which noun in the cluster should be considered as an adjective.

Conclusions will be compared with relevant contemporary literature. This will produce a twofold result. It allows for a fresh approach to genitive case usage. Further, it will provide a set of principles to apply to resolve ambiguous genitive constructions.

Basic Tools

The Greek text of the NT used in this work is the 28th edition of *Novum Testamentum Graece* (NA[28]). The initial data Ghassan Khalaf used for the study used all genitive forms searched using software from the Gramcord Institute.[78] He isolated

---

78 https://www.gramcord.org

and identified all the adnominal genitive constructions. I [J. William Johnston] checked, corrected, and supplemented this data by more recent computer tools and databases available from Logos Bible Software. In addition to grammatically tagged electronic editions of NA[28], the syntactical databases from OpenText.org, *Lexham Syntactic New Testament Database*, and *Cascadia Syntax Graphs of the NT* were used to double-check the findings.[79] English translations of Greek phrases in this volume are the author's or editor's unless otherwise noted. Translations from published Bible versions will be noted with appropriate abbreviations.

Bibliography

Carson, D. A. *Exegetical Fallacies.* 2nd ed. Grand Rapids: Baker, 1996.

Chamberlain, William Douglas. *An Exegetical Grammar of the Greek New Testament.* New York: Macmillan, 1941. Reprint, Grand Rapids: Baker, 1979.

Fitzmyer, Joseph A. *Romans: A New Translation with Introduction and Commentary.* Anchor Yale Bible 33. New York: Doubleday, 1993.

Green, Samuel G. *Handbook to the Grammar of the Greek Testament.* rev. and imp. ed. New York: Revell, 1904.

Jewett, Robert, with the assistance of Roy David Kotansky. *Romans: A Commentary.* Edited by Eldon Jay Epp. Hermeneia. Minneapolis: Fortress, 2007.

Louw, Johannes P. *Semantics of New Testament Greek.* Atlanta: Scholars Press, 1982.

Melick, Richard R., Jr. *Philippians, Colossians, Philemon.* New American Commentary 32. Nashville: Broadman, 1991.

Michaelis, Wilhelm. "πάθημα." Pages 930–35 in *Theological Dictionary of the New Testament.* Edited by Gerhard Friedrich. Translated by Geoffrey W. Bromiley. vol. 5. Grand Rapids: Eerdmans, 1967.

Moulton, Harold K. "Of," *Bible Translator* 19.1 (1968): 18–25. doi:10.1177/000608446801900105.

Nida, Eugene A. *Toward a Science of Translating: With Special Reference to Principles and Procedures Involved in Bible Translating.* Leiden: Brill, 1964.

Nida, Eugene A. and Charles R. Taber. *The Theory and Practice of Translation.* Helps for Translators 8. Leiden: Brill, 1969. Reprint, 1982.

---

79 *The OpenText.org Syntactically Analyzed Greek New Testament* [software], ed. Stanley Porter et al. (Bellingham, WA: Logos Bible Software, 2006); *The OpenText.org Syntactically Analyzed Greek New Testament: Clause Analysis* [software], ed. Stanley Porter et al. (Bellingham, WA: Logos Bible Software, 2006); *The Lexham Syntactic Greek New Testament* [software]; *The Lexham Syntactic Greek New Testament: Sentence Analysis* [software], ed. Albert L. Lukaszewski and Mark Dubis (Bellingham, WA: Logos Bible Software, 2009); Andi Wu and Randall Tan, *Cascadia Syntax Graphs of the New Testament* [software] (Bellingham, WA: Lexham Press, 2009).

Nikiforidou, Kiki. "The Meanings of the Genitive: A Case Study in Semantic Structure and Semantic Change," *Cognitive Linguistics* 2.2 (1991): 149–205. https://www.degruyter.com/view/j/cogl.1991.2.issue-2/issue-files/cogl.1991.2.issue-2.xml.

O'Brien, Peter T. *The Epistle to the Philippians: A Commentary on the Greek Text.* New International Greek Testament Commentary. Grand Rapids: Eerdmans, 1991.

Perschbacher, Wesley J. *New Testament Greek Syntax: An Illustrated Manual.* Chicago: Moody Press, 1995.

Porter, Stanley E. "The Adjectival Attributive Genitive in the New Testament: A Grammatical Study," *Trinity Journal* 4.1 (1983): 3–17.

Rydbeck, Lars. "What Happened to New Testament Greek Grammar after Albert Debrunner?," *New Testament Studies* 21.3 (1975): 424–27.

Smyth, Herbert Weir. *Greek Grammar.* Revised ed. by Gordon M. Messing. Cambridge: Harvard University Press, 1956.

Stolk, Joanne Vera. "Dative by Genitive Replacement in the Greek Language of the Papyri: A Diachronic Account of Case Semantics," *Journal of Greek Linguistics* 15.1 (2015): 91–121. doi:10.1163/15699846-01501001.

The Faith of Jesus Christ: Exegetical, Biblical, and Theological Studies. Edited by Michael F. Bird and Preston M. Sprinkle. Peabody, Mass: Hendrickson, 2010.

The Lexham Syntactic Greek New Testament [software]. Edited by Albert L. Lukaszewski and Mark Dubis. Bellingham, WA: Logos Bible Software, 2009.

The Lexham Syntactic Greek New Testament: Sentence Analysis [software]. Edited by Albert L. Lukaszewski and Mark Dubis. Bellingham, WA: Logos Bible Software, 2009.

The OpenText.org Syntactically Analyzed Greek New Testament [software]. Edited by Stanley Porter et al. Bellingham, WA: Logos Bible Software, 2006.

The OpenText.org Syntactically Analyzed Greek New Testament: Clause Analysis [software]. Edited by Stanley Porter et al. Bellingham, WA: Logos Bible Software, 2006.

Thrall, Margaret E. *A Critical and Exegetical Commentary on the Second Epistle of the Corinthians.* 2 vols. International Critical Commentary. London: T&T Clark, 1994.

Waltke, Bruce K. and Michael Patrick O'Connor. *An Introduction to Biblical Hebrew Syntax.* Winona Lake, IN: Eisenbrauns, 1990.

Wu, Andi and Randall Tan. *Cascadia Syntax Graphs of the New Testament* [software]. Bellingham, WA: Lexham Press, 2009.

CHAPTER ONE

The Pauline Corpus as a Model

This study will confine itself to the Pauline corpus. The Pauline corpus was chosen primarily because of the variety of ways the genitive is used in this group of writings. The diversity of usage in the Paul's letters mirrors that found in the whole NT, for, as Robertson so pithily observes, "To go into detail with Paul's writings would be largely to give the grammar of the N. T."[1] So it stands to reason there is sufficient cohesion of genitive usage to make the study of this body as representative of the whole.

In spite of denials of the authenticity of the Pastorals, Ephesians, Colossians, and 2 Thessalonians,[2] the thirteen letters from Romans to Philemon constitute the *corpus Paulinum*. The question of authenticity for some of the Pauline letters is, of course, not settled for either side.[3] It is not the aim of this book to prove or

---

1   Robertson, *Grammar*, 130. This also is my own [Ghassan Khalaf's] impression as a result of my analysis of the genitives in Paul.
2   Donald Guthrie, *New Testament Introduction*, 4th ed. (Downers Grove: IVP, 1990), 1011; Raymond E. Brown, *An Introduction to the New Testament*, AYBRL (New York: Doubleday, 1997), 407; D. A. Carson and Douglas J. Moo, *An Introduction to the New Testament* (Grand Rapids: Zondervan, 2005), 337.
3   Statements about the authorship of Ephesians are an example of such discussion: Moule, *Idiom Book*, 201; see also Turner, MHT$_4$ 84. On the Pastorals, Donald Guthrie (*NT Introduction*, 646) observes:

disprove either of the two positions, but rather to elucidate the meaning of the genitive constructions in the entire corpus. At any rate, authorship considerations will not affect the conclusions about case usage. Since much of the discussion about authenticity centers on word usage, comparing the way genitive constructions are used between the disputed and undisputed letters of Paul may provide additional data for that discussion. Since our study concerns the usage of the genitive in NT Greek, it would be ideal to examine the entire NT, but limitations are needed. Luke, John, and Paul are among the writers who have sufficient corpora of material for our research. Luke's writings are the longest among the three and his use of the genitive frequently displays Semitic influence.[4] But the Lukan corpus should be studied on its own merits, especially in the Book of Acts. John's simple style generally makes his use of the genitive less diverse and less ambiguous than Paul's. The Pauline corpus presents a field for investigating adnominal genitives for reasons taken up in this chapter.

Distinctive Style

Moule and Turner in particular have examined the characteristic literary features of each of the writers of the NT, agreeing that Paul has a distinct style.[5] A. T. Robertson observes, "in the four groups of [Paul's] letters each group has a style and to some extent a vocabulary of its own, yet, as in Shakespeare's plays, there is the stamp of the same tremendous mind."[6]

The Greek of the OT seems to have had a greater effect on Paul than other writers. This is indicated by his numerous direct quotations from the Greek Bible. Nigel Turner says, "The Greek of the Paulines is Jewish, much influenced by the Septuagint. Its verbosity may derive from Paul's predilection for chiasmus and Old Testament parallelism."[7] Turner defends his position against those who think there is little Semitic influence in Paul's literary style. He argues:

> In spite of the acknowledged differences between the pastorals and Paul's other epistles, the traditional view that they are authentic writings of the apostle cannot be said to be impossible, and since there are greater problems attached to the alternative theories it is most reasonable to suppose that the early church was right in accepting them as such.

4   For instance, James R. Edwards (*The Hebrew Gospel and the Development of the Synoptic Tradition* [Grand Rapids: Eerdmans, 2009], 142) identifies 703 Semitisms, 653 of which are found in the uniquely Lukan material or in the Lukan additions to the triple tradition.

5   See MHT$_4$ 2–3; Moule, *Idiom Book*, 2–3.

6   Robertson, *Grammar*, 128. Turner echoes similar sentiments in MHT$_4$ 3.

7   MHT$_4$ 3.

We need not suppose that the Semitisms and Aramaisms are due to his thinking in Aramaic while writing in Greek, for he was probably brought up to speak Greek from childhood .... There is very strong evidence for LXX influence, despite Moulton's surprising opinion that it did not exert much influence on Paul's style, much less was its diction copied. Nageli, Guillemard and others, on the contrary, saw the Pauline Hebraisms as entirely due to Paul's use of the LXX. Everywhere there are verbal similarities with it.[8]

To illustrate the extent of LXX influence on Paul's style, Turner refers to Paul's use of the genitive:

> Even the so-called "literary" parts of Paul's letters owe their style mainly to Hebrew or to the LXX. Thus, even the neuter adjectives with dependent genitive (e.g. *the impossible things of the law*) (Rom 8:3) [sic] which is not found in the papyri, but in the higher Koine of Strabo and Josephus, is a feature of the free Greek of the LXX (2–4 Maccabees).[9]

Christopher Stanley's comprehensive study of Paul's citations from the OT concludes "his primary text" is the LXX, even though at times there are significant differences with that tradition.[10] A balanced view takes into consideration the two elements in Paul's upbringing: Hellenistic and Hebraic. Walter Lock, in a review of the work of Theodor Nägeli, explains:

> The Apostle writes in the style natural to a Greek of Asia Minor adopting the current Greek of the time, borrowing more or less consciously from the ethical writers of the time, framing new words or giving a new meaning to old words .... His choice of vocabulary is therefore much like that of Epictetus save that his intimate knowledge of the LXX has modified it by the introduction of words or phrases which have arisen from the necessity of translating Hebrew.[11]

Certainly, Paul was well versed in the Greek language as a Roman citizen born in Asia Minor (cf. Acts 21:37–39; 22:3a), and was well schooled in Aramaic and Hebrew as a student in Jerusalem under the Jewish scholar Gamaliel (Acts 21:40; 22:2–3). He was well acquainted with the Septuagint (LXX), as his numerous

---

8   MHT₄ 89.

9   MHT₄ 86–87.

10 Christopher D. Stanley, *Paul and the Language of Scripture: Citation Technique in the Pauline Epistles and Contemporary Literature*, SNTSMS 69 (Cambridge: Cambridge University Press, 1992), 254

11 Walter Lock, "The Language of St. Paul," *JTS* 7.26 (1906): 298, doi:10.1093/jts/os-VII.26.297. The work under review is Theodor Nägeli, *Der Wortschatz des Apostels Paulus*, Beitrag zur sprachgeschichtlichen Erforschung des Neuen Testaments (Göttingen: Vandenhoeck & Ruprecht, 1905). Robertson notes this argument (*Grammar*, 131).

quotations from the Old Testament show. Paul relied on the Septuagint as his Bible for study, devotion, and preaching. Bruce N. Fisk concludes the full discussion of Paul's education:

> It is clear … that Paul could read and write Greek, was thoroughly versed in the Greek Bible, and was comfortable in the role of interpreter. All of this suggests a thoroughly Jewish education involving extended exposure to Israel's sacred texts, postbiblical traditions, and interpretive approaches …. when we examine … Paul's arguments, we find … also clear signs of Hellenistic influence … and contemporary Greco-Roman rhetoric.[12]

Extensive Use of the Genitive

The frequency of the adnominal genitive constructions in the Pauline corpus is remarkable. Nigel Turner theorizes the reason for the high concentration of substantives overall in Paul:

> [Paul] chose substantives rather than verbs or adjectives to describe Christ's relationship with those who are *en Christo*, and delicately turned away from activity to existence, his idiom subconsciously following his theology. What was once activity and growth and movement has now become identification. Verb and adjective cease to be appropriate, supplanted by the substantive idiom.[13]

How extensive is Paul's usage of the genitive in his writings? John Beekman and John Callow provide an answer:

> A quick survey would indicate the frequency may well be higher than once per verse in Paul's Epistles. It seems reasonable to assume, therefore, that the translator is likely to encounter a genitive phrase of this type about twice in every three verses, if not more often.[14]

A statistical survey applied to the adnominal genitive constructions in Ephesians reveals that they appear quite frequently in that letter. There are 155 verses in Ephesians and at least 160 adnominal genitives of two-, three- and four-word constructions. That means that an adnominal genitive construction occurs in every 0.97 verse in Ephesians.

---

12 Bruce N. Fisk, "Paul: Life and Letters," in *The Face of New Testament Studies: A Survey of Recent Research*, ed. McKnight Scot and Grant R. Osborne (Grand Rapids: Baker, 2004), 307–8.

13 Nigel Turner, *Grammatical Insights into the New Testament* (Edinburgh: T&T Clark, 1966), 119.

14 Beekman-Callow, 249.

On a wider scale, a statistical survey applied to the adnominal genitive constructions that occur in the thirteen letters of the Pauline corpus indicates exactly the same percentage of the adnominal genitive occurrence in Ephesians. The total number of verses in the Pauline corpus in the main text of NA^{28} is 2,031. The total number of adnominal genitives of two-word, three-word and four-word constructions is about 1,800 (of course, many verses have multiple adnominal constructions). These figures flesh out the intuitions of Beekman and Callow and confirm the extensive usage of adnominal genitives in the Pauline corpus.

Frequent Genitive Clusters

The Pauline corpus contains the largest proportional number of genitive clusters (i.e. three- and four-word constructions) that occurs in any group of writings in the New Testament except 1 Peter and 2 Peter. Paul is fond of accumulating nouns and substantives together in one chain of structure creating what is called "concatenation of genitives." Alexander Buttmann has pointed this out,

> The union of substantives, especially abstract terms, by the Genitive relation is employed with fondness by some of N. T. writers, particularly by Paul in his doctrinal argumentations ... so that two, three, yes four, Genitives stand in immediate dependence one upon another. Such an accumulation of Genitives is manifestly avoided by the native Greeks, because it easily begets ambiguity (see e.g. [1 Thess 1:3; Rom 11:33], etc.).[15]

Blass and Debrunner under the heading "Concatenation of Genitives with Different Meanings" refer to the ambiguity arising from multiple proximate adnominal genitives by saying, "generally one genitive is dependent on another, whereby an author, particularly Paul, occasionally produces a quite cumbersome accumulation of genitives."[16] A. T. Robertson also states that "Paul in particular is fond of piling up genitives."[17] A list of three- and four-word genitive constructions appears at the ends of Chapter Five and Six (respectively), to which the reader can refer for examples.

---

15   Buttmann, *Grammar*, 154.
16   BDF §168, p. 93.
17   Robertson, *Grammar*, 503

Wide Range of Meanings

Adding a noun to a noun in a genitive construction produces a meaning based on the literary characteristics of the nouns and the kind of the relationship between them. This operation, if repeated with changing nouns and relations, produces a vast variety of meanings with many derivative nuances.[18] Turner comments on Paul's rich use of the genitive and says that both subjective and objective genitive phrases are everywhere in his Epistles.[19] Adolf Deissmann thinks that Paul's use of the genitive transcends all rules about subjective and objective; so much so that in relation to Christ and his people it should be termed a "mystic genitive."[20] Grammarians and theologians recognize the wide versatility of Paul's genitive use.

The Need for Careful Exegesis

Nigel Turner points out that much of Paul's use of the genitive "is controversial."[21] He also assumes that any analysis of the genitive in Paul's writings must be guided by context. He says:

> Indeed, so rich is Paul's compression of language with genitive that the attempt to define too narrowly the various types of genitive is vain; they all denote a relationship which is amplified by the context.[22]

Such interpretive difficulties have a witness in Harold K. Moulton, who points to 2 Cor 13:13, ἡ κοινωνία τοῦ ἁγίου πνεύματος *the fellowship of the Spirit*. He asks, "Is Paul thinking of our fellowship with one another, or of our fellowship with the Spirit? Or are we on the wrong track when we try to suggest contrasting categories of this nature?"[23] His reply: "Perhaps Paul had both thoughts in mind as he penned this genitive."[24] Such ambiguity even in interpretation of Paul's difficult phrases is ubiquitous, even among seasoned NT scholars.

---

18 There are about thirty different meanings of the two-word adnominal genitives used in the Pauline corpus. See Chapter Three.

19 MHT₄ 84.

20 Adolf Deissmann, *St. Paul: A Study in Social and Religious History*, trans. Lionel R. M. Strachan (New York: Hodder & Stoughton, 1912), 140–41. Robertson (*Grammar*, 501) mentions the category with perhaps a suspicious air.

21 MHT₃ 90.

22 MHT₄ 212.

23 Harold K. Moulton, "Of," *Bible Translator* 19.1 (1968): 25.

24 Moulton, "Of," 25.

Another example is εἰς ἔπαινον δόξης τῆς χάριτος αὐτοῦ *to the praise of the glory of his grace* (Eph 1:6). The key to interpreting this construction can be found in a synonymous phrase εἰς δόξαν καὶ ἔπαινον θεοῦ (Phil 1:11). Turner suggests that εἰς ἔπαινον δόξης τῆς χάριτος αὐτοῦ in Eph 1:6, could mean "for the praise and the glory of his grace."[25] This kind of genitive we have categorized under the cumulative genitive.[26] Many such examples can be cited in Paul's writings that need careful exegesis in order to reach sound interpretation.

Paul's Use of the Genitive Is Typical

One other reason for choosing the Pauline corpus is that the diversity of meanings found for the genitive there constitutes a model for studying the whole New Testament. As we have noted before, Robertson's judgment is right when he says, "To go into detail with Paul's writings would be largely to give the grammar of the N.T."[27] After defining the reasons for selecting the Pauline corpus for investigating the adnominal genitive constructions in the NT the way is open now for surveying the meanings of the genitive in NT Greek grammars.

Bibliography

Brown, Raymond E. *An Introduction to the New Testament.* Anchor Yale Bible Reference Library. New York: Doubleday, 1997.

Carson, D. A. and Douglas J. Moo. *An Introduction to the New Testament.* Grand Rapids: Zondervan, 2005.

Deissmann, Adolf. *St. Paul: A Study in Social and Religious History.* Translated by Lionel R. M. Strachan. New York: Hodder & Stoughton, 1912.

Edwards, James R. *The Hebrew Gospel and the Development of the Synoptic Tradition.* Grand Rapids: Eerdmans, 2009.

Fisk, Bruce N. "Paul: Life and Letters." Pages 283–325 in *The Face of New Testament Studies: A Survey of Recent Research.* Edited by Scot McKnight and Grant R. Osborne. Grand Rapids: Baker, 2004.

Guthrie, Donald. *New Testament Introduction.* 4th ed. Downers Grove: IVP, 1990.

Lock, Walter. "The Language of St. Paul," *Journal of Theological Studies* 7.26 (1906): 297–99. doi:10.1093/jts/os-VII.26.297.

---

25 See MHT₃ 218.
26 See Chapters Five to Six.
27 Robertson, *Grammar*, 130.

Moulton, Harold K. "Of," *Bible Translator* 19.1 (1968): 18–25. doi:10.1177/000608446801900105.

Nägeli, Theodor. *Der Wortschatz des Apostels Paulus.* Beitrag zur sprachgeschichtlichen Erforschung des Neuen Testaments. Göttingen: Vandenhoeck & Ruprecht, 1905.

Stanley, Christopher D. *Paul and the Language of Scripture: Citation Technique in the Pauline Epistles and Contemporary Literature.* Society for New Testament Studies Monograph Series 69. Cambridge: Cambridge University Press, 1992.

Turner, Nigel. *Grammatical Insights into the New Testament.* Edinburgh: T&T Clark, 1966.

CHAPTER TWO

The Genitive in New Testament Grammars

In Chapter One the reasons for choosing the Pauline corpus as a model for investigating adnominal genitive constructions in the whole New Testament were defined. As a preliminary step towards the categorization of the adnominal genitive in Paul's letters, we will survey NT grammars. The purpose of this survey is to evaluate the genitive usage categories and the principles for interpretation each author advances. Recognition of the historical development of genitive case analysis will facilitate the production of a more satisfactory taxonomy and point the way for future work.

The New Testament grammars (typically *reference* grammars as distinct from introductory textbooks) here reviewed were selected either for their scholarship or historical value. The genitive categories will be surveyed chronologically, beginning with G. B. Winer in the middle of the nineteenth century, and ending with D. B. Wallace at the end of the twentieth century. Since our study is concerned with adnominal genitives, we will limit discussion to those uses. The reference grammar, by its very nature, is imitative of its predecessors as scholars stand on the shoulders of their forebears in one way or another; it is no surprise that most of the category labels (and their definitions) overlap. This trend culminates in Wallace's thorough and well-organized treatment of the genitive case from a five-case point of view. The present work seeks to extend Wallace's work by incorporating the best elements of the streams that run through the works surveyed. We will not offer a complete analysis of each grammar's presentation. The structure or grouping each author uses in systematizing genitive case uses varies—often widely. We are interested in the general shape of these categories and whether each author recognizes the special problems clustered genitives present to interpretation. Naturally, a recurring theme will also be the ablative-genitive distinction, the treatment of which is largely influenced by whether an author holds to a five-case or an eight-case system. Unlike eight-case system proponents, who see ablative and genitive as distinct cases that happen to share the same forms, five-case system proponents instead see the ablative as a function of the genitive case.

The survey of Greek grammars in this chapter will conclude with two features: (1) a list of all the meanings of the genitive grammarians propose followed by (2) a brief outline of interpretive principles they suggest.

G. B. Winer

George Benedikt Winer's *Grammatik des neutestamentlichen Sprachidioms* first appeared in print from Leipzig in 1822. Testimony to Winer's enduring influence can be seen in the multitude of editions and revisions published afterwards. The second revised and much enlarged edition of appeared in 1825, with the sixth edition—the last of the editions directly from Winer—translated into English by W. F. Moulton (3rd ed. 1882).[1] Lünemann's revision of the seventh German edition was not much different (English translation by E. Masson and J. H. Thayer, 1904). Once Paul Schmiedel took over the production of the eighth German edition, the work marks a departure from its predecessors—and relevantly for our discussion, particularly on Winer's view that the basic meaning of the genitive case is ablatival (see below). So, this discussion will proceed from Moulton's translation of

---

1   Georg Benedikt Winer, *Grammatik des Neutestamentlichen Sprachidioms: Als einzig sichere Grundlage der neutestamentlichen Exegese* (Leipzig: Vogel, 1822); This first edition is a much shorter work than subsequent editions. Georg Benedikt Winer, *Grammatik des neutestamentlichen Sprachidioms: Als sichere Grundlage der neutestamentlichen Exegese*, 2nd ed. (Leipzig: Vogel, 1825). *A Treatise on the Grammar of New Testament New Testament Greek: Regarded as a Sure Basis for New Testament Exegesis*, 3rd ed., trans. W. F. Moulton (Edinburgh: T&T Clark, 1882). The relevant portion of the grammar is §30, spanning pp. 230–60. Page references will be to this edition. Moulton's preface indicates the translation was based on the 6th German ed. This would put it before the 8th German ed. revised by P. W. Schmiedel (referenced by BDF as "W-S"); idem., *Grammatik des neutestamentlichen Sprachidioms*, 8th ed., ed. Paul Wilhelm Schmiedel, 2 vols. (Göttingen: Vandenhoeck & Ruprecht, 1894).

the sixth German edition. To avoid an unnecessary proliferation of reference notes in this chapter, page numbers for grammars we discuss will appear in parentheses. Winer is convinced that "the genitive is unquestionably the *whence-case*" (230),[2] thus emphasizing the ablatival sense as the most basic sense of the genitive, extending this idea broadly to the idea of "*dependence on* or *belonging to*" (231), often using the expression "simple genitive of dependence" (243) to compare his category distinctions. He suggests other uses can be explained as a departure from this ablatival nature (255). Winer presents plenty of practical examples of usage. These examples are helpful as a guide for identifying the meaning of ambiguous genitives. He states also that in order to understand any difficult genitive phrase one should do that through exegesis and cautious use of parallel passages (232).

Winer identifies many categories of genitive usage that are standard fare for later grammarians. For ease of use and presentation, we will assume "genitive of" precedes the category name or that "genitive" follows, as style demands. For Winer, these include objective/subjective, time, content (which he calls "place" [where something is stored]), kindred, partitive (whole/class/sphere), destination, and apposition (meaning *of apposition* as distinct from merely being *in* apposition).

Winer is perhaps the first to handle how to interpret genitive clusters. He observes when three genitives are connected together "one of the substantives often represents an adjectival notion" (238), citing τὸν φωτισμὸν τοῦ εὐαγγελίου τῆς δόξης τοῦ Χριστοῦ (2 Cor 4:4), and εἰς ἔπαινον δόξης τῆς χάριτος αὐτοῦ (Col 1:13). In both of these examples, he judges δόξης to be adjectival. Winer presents one other principle of interpreting the genitive (239):

> when the genitive stands before the governing noun, either (a) It belongs equally to two nouns as in [Acts 3:7 TR] αὐτοῦ αἱ βάσεις καὶ τὰ σφυρά· [John 11:48 ἡμῶν καὶ τὸν τόπον καὶ τὸ ἔθνος]: or (b) It is emphatic: [1 Cor 3:9] θεοῦ γάρ ἐσμεν συνεργοί, θεοῦ γεώργιον, θεοῦ οἰκοδομή ἐστε.

---

2   "Der Genitiv ist unbestritten der Wohercasus" (*Grammatik des neutestamentlichen Sprachidioms: Als sichere Grundlage der neutestamentlichen Exegese*, 6th corr. and enl. ed. [Leipzig: Vogel, 1855], 166; it is retained in Lünemann's 7th ed. *Grammatik des neutestamentlichen Sprachidioms: Als sichere Grundlage der neutestamentlichen Exegese*, 7th corr. and enl. ed. by Gottlieb Lünemann [Leipzig: Vogel, 1867], 174). This confident statement is somewhat muted by Masson and Thayer's translation, "The Genitive is acknowledged to be the *whence*-case" (*A Grammar of the Idiom of the New Testament: Prepared as a Solid Basis for the Interpretation of the New Testament*, 7th ed. enl. and impr. by Gottlieb Lünemann, trans. Edward Masson and Joseph Henry Thayer [Andover, MA: Draper, 1904], 184), and is altogether missing from Schmiedel's 8th German ed.

Winer regularly uses the method of examining parallel passages. This is an early major contribution of understanding the genitive. Hints of what is later recognized as transformational grammar appear in Winer's discussion.

A. Buttmann

Translator J. H. Thayer's 1878 preface commends the work of the German grammarian Philip Karl Buttmann (1764–1829), "whose Grammars ... have rendered the name familiar wherever Greek is studied."[3] Philip Buttmann's grammars include a shorter *Griechische Schulgrammatik* (5th ed. 1819) and a more expanded volume *Griechische Grammatik* (22nd ed. 1869),[4] a work carried on and expanded by his son Alexander Buttmann.[5] The younger Buttmann looks to provide an account of NT Greek usage "in so far as it differs from ordinary usage" (x), and so his treatment of the genitive appears to lack a clear outline. His specific categories of adnominal usage seem very much indebted to Winer: subjective/objective, country, separation (whence-case), partitive, adjectival, time, place. Yet he does not evidently share Winer's view of the genitive as primarily ablatival. He seems less interested in classifying adnominal usage than in proposing helpful principles for construal.

Buttmann begins by taking as proven by other grammarians that the subjective and the objective genitive categories exist, so one must allow for either possibility in exegesis, even if grammarians and interpreters disagree. Like Winer before him, Buttmann calls attention to the importance of context and authorial usage in parallel passages informing the exegete's judgment on whether a given genitive is subjective or objective (154–55). But before discussing specific categories of usage, Buttmann remarks first on the ubiquity of adnominal genitives in the NT, noting that the author of Revelation and Paul both stand out in this regard, "that two, three, yes four, Genitives stand in immediate dependence one upon another ... [something] manifestly avoided by the native Greeks, because it easily begets ambiguity" (154; citing 1 Thess 1:3; Rom 11:33 as examples).

Buttmann notices how the genitive substantive is used adjectivally (e.g., Rom 1:26 πάθη ἀτιμίας *dishonoring passions* [his rendering]). While this usage is not unknown to Greek, this sense is encouraged under the influence of Semitic

3 Alexander Buttmann, *A Grammar of the New Testament Greek*, trans. J. H. Thayer (Andover: Draper, 1880), v.

4 Philipp Karl Buttmann, *Griechische Schulgrammatik* (Berlin: Mylius, 1819); Philipp Karl Buttmann, *Griechische Grammatik*, ed. Alexander Buttmann, 22nd ed. (Berlin: Dümmler, 1869).

5 Buttmann, *Grammar*, 154–71. The work was reprinted by the publisher in 1891, without any changes to the pagination.

languages such as Hebrew. This is seen, he says, in frequent usage of expressions where τέκνον or υἱός appear as head nouns characterized by a genitive (Buttmann [161–62] cites e.g., τοὺς υἱοὺς τῆς ἀπειθείας "sons of disobedience" [ESV] Eph 5:6; τέκνα φωτός "children of light" [ESV] Eph 5:7; cf. BDAG "prob[ably] a Hebraism in the main"[6]).

Buttmann's real contribution lies in his method for understanding the genitive in clusters (155). He distinguishes between genitives that (a) "depend on one another" and those that (b) "depend on one and the same substantive" (155). In the first category (a), expressions like τῇ ἀπεκδύσει τοῦ σώματος τῆς σαρκός *the putting off of the body of flesh* (Col 2:11) should be evaluated in the order they appear in the text because they depend on one another in that order. In the second category (b), when the final term is a "personal (possessive) term" the construction "easily unites with its predecessor into one whole" (155). Buttmann offers Col 1:13 τὴν βασιλείαν τοῦ υἱοῦ τῆς ἀγάπης αὐτοῦ *the kingdom of the son of his love* as an example of this rule in action. He readily admits, however, that Ὦ βάθος πλούτου καὶ σοφίας καὶ γνώσεως θεοῦ *O the depths of the wealth and wisdom and knowledge of God* (Rom 11:33) is much more difficult a text, since σοφίας and γνώσεως could depend only on πλούτου or could depend "together with πλούτου upon βάθος" (155). He adds to this second category that genitives can appear before (e.g., 2 Cor 5:1 ἡ ἐπίγειος ἡμῶν οἰκία τοῦ σκήνους) and after (e.g., Phil 2:30 τὸ ὑμῶν ὑστέρημα τῆς πρός με λειτουργίας) the *nomen regens*.

S. G. Green

The publication of S. G. Green's *Handbook to the Grammar of the Greek Testament* spans the end of the nineteenth and the beginning of the twentieth century.[7]

---

6 BDAG 1025 s.v. υἱός 2cβ.

7 Samuel G. Green, *Handbook to the Grammar of the Greek Testament*, rev. and imp. ed. (New York: Revell, 1904), 207–22. The discussion in this section derives from the 1904 edition. Green's revised edition was completed in 1885, revised mainly by his son, S. Walter Green, with a shift from the *Textus Receptus* to the Westcott-Hort NT and the addition of references to the Revised Version (xii). Different dates for successive editions seem only to differentiate British and American printings of the volume. The structure of the sections is identical, with the genitive case discussion beginning with §246 and ending with §275. Only slight differences separate the 1876 and 1907 editions (clarifying phrases seem the extent of the changes). Pagination differences between the editions seem due to font size and page layout. The 1907 edition employs a more user-friendly bold type to set key words and definitions. The examples given in each section are nearly identical, with some examples from the 1876 edition withdrawn from the 1907 edition.

Green's treatment has the virtue of including a rich variety of illustrative examples of genitive usage in context, but his categories of usage for adnominal genitives follows familiar contours: origin (what most would call "subjective"), separation (or ablation), possession, attribute (or quality), apposition partition, object, relation.

Green displays the influence of Winer when he says, "The fundamental meaning of the case as denoting *whence* is very apparent" (§254 p. 212), referring to the categories he lists as "modifications" from this basic meaning (§246 p. 207). Green also follows Winer in including the ablative usage of the genitive under the genitive of separation.

Like many other grammarians, Green notes the usual word order has the genitive noun following the head noun, and also the application of Apollonius's Canon[8] to the relationship (without naming Apollonius). He also notices the difference between classical Greek's tendency to put an articular genitive phrase in attributive position, and notes this word order is "rarely followed." The phrase ἡ τοῦ θεοῦ μακροθυμία *the patience of God* (1 Pet 3:20) is one such example (§260 p. 215).

After noting that genitives typically follow what they modify, Green comes close to recognition of genitive use in clusters when he notes word order with genitive pronouns. Following Winer, he says genitive may precede, "When one Genitive belongs to more than one substantive" noting the same example Winer cites from Acts 3:7 (TR). In other instances, the position of the genitive may indicate emphasis (e.g., Phil 2:25 ὑμῶν δὲ ἀπόστολον) or primacy (Rom 11:13 ἐθνῶν ἀπόστολος with emphasis on *of the Gentiles*; §260 p. 215).

J. H. Moulton

James Hope Moulton set out at the beginning of the twentieth century to produce a series of volumes on the grammar of the NT, beginning just as the discoveries of papyrus documents in Greek close in date to NT books were coming to light. The third edition of the work appeared in 1908.[9] Moulton is concise in presenting the syntax of the genitive which is in harmony with his goal expressed in the introduction: "I make no attempt at exhaustiveness, and often omit important subjects

---

8 Apollonius Dyscolus, *Syntax* 1.140. For translation and commentary on the formulation of the rule, see Householder, *Apollonius*, 78. The rule is cited by MHT₃ 180. For discussion, see Wallace, *ExSyn*, 239–40.

9 James Hope Moulton. *Prolegomena*, vol. 1 of *A Grammar of New Testament Greek*, 3rd ed. (London: T&T Clark, 1908). This work is designated in the abbreviations list of the present work as MHT₁. Robertson notes, in the 1919 preface to the 3rd ed. of his *Grammar* (xviii), Moulton "fell a victim in April, 1917, in the Mediterranean Sea, to the German submarine."

THE GENITIVE IN NEW TESTAMENT GRAMMARS | 33

on which I have nothing new to say" (x). Accordingly, his treatment of the genitive case spans only a few pages (72–74). Moulton criticizes Winer's whence-case view of the genitive as "utterly obsolete" (72). On the subjective/objective genitive, he insists that the decision "is entirely one of exegesis, not of Grammar" (72).

To Moulton, "The Greek Genitive is syncretic; and the ablative ... is responsible for a part of the uses of the genitive in which it was merged" (72). Moulton believes that the Greek language in prehistoric times lost three out of the primitive seven cases, one of them the ablative, although that case survived in Sanskrit. "The purely local cases," he writes explaining why the ablative, locative, and instrumental disappeared, "in which the meaning could be brought out by a place-adverb (for this purpose called preposition), sacrificed their distinct forms and usages" (61). Moulton seems in agreement with Buttmann who points to the preference for prepositions to express the meaning of the simple case, as in the partitive genitive expressed with ἐκ.[10] This trajectory finds expression in other prepositions such as κατά being used in a genitive "sense" such as τὴν καθ᾽ ὑμᾶς πίστιν *the according-to-you faith* (Eph 1:15), which would be the equivalent of ἡ πίστις ὑμῶν *your faith* (Rom 1:8).[11]

Finally, we should say, Moulton suggests (73–74) a different category name "genitive of definition" (like the adjectival genitive) that accounts for many phrases in use in the NT that appear to come directly from Hebrew (citing F. Blass who says they "obviously take their origin from Hebrew"[12]), e.g., καρδία πονηρὰ ἀπιστίας *a wicked heart of unbelief* (Heb 3:12).

A. T. Robertson

The fourth edition of A. T. Robertson's hefty tome *A Grammar of the Greek New Testament in the Light of Historical Research* appeared in print in 1923.[13] Its influence as a reference grammar continues to today, nearly a century afterwards. Robertson's approach to the subject of case is historical and comparative, pointing to Sanskrit's combination of genitive and ablative forms in the singular and stating

---

10 Buttmann, *Grammar*, 158.

11 Buttmann, *Grammar*, 156.

12 Friedrich Blass, *Grammar of New Testament Greek*, 2nd ed., trans. Henry St. John Thackeray (London: Macmillan, 1905; repr., 1911), 98. Blass cites πάθη ἀτιμίας (Rom 1:26). We will consider Blass's contribution in connection to Debrunner (see below).

13 A. T. Robertson, *A Grammar of the Greek New Testament in the Light of Historical Research*, 4th ed. (New York: Hodder & Stoughton, 1923; repr., Nashville: Broadman & Holman, 1934), 491–520.

that the "Greek genitive has taken over the function of the ablative" (247–48). Thus, Robertson views the genitive and the ablative as two cases with one form. Joining Moulton in criticism of Winer about the genitive being the "whence-case," he suggests instead that the genitive case is the specifying case (493), the ablative is the whence-case (492). Though the genitive case "adheres to its technical root-idea," Robertson cautions, that "the error must not be made of mistaking the translation of the resultant whole for the case itself" (493–4).

Robertson presents a detailed outline in his section on adnominal genitive categories: possessive, attributive, predicate, apposition (definition), subjective, objective, relationship (membership), partitive. His last two headings, "The Position of the Genitive" and "Concatenation of Genitives" are more focused on syntax than on the semantics, making them seem somewhat out of place in a list like the preceding eight categories. But word order and clustering of genitives are important factors to consider in interpretation, requiring special treatment.

Like other grammarians before him, Robertson notes the tendency of Greek authors to put the dependent genitive after its head noun, but also cites the same example (τὸν συστρατιώτην μου, ὑμῶν δὲ ἀπόστολον Phil 2:25) that Winer does to illustrate a pre-positioned genitive indicating a "sharp contrast" (502).

Robertson, insisting on separating the ablative from the genitive, leaves the partitive with the genitive. One might expect him to associate it with the ablative. Robertson explains that if the partitive idea is used without a preposition, it is genitive; and if it is used with a preposition, it refers to source and comes logically under the ablative (502). H. E. Dana and J. R. Mantey follow A. T. Robertson in this matter.[14] Brooks and Winbery classify the partitive under the ablative.[15] Also, A. T. Robertson includes "the predicate genitive" under "the genitive with substantives" rather than "the genitive with verbs," as Goodwin, the classical Greek scholar, does.[16]

Robertson makes a lasting contribution in providing several methods to interpret genitive constructions. The genitive case pretty well sticks to "its technical root-idea" of specification (493), but is shaped by its contexts (496, 500). Three elements should be considered in explaining the genitive: (1) The root-idea of the case; (2) The context: the words that are used with it; (3) History: Robertson regards μετοικεσίαν Βαβυλῶνος (Matt 1:12), "removal to Babylon," as an example

---

14 Dana-Mantey, 79–80.

15 One might expect Brooks and Winbery to follow Robertson in this regard, since they too see the genitive and the ablative as two cases with one form. But, they classify the partitive under the ablative. See Brooks-Winbery, 28.

16 William W. Goodwin, *Greek Grammar*, Rev. and enl. ed. (Boston: Ginn, 1900), 232.

of how historical information helps in understanding the meaning of the genitive (494). In this instance, the genitive is woodenly rendered "removal of Babylon." The genitive "Babylon" cannot be determined whether it is subjective or objective without the historical information about the exile in the OT (e.g., Dan 1:1–4). The genitive must be interpreted carefully because of the great latitude in the ways it is used. Again, the context must decide (501).

When it comes to the ablative, it is "rare with substantives" but it is evident in examples such as Rom 10:12 διαστολὴ Ἰουδαίου τε καὶ Ἕλληνος *difference between Jew and Greek* and 2 Cor 4:7 τοῦ θεοῦ of ἡ ὑπερβολὴ τῆς δυνάμεως ᾖ τοῦ θεοῦ *[that] the extraordinary quality of the power be of God* (514). Robertson also separates such usage from the ablative with adjectives, among which he considers as ablative usage (515–16): ξένοι τῶν διαθηκῶν *strangers from the covenants* (Eph 2:12), ἀγαπητοῖς θεοῦ *beloved of God* (Rom 1:7), διδακτοῖς πνεύματος *taught of the Spirit* (1 Cor 2:13), and κλητοὶ Ἰησοῦ Χριστοῦ *called of Jesus Christ* (Rom 1:6). Even those who do not agree with Robertson's eight-case viewpoint can still benefit from the thoughtful discussion and copious examples.

H. E. Dana and J. R. Mantey

H. E. Dana and J. R. Mantey released their well-known and widely-used Greek textbook in 1927.[17] Their categories for the genitive and ablative follow the contours of their predecessors, especially A. T. Robertson, following him in an eight-case view of Greek. Their adnominal genitive categories include: description, possession, relationship, objective/subjective (descriptively grouped under the head "genitive with nouns of action"), apposition, partitive. Their adverbial genitive categories, unconvincingly, include: time, place, and reference. C. F. D. Moule is right to associate the genitive of quantity with those of time and place.[18] Under the ablative they list separation, source, means, and comparison. "The basal function of the genitive," they declare, "is to define." Like the accusative, the genitive restricts the substantive if modifies, but "as to kind, while the accusative limits as to extent" (73).

Dana and Mantey, admitting their analysis is not exhaustive, omit mention of certain genitive uses such as the genitive of direction, purpose, or quality (75). Neither do they mention the predicate genitive, possibly due to their tendency

---

17 H. E. Dana and Julius R. Mantey, *A Manual Grammar of the Greek New Testament* (New York: Macmillan, 1927; repr., 1957), 72–83.

18 Moule, *Idiom Book*, 39.

to avoid a full treatment of the genitive with verbs. Overall, their organization of the discussion leaves much to be desired, since Dana and Mantey have not sufficiently indicated which of these categories have syntactical ambiguities, nor do they offer any guidance to the reader on the interpretation of problematic genitive constructions, nor mention the genitive in concatenation.

F. Blass and A. Debrunner

Friedrich Blass's *Grammatik des neutestamentlichen Griechisch* first appeared in October 1896.[19] Its most famous appearance in English translation came through the efforts of Robert Funk in 1961.[20] Rich with examples and applications for important genitive phrases taken from a variety of contexts, the adnominal categories are clearly distinct in presentation from other categories (except perhaps that the genitive with substantival adjectives is treated under a separate heading): origin and relationship, objective (or subjective), partitive, quality, direction and purpose, and content and appositive.

Blass and Debrunner list the concatenation of genitives with the adnominal genitive (§168 p. 93). One might have wished for a special treatment rather than including it here, but since concatenation involves adnominal uses, one can understand the organizational decision. Some uses of the genitive are conspicuously absent from BDF's headings, such as the possessive genitive and subjective genitive, but digging deeper usually reveals a corresponding opposite. The possessive

---

19 So translator Henry St. John Thackeray in the preface to the 2nd English ed. Blass, *Grammar*, v. The 4th German ed. marked the beginning of Albert Debrunner's editorial control, through its 9th ed. (So Frederick W. Danker, *Multipurpose Tools for Bible Study*, Rev. and exp. ed. [Minneapolis: Fortress, 2003], 115).

20 F. Blass and A. Debrunner, *A Greek Grammar of the New Testament and Other Early Christian Literature*, trans. and ed. Robert W. Funk from the 9th–10th German ed. (Chicago: University of Chicago Press, 1961), pp. 89–100. The German editions (18th ed. 2001) continued to undergo revision (starting with the 14th) under Friedrich Rehkopf (Friedrich Blass and Albert Debrunner, *Grammatik des neutestamentlichen Griechisch*, ed. Friedrich Rehkopf, 14th ed. [Göttingen: Vandenhoeck & Ruprecht, 1976]; Friedrich Blass and Albert Debrunner, *Grammatik des neutestamentlichen Griechisch*, ed. Friedrich Rehkopf, 18th ed. [Göttingen: Vandenhoeck & Ruprecht, 2001], which appears to be a reprint of the 14th) [BDR]. The German 18th edition does not add anything to the discussion not already covered here, but there is a certain pithiness to the language which make the German a bit more easily understood. E.g., §168(1) "Nicht oft sind zwei Gen. vom gleichen Nomen abhängig, das dann zwischen ihnen zu stehen pflegt" (p. 138). cf. "Two genitives dependent on the same noun—which then usually stands between them—do not occur very often" (p. 93).

genitive is treated under the genitive of relationship and the subjective under the objective genitive. The genitive of separation, occurring mostly with verbs is treated in the adverbial genitive section with the note that prepositions ("ἀπό or ἐκ") are more likely to do the job in such instances (§180 p. 97).

Like Winer, BDF presents two general syntactical principles for interpreting adnominal concatenate genitive constructions (§168 p. 93). The first is that when a noun has two dependent genitives, the noun "usually stands between them" (e.g., the word οἰκία in ἡ ἐπίγειος ἡμῶν οἰκία τοῦ σκήνους 2 Cor 5:1 has the dependent pronoun ἡμῶν and the genitive of apposition τοῦ σκήνους), this, they say, is infrequent. It actually seems that examples of this word order typically involve a personal pronoun (e.g., μνημονεύοντες ὑμῶν τοῦ ἔργου τῆς πίστεως 1 Thess 1:3; τὸ ὑμῶν ὑστέρημα τῆς πρός με λειτουργίας Phil 2:30 [cf. 1 Thess 3:10]). More commonly, however,

> one genitive is dependent on another, whereby an author, particularly Paul, occasionally produces a quite cumbersome accumulation of genitives; to facilitate clarity in such cases, the governing genitive must always precede the dependent genitive ... which also corresponds to Hebrew usage: [2 Cor 4:4] τὸν φωτισμὸν τοῦ εὐαγγελίου ('the light emanating from the Gospel') τῆς δόξης (content) τοῦ Χριστοῦ (BDF §168 p. 93).[21]

This is essentially saying that the dependent genitive should be taken in successive order in pairs. In the more detailed exegetical discussion, BDF offers the observation, "The last gen. is usually possessive" (§168(2) p. 93). As examples Blass and Debrunner offer εἰς ἔπαινον δόξης τῆς χάριτος αὐτοῦ *to the praise of the glory of his grace* (Eph 1:6); εἰς ἔπαινον τῆς δόξης αὐτοῦ *to the praise of his glory* (Eph 1:12); τῆς ὑπομονῆς τῆς ἐλπίδος τοῦ κυρίου ἡμῶν *the perseverance of the hope of our Lord* (1 Thess 1:3) and other instances (Eph 1:18, 19, 4:13, Col 2:12).

M. Zerwick

Maximilian Zerwick's is a useful grammar focused on issues that have value for interpretation.[22] The categories he uses are familiar, though the organization is different from its predecessors. His adnominal categories include: general (by which

---

21 This sentiment is not altogether different from what we have already seen in BDF's predecessors. See also Herbert Weir Smyth, *A Greek Grammar for Colleges* (New York: American Book Company, 1920), §1338 pp. 319–20; idem., *Greek Grammar*, rev. ed. by Gordon M. Messing (Cambridge: Harvard University Press, 1956). The pagination and wording for Gordon M. Messing's 1956 revision of the volume is identical in this section.

22 Maximillian Zerwick, *Biblical Greek: Illustrated by Examples*, trans. Joseph Smith, SPIB 114 (Rome: Pontifical Biblical Institute, 1963), §§36–50 pp. 12–19. [Zerwick, *Biblical Greek*]

he means subjective or objective), "Hebrew" (attributive or qualitative), relation, epexegetic. Zerwick includes a section titled "Multiplicity of genitives" (§47 p. 18) that mirrors that of BDF/BDR. Under the "Hebrew" genitive he concentrates on the adjectival genitive, considering it as a Semitic manner of expression. Under the "epexegetic" genitive he treats the appositive genitive with some interesting examples. It seems strange that he omits reference to any ablatival uses of the genitive and confines his treatment to certain limited aspects of the genitive case.

In some difficult instances, Zerwick is not satisfied with the classification of genitive meanings as they appear in traditional grammars. In his opinion, the genitive construction has several interrelations, so if a particular construction is classified under a given neat genitive usage category, the interpreter might be cut off from a complete exploration of the possibilities, such as in ἡ γὰρ ἀγάπη τοῦ Χριστοῦ συνέχει ἡμᾶς *for the love of Christ compels us* (2 Cor 5:14). Zerwick finds that objective ("Paul's love for Christ") does not do the text justice; nor does the subjective ("Christ's love for us") fully explain it either, "because the love in question is a living force working in the spirit of the apostle." Zerwick opines, "we must beware lest we sacrifice to clarity of meaning part of the fullness of the meaning" (§36 p. 13).

Yet there seems to be a bit of prevarication in Zerwick's insistence that the example cited above is both subjective and objective at the same time. Or yet with the example εὐαγγέλιον τοῦ Χριστοῦ being seen as *simultaneously* subjective and objective ("because it is both, and yet more" §37 p. 13).[23] True, either meaning is possible, and in different contexts can certainly be different.

In making his case, Zerwick gives no reference or context where εὐαγγέλιον τοῦ Χριστοῦ occurs. Contextual examination makes it clearer that an objective genitive is apparent in most of the passages εὐαγγέλιον τοῦ Χριστοῦ appears (Rom 15:19; 1 Cor 9:12; 2 Cor 2:12; 9:13; 10:14; Gal 1:7; Phil 1:27; 1 Thess 3:2): "proclaiming Christ." To be sure, Christ is the author of the gospel (c.f. Rom 1:1 εὐαγγέλιον θεοῦ; see the *genitive of authorship* in Chapter Four), but I think an effort must be made to find a specific sense in a specific context.

C. F. D. Moule

C. F. D. Moule's concise observations about the Greek language do not make for a reference grammar, but he certainly has much to give the reader.[24] He modestly

---

23 Nigel Turner seems to have followed Zerwick uncritically when he makes the same claim in MHT₃ 210.

24 C. F. D. Moule, *An Idiom Book of New Testament Greek*, 2nd ed. (Cambridge: Cambridge University Press, 1959), 37–43. [Moule, *Idiom Book*]

offers "some guide to the translation of some of the more obscure and ambiguous uses" (37) of the genitive. Moule is probably first to name the "distinguishing genitive" as a category. He says (38),

> The chief thing to remember is that the Genitive often practically does the duty of an adjective, distinguishing two otherwise similar things; e.g. 'to which of many men called James do you refer?' Answer: 'To the Zebedaean—the James who was Zabdi's son': [Matt 4:21] Ἰάκωβον τὸν τοῦ Ζεβεδαίου.

This new shade of meaning will be given the suitable name "the genitive of identification" by Beekman and Callow.[25]

Moule includes "the genitive of separation" in his presentation, describing it as, genitive "in form; but its meaning justifies its description by grammarians as Ablative" (41). Moule's treatment is concise, rich, and direct. His work complements the other scholarly NT Greek grammars. Moule treats the genitive and its variety of uses in several places, such as, "Accusative and Genitive—Disputed Territory," (36) "The Articular Infinitive with the Article in the Genitive" (128–29), "Semitic Adjectival Genitive" (174–76).

Moule points to context as a basic factor in determining the meaning of the genitive (40). He also states concerning the relationship between the subjective and possessive Genitive that "The Subjective Genitive merges indistinguishably into the possessive Genitive" (40), of which ἡ σοφία τοῦ θεοῦ *the wisdom of God* (1 Cor 1:21) as an illustration.

Nigel Turner

Nigel Turner continued the series of volumes started by J. H. Moulton and W. F. Howard, with his *Syntax* volume being the most important to our study.[26] Turner's categories include: true genitive: possessive, partitive, objective/subjective, relationship, quality, material, epexegetical (appositive). The section on ablatival genitives really deals with the genitive of separation.

Turner sees one case—the genitive, but he divides usage into two headings: the true genitive and the ablatival genitive. He, like Robertson, presents a clear division of the two aspects of the genitive (though Robertson, of course, sees a different *case* in the genitive forms). Readers of previous grammars might find some of the

---

25 Beekman-Callow, 255.
26 Nigel Turner. *Syntax*, vol. 3 of *A Grammar of New Testament Greek* (London: T&T Clark, 1963) 207–19. [MHT₃]

changes to category names somewhat odd. Unlike other grammarians' designation of "genitive of relationship," he includes this usage under the "possessive genitive" (207). Instead, he uses "genitive of relationship" to describe a general relationship between the nouns in the construction (212), closer to what Wallace calls "descriptive genitive."[27]

Under the heading of ablatival genitives, Turner takes up the topic of genitives "with adjectives and adverbs," approaching it from semantic consideration of the adjectives (such as "sharing ... fullness ... worthiness and guilt" etc. 215) but he is not clear about whether the adjectives in question are substantival or not (he does, however comment after citing the example κοινωνοὶ τοῦ θυσιαστηρίου [1 Cor 10:18] "substantival κοινωνός" 215).

Turner includes a section on the concatenation of genitives which draws extensively on BDF/BDR: "Rather rarely two genitives depend on the same noun, which then usually stands between them," citing all the examples of BDF/BDR (218; cf. BDR §168 p. 138; BDF §168 p. 93). He continues with the same general dictum that "more commonly ... one gen. is dependent on the other, the result being sometimes a clumsy accumulation" and that they should be taken in successive order (218).

Turner points to the value of context for deciding the meaning of the genitive: "The relationship expressed by the genitive is so vague that it is only by means of the context and wider considerations that it can be made definite" (207). Regrettably, he does not mention any of the factors he has in mind. Turner's treatment of the genitive is rich in references, examples, and applications; but sometimes it appears as if he used them randomly.

J. A. Brooks and C. L. Winbery

James A. Brooks and Carlton L. Winbery offer an introductory syntax based on an eight-case model.[28] In the fabric of their treatment, Brooks and Winbery include all the prepositions and the adverbial prepositions used with genitive-ablative forms with the genitive and ablative constructions which have the substantive without a preposition. Brooks and Winbery mention all possible uses of the genitive and the ablative. They analyze even some meanings that are hardly touched by

---

27 Wallace, *ExSyn*, 79.

28 James A. Brooks and Carlton L. Winbery, *Syntax of New Testament Greek* (Lanham, MD: University Press of America, 1979), 7–29. [Brooks-Winbery]

other grammarians (e.g., genitive of association, of attendant circumstances, and of oaths. The ablative of cause, of rank, of position, and of purpose; 18, 26–28).

It seems that Brooks and Winbery attempt to make their treatment a complete guide or manual for the uses of the genitive and ablative, with substantives as well as with both proper and improper prepositions. In their treatment they mix the substantival uses of the genitive-ablative with the prepositional uses, as if the prepositional uses of genitive-ablative are case uses. We may question this procedure with Wallace's statement *"the use of a particular preposition with a particular case never exactly parallels—either in category possibilities or in relative frequency of nuances—the use of a case without a preposition."*[29] To this we may add the observation of Chrys Caragounis that prepositions strengthen the meaning of the Greek cases especially in the New Testament and are used "for the sake of greater clarity." He gives examples about how ἐκ and ἀπό are used to strengthen the partitive genitive, and διά to show the genitive of cause.[30] For instance, ἀπέχεσθαι ὑμᾶς ἀπὸ τῆς πορνείας *your keeping from fornication* (1 Thess 4:3), where the expectation in earlier Greek would have been ἀπέχεσθαι ὑμᾶς τῆς πορνείας, leaving the preposition only on the verb.

Brooks and Winbery's treatment omits any mention of genitives in concatenation. The absence of such an important aspect of genitive usage is an unfortunate shortcoming in a guide to New Testament Greek syntax. Brooks and Winbery are somewhat haphazard with their organization, treating together the genitive absolute (16) and the genitive of direct object (19; where one would expect it to be treated with verbs). There are a few hidden gems in their treatment, though. They add a category not usually treated in other grammars, the genitive of advantage, which means, "on behalf of whom or on behalf of which something is done ... θύραν τοῦ λόγου (Col 4:3) ... a door *for the word*" (17). Regrettably, though, Brooks and Winbery present no methods or guiding principles for interpreting the genitive.

---

29 Wallace, *ExSyn*, 361–62 [emphasis original].

30 Chrys C. Caragounis, *The Development of Greek and the New Testament: Morphology, Syntax, Phonology, and Textual Transmission* (Tübingen: Mohr Siebeck, 2004; repr., Grand Rapids: Baker, 2008), 143–44.

S. E. Porter

Stanley E. Porter offers his work for the student making the transition from elementary Greek to the more advanced study of syntax.[31] His discussion of the genitive helpfully begins with the statement, "The genitive case has been variously described as the case of origin [Winer], definition or description [Dana-Mantey, Brooks-Winbery], specification [Robertson], or restriction [Louw]" (92), preferring the last as a starting point for the basic meaning of the case. Coming from a five-case system (81), Porter puts the ablative-type usage under the aegis of the genitive case.

Porter's treatment, though concise, is informative, demonstrating how complicated interpreting the genitive can be. Porter gives voice to the frustration of establishing a firm scheme for analyzing the meanings and section headings of the genitive case when he suggests somewhat tongue-in-cheek: "the number of classificatory schemes of the genitive are almost as many as the various classifications themselves" (92). For Porter, these categories for adnominal usage include: quality (definition or description), partitive, possession (ownership, origin or source), apposition, objective/subjective. With adjectives and verbs, the categories of comparison, value (or price), time (or space) also appear.

Porter reviews very briefly, but in succinct detail, elements of the "recurring debate" (95) over the phrase πίστεως Ἰησοῦ Χριστοῦ *faith* [*of* / *in*] *Jesus Christ* (Rom 3:22):

> The debate is often put in terms of whether the genitive is (a) subjective (or source or origin) and rendered 'faith of Jesus Christ', 'faith given by Jesus Christ', or even 'Jesus Christ's faithfulness', or (b) objective and rendered 'faith in Jesus Christ', or (c) both. Semantic or syntactical analysis alone will not solve the problem; context must decide. Commentators weigh such factors as whether suitable parallels are found in Romans 4 with reference to Abraham's faith, whether reference to 'to all who believe' (v. 22) is redundant, whether Christ's faithfulness is an issue for Paul in Romans, and whether and in what way Paul's emphasis is on God's righteousness. (95)

Porter surprisingly does not mention the adjectival or "Hebrew genitive" which Zerwick popularized,[32] but he indicates he is unconvinced of widespread Semitic effect on the language of the NT, and doubtful "any hypothetical linguistic

---

31 Stanley E. Porter, *Idioms of the Greek New Testament*, 2nd ed., Biblical Languages—Greek 2 (Sheffield: JSOT Press, 1994), 14. The treatment of the genitive case spans pp. 92–97. [Porter, *Idioms*]

32 Zerwick, *Biblical Greek*, §40 p. 14.

background" is of much help at any rate (13). Unfortunately, he omits discussion of genitive clusters; his discussion in an "idiom" book would have been most welcome.

R. A. Young

Richard A. Young offers, as the subtitle suggests, "an exegetical approach."[33] For him, "it seems best to categorize the genitive by its syntactic and semantic functions as evidenced in usage rather than by the form's historical meaning" (23). This is in line, too, with Porter's synchronic approach as well as Wallace's.[34]

Young's classification scheme for adnominal genitives offers three main categories. The first is "Genitives Functioning as Adjectival Phrases" (23), under which appear these uses: description, attributive, possession, relationship, content, material, and partitive. The second main category is "Genitives Functioning in Deep Structure Event Clauses" (29) under which appear: subjective/objective, verbal genitive, and compound verbal genitive. The third category is "Genitives Functioning as Adverbial Phrases" (33), under which appear genitives of time, space, disassociation, manner, comparison, price, reason, purpose, means, and reference. Some of these last uses might appear to be categories used with verbs, but Young gives adnominal examples in all of them, even if some of the examples are debatable. For instance, Young classifies ἐκ μισθοῦ τῆς ἀδικίας (Acts 1:18) "the wages of iniquity" as a genitive of means, i.e., "the money Judas received by means of his wicked act" (38).

Under this second main category the categories reflect a transformational grammar approach, in which the relationship between the head noun and the dependent genitive is brought out by transforming the expression into "an underlying kernel clause" (29). The subjective/objective usage is familiar. But the categories he classes as "verbal genitive" need some explanation as a new departure in the discussion thus far. If the dependent genitive "is a verbal noun, it represents a deep structure verb" (31). Young cites (*inter alia*) as examples of this idea: τοῦ σώματος τοῦ θανάτου *the body of death* (Romans 7:24) "the body which will die;" τοῖς υἱοῖς τῆς ἀπειθείας· *sons of disobedience* (Ephesians 2:2) "the people who disobey God;" ἡμέραν ἀπολυτρώσεως *day of redemption* (Ephesians 4:30) "the day in which God redeems his people" (32 [Young's translations in quotes]). The situation is further complicated when both nouns in the construction are verbal nouns ("compound verbal

---

33 Richard A. Young, *Intermediate New Testament Greek: A Linguistic and Exegetical Approach* (Nashville: Broadman & Holman, 1994), 23–41.

34 Porter, *Idioms*, 13; Wallace, *ExSyn*, 4.

genitive" 32), where two verbs must be used (33) such as in εἰς ὑπακοὴν πίστεως (Rom 1:5) "to believe and obey" (TEV).

Young minimizes the value of the ablative function of the genitive by classifying it as a subtype of the genitive of space, which is according to Young's division under the adverbial function of the genitive (34–35). Even the "genitive of disassociation" that he creates does not adequately deal with the separation function it deserves (35).

Young's treatment of the appositive genitive does not follow his new approach in categorizing the genitive meanings. Instead of dividing the appositive into nominal use (proper noun constructions), adjectival use (adding a definition or description), and metaphorical use (e.g., *crown of life* Jas 1:12), Young, unnecessarily, divides his treatment by case usage (39).

Under the "Attributive Genitive" Young touches the use of genitive in clusters, an area usually neglected by grammarians. He discusses some examples of the ambiguity created by such chain-constructions and a solution suggested by Beekman and Callow that "the best way to unravel them is to work backward, determining each relation in reverse order" (25).[35]

D. B. Wallace

Daniel B. Wallace's *Greek Grammar Beyond the Basics: An Exegetical Syntax of the New Testament* began as a collection of syntax notes for students in the late 1970s,[36] and its publication in 1996 marks a milestone for the present study. More than eighty years passed from the issue of the first edition of Robertson's voluminous grammar in 1914, until 1996, when Wallace published his 800+-page grammar. Just as Robertson concluded the genitive investigation of the nineteenth century, Wallace concludes the genitive investigation of the twentieth century.

Wallace presents the most comprehensive treatment of the genitive case since A. T. Robertson's. By way of comparison, Robertson's treatment of the genitive and ablative covers twenty-eight pages, while Wallace's treatment of the genitive (ablative is included) spans sixty-three. If this difference reveals anything, it reveals the amount of progress made in the last eighty years in NT grammar, and precisely with regard to the genitive case.

---

35 See Beekman-Callow, 359–60.

36 Daniel B. Wallace, *Greek Grammar Beyond the Basics: An Exegetical Syntax of the New Testament* (Grand Rapids: Zondervan, 1996), x. The discussion of the genitive case spans pp. 72–136.

Wallace, like Young, categorizes the meanings of the genitive case by their syntactic and semantic functions. The meanings of the genitive appear in five categories, namely: the adjectival, the ablatival, the verbal, the adverbial, and a sort of catch-all category, "genitive after certain words" (131), which reveals the difficulty of categorizing the diversity of nuances of the genitive case. This method of categorizing the genitive uses helps to identify the main functions of the case, and eventually enable the branches to grow organically from their respective roots.

Wallace's presentation of the genitive material is orderly and easily understood. He demonstrates every meaning of the genitive in one way or another in usable sections: (a) Definition; (b) Key(s) to identification; (c) Amplification, clarification, or simplification; (d) Semantics; and (e) Illustrations.

Under "definition" Wallace specifies meaning and usage. In "Key(s) to identification" he suggests possible English glosses to use in translating the meaning of the genitive in an appropriate way, a kind of initial check at understanding. Under a section called "amplification," "clarification," or "simplification," Wallace elaborates the definition and provides helps to make the identification clear. In the section called "Semantics," Wallace investigates the effect the structure of the genitive construction has on meaning. For example, he asks if there is any verbal meaning inherent in the nominal phrases of the subjective or objective genitive. Elsewhere he compares uses of the genitive in order to discover the nuances that are distinct to each genitive category. Under "Illustrations," provides ample NT examples to demonstrate the construction. An example of this in action is his treatment of the genitive of apposition on pp. 95–100. Wallace amplifies his discussion with proper applications and extensive footnotes with a wealth of information and charts. His classification of the whole material is superb. It is organized by a master teacher and is very useful as a tool for pedagogical purposes.

Under the "Verbal Genitive" Wallace inserts a subtitle he calls "Plenary Genitive." In the definition he says that in this case "the genitive is *both* subjective and objective" (119). At first glance the idea might seem absurd that a particular instance of a genitive case usage might have opposite meanings, and that those opposite meanings could be intended at the same time *by the author*. But those opposite meanings are opposites of *direction*, not of opposites of *contradiction*. Wallace works harder than Zerwick to bring out this difference.[37] In the example, say of ἡ ἀγάπη τοῦ Χριστοῦ *the love of Christ* (2 Cor 5:14), may refer to Christ's love for believers, or to believers' love for Christ, but these opposites are not contradictory. It is important to note Wallace's careful wording, "If *both* ideas seem to fit in a

---

37 See Zerwick, *Biblical Greek*, §36 p. 13.

given passage, *and do not contradict but rather complement one another.*"[38] We must allow biblical authors to be intentionally elastic at times.

Wallace mentions the use of genitive in concatenation, or in clusters, only once to illustrate a particular point (87–88), but it is valuable, and we will take it up in Chapter Four. The use of genitive with clusters (three-word and four-word genitive constructions) needs a thorough investigation with more definitions and illustrations.

Conclusion

The fourteen grammars taken up by this chapter represent the bulk of treatments of NT Greek. Naturally, other grammars have appeared in the past several decades, like those of A. T. Robertson and W. Hersey Davis, W. D. Chamberlain, J. Harold Greenlee, W. G. MacDonald, Kendell H. Easley, and Wesley J. Perschbacher.[39] We have not discussed these because the analyses of the genitive represented in them do not differ substantially from the work of various scholars presented in this chapter.

The genitive material examined in this chapter reveals a constructive and progressive development in presentations of the genitive. Instead of the haphazard treatment of the early grammarians, an analytical and orderly outlining appears in more recent grammars. The most serious shift in the treatment of the genitive came with J. H. Moulton's and A. T. Robertson's correction of G. B. Winer. Winer argued that the genitive case is primarily the whence-case (source or origin). Moulton and Robertson affirm that the genitive case is the specifying case. Such an understanding of the genitive released new possibilities for defining more accurately the genitive usage in its various classifications. The two most important

---

38 Wallace, *ExSyn*, 120. [emphasis original]

39 A. T. Robertson and W. Hersey Davis, *A New Short Grammar of the Greek Testament* (New York: Harper & Brothers, 1931; repr., Grand Rapids: Baker, 1977); William Douglas Chamberlain, *An Exegetical Grammar of the Greek New Testament* (New York: Macmillan, 1941; repr., Grand Rapids: Baker, 1979); J. Harold Greenlee, *A Concise Exegetical Grammar of New Testament Greek*, 5th ed. (Grand Rapids: Eerdmans, 1986); William Graham MacDonald, *Greek Enchiridion: A Concise Handbook of Grammar for Translation and Exegesis* (Peabody, MA: Hendrickson, 1986); Kendell H. Easley, *User-Friendly Greek: A Common Sense Approach to the Greek New Testament* (Nashville: Broadman & Holman, 1994); Wesley J. Perschbacher, *New Testament Greek Syntax: An Illustrated Manual* (Chicago: Moody Press, 1995). Greenlee has re-released his grammar even more recently. See J. Harold Greenlee, *A Concise Exegetical Grammar of New Testament Greek*, 6th ed. (Wilmore, KY: First Fruits, 2012).

features resulting from this examination of genitive classifications are the following cumulative outline of usage and some briefly stated principles of interpretation.

Cumulative Outline of Usage

This outline embodies all the analyses presented in this chapter and reflects the process of growing understanding of successive grammars throughout the past century. The section headings of the two main meanings of the genitive in the outline of the first list (the syntactical) are borrowed from A. T. Robertson and Nigel Turner. They represent the spirit of the whole treatment of this chapter. The outline contains the main uses of the genitive. Synonymous terms that are used by different grammarians are listed alongside the main entry.

The True Genitive

- possessive genitive, or of ownership
- genitive of definition
- genitive of relationship, or kindred, or social
- genitive of identification
- genitive of country
- adjectival, or "Hebrew" genitive
- attributive genitive
- attributed genitive
- descriptive genitive
- qualitative genitive
- subjective genitive, or of production
- objective genitive, or of subordination, or of product
- plenary genitive (subjective and objective)
- genitive of destination, or direction, or purpose
- appositive genitive (epexegetic)
- genitive of time
- genitive of place, or space
- genitive of content, or material
- genitive of quantity, or value, or price
- genitive of measure
- genitive of reference
- genitive of advantage
- genitive of association
- genitive of attendant circumstances
- genitive of oaths

The Ablatival Genitive

- genitive of separation, or departure, or disassociation
- genitive of cause, or reason
- genitive of origin, or source
- partitive genitive
- genitive of comparison
- genitive of exchange
- genitive of agency, or means

Principles for Interpretation

The second concluding feature of this chapter, as important as the first, is the suggestions presented by grammarians concerning how to interpret the genitive when it is ambiguous. Underneath it all is a body of suggestions that comprises a good basis for a detailed list to be used as a guide for interpreting the genitive. We can summarize the requirements of adnominal genitive interpretation thus:

1. Thorough exegesis
2. Giving attention to the root-idea of the genitive
3. Considering the verbal idea included in the governing substantive
4. Considering the force of prepositions in determining the meaning of the genitive construction
5. Considering the context (both literary and historical) and what it suggests
6. Considering the internal connection in every passage
7. Comparing parallel expressions and passages
8. In multiple genitives, the governing genitive comes regularly before the dependent genitive

These principles are the result of diligent and insightful study by leading grammarians. Every point in the above list needs an explanation and an illustration. That task will be addressed in a coming chapter.

Bibliography

Blass, Friedrich. *Grammar of New Testament Greek.* Translated by Henry St. John Thackeray. 2nd ed. London: Macmillan, 1905. Reprint, 1911.

Blass, Friedrich and Albert Debrunner. *Grammatik des neutestamentlichen Griechisch.* Edited by Friedrich Rehkopf. 18th ed. Göttingen: Vandenhoeck & Ruprecht, 2001. [BDR]

Buttmann, Alexander. *A Grammar of the New Testament Greek.* Translated by J. H. Thayer. Andover: Draper, 1880. [Buttman, *Grammar*]

Buttmann, Philipp Karl. *Griechische Schulgrammatik.* Berlin: Mylius, 1819. https://www.google.com/books/edition/Griechische_Schulgrammatik/TCRGAAAAcAAJ.

Buttmann, Philipp Karl. *Griechische Grammatik.* Edited by Alexander Buttmann. 22nd ed. Berlin: Dümmler, 1869. https://archive.org/details/philippbuttmann00butt/page/n3.

Caragounis, Chrys C. *The Development of Greek and the New Testament: Morphology, Syntax, Phonology, and Textual Transmission.* Tübingen: Mohr Siebeck, 2004. Reprint, Grand Rapids: Baker, 2008.

Chamberlain, William Douglas. *An Exegetical Grammar of the Greek New Testament.* New York: Macmillan, 1941. Reprint, Grand Rapids: Baker, 1979.

Danker,FrederickW.*MultipurposeToolsforBibleStudy.*Rev.andexp.ed.Minneapolis:Fortress,2003.

Goodwin, William W. *Greek Grammar.* Rev. and enl. ed. Boston: Ginn, 1900.

Green, Samuel G. *Handbook to the Grammar of the Greek Testament.* rev. and imp. ed. New York: Revell, 1904.

Smyth, Herbert Weir. *A Greek Grammar for Colleges.* New York: American Book Company, 1920.

Smyth, Herbert Weir. *Greek Grammar.* Revised ed. by Gordon M. Messing. Cambridge: Harvard University Press, 1956.

Winer, Georg Benedikt. *Grammatik des neutestamentlichen Sprachidioms: Als sichere Grundlage der neutestamentlichen Exegese.* 6th corr. and enl. ed. Leipzig: Vogel, 1855 https://www.google. com/books/edition/Grammatik_des_neutestamentlichen_Sprachi/ 62loAAAAcAAJ?hl= en&gbpv=1&pg=PP7&printsec=frontcover.

Winer, Georg Benedikt. *Grammatik des neutestamentlichen Sprachidioms: Als sichere Grundlage der neutestamentlichen Exegese.* 7th corr. and enl. ed., Gottlieb Lünemann ed. Leipzig: Vogel, 1867 https://www.google.com/books/edition/Grammatik_des_neutestamentlichen_Sprachi/ MWsOAAAAQAAJ?hl=en&gbpv=1&pg=PR2&printsec=frontcover.

Winer, Georg Benedikt. *A Treatise on the Grammar of New Testament New Testament Greek: Regarded as a Sure Basis for New Testament Exegesis.* Translated by W. F. Moulton. 3rd ed. Edinburgh: T&T Clark, 1882. [Winer, *Grammar*]

Winer, Georg Benedikt. *Grammatik des neutestamentlichen Sprachidioms.* 8th ed., ed. Paul Wilhelm Schmiedel. 2 vols. Göttingen: Vandenhoeck & Ruprecht, 1894.

Winer, Georg Benedikt. *A Grammar of the Idiom of the New Testament: Prepared as a Solid Basis for the Interpretation of the New Testament.* Translated by Edward Masson and Joseph Henry Thayer. 7th ed. enl. and impr. by Gottlieb Lünemann. Andover, MA: Draper, 1904 http:// books.google.com/books?id=AE85AQAAMAAJ.

Young, Richard A. *Intermediate New Testament Greek: A Linguistic and Exegetical Approach.* Nashville: Broadman & Holman, 1994.

CHAPTER THREE

The Semantics
of Adnominal Genitives

In Chapter Two the major NT Greek reference grammars of the last hundred or so years were surveyed and evaluated. In this chapter, our goal is to investigate the growing influence of semantics (as a branch of linguistics) on Bible interpretation, mainly concerned with "the science of meaning."[1] Stanley E. Porter and Matthew B. O'Donnell point to James Barr's monograph *The Semantics of Biblical Language* as one of the key influences for raising awareness of semantics for Bible scholars.[2]

Technically speaking, there is a difference between the overlapping terms *semantics* and *pragmatics*. Margarita Goded Rambaud offers this distinction: "semantics deals with conventional meaning, that is to say, with those aspects of meaning which do not vary much from context to context, while pragmatics deals

---

1   F. R. Palmer (*Semantics*, 2nd ed. [Cambridge: Cambridge University Press, 1981], 1) credits the first application of a Greek neologism *sémantique* to Michel Bréal, a French linguist whose book *Semantics: Studies in the Science of Meaning* appeared in English in 1900 (Michel Bréal, *Semantics: Studies in the Science of Meaning*, trans. Nina Cust [New York: Holt, 1900]).

2   James Barr, *The Semantics of Biblical Language* (London: Oxford University Press, 1961; repr., Eugene, OR: Wipf & Stock, 2004); See Stanley E. Porter and Matthew Brook O'Donnell, "Semantics and Patterns of Argumentation in the Book of Romans: Definitions, Proposals, Data and Experiments," in *Diglossia and Other Topics in New Testament Linguistics*, ed. Stanley E. Porter, JSNTS 193; SNTG 6 (Sheffield: Sheffield Academic Press, 2000), 154.

with aspects of individual usage and context-dependent meaning."[3] In the more recent past, NT scholars have begun to explore how words mean what they mean in context. Goded Rambaud's tension between semantics and pragmatics can be seen in what Wallace calls "semantic situation" and the difference between "affected" (or "real-life") and "unaffected" ("the meaning of the construction in a vacuum") meaning.[4] To put it another way, Stanley Porter points out three sources of meaning:

> These include [1] the meaning contributed by context in a given instance ... [2] the meaning contributed by particular syntactical features ... and [3] the meaning contributed by the fundamental semantics of a case as part of the Greek case system ... As a result, *Greek cases are subject to a three-tiered analysis, including the meaning of the form, syntax and context.*[5]

This chapter is a treatment of the semantics of the genitive case found in the Pauline epistles. Thus, this and the previous chapter are complementary; both aim at understanding the genitive comprehensively.

Short History of Linguistic Theory

In order to understand fully the need of applying the results of semantics to the New Testament Greek studies, there must be awareness of what happened to the study of the grammar of New Testament Greek in the last two centuries.

The period of scientific study of the New Testament Greek grammar, which started in the beginning of the nineteenth century, is long enough to permit making some observations. Daryl D. Schmidt, for example, observes a cause-effect relationship between linguistic theories and the development of theories of NT Greek grammar. He notices that each change in understanding the Hellenistic Greek grammar has been occasioned by a new linguistic theory. He says:

> The study of grammar in the modern era has gone through several momentous periods, and each one has been conditioned primarily by a preceding change in linguistic theory. In each case the change has occurred rather suddenly and has had a

---

3   Margarita Goded Rambaud, *Semantics*, Unidades Didácticas (Madrid: Universidad Nacional de Educación a Distancia, 2010), 22.
4   Wallace, *ExSyn*, 2.
5   Porter, *Idioms*, 81–82. [emphasis is original; enumeration added]

revolutionary effect on the study of grammar. The study of Hellenistic Greek grammar has followed this same pattern.[6]

Schmidt observes four linguistic periods that occurred in the study of Hellenistic Greek grammar in the last two centuries. These periods are (1) rationalist, (2) comparative-historical, (3) structuralist, and (4) transformational-generative.[7] These useful demarcations will guide our discussion in describing the changing approaches of grammars presented in Chapter Two.

Rationalistic

The rationalistic period dominated in the first half of the nineteenth century, with G. B. Winer leading the way. Daryl Schmidt notes that Gottfried Hermann and his school, who were concerned with rational philology, influenced Winer.[8] Winer sought to break the study of the NT free from the chains of "a perverted philology" that failed to recognize the language of the NT was "a *living* idiom."[9] A. T. Robertson lauds Winer's success as a tenacious grammarian who gained a broad influence, both during and beyond his lifetime.[10]

Comparative-Historical

The comparative-historical school dominated NT grammatical studies in the second half of the nineteenth century and in the first quarter of the twentieth century. Friedrich Blass, Albert Debrunner, James H. Moulton and A. T. Robertson were the creative thinkers who applied this method to the NT. Robertson names Franz Bopp as the pioneer of the field of comparative philology.[11] Those grammarians' linguistic focus on Indo-European languages led to broad emphases involving the comparison of NT Greek with classical Greek (BDF follows this

---

6   Daryl D. Schmidt, *Hellenistic Greek Grammar and Noam Chomsky: Nominalizing Transformations*, SBLDS 62 (Chico, CA: Scholars Press, 1981), 1.

7   Schmidt, *Hellenistic Greek Grammar*, 3; See also David Alan Black, "The Study of New Testament Greek in the Light of Ancient and Modern Linguistics," in *Interpreting the New Testament: Essays on Methods and Issues*, ed. David Alan Black and David S. Dockery (Nashville: Broadman & Holman, 2001), 230–52.

8   Schmidt, *Hellenistic Greek Grammar*, 3.

9   Winer, *Grammar*, xxi.

10 Robertson, *Grammar*, 4.

11 Robertson, *Grammar*, 10. As Schmidt notes this transformation was driven by "a change in linguistic theory and the discovery of new texts" ("The Study of Hellenistic Greek Grammar in the Light of Contemporary Linguistics," *Perspectives in Religious Studies* 11.4 [1984]: 29).

model), combined with the comparison of other Hellenistic Greek, such as the LXX, papyri, and the like.[12] The use of comparative philology paved the way for a more scientific approach to the study of language.

Structuralist

Structuralism was a main influence on grammatical study in the first half of the twentieth century. John Lyons credits structuralism's origins to Swiss linguist Ferdinand de Saussure, while Anthony Thiselton adds Charles Peirce as a co-founder.[13] This approach to language posits a structure or system from which words are chosen in relation to each other (rather than arbitrarily used), and that there is a degree of objectivity possible in the analysis of this structured system.[14]

One of the key developments of this method is the recognition that the study of language is more than just consideration of individual words. The structuralist approach works to group words into the smallest meaningful units for "immediate constituent analysis."[15] This combination of words into units is what Black describes as "structural meaning" as distinct from "lexical meaning."[16] The structural meaning, or the meaning of words in their immediate context, is one of the keys needed for working with adnominal genitives. Structuralism has been successfully applied to the study of the NT by scholars like Robert Funk, Peter Cotterell, Max Turner, David Black, Daniel Patte, and Gordon Fee.[17]

---

12   See Schmidt, *Hellenistic Greek Grammar*, 6, 7, 10.

13   John Lyons, *Introduction to Theoretical Linguistics* (Cambridge: Cambridge University Press, 1968), 38; Anthony C. Thiselton, *New Horizons in Hermeneutics* (Grand Rapids, MI: Zondervan, 1992), 83.

14   Anthony C. Thiselton, *Hermeneutics: An Introduction* (Grand Rapids: Eerdmans, 2009), 195–96. Peter Cotterell and Max Turner (*Linguistics and Biblical Interpretation* [Downers Grove: IVP, 1989], 29) helpfully distance *structuralism* in the study of language from the application of the term to social anthropology in the work of authors like Claude Levi-Strauss.

15   David Alan Black, *Linguistics for Students of New Testament Greek: A Survey of Basic Concepts and Applications*, 2nd ed. (Grand Rapids: Baker, 1995), 100.

16   Black, *Linguistics*, 97.

17   Robert W. Funk, *A Beginning-Intermediate Grammar of Hellenistic Greek*, 2nd ed. (Missoula, MT: Scholars Press, 1973); David Alan Black, *Linguistics*; Daniel Patte, "Structural Criticism," in *To Each Its Own Meaning: An Introduction to Biblical Criticisms and Their Application*, ed. Stephen R. Haynes and Steven L. McKenzie, Rev. and exp. ed. (Louisville: Westminster John Knox, 1999), 183–200; David Alan Black, "The Study of New Testament Greek in the Light of Ancient and Modern Linguistics," in *Interpreting the New Testament: Essays on Methods and Issues*, ed. David Alan Black and David S. Dockery (Nashville: Broadman & Holman, 2001), 230–52; Gordon D. Fee, *New Testament Exegesis: A Handbook for Students and Pastors*, 3rd ed. (Louisville: Westminster John Knox, 2002).

Transformational-Generative

The fourth stage of Schmidt's historical overview is "the transformational-generative theory" of Noam Chomsky, whose linguistic studies have had broad effect in many disciplines. Put simply, Chomsky's generative grammar theory posits that language has "surface structures" (the arrangement of the words) that are interpreted by the hearer into "deep structures" by rules that can be observed and formulated by linguistic investigation such that the understanding of the meaning of an utterance or sentence is not simply a matter of purely *grammatical* or *lexical* study, but must be *semantically* oriented.[18] This insight into semantic relationships becomes important to our study, since, as Wallace puts it, the key word *of* often used to render the genitive case, *"covers a multitude of semantic relationships."*[19] Schmidt applies the results of Chomsky's theory to the language of the NT. So, approaches to the study of NT grammar generally tend to follow the currently fashionable linguistic theory.[20]

From Dictionary to Meaning

From another perspective, this development may be viewed in terms of four other successive stages: (1) lexical, (2) grammatical, (3) syntactical, and (4) semantic.

Lexical

This stage corresponds to the rationalist philology period, where emphasis was placed upon the lexical meaning of words. Definitions came from discovering the roots of words and the relationship between letters in the same word. In this period comparative philology emerged as the dominant force. Its concern was directed towards comparing NT Greek with classical Greek. Four pioneers of Greek grammar who represent this stage were Winer, Buttmann, Blass, and Debrunner.[21]

---

18 Noam Chomsky, *Studies on Semantics in Generative Grammar*, JLSM 107 (The Hague: Mouton, 1972), 66–70.
19 Wallace, *ExSyn*, 75 [emphasis original].
20 Schmidt, *Hellenistic Greek Grammar*, 41–65.
21 See Stanley E. Porter, "Greek Grammar and Syntax," in *The Face of New Testament Studies: A Survey of Recent Research*, ed. McKnight Scot and Grant R. Osborne (Grand Rapids: Baker, 2004), 78–79.

Grammatical

In this stage, the focus concentrated on the relationship between words and phrases, and the logical consequences of this relationship. There were in-depth investigations of moods, tenses, and cases. Burton represents very well this field of grammatical work.[22] Grammarians searched deeply in languages and in their comparative history seeking a better understanding of grammatical constructions.

A. T. Robertson felt the comparative study of Sanskrit (the mother of Indo-European languages) was indispensable to the study of Greek.[23] J. H. Moulton compared contemporary documentary papyri with New Testament Greek.[24] And Nigel Turner directed his attention—on the reasonable assumption of the Hebrew background of the NT writers—towards Semitic influence on New Testament Greek.[25] Turner was influenced in this approach by C. C. Torrey and Matthew Black, who emphasized the Aramaic background of the Greek Gospels.[26] Joseph A. Fitzmyer—following Turner—wrote extensively on the Semitic background of the NT.[27]

On another level, grammarians following Moulton's *Prolegomena*[28] avoided syntax and exegesis in order to save their conclusions from any subjectivity. Besides, they were convinced that correct exegesis is built on correct understanding of grammatical constructions.

Grammarians, however, soon noticed that the meaning of words exceeds what the grammatical constructions can explain, although the two are inseparable and dependent on each other. Chomsky's question remains valid even today: "How can you construct a grammar with no appeal to meaning?"[29]

---

22 Ernest De Witt Burton, *Syntax of the Moods and Tenses in New Testament Greek*, 3rd ed. (Chicago: University of Chicago Press, 1898).

23 Robertson, *Grammar*, 39.

24 MHT₁ 3.

25 Porter, "Greek Grammar and Syntax," 80–82. e.g., MHT₃ 4, 347; MHT₄ 37.

26 Charles C. Torrey, *Our Translated Gospels: Some of the Evidence* (London: Hodder & Stoughton, 1936); Matthew Black, *An Aramaic Approach to the Gospels and Acts*, 3rd ed. (Oxford: Clarendon, 1967; repr., Peabody, MA: Hendrickson, 1998). See esp. MHT₄ 11.

27 Fitzmyer's work, originally published in the 1970s, has been reissued in a two-volume collection: Joseph A. Fitzmyer, *Essays on the Semitic Background of the New Testament*, vol. 1 of *The Semitic Background of the New Testament* (Grand Rapids, MI: Eerdmans, 1997); and *A Wandering Aramean: Collected Aramaic Essays*. vol. 2 of *The Semitic Background of the New Testament*, combined ed. (Grand Rapids: Eerdmans, 1997).

28 MHT₁.

29 Noam Chomsky, *Syntactic Structures*, 2nd ed. (Berlin: de Grutyer Mouton, 2002), 93.

Syntactical

After establishing the standard NT grammars at the beginning of the twentieth century, grammatical science did not stand still. A new dimension opened: the study of syntax.

Nothing demonstrates the insufficiency of grammar alone to comprehend the full meaning of language as much as the usage of the genitive. That is why grammars give more space to genitive's grammatical uses and syntax than to other cases. In this period, which is parallel to Schmidt's "structural period" (see above), NT grammarians were busy "constructing" or "outlining" the parts of speech, which are the essential items of any real grammar. NT grammar in this stage became more analytical. This can be seen clearly by comparing the outlines of genitive syntactic analyses summarized in Chapter Two. One can see the development of these outlines from simple constructions to more sophisticated analyses.

Semantic

Although semantics as a theory of meaning began to develop in the early 1900s, it did not affect the studies of NT Greek syntax until the middle of the twentieth century. As developing linguistic theories had influenced biblical interpretation in the past, semantics began to exert influence in biblical hermeneutics in this period.

Semantics is concerned with "signification"—the meaning of phrases and sentence constructions.[30] As J. P. Louw puts it, "the study of the structure of meaning."[31] In this capacity it offers a valuable method for interpreting and analyzing genitive constructions. Syntax and semantics are complementary methods for interpreting the genitive. Distinguishing between syntax and semantics is not an easy matter. Chomsky refers to this difficult area, "There is no aspect of linguistic study more subject to confusion and more in need of clear and careful formulation than that which deals with the points of connection between syntax and semantics."[32]

These four periods (or stages) of the study of language developed organically, with each system building upon the preceding one. It seems that there is no end to linguistic theorization. D. A. Black says, "Already linguists on the forefront of knowledge are developing new systems and expanding present ones .... This merely proves the obvious: since language is changing constantly, no system of grammar will ever become the final and ultimate one."[33]

---

30 James Barr says, "By 'semantics' I understand the study of signification in language" (*Semantics*, 1).
31 Johannes P. Louw, *Semantics of New Testament Greek* (Atlanta: Scholars Press, 1982), 1.
32 Chomsky, *Syntactic Structures*, 93.
33 Black, *Linguistics*, 117–18.

Works on syntax, semantics, and pragmatics have been developed and have gained ground at the beginning of the third Millennium. Phrases such as "word order and meaning," "phrase structure trees," "principle of compositionality," "textual mechanisms," and how to solve "structural ambiguity," emerged in many general and technical linguistic works.[34] Needless to say that there is an interrelation between linguistics and philosophy from one side and Bible language and theology from the other side. Both sides are benefiting greatly from hearing the questions the other party is raising.

L. Roland Ross describes the value and role of modern linguistics in advancing biblical interpretation and translation, he says:

> Linguistics played an important role in Bible translation in the twentieth century ….
> Throughout the century, increasingly sophisticated tools were developed for studying languages from the sound the sentence: phonetics, phonology, morphology and syntax …. the newer subdisciplines of linguistics such as typology, pragmatics, sociolinguistics, discourse analysis and cross-cultural semantics have an enormous contribution to make in Bible translation.[35]

Now, after demonstrating these four systems successively, it is necessary to see the contribution of semantics to the problem of the genitive in the NT, precisely in the letters of Paul.

The Genitive in the Era of Semantics

Meaning can be expressed through many vehicles; one of them is language. Semantics is the science of discovering the meaning that is expressed through language, whether spoken or written. For our purpose, semantics is applied to the written documents of the NT. Written texts are composed of words, phrases, sentences, and passages, all interrelated. Phrases are composed of words. Sentences are composed of phrases. Likewise, passages are composed of sentences. Genitive constructions fit into the level of phrases, since a genitive construction is composed

---

34 Here are some examples of such works: L. Ronald Ross, "Advances in Linguistic Theory and Their Relevance to Translation," in *Bible Translation: Frames of Reference*, ed. Timothy Wilt (Manchester: St. Jerome, 2002; repr. London: Routledge, 2014), 113–52; Jacob L. Mey, *Pragmatics: An Introduction*, 2nd ed. (Oxford: Blackwell, 2001), 237–61; Georgios Tserdanelis and Wai Yi Peggy Wong, eds. *Language Files: Materials for an Introduction to Language and Linguistics*, 9th ed. (Columbus: Department of Linguistics, Ohio State University, 2004), 183–261.
35 Ross, "Advances in Linguistic Theory," 152.

of more than one word and is less than a complete sentence, although sometimes a genitive phrase may contain—semantically—a complete sentence. For example, a genitive phrase may imply a complete sentence as in Eph 1:4 πρὸ καταβολῆς κόσμου *before the foundation of the world* i.e., before God had founded the world.

The adnominal genitive construction may consist of two, three, or four (occasionally more) words. Meaning can be investigated semantically by studying the relationships between the words of the genitive phrase, however many words are joined syntactically in a construction. In order to understand the genitive construction fully, words and sentences which are found in a passage (the context) must be investigated. Thus, the concentration will be on the genitive construction (the phrase structure), without forgetting that semantics deals with all levels of a given text.

Many biblical scholars have written about semantics, but few have covered the genitive in their treatment of the subject matter. Scholars like W. L. Wonderly, E. A. Nida, C. R. Taber, J. Beekman, J. Callow, and J. P. Louw apply Noam Chomsky's transformational grammar in analyzing the grammatical structures. The following is a chronological survey of the treatment of the genitive by those biblical scholars and others in the last half century or so.

William L. Wonderly

William Wonderly seeks a method of eliminating structural ambiguity by using a transform that makes the intended meaning explicit, offering several examples of genitive case disambiguation,[36] a pair of which we will offer here. One of the key things he emphasizes in his examples is that the translator's choice of one rendering over another eliminates other possible construals. Take, for instance, ὑμεῖς ἐστε τὸ φῶς τοῦ κόσμου *you are the light of the world* (Matt 5:14); to render it "You are like light for the whole world" (TEV) eliminates the source genitive construal, "Light belonging to (or emanating from) the world." The warning about a neophyte pastor, εἰς κρίμα ἐμπέσῃ τοῦ διαβόλου [*so that*] *he may* [*not*] *fall into the condemnation of the devil* (1 Tim 3:16), rendered "so that he will not swell up with pride and be condemned, as the Devil was" (TEV), eliminates the possible source or subjective genitive: "be condemned by the devil." These examples show the value of transformation in making the meaning of the genitive clear, and at the same time, how unintended meanings are eliminated. This is done by transforming a structural phrase into an explicit sentence.

---

36 William L. Wonderly, *Bible Translations for Popular Use*, HFT 7 (London: United Bible Societies, 1968), 163.

Harold K. Moulton

H. K. Moulton's unassumingly titled—but important—article "Of," advances the idea that the possessive is not the main meaning of the genitive.[37] His main contribution is in pointing to the realization that genitive phrases have sometimes a wider meaning than accounted for in the traditional definitions. Regarding the phrase: "the spirit of your mind" in Eph 4:23, Moulton raises a question about how spirit and mind are connected, answering:

> Both N.E.B. and T.E.V. think that the connection is best made by 'and', not 'of'. They have 'mind and spirit', 'hearts and minds'. Armitage Robinson speaks of 'the spiritual principle of the mind', and the early 18th century commentator, Bengel, writes with characteristic succinctness 'spiritus est intimum mentis', 'the spirit is the intimate part of the mind' …. Paul is writing of the very center of our mind, where alone true renewal can take place.[38]

This is just one illustration; Moulton, however, reflects further on genitive phrases like "the abomination of desolation" (Matt 24:15); "the testimony of Christ" (1 Cor 1:6); "the hope of righteousness" (Gal 5:5); and "faith of God" (Mark 11:22). When he comes to 2 Cor 13:13, "the fellowship of the Holy Spirit", he says, "Is Paul thinking of our fellowship with one another, or of our fellowship with the Spirit? … Perhaps Paul had both thoughts in mind as he penned this genitive."[39] Here Moulton is asking the right questions and presenting the right answer, which is found in the immediate context:

> This could mean 'fellowship among believers, which is the gift of the Holy Spirit.' In that way it would be parallel in construction with the two previous genitive phrases: 'the grace which comes from the Lord Jesus Christ' and 'the love which comes from God.'[40]

Moulton calls for looking beyond the grammatical construction, to the wider meaning of words when they have special relations.

Nida and Taber

Eugene A. Nida and Charles R. Taber interact with Chomsky's transformational grammar from a conviction in contrast to Chomsky's denial of a relation between

---

37 Harold K. Moulton, "Of," *Bible Translator* 19.1 (1968): 18–25.
38 Moulton, "Of," 22–23.
39 Moulton, "Of," 25.
40 Moulton, "Of," 25.

grammar and meaning,[41] "Even a comparison of *John hit Bill* and *Bill hit John* should convince us that grammar has some meaning, for it is the first word which performs the action of the second word."[42]

But grammar alone does not establish all meanings, because "the same grammatical construction may have many different meanings,"[43] like the ubiquitous *A of B* formula in English, where A and B are nouns, as in the *foundation of the world* (Eph 1:4):

> In the case of *the foundation of the world* … there is an immediate confusion, for *foundation* normally identifies an object, e.g., the foundation of the house, but we know that this is not what is meant in Ephesians 1:4 …. We conclude, therefore, that *foundation* must in this instance not be an object, but an event, and that it should actually be translated as "creation." This interpretation is further strongly supported by the presence of the preposition *before*, which expresses time relations between events. We can then readily understand the relationship between the parts as "creating the world"; that is to say, the second element B is the goal of the first. But the first element also implies a subject, namely, God, so that the entire expression is really equivalent to "(God) creates the world." And an appropriate formula could be "X does A to B," or "B is the goal of A."[44]

The following is a selection of examples Nida and Taber present, using their kernel transformations in quotation marks. I have supplied verse references:

- *the will of God* (Eph 1:1), "God wills."
- *the Holy Spirit of promise* (Eph 1:13) "(God) promises the Holy Spirit."
- *the God of peace* (Rom 15:33), "God produces peace."
- *the day of preparation* (Matt 27:62) "the day when (people) prepare (for the Sabbath)."
- *the remission of sins* (Mark 1:4), "(God) forgives (the people's) sins."[45]

Kernels, they say, "are the basic structural elements out of which the language builds its elaborate surface structures."[46] Genitive constructions are transformed into verbal sentences, so that events are expressed as verbs. The operation of restructuring expressions in order to be clear and least ambiguous is the goal of

---

41 See Chomsky, *Syntactic Structures*, 93, 106.
42 Eugene A. Nida and Charles R. Taber, *The Theory and Practice of Translation*, HFT 8 (Leiden: Brill, 1969; repr., 1982), 35.
43 Nida and Taber, *Theory and Practice*, 35.
44 Nida and Taber, *Theory and Practice*, 36.
45 Nida and Taber, *Theory and Practice*, 35–36.
46 Nida and Taber, *Theory and Practice*, 39.

transformational grammar. Some nouns are action words, like *creation* and *faith*; others like *stove* or *tree* have no verbal idea. When the implicit power of the verb in nouns is made explicit, the meaning of the kernel will be clear. The same happens when objects are expressed as nouns and abstracts (quantities and qualities) as adjectives or adverbs.

Nida and Taber attempt to solve the problem of figurative meanings created by an extension of the main sense of a word.[47] They offer some suggestions about how to understand figurative genitive expressions. The "kingdom of heaven," for example, does not refer to a geographical place because Matthew uses heaven as metonymy for God. "Sons of disobedience" (Eph 2:2), means simply "people who disobey (God)." "Children of wrath" (Eph 2:3) refers to persons who "experience the wrath of God."[48] The value of Nida and Taber's treatment lies in relating transformational grammar to the science of translating the Bible. Applying transformation principles to the genitive case in the NT illuminates many ambiguous genitive expressions.

Beekman and Callow

John Beekman and John Callow treat the genitive problem in a chapter and an appendix in their guide for Bible translators, *Translating the Word of God*.[49] Their work is particularly useful for the purpose of our study, its main contribution being a harmonious synthesis of syntax and semantics. Just as lexicography and grammar are related, so also syntax and grammar; like links in a chain, interdependent with the other.[50] Beekman and Callow's transformational grammar approach is evident in the statement, "the most useful way of identifying the actual sense of a given genitive is to restate its meaning by means of one or more propositions" (251). Benefitting from the work of Nida and Taber, they apply the principles of transformational grammar without using its technical terminology. The reader finds on offer a detailed well-constructed outline of the meanings and uses of the syntax of the genitive case. The major divider in the taxonomy is whether the genitive

---

47 Nida and Taber, *Theory and Practice*, 87–88.

48 Nida and Taber, *Theory and Practice*, 89.

49 John Beekman and John Callow, *Translating the Word of God* (Grand Rapids: Zondervan, 1974), 249–66, 358–62. [Beekman-Callow]

50 For a similar treatment, see Mildred L. Larson, *Meaning-Based Translation: A Guide to Cross-Language Equivalence* (Lanham, MD: University Press of America, 1984), 228–33. The second edition has a special treatment of genitive constructions: idem., *Meaning-Based Translation: A Guide to Cross-Language Equivalence*, 2nd ed. (Lanham, MD: University Press of America, 1998), 249–51.

construction can be restated as a "state" proposition (a stative verb used in the representation of the idea) or an "event" proposition (where there is usually a transitive verb).

The category of "state propositions" (251–57) covers many uses of the genitive which we have already seen in the traditional grammars: possession, partitive-wholative, attributive, degree, kinship, role, location, identification, content, and material. These uses are usually restated quite simply. For instance, *the house of Philip* (Acts 21:8) is "Philip's house" (252). At the risk of being accused of hairsplitting, we might add (to make it a proposition), "Phillip *has* a house." The category of role (254) is a bit different from how some NT grammars have organized their usage. An example of the role category is τοῦ κυρίου ἡμῶν *the Lord of us* (Col 1:3), "our Lord," or τὸν θεὸν Ἰσραὴλ *God of Israel* (Matt 15:31), "Israel's God." This analysis is somewhat complicated by the fact that this kind of example can imply an event or activity "the God whom Israel *worships*" (254n10).

The category of "event propositions" (257–65) subdivided into those in which the event is explicit (257–61) and those in which the event is implied (261–65), covers those categories usually found in sections such as Wallace's "Verbal Genitive,"[51] like subjective and objective. But instead of traditional labels, the linguistic terms *agent* and *experiencer* appear (258). Beekman and Callow offer an insight about the semantic attribute of abstraction, where the genitive substantive is an abstraction rather than a thing. An example is τὴν ἀγάπην τῆς ἀληθείας *the knowledge of the truth* (2 Thess 2:10), "(they) love *that which* is true," which they classify as "content" (260). The usages classified as time, manner, and degree appear under the category of event propositions in their taxonomy (260–61). The implicit event category includes usages termed "goal," "manner," "time," "recipient," and "agent" (261–63). An example of the "goal" category (where the genitive is the agent) is a ἀνθρώπου … διαθήκην *will … of man* (Gal 3:15), "a will which a man *made*." Another is τῶν θυσιῶν αὐτῶν *their sacrifices* (Luke 13:1), "the sacrifices which they *were offering* (to God)" (261). An example of the "recipient" category is τὸν ἄρτον τῶν τέκνων *the bread of the children* (Matt 15:26), "the bread which is *to be given* to the children" (262).

Some genitive uses involve restatement as two propositions (263–65), further divided into situations where both events are explicit (263–64) and those where only one is explicit, and those where no events are stated (265). In the first category (both explicit) the restatement can involve "sequence" such as ἀνάστασιν ζωῆς *resurrection of life* (John 5:29), "(people) will rise *and then* (they) will live"; or "result-reason," such as τοῦ ἔργου τῆς πίστεως *the work of faith* (1 Thess 1:3), "(you)

---

51 Wallace, *ExSyn*, 112–22.

work *because* (you) believe (in God/Christ)" (264). Other categories involve "content" (close to objective genitive here, too), "generic-specific" (epexegetical), and "circumstance" (description). In the category of "no explicit events," the example Beekman and Callow offer is μισθοῦ τῆς ἀδικίας *reward of wickedness* (Acts 1:18) "he received a reward because he acted wickedly" (265).

In Appendix D (358–62), Beekman and Callow treat briefly what is called in the Greek grammars "Concatenation of Genitives," and the figures of speech[52] involved in the genitive construction. The authors apply the principles of semantics to the concatenation of genitives, and thus reveal the variety of meanings possible in the genitive construction, as well as indicating how to reconstruct the kernel sentences implicit in each construction. They work with genitive cluster constructions with the goal of showing the relationships between the multiple kernel units contained in each construction in order to establish the full meaning. We have already seen their influence in Richard Young's grammar (see Chapter Two).

J. P. Louw

When it comes to the application of semantics to biblical literature, Johannes P. Louw's name stands out. For instance, he and Eugene Nida collaborated to produce the *Greek-English Lexicon of the New Testament: Based on Semantic Domains.*[53] However, it is one of his earlier works, *Semantics of New Testament Greek*, that interests us here.[54] Though not treating the genitive specifically, he has many illustrations of genitive usage. In particular, his method of dividing sentences into constituent elements helps make the steps needed to disambiguate genitive phrases, which "can be better understood if the semantic parts of speech are reduced to transformations which make their kernel structure explicit" (81).

"In Eph 1:13," he writes, "the words τὸ εὐαγγέλιον τῆς σωτηρίας ὑμῶν 'the gospel of your salvation' immediately raises [*sic*] the question what the meaning of *the group* τῆς σωτηρίας ὑμῶν would be" (77 [emphasis added]). Louw helpfully states that grappling with the *word group* is a key task. It is the transformation of the surface structure of the phrase to its deep structure that constitutes Louw's method.

---

52 "Figures of speech such as metonymy, synecdoche, metaphor, and euphemism" (Beekman-Callow, 360).

53 Johannes P. Louw and Eugene Albert Nida, *Greek-English Lexicon of the New Testament: Based on Semantic Domains*, 2nd ed., 2 vols. (New York: United Bible Societies, 1996).

54 Louw, *Semantics of New Testament Greek* (Atlanta: Scholars Press, 1982).

At the surface, the genitive pronoun in τῆς σωτηρίας ὑμῶν can be subjective ("you save something") or objective ("something/someone saves you"). That much can be achieved with traditional grammar. But transformational grammar notices that because the semantic sense of the noun σωτηρία implies an event, the phrase τῆς σωτηρίας ὑμῶν resolves as an embedded sentence: σῴζει ὑμᾶς (77–78). Louw observes the contextual factor, "The connection of this group with τὸ εὐαγγέλιον results in making [the objective sense] more probable" (78), i.e., that the *readers* are not producing the action of salvation; something else must be the agent. Louw then looks to τὸ εὐαγγέλιον as the subject of the verb of the implied. Thus, the surface structure of τὸ εὐαγγέλιον τῆς σωτηρίας ὑμῶν resolves to the deep structure τὸ εὐαγγέλιον σῴζει ὑμᾶς (79).

Louw analyzes (80–83) the following genitives thus: τὸ βάπτισμα τὸ Ἰωάννου (Matt 21:25) "John baptizes (people)." θέλημα θεοῦ (Eph 1:1) "God wills." ἡ ἐντολὴ τοῦ θεοῦ (Mark 7:8) "God commands." τὸ πνεῦμα τῆς ἐπαγγελίας τὸ ἅγιον (Eph 1:13) "the Holy Spirit which God promised." τὸ εὐαγγέλιον τῆς χάριτος (Acts 20:24) "the good news of grace." Paul preaches the gospel; God shows kindness. τὸ πνεῦμα τῆς ἀληθείας (John 14:17) "the Spirit is true."[55] Thus Louw captures for us the essence of the concern of semantics that looks beyond the surface structure of genitive constructions.

Conclusion

This chapter has surveyed the era of semantics in the field of New Testament Greek, which has now covered half a century. The survey started with William L. Wonderly, then continued chronologically to Harold K. Moulton, Eugene A. Nida and Charles R. Taber, John Beekman and John Callow, and finished with J. P. Louw. These were the pioneers in treating the genitive case constructions according to semantic principles. They applied Chomsky's transformational grammar to the language of the NT looking for help to understand ambiguous genitive phrases.

To think, though, that transformational grammar is the one method that will solve all problems would be simplistic. Transformational grammar does not have a master key that opens all locks. Understanding the problem is one thing; solving it is another. Every case of interpretation demands deep and complete exegetical work with every tool available to the interpreter brought to bear. Kernel analysis can accomplish only part of the task. "Kernel analysis," Cotterell and Turner

---

55 Louw, *Semantics*, 80–83.

remind us, "provides us with a list of the basic propositions stated by the discourse .... *but it does not tell us how the propositions are related.*"[56] This goal is the ambition of the following three chapters in unpacking the genitive constructions observed.

Bibliography

Barr, James. *The Semantics of Biblical Language*. London: Oxford University Press, 1961. Reprint, Eugene, OR: Wipf & Stock, 2004.

Black, David Alan. *Linguistics for Students of New Testament Greek: A Survey of Basic Concepts and Applications*. 2nd ed. Grand Rapids: Baker, 1995.

Black, David Alan. "The Study of New Testament Greek in the Light of Ancient and Modern Linguistics." Pages 230–52 in *Interpreting the New Testament: Essays on Methods and Issues*. Edited by David Alan Black and David S. Dockery. Patte, Daniel. "Structural Criticism." Pages 183–200 in *To Each Its Own Meaning: An Introduction to Biblical Criticisms and Their Application*. Edited by Stephen R. Haynes and Steven L. McKenzie. Rev. and exp. ed. Louisville: Westminster John Knox, 1999. Nashville: Broadman & Holman, 2001.

Black, Matthew. *An Aramaic Approach to the Gospels and Acts*. 3rd ed. Oxford: Clarendon, 1967. Reprint, Peabody, MA: Hendrickson, 1998.

Burton, Ernest De Witt. *Syntax of the Moods and Tenses in New Testament Greek*. 3rd ed. Chicago: University of Chicago Press, 1898.

Chomsky, Noam. *Studies on Semantics in Generative Grammar*. Janua linguarum, Series minor 107. The Hague: Mouton, 1972.

Chomsky, Noam. *Syntactic Structures*. 2nd ed. Berlin: de Gruyter Mouton, 2002.

Cotterell, Peter and Max Turner. *Linguistics and Biblical Interpretation*. Downers Grove: IVP, 1989.

Fee, Gordon D. *New Testament Exegesis: A Handbook for Students and Pastors*. 3rd ed. Louisville: Westminster John Knox, 2002.

Fitzmyer, Joseph A. *Essays on the Semitic Background of the New Testament*. vol. 1 of *The Semitic Background of the New Testament*. Combined ed. Grand Rapids, MI: Eerdmans, 1997.

Fitzmyer, Joseph A. *A Wandering Aramean: Collected Aramaic Essays*. vol. 2 of *The Semitic Background of the New Testament*. Combined ed. Grand Rapids: Eerdmans, 1997.

Funk, Robert W. *A Beginning-Intermediate Grammar of Hellenistic Greek*. 2nd ed. Missoula, MT: Scholars Press, 1973.

Goded Rambaud, Margarita. *Semantics*. Unidades Didácticas. Madrid: Universidad Nacional de Educación a Distancia, 2010.

Larson, Mildred L. *Meaning-Based Translation: A Guide to Cross-Language Equivalence*. Lanham, MD: University Press of America, 1984.

Larson, Mildred L. *Meaning-Based Translation: A Guide to Cross-Language Equivalence*. 2nd ed. Lanham, MD: University Press of America, 1998.

---

56 Cotterell and Turner, *Linguistics*, 196. [emphasis added]

Louw, Johannes P. *Semantics of New Testament Greek.* Atlanta: Scholars Press, 1982.

Louw, Johannes P. and Eugene Albert Nida. *Greek-English Lexicon of the New Testament: Based on Semantic Domains.* 2 vols. 2nd ed. New York: United Bible Societies, 1996.

Lyons, John. *Introduction to Theoretical Linguistics.* Cambridge: Cambridge University Press, 1968.

Mey, Jacob L. *Pragmatics: An Introduction.* 2nd ed. Oxford: Blackwell, 2001.

Moulton, Harold K. "Of," *Bible Translator* 19.1 (1968): 18–25. doi:10.1177/000608446801900105.

Nida, Eugene A. and Charles R. Taber. *The Theory and Practice of Translation.* Helps for Translators 8. Leiden: Brill, 1969. Reprint, 1982.

Palmer, F. R. *Semantics.* 2nd ed. Cambridge: Cambridge University Press, 1981.

Patte, Daniel. "Structural Criticism." Pages 183–200 in *To Each Its Own Meaning: An Introduction to Biblical Criticisms and Their Application.* Edited by Stephen R. Haynes and Steven L. McKenzie. Rev. and exp. ed. Louisville: Westminster John Knox, 1999.

Porter, Stanley E. "Greek Grammar and Syntax." Pages 76–103 in *The Face of New Testament Studies: A Survey of Recent Research.* Edited by Scot McKnight and Grant R. Osborne. Grand Rapids: Baker, 2004.

Porter, Stanley E. and Matthew Brook O'Donnell. "Semantics and Patterns of Argumentation in the Book of Romans: Definitions, Proposals, Data and Experiments." Pages 154–204 in *Diglossia and Other Topics in New Testament Linguistics.* Edited by Stanley E. Porter. Journal for the Study of the New Testament Supplement Series. 193; Studies in New Testament Greek 6. Sheffield: Sheffield Academic Press, 2000.

Ross, L. Ronald. "Advances in Linguistic Theory and Their Relevance to Translation." Pages 113–52 in *Bible Translation: Frames of Reference.* Edited by Timothy Wilt. Manchester: St. Jerome, 2002. Reprint, London: Routledge, 2014.

Schmidt, Daryl D. *Hellenistic Greek Grammar and Noam Chomsky: Nominalizing Transformations.* Society of Biblical Literature Dissertation Series 62. Chico, CA: Scholars Press, 1981.

Schmidt, Daryl D. "The Study of Hellenistic Greek Grammar in the Light of Contemporary Linguistics," *Perspectives in Religious Studies* 11.4 (1984): 27–38.

Thiselton, Anthony C. *New Horizons in Hermeneutics.* Grand Rapids, MI: Zondervan, 1992.

Thiselton, Anthony C. *Hermeneutics: An Introduction.* Grand Rapids: Eerdmans, 2009.

Torrey, Charles C. *Our Translated Gospels: Some of the Evidence.* London: Hodder & Stoughton, 1936. https://archive.org/details/OurTranslatedGospelsCCTorrey/page/n1.

Tserdanelis, Georgios and Wai Yi Peggy Wong, eds. *Language Files: Materials for an Introduction to Language and Linguistics.* 9th ed. Columbus: Department of Linguistics, Ohio State University, 2004.

Wonderly, William L. *Bible Translations for Popular Use.* Helps for Translators 7. London: United Bible Societies, 1968.

CHAPTER FOUR

Adnominal Two-Word Genitive Constructions

Introduction

In Chapter Two we undertook a summary of NT Greek grammars. These grammars were researched for identifying the meanings of genitive adnominal constructions. In Chapter Three, we took up the genitive in the light of semantics. In the present chapter, our aim is to begin to classify the range of meanings of the genitive case in the Pauline corpus. All that has been gained in relation to genitive meanings from previous chapters will be applied here.

The focus in this study is adnominal constructions. Other uses of the genitive case, such as genitive with verbs and genitive with prepositions have been excluded. The first reason for this limitation is that the use of genitives with verbs is the same kind of modification to meaning as the accusative case, and the meaning of genitives with prepositions is identified lexically. The second reason for our focus on adnominal genitives is that the genitive with verbs or prepositions rarely create any problems for construal. Syntactic problems emerge when substantives are added to each other successively.

Scrutinizing every genitive construction consisting of two or more substantives in the letters of Paul is not an easy task. Nevertheless, such a survey is an unavoidable task if the aim is to construct a comprehensive list of the syntactic meanings of the genitive. In order to achieve that goal, a complete list of genitive forms, extending from Romans to Philemon, has been processed, and genitive constructions consisting of two, three, and four (or—in a few instances—more) substantives have been identified and classified.

It is important to take note of the difficulty in providing precise statistics. For the most part, counting adnominal genitives is a straightforward syntactical task: find the nominals with dependent genitives. In the expression κατὰ τὰ ἔργα αὐτοῦ (Rom 2:6) there is a head noun with one dependent genitive. But other factors will complicate the analysis. Take, for instance, θλῖψις καὶ στενοχωρία ἐπὶ πᾶσαν ψυχὴν ἀνθρώπου τοῦ κατεργαζομένου τὸ κακόν, Ἰουδαίου τε πρῶτον καὶ Ἕλληνος· (Rom 2:9). ψυχὴν ἀνθρώπου is clearly enough a two-word construction. But how do we account for situations involving ellipsis? The rest of the verse resolves to something like [ψυχὴν] ... Ἰουδαίου ... [ψυχὴν] Ἕλληνος. Or should this be counted (because of the connective conjunctions) as a four-word construction? In the interest of simplicity, we count these as multiple instances of two-word constructions with implied head words. The key factor in counting is whether the genitives are added to the head noun or whether they are chained together by juxtaposition.

There are about 1,800 two-word genitive constructions in the Pauline corpus.[1] Clusters of genitives are much less frequent. There are 181 three-word genitive constructions in Paul (see Chapter Five and the list at its end) and 29 four-word genitive constructions in the NT, 17 of them in Paul (see Chapter Six and its list).

In order to analyze properly all the syntactic meanings of adnominal genitives according to the categorization of genitive constructions mentioned above, this chapter will deal with *two-word* genitive constructions, while *three-word* genitive constructions will be dealt with in Chapter Five, and *four-word* genitive constructions in Chapter Six. There are a few other constructions of larger groupings which will be covered there as well.

For our purposes, the two-word genitive construction—as the label suggests—is a two-word construction in which one of the two is a genitive. The genitive in such a construction must be a genitive by virtue of being appended to another substantive, without a preposition or an adverb.[2] In Wallace's taxonomy, the

---

1   This is an approximation, since not everyone would agree on the groupings of specific constructions. For the most part, however which constructions would count as two-word are fairly straightforward.

2   For example to use a hypothetical phrase that does not occur in the NT: κατὰ τῶν εὐαγγελίων τοῦ θεοῦ, where, τῶν εὐαγγελίων has a genitive form by virtue of the preposition κατά; the genitive in our N-Ng construction is τοῦ θεοῦ. Wallace (*ExSyn*, 77n17), says: "Some grammarians mix the naked case uses with those of preposition + case (e.g., Brooks-Winbery, 7–64). This only confuses the issue and promotes a great deal of exegetical misunderstanding."

construction is notated N-N${}_g$.[3] This notation is useful, even when the N${}_g$ precedes
its N (e.g., θεοῦ γὰρ διάκονός ἐστιν Rom 13:4). As we are using the designation *two-word* to describe constructions, it is important to note that the designation focuses
on the main terms, ignoring articles, any intervening postpositive conjunctions,
or any adjectival elements. It also ignores any genitives in simple apposition. For
instance, in the prepositional phrase διὰ τοῦ κυρίου ἡμῶν Ἰησοῦ Χριστοῦ (Rom 5:1),
τοῦ κυρίου is the head noun (or N or *nomen regens*), and is genitive only because it is
the object of the preposition διά. The N${}_g$ (or *nomen rectum*) is ἡμῶν. The appositive
Ἰησοῦ Χριστοῦ is genitive in simple apposition to the head noun in the preceding
construction, and is not counted as part of the two-word construction.

Adnominal Genitive Meanings

Usually, both words in a two-word genitive construction are important, but the
focus is placed upon the appended genitive for identification. For example, in the
two following constructions: *the peace of God* (ἡ εἰρήνη τοῦ θεοῦ Phil 4:7), and *the
God of peace* (ὁ θεὸς τῆς εἰρήνης Phil 4:9; Rom 16:20). In *peace of God*, the genitive is termed a genitive of source or a subjective genitive, while in *the God of
peace*, it is called a descriptive genitive. In the final analysis, it may be that these
two constructions have roughly the same meaning, that is: God is the source of
peace, and God bestows it. Nevertheless, the description of the genitive construction must be centralized in the appended word, for therein lies the weight of the
genitive construction.

Since this work is concerned with Paul's usage of the genitive, the categories
adopted are limited by that consideration. For adnominal genitive usage, these
five principal categories apply: (1) genitive of definition, (2) adjectival genitive,
(3) objective genitive, (4) subjective genitive, and (5) ablatival genitive. Some may
consider "the adjectival genitive" category a part of "the genitive of definition," or
vice versa, as Wallace suggests.[4] While the last two headings (i.e., the subjective
genitive and the ablatival genitive), may seem to be interwoven with each other;
yet, they remain distinct.

---

3 Wallace *ExSyn*, 75.
4 Wallace, *ExSyn*, 72.

Genitive of Definition

The primary meaning of the genitive case consists of a substantive added to another substantive in order to define it. Although description is also an important function of the genitive, definition is closer to the real nature of the genitive. Grammarians continue to debate the nature of the definition usage of the genitive. Robertson considers the genitive of definition to be the same as the appositive, but genitive of apposition is in fact just a subset meaning under the definition category,[5] as Moule has rightly described it.[6] The following are the applications.

The genitive in the phrase ἐν δεξιᾷ τοῦ θεοῦ *at the right hand of God* (Rom 8:34), defines at whose right hand Christ sits. The genitive ὁ οἰκονόμος τῆς πόλεως *the treasurer of the city* (Rom 16:23), defines the treasurer and shows his position in the city. In ἀποστόλους Χριστοῦ *apostles of Christ* (2 Cor 11:13), Χριστοῦ defines the identity of those apostles; they are Christ's. Likewise, in the following phrases the genitive is one of definition: τῷ Μωϋσέως νόμῳ *the law of Moses* (1 Cor 9:9), πνεύματι θεοῦ *the Spirit of God* (2 Cor 3:3), ἡ ζωὴ τοῦ Ἰησοῦ *the life of Jesus* (2 Cor 4:10), τῇ βασιλείᾳ τοῦ Χριστοῦ *the kingdom of Christ* (Eph 5:5), φωνῇ ἀρχαγγέλου *the voice of the archangel* (1 Thess 4:16), τὸν ναὸν τοῦ θεοῦ *the temple of God* (2 Thess 2:4); λόγου θεοῦ *the word of God* (1 Tim 4:5), and ὁ τοῦ θεοῦ ἄνθρωπος *the man of God* (2 Tim 3:17).

The genitives in the examples already mentioned are strictly those of definition, but the genitive of definition, as a main function of the genitive, encompasses a larger variety of uses which must be classified under it. Meanings of the genitive may overlap in categories between titles and subtitles or between each group of them respectively. This is natural due to the narrowness of margin that limits the relationship among genitive uses.

Possessive Genitive

The possessive genitive, a subcategory of the genitive of definition, is very common in the New Testament.[7] In a sense, every genitive used to express ownership could be classified as possessive.[8] The possessive genitive shows who possesses whom or who possesses what. It indicates also the idea of belonging.[9] Paul seldom uses

---

5   Robertson, *Grammar*, 498.
6   Moule, *Idiom Book*, 38.
7   Wallace, *ExSyn*, 81.
8   "The genitive of possession modifies the head noun by identifying the person who owns it" (Richard A. Young, *Intermediate New Testament Greek: A Linguistic and Exegetical Approach* [Nashville: Broadman & Holman, 1994], 25). See also Porter, *Idioms*, 93.
9   Brooks-Winbery, 8.

the possessive genitive to express ownership of material things, but in numerous instances he applies the possessive to abstracts or human relationships. He, also, uses the possessive genitive regularly to describe the relation of the body with its parts.

In Paul's writings, for example, material things may be possessed: Nympha owns a house; it is οἶκον αὐτῆς *her house* (Col 4:15). A table for a banquet ἡ τράπεζα αὐτῶν (Rom 11:9) may be obtained. Paul speaks as though his prison restraints μου τῶν δεσμῶν *my chains* (Col 4:18) belong to him.

An abstract principle also can be possessed, such as: "gospel" in τὸ εὐαγγέλιόν μου (*my gospel* Rom 2:16), salvation, in ἑαυτῶν σωτηρίαν "your own salvation" (ESV; Phil 2:12), and faith, in ἡ πίστις ὑμῶν *your faith* (2 Thess 1:3).

A person—in a loose sense—may be possessed by or belong to another person. Paul says that he is a *slave of Christ* Χριστοῦ δοῦλος (Gal 1:10)[10] and urges Timothy to be a good *soldier of Christ* στρατιώτης Χριστοῦ (2 Tim 2:3). A companion may belong to fellow travelers, as Titus is our *fellow traveler* (συνέκδημος ἡμῶν 2 Cor 8:19). A group of people may belong to a person as a leader, such as *Christ's apostles* (Χριστοῦ ἀπόστολοι 1 Thess 2:7).

Even God may be called *my God* (τῷ θεῷ μου Phlm 4). The genitive pronoun could be subjective, *the God whom I worship*, or objective, *the God who created me*, but it better here to stress the idea of belonging to God. For Paul, God is a personal God.[11] This idea of belonging to God leads to confirm a phase of meaning that should be called the *exclusive* meaning of the possessive genitive, as to say "He is my *only* God" or "I belong to God alone." The *exclusive* emphasis of the genitive may be seen in λαόν μου *my people* (Rom 9:25), a possession not shared by other "gods"; τὰς ἑαυτῶν γυναῖκας *their own wives* (Eph 5:28), the wives must be, exclusively, the object of their husbands' love.

It is difficult to decide whether the genitive is possessive or appositional in expressions such as τὸ ὄνομα τοῦ θεοῦ *the name of God* (Rom 2:24; 1 Tim 6:1),[12]

---

10   In his discussion of Paul as a servant of Christ, K. H. Rengstorf, says: "Christ has won Paul from the world and made him His possession" (*TDNT* 2:277 s.v. δοῦλος κτλ.).

11   James D. G. Dunn says the possessive "underlines the personal character of Paul's devotion, probably in (un)conscious echo of typical Psalm speech (Pss. 3:7; 5:2; 7:1, 3, 6; 13:3; 18:2, 6, 21, 28–29, etc.)" (*The Epistles to the Colossians and to Philemon: A Commentary on the Greek Text*, NIGTC [Grand Rapids: Eerdmans, 1996], 316).

12   "The expression, 'the name of God,' refers to all that God is in His matchless Person as deity" (Kenneth Samuel Wuest, *The Pastoral Epistles in the Greek New Testament* [Grand Rapids: Eerdmans, 1953], 90). "τὸ ὄνομα τοῦ θεοῦ, 'the name of God,' is that by which God makes himself known … (cf., e.g., Ex 20:7)" (George W. Knight, *The Pastoral Epistles: A Commentary on the Greek Text*, NIGTC [Grand Rapids: Eerdmans, 1992], 245).

and τὸ ὄνομα Παύλου *the name of Paul* (1 Cor 1:13). In the first phrase, if the word *God* were considered a general name for the deity, then the meaning would be possessive; but if the word *God* were used as the name for the deity itself, then the meaning would be appositional. In the second phrase, the meaning of the genitive depends on what is understood by *the name of Paul*. If it is understood as "the name (which is) Paul," it would be appositional, but if we understand it as "the name (that belongs to me) Paul," then it would be possessive.

Words referring to parts of the body would also fit the possessive classification better than the partitive.[13] Body parts, after all, "belong" to the body.[14] In a phrase like ἁγίων πόδας *feet of saints* (1 Tim 5:10), the stress should be on the genitive, not on the noun that precedes it. The word *saints* is genitive and the *feet* belong to the saints. The genitive must be possessive rather than partitive.[15]

The following are other examples of Paul's use in reference to the parts of the body: ὁ λάρυγξ αὐτῶν *their throat* (Rom 3:13); ταῖς γλώσσαις αὐτῶν *their tongues* (Rom 3:13); τὰ χείλη αὐτῶν *their lips* (Rom 3:13); τὰς χεῖράς μου *my hands* (Rom 10:21); τὸν νῶτον αὐτῶν *their back* (Rom 11:10); τῇ ἑαυτῶν κοιλίᾳ *their belly* (Rom 16:18); τὰ μέλη τοῦ Χριστοῦ (1 Cor 6:15), *the members of Christ*; ἐν προσώπῳ Ἰησοῦ *in the face of Jesus* (2 Cor 4:6); τὸ στόμα ἡμῶν *our mouth* (2 Cor 6:11); τοῖς σπλάγχνοις ὑμῶν *your bowels* (2 Cor 6:12); κοιλίας μητρός *mother's womb* (Gal 1:15); τοὺς ὀφθαλμοὺς ὑμῶν *your eyes* (Gal 4:15); τοῦ αἵματος αὐτοῦ *his blood* (Eph 1:7); τὰ γόνατά μου *my knees* (Eph 3:14); and τὴν ὀσφὺν ὑμῶν *your waist* (Eph 6:14). About this usage Green remarks: "The genitives of the personal pronouns are mostly employed in this sense instead of the possessive adjectival forms."[16]

Likewise, the following are genitival phrases that refer to elements of human personality: τὰ σώματα αὐτῶν *their bodies* (Rom 1:24); τῆς συνειδήσεώς μου *my conscience* (Rom 9:1); τῆς ψυχῆς μου *my soul* (Rom 16:4); νοῦν κυρίου *the mind of the Lord*

---

13 See below under *Partitive Genitive* in the ablative categories.

14 On the idea that parts of a whole are like the whole's possessions. See Kiki Nikiforidou, "The Meanings of the Genitive: A Case Study in Semantic Structure and Semantic Change," *Cognitive Linguistics* 2.2 (1991): 172–74, https://doi.org/10.1515/cogl.1991.2.2.149.

15 See the rule of differentiation between the possessive and the partitive at the subheading *Partitive Genitive* below.

16 Samuel G. Green, *Handbook to the Grammar of the Greek Testament*, rev. and imp. ed. (New York: Revell, 1904), 212. As Chiara Gianollo observes, most of these kind of body-part possessive ideas "can be conceptualized as inalienable" ("External Possession in New Testament Greek," *JLL* 11.1 [2010]: 110, doi:10.1515/joll.2010.11.1.101). In fact, forms of ἐμός only appear 21 times in the Pauline epistles.

(1 Cor 2:16); ὁ ἡμῶν ἄνθρωπος *our man (nature)* (2 Cor 4:16); τοῦ πνεύματος ὑμῶν *your spirit* (Gal 6:18); and αὐτῶν ὁ νοῦς *their mind* (Titus 1:15).

Even the things the body does, or produces, or suffers from, become its possession, or belong to the whole being, such as tears, milk, voice, and illness. Here are some examples: τοῦ γάλακτος τῆς ποίμνης *the milk of the flock* (1 Cor 9:7); τὴν φωνήν μου *my voice* (Gal 4:20); τὰ στίγματα τοῦ Ἰησοῦ *the marks of Jesus* (Gal 6:17); τὰς πυκνάς σου ἀσθενείας *your illnesses* (1 Tim 5:23); and σου τῶν δακρύων *your tears* (2 Tim 1:4). Some of these genitives may be classified under the genitive of source, but it is more likely that they fit into the possessive genitive classification.

Genitive of Relationship

This genitive of relationship may be categorized under other genitive classifications such as the possessive, the origin, the derivative, or the genitive of identification. Its application, however, demands a special heading, because it has "a special application" as Robertson remarks.[17] The genitive of relationship is called as such, because it is concerned with familial or marital relationship. It relates a person to another or a group of persons to their people.[18] The genitive of relationship may be divided into two sections: (a) *physical relationship* and (b) *figurative relationship*.

Physical Relationship

In this context *physical relationship* denotes some sort of family relationship. Winer named this usage "the genitive of kindred."[19] This kind of genitive names a person by the father's name, as in Σίμων Ἰωάννου *Simon son of John* (John 21:15); or the mother's name, as in Μαρία ἡ Ἰωσῆτος *Mary the mother of Joses* (Mark 15:47); a wife by her husband's name: Μαρία ἡ τοῦ Κλωπᾶ *Mary the wife of Clopas* (John 19:25); and possibly a person by his brother's name: Ἰούδας Ἰακώβου *Judas the brother*[?] *of James* (Acts 1:13).[20] In these examples the implied relationship *son, mother, wife, brother*, and the like are supplied by the reader.

Such usage of the genitive for family relationship is absent from the Pauline corpus. However, Paul sometimes uses the article to refer to family or household relationship, as in τοὺς ἐκ τῶν Ἀριστοβούλου *those from Aristobulus's people* (Rom

---

17 Robertson, *Grammar*, 501.
18 See BDF §162 p. 89; Young, *Intermediate Greek*, 25–26.
19 Winer, *Grammar*, 237.
20 Though most see the expression as "son of James" here. But BDAG 479 s.v. Ἰούδας 5 concedes, "ἀδελφός might also be supplied."

16:10) and τοὺς ἐκ τῶν Ναρκίσσου *those from Narcissus's people* (Rom 16:11); but these are not "pure" adnominal genitive constructions because of the preposition ἐκ.

Paul uses the genitive of relationship in two ways: (1) *general relationship* as in τὸν Στεφανᾶ οἶκον *the house of Stephen* (1 Cor 1:16; 16:15); τῷ ʼΟνησιφόρου οἴκῳ *the house of Onesiphorus* (2 Tim 1:16); τῶν συγγενῶν μου *my fellow countrymen* (Rom 9:3); and μου τὴν σάρκα *my flesh* (Rom 11:14). These last two expressions refer to Paul's people; but ὑπὸ τῶν Χλόης *by those of Chloe* (1 Cor 1:11) may refer to Chloe's slaves or workers.[21] The second way Paul uses the genitive of relationship may be classified as (2) *direct relationship*, such as τοῖς γονεῦσιν ὑμῶν *your parents* (Eph 6:1), τὰ τέκνα ὑμῶν *your children* (Eph 6:4), and ὁ ἀνεψιὸς Βαρναβᾶ *the cousin of Barnabas* (Col 4:10). Paul also uses the following genitive phrases for direct relationship: οἱ ἀδελφοὶ τοῦ κυρίου *the brothers of the Lord* (1 Cor 9:5); μητρός μου *my mother* (Gal 1:15); ἐν τῇ μάμμῃ σου Λωΐδι καὶ τῇ μητρί σου Εὐνίκῃ *in your grandmother Lois and your mother Eunice* (2 Tim 1:5).

The figurative nature of πατέρα περιτομῆς *father of circumcision* (Rom 4:12) makes it more complicated to interpret, but it too fits the genitive of relationship category. Exactly how it fits this category depends on how the noun περιτομή can be taken. If the noun refers to the rite of circumcision, Abraham, is figuratively "the father of circumcision" (KJV ASV NASB), and thus the source of this ritual, the one who started it, in a figurative extension of the genitive of physical relationship.[22] However, if περιτομή is to be understood as a reference to the people group so designated, then Abraham is seen as "the father of the circumcised" (NRSV REB TEV NAB NET NIV ESV CSB), presumably those who are by faith the circumcised in heart (Rom 2:29). But this understanding would seem opposed to what is "clearly referring to a group with Jewish identity" since οὐκ ἐκ περιτομῆς μόνον *not from the circumcision alone* is contrasted with the group who *walk in the footsteps* of Abraham's faith.[23]

---

21 See Richard C. H. Lenski, *The Interpretation of St. Paul's First and Second Epistles to the Corinthians* (Minneapolis: Augsburg, 1937), 41; Gordon D. Fee, *The First Epistle to the Corinthians*, Rev. ed., NICNT (Grand Rapids: Eerdmans, 2014), 55n33.

22 Leon Morris, taking περιτομή as the rite of circumcision, transmits Lightfoot's opinion, "Lightfoot comments, 'The genitive περιτομῆς does not describe Abraham's progeny, as many commentators take it, but his own condition.' He was 'a father belonging to circumcision, himself circumcised'" (*Romans*, PNTC [Grand Rapids: IVP, 1988], 204n49).

23 Robert Jewett, with the assistance of Roy David Kotansky, *Romans: A Commentary*, ed. Eldon Jay Epp, Hermeneia (Minneapolis: Fortress, 2007), 320.

Figurative Relationship

Figurative relationship refers to the intimate relationship that transcends physical or family relationship. It is the relationship between God and his Son, and between God and human beings who believe in Him. In this regard, Paul uses expressions such as υἱοὶ θεοῦ *sons of God* (Rom 8:14) and τέκνα θεοῦ *God's children* (Rom 8:16). He also refers to God as πατρὸς ἡμῶν *our Father* (1 Cor 1:3; 2 Thess 2:16), and to Christians as οἰκεῖοι τοῦ θεοῦ *household members of God* (Eph 2:19).

Concerning the relationship between God the Father and his Son Jesus Christ, the expression *Son of God* appears in three different structural configurations in Paul's epistles: ὁ τοῦ θεοῦ υἱός (2 Cor 1:19), υἱοῦ θεοῦ (Rom 1:4), and τοῦ υἱοῦ τοῦ θεοῦ (Gal 2:20; Eph 4:13), with no discernable difference in meaning. Other terms that express this relationship include ὁ θεὸς καὶ πατὴρ τοῦ κυρίου ἡμῶν Ἰησοῦ Χριστοῦ *the God and Father of our Lord Jesus Christ* (2 Cor 1:3; 11:31; Eph 1:3) and ὁ θεὸς τοῦ κυρίου ἡμῶν *the God of our Lord* (Eph 1:17). Exactly what expressions like the latter mean about the relationship between God and his Son is difficult to pin down. Does Paul here use the genitive objectively, affirming Jesus's subordinate status to God[24] (i.e., God sent Christ to the world), or does he meant it subjectively: the God whom the Lord Jesus declares, or worships?[25] If the genitive is subjective, it may also mean that Jesus came to reveal God in a special way.[26] It seems that Paul is using an OT formula for the name of God: "the God of Abraham, the God of Isaac, and the God of Jacob" (Exod 3:15).[27] Any attempt to interpret these genitives must recognize that Paul's theological terms resist being squeezed into a box of precise grammatical terminology.

Genitive of Identification

The genitive of identification fits properly within the genitive of definition. It is described here under separate title because its function is "distinguishing two otherwise similar things,"[28] or to focus on one part of the two elements of the

---

24   R. H. Strachan notes, "Paul … consistently recognizes the subordination of Christ to God" (*The Second Epistle of Paul to the Corinthians*, MNTC [London: Hodder & Stoughton, 1935; repr., Eugene, OR: Wipf & Stock, 2008], 45).

25   Robert G. Bratcher and Eugene Albert Nida, *A Handbook on Paul's Letter to the Ephesians*, UBSHS (New York: United Bible Societies, 1982), 30.

26   As A.T. Lincoln observes, the phrase "characterizes God as the Christian God, the one uniquely associated with Christ" (*Ephesians*, WBC 42 [Dallas: Word, 1990], 56).

27   Paul Barnett says: "In the hands of the now-converted Paul the 'God of *our fathers*' is identified as 'the God and Father of *our Lord Jesus Christ*'" (*The Second Epistle to the Corinthians*, NICNT [Grand Rapids: Eerdmans, 1997], 67).

28   Moule, *Idiom Book*, 38.

parallel, whether it is two or more comparable persons or things. As a matter of fact, the phrase ποτήριον κυρίου *the cup of the Lord* (1 Cor 10:21) could be called simply a genitive of definition, but since it is mentioned with a counter-parallel phrase ποτήριον δαιμονίων *the cup of demons* (1 Cor 10:21), it is more appropriate to call it a "genitive of identification." The same verse has τραπέζης κυρίου *the table of the Lord* in contrast to τραπέζης δαιμονίων *the table of demons*. Aside from genre considerations (such as poetry), when a genitive occurs in antithetical parallelism as these examples do, it is better to classify it with the same syntactical force as its counterpart in the parallel.

It is necessary to give more examples to illuminate this nuance. In the phrase ἐκ σπέρματος Δαυίδ *from the lineage of David* (Rom 1:3; 2 Tim 2:8) Δαυίδ is a genitive of definition. But if Paul were stressing the excellency of Jesus' coming from David's lineage over another lineage, then it should be classified as genitive of identification. Likewise, the phrase αἱ ἐκκλησίαι τῶν ἐθνῶν *the churches of the gentiles* (Rom 16:4), refers to the gentile churches as distinguished from the Judean churches ταῖς ἐκκλησίαις τῆς Ἰουδαίας *the churches of Judea* (Gal 1:22). Likewise, τῇ ἐκκλησίᾳ Θεσσαλονικέων *the Thessalonian church* (1 Thess 1:1) and αἱ ἐκκλησίαι τῆς Ἀσίας *the churches of Asia* (1 Cor 16:19), could also be genitives of identification.[29] Other examples may be cited:

- 1 Cor 1:20–21 τὴν σοφίαν τοῦ κόσμου *the world's wisdom* || τῇ σοφίᾳ τοῦ θεοῦ *God's wisdom*
- 1 Thess 2:13 λόγον ἀνθρώπων *the word of humans* || λόγον θεοῦ *the word of God*
- Gal 4:30 ὁ υἱὸς τῆς παιδίσκης *the son of the slave-girl* || τοῦ υἱοῦ τῆς ἐλευθέρας *the freewoman's son*
- 1 Cor 15:49 τὴν εἰκόνα τοῦ χοϊκοῦ *the image of the earthy* || τὴν εἰκόνα τοῦ ἐπουρανίου *the image of the heavenly*
- 1 Cor 2:11 τὸ πνεῦμα τοῦ ἀνθρώπου *the spirit of humanity* || τὸ πνεῦμα τοῦ θεοῦ *the Spirit of God*
- Rom 3:27 νόμου τῶν ἔργων *law of works* || νόμου πίστεως *law of faith*

Sometimes this sort of genitive expressions can be contrasted in situations with similar head nouns, but in different contexts. For example, ἐντολή κυρίου *the Lord's commandment* (1 Cor 14:37; likewise, ἐπιταγὴν κυρίου [1 Cor 7:25]) contrasts with ἐντολαῖς ἀνθρώπων *commandments of people* (Titus 1:14). Also, the expression τὸν Ἰσραὴλ τοῦ θεοῦ *the Israel of God* (Gal 6:16) involves a genitive of identification,

---

29 For more applications from the Gospels and Acts concerning the genitive of identification, see Beekman-Callow, 255n11.

because Paul has in mind a concept that stands in contrast with τὸν Ἰσραὴλ κατὰ σάρκα *Israel according to the flesh* (1 Cor 10:18).

Paul uses several other synonymous terms that can be classified under the genitive of identification, like τῆς πολιτείας τοῦ Ἰσραὴλ *the commonwealth of Israel* (Eph 2:12), and γένους Ἰσραὴλ *the race of Israel* (Phil 3:5), though these two examples could easily classify as genitive of apposition. In Gal 6:10, the expression μάλιστα δὲ πρὸς τοὺς οἰκείους τῆς πίστεως, "and especially for those *of the family of faith*," is used in the same verse in contrast with ἐργαζώμεθα τὸ ἀγαθὸν πρὸς πάντας "let us work for the good *of all*" (NRSV [emphasis added]). The genitive of identification is certain in the last reference, for Paul uses the adverb μάλιστα "*especially* for those of the family of faith" (NRSV [emphasis added]). The expression τὸν αἰῶνα τοῦ κόσμου τούτου *the age of this world* (Eph 2:2) can be set in contrast to Paul's description of the *coming* age of God (cf. 1 Cor 15:24–28). Likewise, the expression ὁ θεὸς τοῦ αἰῶνος τούτου *the god of this age* (2 Cor 4:4) is in contrast with ἐπιταγὴν τοῦ αἰωνίου θεοῦ *the command of the eternal God* (Rom 16:26). The phrase θανάτου σταυροῦ *death of/on a cross* (Phil 2:8) also can be classified as a genitive of identification, for Christ humbled himself and became obedient unto death, "even the death of the cross." Paul identifies Jesus's death by crucifixion as distinct from other means of execution.

When Paul asks God's blessing on τῷ Ὀνησιφόρου οἴκῳ *Onesiphorus's household* (2 Tim 1:16), a certain household, he refers to them exclusively. The genitive is clearly a genitive of identification, since Ὀνησιφόρου stands in emphatic position between the article and noun. Paul greets the church τῇ ἐμῇ χειρὶ Παύλου *with my, Paul's, hand* (1 Cor 16:21), "in part to assure his readers of the authenticity of the letter, more probably ... as a sign of affection and indication of his desire and longing for personal presence in Corinth."[30] In 2 Cor 4:13, τὸ αὐτὸ πνεῦμα τῆς πίστεως *the same spirit of faith* the identity of the spirit is defined by τὸ αὐτό, hence a genitive of identification.[31] The wealth of references quoted in the examples above justify giving special attention to the genitive of identification as a specific nuance to the broader genitive of definition category.

---

30 Anthony C. Thiselton, *The First Epistle to the Corinthians: A Commentary on the Greek Text*, NIGTC (Grand Rapids, MI: Eerdmans, 2000), 1347.

31 As Victor Paul Furnish says, "Paul means to identify the *Spirit of faith* he has experienced with *the same* one known to the psalmist from whom he proceeds to quote." *II Corinthians*, AB 32A [Garden City, N.Y.: Doubleday, 1984; repr., New Haven: Yale University Press, 2008], 258.

Genitive of Location

The genitive of location occurs when the noun in the genitive is a geographical place name[32] or nouns that indicate a state or a sphere in which a person abides, a group of people dwells, an incident takes place, or where a piece of land is located. This category overlaps with the partitive genitive and the genitive of apposition, since in those uses, the noun in the genitive is often a place name of some sort. There is also overlap with what Wallace considers a genitive of sphere/place, though he seems to limit this category to genitives related to verbs.[33] Rendering these genitive expressions in English likely requires spatially oriented prepositions such as *among, between, in, inside, at, where, within which.*[34]

For practical purposes, it is useful to divide the genitive of location or the locative usage of the genitive into two sections: (a) *geographical location*, and (b) *metaphorical location*. Uses detailed in the first section are more straightforward since they involve obvious geographical designations. In the second section, the location or sphere is more conceptual than geographical.

Geographical Location

There are several geographical terms occurring in the genitive case in the letters of Paul. The following are some examples: ἀπαρχὴ τῆς Ἀσίας "first convert in Asia" (Rom 16:5 REB ESV); ἀπαρχὴ τῆς Ἀχαΐας "first converts in Achaia" (1 Cor 16:15 NRSV TEV REB ESV); ταῖς ἐκκλησίαι τῆς Γαλατίας "the churches in Galatia" (1 Cor 16:1 REB) αἱ ἐκκλησίαι τῆς Ἀσίας "the churches in Asia" (1 Cor 16:19); ταῖς ἐκκλησίαις τῆς Μακεδονίας "the churches in Macedonia" (2 Cor 8:1 REB); ταῖς ἐκκλησίαις τῆς Ἰουδαίας "the churches in Judea" (Gal 1:22 RSV); and ὄρους Σινᾶ *a mountain in Sinai* (Gal 4:24). Also to be considered here is the more general expression τὰ κατώτερα μέρη τῆς γῆς *the lower parts of the earth* (Eph 4:9). This genitive is still locational in its sense regardless of the other nuances it might fit. There are three possible nuances: (1) partitive (*the lower parts of the earth*), (2) comparative (*the parts lower than the earth*), or (3) appositional/epexegetical (*the lower parts, that is, the earth*).[35]

---

32 A useful index of this broad category is the group of nouns classified as geographic terms, as in, for instance, LN §1: "Geographic Objects and Features," or LN §93 "Names of Persons and Places."

33 See Wallace, *ExSyn*, 122–24.

34 This list was gleaned from several keyword identifiers in Wallace, *ExSyn*, 124.

35 See also these two meanings of the genitive under the ablative category at the end of this chapter. For the grammatical discussion, see Wallace, *ExSyn*, 99–100. Wallace opts for the genitive of

Metaphorical Location

There are some other locational genitive expressions in Paul's writings referring to a sphere or realm other than a geographical or physical location. For example, Phoebe is described as διάκονον τῆς ἐκκλησίας *a servant in the church* (Rom 16:1) at Cenchreae.[36] Jesus Christ is μεσίτης θεοῦ καὶ ἀνθρώπων *mediator between God and people* (1 Tim 2:5). This example is not easily classified into the ordinary uses of the genitive.[37] Also, τὰ κρυπτὰ τοῦ σκότους "the hidden things of darkness" (1 Cor 4:5 KJV) is rendered "the things hidden in darkness" by several versions (RSV NIV NAB ESV).[38] But Turner argues that this is a subjective genitive: *the darkness which hides.*[39] Another appropriate example for *metaphorical location* is ἀγῶνα τῆς πίστεως *struggle of faith* (1 Tim 6:12), where faith is the sphere: the fight is a fight *in the course* of faith.[40] The expression τὴν ὑμῶν προκοπὴν καὶ χαρὰν τῆς πίστεως *your progress and joy of faith* (Phil 1:25) is difficult to assess. Richard Melick takes the genitive as objective: "progress and joy directed toward their faith."[41] Markus Bockmuehl notes a possible subjective sense as the "human response" to the gospel, but tentatively suggests "quite possibly both [objective and subjective] are meant."[42] Fee says that "most likely it is a 'genitive of reference' ... thus, 'progress and joy, both with regard to the faith.'" As an alternative he refers to the article that controls both nouns τὴν προκοπὴν καὶ χαρὰν and suggests "your faith's

---

apposition, while Harold Hoehner (*Ephesians: An Exegetical Commentary* [Grand Rapids: Baker Academic, 2002], 533–36) favors the partitive. Both view the comparative sense as unlikely.

36 Where ἐκκλησία designates "a local organized Christian community" (Joseph A. Fitzmyer, *Romans: A New Translation with Introduction and Commentary*, AB 33 [New York: Doubleday, 1993], 729). Gie Vleugels sees the genitive as objective: *she serves the church* (personal correspondence with Ghassan Khalaf, April 2000). See also REB. Jewett points to a leadership role for her in the church (Jewett, *Romans*, 944).

37 Wallace, *ExSyn*, 135.

38 As Gordon Fee puts it, "The motives that lie behind the visible actions" (*1 Corinthians*, 178). C. K. Barrett handles the expression similarly (*The First Epistle to the Corinthians*, BNTC [Peabody, MA: Hendrickson, 1968], 103).

39 MHT₃ 14; cf. "the darkness itself which hides" Nigel Turner, *Grammatical Insights into the New Testament* (Edinburgh: T&T Clark, 1966), 132.

40 See TEV and Wuest, *Pastoral Epistles*, 99.

41 Richard R. Melick, Jr., *Philippians, Colossians, Philemon*, NAC 32 (Nashville: Broadman, 1991), 87n102; Gordon D. Fee, *Philippians*, IVPNTC 11 (Downers Grove: IVP, 1999), 73.

42 Markus Bockmuehl, *The Epistle to the Philippians*, BNTC (London: Black, 1997), 94. G. Walter Hansen (*The Letter to the Philippians*, PNTC [Grand Rapids: Eerdmans, 2009], 90–91) similarly notes the presence of both objective (1:27 faith in the gospel) and subjective (1:29 believing in him) elements in the context.

progress and joy."[43] It seems best to take "in the faith" as the metaphorical space or the sphere (genitive of location) in which Christians grow and rejoice. The very similar expression in Rom 15:13 χαρᾶς καὶ εἰρήνης ἐν τῷ πιστεύειν, "joy and peace in believing" is a parallel using ἐν that supports the genitive of location for Phil 1:25. A plethora of English translations (RSV NRSV REB TEV NIV NJB NET ESV CSB) render the expression "progress and joy in the faith." But in this matter, the English preposition *in* can represent Fee's "genitive of reference"[44] view or a genitive of location. In some situations, there is probably little semantic distance between the two categories.

The above examination of the locative usage of the genitive shows that it deserves a proper place among the semantic range of the genitive case, and it fits properly under the genitive of definition, which covers a variety of similar genitive uses.

Genitive of Association

The genitive of association indicates a notion of parallelism or company (accompanying) and can be rendered by using adverbs such as: *by*, *with*, or *along with*. Citing John 6:66 and Mark 1:13 as examples, Brooks and Winbery declare, "Association is expressed in the genitive case only by the substantive with the preposition μετά."[45] This definition is inadequate. Wallace provides a clearer understanding of associative usage of the genitive without prepositions:

> The head noun to which this kind of genitival use is connected is normally prefixed with συν-. Such compound nouns naturally lend themselves to the associative idea. As well, some nouns and adjectives already embrace lexically the idea of "in association with" and hence can take a genitive of association without συν- prefixed to them.[46]

This definition has relevance for adnominal constructions involving substantival adjectives in this associative semantic domain. It is worth noting the examples Wallace cites for συν- prefixed head word constructions in the Pauline corpus. First are clear examples: συγκληρονόμοι Χριστοῦ *co-heirs with Christ* (Rom 8:17), συμπολῖται τῶν ἁγίων *fellow-citizens with the saints* (Eph 2:19), συμμέτοχοι αὐτῶν *co-partakers with them* (Eph 5:7), and ὁ συναιχμάλωτός μου *fellow prisoner with me* (Col 4:10). These are debated examples: σύμβουλος αὐτοῦ *his counselor* (or *counselor*

---

43 Gordon D. Fee, *Paul's Letter to the Philippians*, NICNT (Grand Rapids: Eerdmans, 1995), 153n15.
44 For which, see Wallace, *ExSyn*, 127–28.
45 Brooks-Winbery, 18.
46 Wallace, *ExSyn*, 128–29.

with him Rom 11:34); θεοῦ συνεργοί *God's fellow-workers* (or *fellow-workers with God* 1 Cor 3:9); συμμιμηταί μου *imitators of me* (or *imitators with me* Phil 3:17).[47]

The truth of the matter is that Paul does use the genitive of association without prepositions, but very rarely. The first apparent genitive of association without a preposition in the Pauline corpus is τὸ ποτήριον τῆς εὐλογίας *the cup of thanksgiving* (1 Cor 10:16). This expression refers to the prayers *associated* with the offering of the cup at the Lord's Supper. C. K. Barrett translates the expression as follows: "The cup of blessing, *over which* ... we say the blessing (that is, the thanksgiving to God)."[48] Thiselton supports the position of Barrett by taking the genitive to be of association, "people did not 'bless the cup,' but blessed *God* (i.e., with thanksgiving) for what God had provided."[49] Accordingly, τῆς εὐλογίας does not fall under subjective genitive,[50] but under the genitive of association. The blessing or the prayers that go with giving of the cup confirm the meaning of the genitive as that of association.

Another example is ἡ ἄμμος τῆς θαλάσσης (Rom 9:27). The precise meaning of the phrase would be, "the sand by the sea" (TEV NIV). There is good reason here to consider the expression as a genitive of association. Another frequently occurring example of the genitive of association involves the word κοινωνία (and its cognate κοινωνός), which entails both fellowship and partnership.[51] These two meanings are synonymous and are inherent in the lexical meaning of κοινωνία, both denoting a kind of association. Thus, κοινωνοὶ τοῦ θυσιαστηρίου (1 Cor 10:18) is translated "participants [partners REB] in the altar" (REB NIV ESV); κοινωνοὺς τῶν δαιμονίων (1 Cor 10:20) as "participants [partners REB] with demons" (REB NIV ESV). The phrase ὡς κοινωνοί ἐστε τῶν παθημάτων, οὕτως καὶ τῆς παρακλήσεως (2 Cor 1:7) is translated "as you share in our sufferings, so also you [will NET] share in our consolation" (NRSV NET NIV). These examples amply demonstrate that Paul uses the genitive of association without prepositions and that it deserves to be categorized with genitive meanings.

---

47 Wallace, *ExSyn*, 129–30.

48 Barrett, *1 Corinthians*, 231. [emphasis added]

49 Thiselton, *1 Corinthians*, 756 [emphasis original]. Cf. John S. Ruef, *Paul's First Letter to Corinth*, WPC (Philadelphia: Westminster John Knox, 1977), 98.

50 David Garland says specifically that it is "not a subjective genitive" (*1 Corinthians*, BECNT [Grand Rapids, MI: Baker Academic, 2003], 476).

51 See BDAG 552–53 s.v. κοινωνία 1, 4; s.v. κοινωνός 1αβ.

Genitive of Accordance

This usage of the genitive becomes clear when an expression such as "according to" is applied to genitive constructions. The function of this kind of genitive is to limit the standard by which the subject, that is the head word, is measured.

Several genitives of accordance are scattered throughout Paul's letters. It is certain that the genitive construction ἡ τοῦ κόσμου λύπη (2 Cor 7:10) is that of accordance. The literal translation is "the grief of the world," but it means "the grief *according to* the world." This meaning is strongly attested by the parallel expression ἡ κατὰ θεὸν λύπη that occurs here and in v. 11. Most leading Bible versions translate ἡ τοῦ κόσμου λύπη by "worldly grief" or "worldly sorrow" (RSV NRSV NIV NET ESV CSB). The adverbial expression is synonymous with the accordance nuance of the genitive.[52] The NJB has "the world's kind of distress." While the REB aptly translates ἡ τοῦ κόσμου λύπη by "pain borne in the world's way."[53] Both versions show forth the accordance function of the genitive.

Another genitive that bears the meaning of accordance is τὸ μέτρον τοῦ κανόνος (2 Cor 10:13). The KJV translates the genitive phrase literally: "the measure of the rule." This expression may well be translated as "the measure that *agrees with* the limit." REB reads "our sphere is *determined by* the limit," also, NET says precisely: "*according to* the limits" [emphasis added]. These translations render the accordance function of the genitive.[54]

A similar genitive of accordance occurs in Eph 6:4, ἐν παιδείᾳ καὶ νουθεσίᾳ κυρίου. According to F. F. Bruce, the instruction involves imitation of Christ's example and commitment to the principles he embodies.[55] Lincoln comments on this verse: "teach their children ... about Christ and help to shape their lives *in accordance with* it."[56] So,

---

52 These versions' renderings of ἡ κατὰ θεὸν λύπη by "godly grief" or "godly sorrow" show a construal of κατά with the accusative and the function of the genitive as parallel. Commentators note the two expressions are contrastive. See, for instance, Furnish, *II Corinthians*, 388; Ralph P. Martin, *2 Corinthians*, 2nd ed., WBC (Nashville: Nelson, 2014), 232. Cf. Harris, who suggests "sorrow as those of the world experience it" as a possible rendering (*The Second Epistle to the Corinthians: A Commentary on the Greek Text*, NIGTC [Grand Rapids: Eerdmans, 2005], 540).

53 TOB reads, "La tristesse selon ce monde."

54 See an informative discussion of the meaning of τὸ μέτρον τοῦ κανόνος in Furnish, *II Corinthians*, 471.

55 F. F. Bruce, *The Epistles to the Colossians, to Philemon, and to the Ephesians*, NICNT (Grand Rapids: Eerdmans, 1984), 399.

56 Lincoln, *Ephesians*, 408. [emphasis added]

the meaning of the genitive would be "the instruction that is *in agreement with* Christ's precepts."[57]

There is a good example of the genitive of accordance in πρὸς οἰκοδομὴν τῆς χρείας (Eph 4:29). The following translations denotes accordance: "according to their needs" (NIV),[58] "as fits the occasion" (RSV ESV), "as there is need" (NRSV), and "as occasion offers" (NJB). Robinson says: "The meaning here is, 'for building up as the matter may require,' or *'as need may be.'*"[59] Thielman admits this genitive phrase is difficult when it is taken literally, since it might give the impression of exacerbating the need, going on to classify it as qualitative genitive ("needed upbuilding"), or genitive of reference ("upbuilding with reference to the need"). Here he comes close to the genitive of accordance.[60]

Some classify the phrase τὴν αὔξησιν τοῦ θεοῦ *the growth of God* (Col 2:19) as merely a subjective genitive, "grows as God causes it to grow" (NIV), or "a growth that is from God" (NET ESV RSV NRSV), "a growth from God" (CSB), although it may well be a genitive of accordance. NEB and REB, render the genitive as follows: "grows according to God's design." Both versions point to the genitive of accordance. WB has also indicated the same direction: "grows as God meant it to grow." Melick has summed it up succinctly: "The goal is to grow with 'God's growth.'"[61] The accordance usage of the genitive has enough weight to deserve a separate subheading in the definition classification of genitive usage.

Ascription-Recipient Genitive (Ascribed-to Genitive)

There are many genitive phrases in Paul's letters which could be assigned as genitive of definition, such as ὀργὴ θεοῦ *wrath of God* (Rom 1:18), θεοῦ δικαιοσύνην *God's righteousness* (Rom 3:5), and ἡ ἀλήθεια τοῦ θεοῦ *the truth of God* (Rom 3:7). Yet, these genitive phrases and the like have special aspects warranting a separate treatment.

---

57 Markus Barth, in his translation of Eph 6:4, seems to see the genitive κυρίου as subjective: "but bring them up the way the Lord disciplines and corrects [you]." However, his rendering "the way" (*Ephesians*, 2 vols., AB 34–34A [New Haven: Yale University Press, 1974], 754) seems to construe it as accordance. T. K. Abbott says, "not 'concerning the Lord,' ... but the subjective genitive; the Lord is regarded as the guiding principle of the education" (*A Critical and Exegetical Commentary on the Epistles to the Ephesians and to the Colossians* [Edinburgh: T&T Clark, 1897; repr., 1964], 178).

58 The leading Arabic Bible, Boustani-Van Dyck, has "according to need."

59 John A. T. Robinson, *Commentary on Ephesians: The Greek Text with Introduction Notes and Indexes*, 2nd ed. (London: Macmillan, 1904; repr., 1909), 193.

60 Frank Thielman, *Ephesians*, BECNT (Grand Rapids: Baker Academic, 2010), 316–17.

61 Melick, *Philippians, Colossians, Philemon*, 273.

The new category name I am coining, "ascription-recipient genitive" is an attempt to describe the exact function of this usage of genitive; for such genitive phrases do not merely contain a defining aspect, but an ascriptive aspect. In the genitive of definition, the genitive is added in order to define the other substantive connected to it, while in the ascription-recipient genitive the head word is used to ascribe a certain value to the genitive.

There are plenty of examples in Paul's writings where certain characteristics are ascribed to persons or things. In the phrase τὸ χρηστὸν τοῦ θεοῦ *the kindness of God* (Rom 2:4), kindness is ascribed to God. In τὴν πίστιν τοῦ θεοῦ (Rom 3:3), faithfulness is ascribed to God, "God's faithfulness" (NIV). Likewise, in the following examples: τῆς δόξης τοῦ πατρός *the glory of the Father* (Rom 6:4), δυνάμει πνεύματος *the power of the Spirit* (Rom 15:13), δυνάμει θεοῦ *the power of God* (2 Cor 6:7), τῆς πραΰτητος καὶ ἐπιεικείας τοῦ Χριστοῦ *the meekness and gentleness of Christ* (2 Cor 10:1), ἡ δύναμις τοῦ Χριστοῦ *the power of Christ* (2 Cor 12:9), ἡ ἀγάπη τοῦ θεοῦ *the love of God* (2 Cor 13:13), τὸ πλοῦτος τοῦ Χριστοῦ *the wealth of Christ* (Eph 3:8), and ἡ σοφία τοῦ θεοῦ *the wisdom of God* (Eph 3:10). In all these examples, the head words are ascribed to the dependent genitives. Moreover, with synonymous repetition: τὸ περισσὸν τοῦ Ἰουδαίου *the advantage of the Jew*, and ἡ ὠφέλεια τῆς περιτομῆς *the benefit of circumcision* (Rom 3:1), advantage and profit are ascribed respectively to the Jew and circumcision. Paul, in his argumentation regarding the wisdom of God in redemption, ascribes for the sake of argument *foolishness* and *weakness* to God (τὸ μωρὸν τοῦ θεοῦ … τὸ ἀσθενὲς τοῦ θεοῦ 1 Cor 1:25), but asserts, paradoxically, that both were able to achieve what wisdom and power of human beings could not.[62]

The value of this feature of the genitive is that it examines the genitive usage from a different angle other than the definition aspect. The emphasis here is not on defining the head word by the genitive, but on "defining" (declaring the attributions of) the genitive by the head word.

Appositive (Epexegetic) Genitive

The appositive usage of the genitive consists of two substantives, one standing in apposition to the other in the genitive construction. This kind of genitive is listed here because it fits well under the genitive of definition category. The function of this type of genitive usage is similar to that of definition. It defines who is who and what is what. Moule discusses the relationship between the genitive of definition and that of apposition, "In certain cases the Defining Genitive represents more

---

62 Barrett, *1 Corinthians*, 56.

than an adjective; it represents nothing less than a second noun in apposition to the first; e.g. [Rom 4:11] σημεῖον ἔλαβεν περιτομῆς."[63]

This relationship also is affirmed by both Robertson and Wallace,[64] who group the genitive of definition in the same title heading as a synonym to the genitive of apposition. The appositive genitive may fittingly be divided into two categories: (a) *substitute usage* and, (b) *epexegetic usage*.

Substitute Usage

The substitute usage of the appositive genitive consists of two or more substantives which occur successively, and each substitute another by being simply put in apposition to it, i.e., "genitive in simple apposition."[65] The best example of the substitute usage is represented in the following phrase: εἰρήνη ἀπὸ θεοῦ πατρὸς ἡμῶν καὶ κυρίου Ἰησοῦ Χριστοῦ *peace from God our Father and from the Lord Jesus Christ* (Rom 1:7). Here, *Father* is an appositive substitute to *God* (i.e., God who is the Father), and *Jesus Christ* is an appositive substitute to *Lord*. The words *Jesus Christ* are in apposition to *Lord* and to each other (i.e., Jesus who is the Christ). In 1 Thess 1:3 we have similar appositional phrases: τοῦ κυρίου ἡμῶν Ἰησοῦ Χριστοῦ ἔμπροσθεν τοῦ θεοῦ καὶ πατρὸς ἡμῶν *our Lord Jesus Christ before our God and Father*. Another example is: Μαρίας τῆς μητρὸς αὐτοῦ *Mary his mother* (Matt 2:11). An important example of the *substitute usage* of the genitive is found in the Apocalypse. There occurs the longest genitival concatenation in the NT: τὴν ληνὸν τοῦ οἴνου τοῦ θυμοῦ τῆς ὀργῆς τοῦ θεοῦ τοῦ παντοκράτορος (Rev 19:15). The literal translation of this verse is: "the press of the wine of the fury of the wrath of God the Almighty." G. K. Beale observes that the "genitive τοῦ θυμοῦ ('the wrath') is appositional, defining the preceding symbol: 'the wine-press, which represents … [the] wrath of God.'"[66] The expression τοῦ θυμοῦ is of the epexegetic variety. The title τοῦ παντοκράτορος stands in simple apposition to τοῦ θεοῦ, *God the Almighty*. This usage of the appositive substitute (in which any noun substitutes another) is common to all cases in Greek, so it is not precisely a genitive issue and does not involve syntactic classification.[67]

---

63 Moule, *Idiom Book*, 38.

64 Robertson, *Grammar*, 498; Wallace, *ExSyn*, 95.

65 Wallace *ExSyn*, 94.

66 Gregory K. Beale, *The Book of Revelation: A Commentary on the Greek Text*, NIGTC (Grand Rapids: Eerdmans, 1999), 963.

67 Wallace itemizes the features of the simple appositive. He says: "An appositional construction involves (1) two adjacent substantives (2) in the same case, (3) which refer to the same person or thing, (4) and have the same syntactical relation to the rest of the clause" (Wallace, *ExSyn*, 48).

Epexegetic Usage

The epexegetic usage of the appositive genitive is more sophisticated than the simple substitute usage, and is restricted to the genitive case. Some grammarians use the term "epexegetic" interchangeably with "appositive" to describe this kind of genitive.[68] The word "Epexegesis" is derived from Greek, and it means "additional explanation or explanatory matter."[69] This label is really the best one to describe this sense of the genitive case.

Here are some well-known examples outside the Pauline corpus for this type of genitive: τοῦ ναοῦ τοῦ σώματος αὐτοῦ (John 2:21) "the temple ... was his body" (REB NIV),[70] τὴν δωρεὰν τοῦ ἁγίου πνεύματος (Acts 2:38) "God's gift, the Holy Spirit" (TEV); and τὸ σημεῖον τοῦ υἱοῦ τοῦ ἀνθρώπου *the sign of the Son of Man* (Matt 24:30), which could mean that the sign is the Son of man himself.[71] Other examples include πόλεις Σοδόμων καὶ Γομόρρας *cities of Sodom and Gomorrah* (2 Pet 2:6), τοῦ οἴνου τοῦ θυμοῦ *the wine of the wrath* (Rev 14:10), τὸ σημεῖον Ἰωνᾶ τοῦ προφήτου *the sign of Jonah the prophet* (Matt 12:39; cf. Luke 11:29) τῆς κοιμήσεως τοῦ ὕπνου *the sleep of slumber* (John 11:13),[72] θεμέλιον μετανοίας *the foundation of repentance* (Heb 6:1 REB, NRSV NJB)[73] and τὸν στέφανον τῆς ζωῆς *the crown of life* (Rev 2:10).

Paul uses the epexegetical genitive extensively. The following discussion exposes a variety of examples: the phrase σημεῖον περιτομῆς *sign of circumcision* (Rom 4:11), means "the sign, which is circumcision,"[74] for the ritual sign made in the flesh is called circumcision, as NIV renders: "he received circumcision as a sign." Likewise, the phrase τῆς δωρεᾶς τῆς δικαιοσύνης *the gift of righteousness* (Rom 5:17) means: "the gift, which consists of righteousness." The phrase ἐπαγγελίας ὁ λόγος *the word of promise* (Rom 9:9) is also an epexegetic genitive, because "the word" here

---

68 "Genitive *of* apposition" Wallace, *ExSyn*, 95; and "epexegetic" (Zerwick, *Biblical Greek*, §45 p. 16).

69 *Merriam-Webster's Collegiate Dictionary*, ed. Frederick C. Mish, 11th ed. (Springfield, MA: Merriam-Webster, 2003), s.v. "epexegesis." See also BDAG 349 s.v. ἐξήγησις.

70 NET note *ad loc.* says, this is a "genitive of apposition, clarifying which temple Jesus was referring to."

71 Zerwick, *Biblical Greek*, §46 p. 17; A. T. Robertson, *Word Pictures in the New Testament* (Nashville: Broadman, 1930), 1:193.

72 "merely to sleep" (NRSV).

73 Paul Ellingworth says: "The context requires" θεμέλιον μετανοίας "to mean 'a foundation which consists of repentance'" (*The Epistle to the Hebrews: A Commentary on the Greek Text*, NIGTC [Grand Rapids: Eerdmans, 1993], 313).

74 Wallace, *ExSyn*, 99. Morris says: "The genitive περιτομῆς means something like 'a sign consisting in circumcision'" (*Romans*, 202n42). Douglas Moo declares, "The word περιτομῆς is an epexegetic genitive: 'the sign that is circumcision.'" (*Romans*, 2nd ed., NICNT [Grand Rapids: Eerdmans, 2018], 294n966).

consists of "the promise."[75] In Rom 15:16, the genitive ἡ προσφορὰ τῶν ἐθνῶν may mean "the offering which the gentiles offer to God" (subjective genitive), that is the contributions sent by Paul from the Macedonians to the poor in Jerusalem (see Rom 15:25–31).[76] But it is fair to say that Paul is using an epexegetic genitive here, meaning that the offering is the Gentiles Paul offers to God.[77] The genitive phrase τὸν ἀρραβῶνα τοῦ πνεύματος *the earnest of the Spirit* (KJV 2 Cor 1:22; 5:5; Eph 1:14), is variously translated, "the Spirit ... as a first installment" (NRSV), "as a guarantee" (ESV), "as a down payment" (NET), "as a deposit, guaranteeing what is to come" (NIV), demonstrating the epexegetic usage of the genitive.[78]

The notoriously ambiguous phrase ἀπὸ κυρίου πνεύματος (2 Cor 3:18) is another example of the appositive genitive. KJV reads "by the Spirit of the Lord," but almost all modern versions render it "from the Lord, who is the spirit" (NJB TEV REB ESV NET NIV CSB; NRSV "from the Lord, the Spirit").[79] The phrase τὴν ἐπαγγελίαν τοῦ πνεύματος *the Spirit of promise* (Gal 3:14) may be an attributed genitive, "the promised Spirit" (ESV), or an epexegetic genitive, "The substance of the 'promise' is the gift of the Spirit."[80] In Gal 5:11 τὸ σκάνδαλον τοῦ σταυροῦ "the

---

75 As Moo notes, "ἐπαγγελίας is thrown to the front of the sentence for emphasis: 'Of the nature of promise is this word'" (*Romans*, 598n145).

76 David J. Downs vigorously defends the subjective meaning of the genitive in Rom 15:16 over the appositional in a well-documented article. See his "'The Offering of the Gentiles' in Romans 15.16," *JSNT* 29.2 (2006): 173–86, doi:10.1177/0142064x06072837. This point is also covered in the revision of his Ph.D. thesis: David J. Downs, *The Offering of the Gentiles: Paul's Collection for Jerusalem in Its Chronological, Cultural, and Cultic Contexts*, WUNT 2/248 (Tübingen: Mohr Siebeck, 2008). See also Chapter Seven for our discussion of Rom 15:16.

77 Moo says: "On this view, the genitive τῶν ἐθνῶν is epexegetic. Not only does this interpretation fit the context well, but it also accords with the probable background for Paul's conception: Isa. 66:19–20, where God proclaims that ... he would ... declare his glory among the nations and 'bring all your people, from all the nations ... as an offering [LXX ἐκ πάντων τῶν ἐθνῶν δῶρον] for the Lord'" (*Romans*, 907n35). See also REB TEV NJB NIV NET. Many adherents support the appositive meaning of the genitive in Rom 15:16. See also: W. Sanday and Arthur C. Headlam, *A Critical and Exegetical Commentary on the Epistle to the Romans*, 5th ed., ICC (Edinburgh: T&T Clark, 1902), 405; John Murray, *The Epistle to the Romans*, 2 vols., NICNT (Grand Rapids: Eerdmans, 1968), 2:210; Jewett, *Romans*, 907–908 esp. 907n57.

78 See a defense for the epexegetic genitive for these references in Harris, *2 Corinthians*, 208. See below for a full discussion of τὸν ἀρραβῶνα τοῦ πνεύματος with the partitive genitive under *Ablatival Genitive*.

79 Barrett (*The Second Epistle to the Corinthians*, BNTC [London: Continuum, 1973], 126) points out other options: "(1) the Spirit of the Lord, (2) the Lord of the Spirit, and (3) a Spirit who is sovereign."

80 F. F. Bruce, *The Epistle to the Galatians: A Commentary on the Greek Text*, NIGTC (Grand Rapids: Eerdmans, 1982), 168.

obstacle which is the cross" (NJB) is a suitable rendering of the genitive. Other phrases like τῆς πολιτείας τοῦ Ἰσραήλ "the community *which is* Israel" (Eph 2:12), τὴν ἀνταπόδοσιν τῆς κληρονομίας "the inheritance ... as a reward" (Col 3:24 [NIV]), and Lohse's "the reward which the 'inheritance' (κληρονομία) constitutes,"[81] are additional witnesses to the same usage of the genitive.

The appositive genitive appears frequently in metaphors and figurative expressions in the Pauline corpus.[82] Note, for example, τὸν θυρεὸν τῆς πίστεως *the shield of faith* (Eph 6:16), where Paul uses the head word "shield" as a metaphor for the genitive "faith." The meaning of the phrase would be "hold faith as if it is a shield." In the same manner, Paul uses τὸν θώρακα τῆς δικαιοσύνης *the breast-plate of righteousness* (Eph 6:14), the breastplate stands for justification. In τὴν περικεφαλαίαν τοῦ σωτηρίου (Eph 6:17), the helmet represents salvation.[83] Likewise, the phrases: θώρακα πίστεως καὶ ἀγάπης *the breastplate of faith and love* (1 Thess 5:8),[84] and ζυγῷ δουλείας "yoke of slavery" (Gal 5:1 NET).[85]

There are some other figures of speech used by Paul for the appositive genitive. In Eph 2:20, τῷ θεμελίῳ τῶν ἀποστόλων καὶ προφητῶν *the foundation of the apostles and prophets*, the *foundation* stands for the apostles and the prophets.[86] In Eph 4:14, ἀνέμῳ τῆς διδασκαλίας *wind of teaching* the wind represents (the chaos of) teaching.[87] In 1 Cor 5:8, ζύμη κακίας *leaven of malice* the leaven is a symbol for malice, and ἀζύμοις ἀληθείας *unleavened [bread] of truth* the unleavened bread stands for truth. In Eph 4:3, τῷ συνδέσμῳ τῆς εἰρήνης *bond of peace* means "the bond which is peace."[88] In Col 1:18, ἡ κεφαλὴ τοῦ σώματος τῆς ἐκκλησίας *head of the body of the church* the body is a metaphor for the church. The NJB, for example, reads

---

81   Edward Lohse, *Colossians and Philemon*, ed. Helmut Koester, trans. William R. Poehlmann and Robert J. Karris, Hermeneia (Philadelphia: Fortress, 1971), 161.

82   As Wallace, *ExSyn*, 95 notes, "the head noun" in this kind of genitive can "be metaphorical in its meaning."

83   See how TEV has translated all the metaphors in Eph 6:14–17.

84   J. E. Frame notes, "The gen. πίστεως and ἀγάπης are appositional" (*A Critical and Exegetical Commentary on the Epistles of St. Paul to the Thessalonians*, ICC [New York: Scribner's, 1912], 187).

85   As D. C. Arichea and E. A. Nida note, "The yoke is an appropriate metaphor for bondage, since an animal under a yoke has to obey its master" (*A Handbook on Paul's Letter to the Galatians*, UBSHS [New York: United Bible Societies, 1976], 119). The appositive genitive could also be a classified as a genitive of description if it is used metaphorically.

86   Markus Barth says the foundation "is the basis consisting of (not laid by) specific servants of God" (*Ephesians*, 1:271). Thielman specifically rejects a subjective genitive view in favor of appositional (*Ephesians*, 180n5).

87   Robert Bratcher and Eugene Nida comment, "This figure of rough waves and strong winds is applied to wrong teachings" (*Ephesians*, 104).

88   Barth, *Ephesians*, 2:428.

"the Head of the Body, that is, the Church." Further evidence of the genitive as appositional is its occurrence with related synonymous phrases, such as: ὑπὲρ τοῦ σώματος αὐτοῦ, ὅ ἐστιν ἡ ἐκκλησία *for his body, which is the church* (Col 1:24), and τῇ ἐκκλησίᾳ ἥτις ἐστὶν τὸ σῶμα αὐτοῦ *the church, which is his body* (Eph 1:22, 23). Paul added τοῦ σώματος to the phrase ἡ κεφαλὴ τοῦ σώματος τῆς ἐκκλησίας "in order to define more precisely the meaning of the figure, ἡ κεφαλὴ τῆς ἐκκλησίας. It shows that the writer is not using κεφαλή vaguely, but with the definite figure of the relation of head to body in his thoughts."[89] The expression τῷ μυστηρίῳ τοῦ Χριστοῦ *the mystery of Christ* (Eph 3:4; Col 4:3) is also reckoned as appositive. The probable meaning is *the mystery whose central topic is Christ*. F. F. Bruce considers the genitive epexegetical. Markus Barth does the same.[90] James D. G. Dunn asserts that *the mystery of Christ* is "the mystery which is Christ."[91] The examples given above indicate how extensively the genitive of apposition (epexegetic genitive) is used in Paul's writings, and that it is an important aspect in the categorization of genitive usage.

Adjectival Genitive

The adjectival genitive is a type of genitive usage limited to description. It is called here "adjectival" in order to define its function and to establish it as a wider category under which several descriptive meanings may be classified. Most genitives contain an adjectival element in their structures. This fact becomes clear upon observation of the real function of the genitive case in all its aspects. As we noted in Chapter Two, Robertson said the genitive is, "the specifying case."[92] Robertson take precautions against misunderstanding: "The genitive does indeed resemble the adjective," he writes, "but it is not adjectival in origin ... the function of the case is largely adjectival ... though the adjective and the genitive are not exactly parallel."[93]

Moule refers to the point of contact where the genitive case and the adjective meet: "The Genitive often practically does the duty of the adjective."[94] Moreover, Wallace adds that the genitive "is more emphatic than a simple adjective would be."[95]

---

89 Thomas Kingsmill Abbott, *A Critical and Exegetical Commentary on the Epistles to the Ephesians and to the Colossians*, ICC 36 (New York: Scribner's, 1903), 211.

90 Bruce, *Colossians, Philemon, Ephesians*, 313n19. Markus Barth writes, "This secret consists of the Messiah" (*Ephesians*, 1:331).

91 Dunn, *Colossians and Philemon*, 263.

92 Robertson, *Grammar*, 493.

93 Robertson, *Grammar*, 493.

94 Moule, *Idiom Book*, 38.

95 Wallace, *ExSyn*, 78.

The adjective as a function is well inherent in the genitive case. Every genitive retains, more or less, some feature of the adjective. Some genitives are completely mere adjectives, like those that are called "Hebrew" genitives. Others have a nuance of adjective; however slight it is. In the following categorization of the adjectival meanings of the genitive, all adjectival functions of the genitive will be treated separately and will be given the attention they deserve.

Descriptive Genitive

It is difficult to set a clear limit between the subhead titles of the adjectival genitive category. The descriptive[96] (or attributive), "Hebrew," and qualitative genitives are listed here under the adjectival genitive, but these can only be distinguished through illuminating illustrations from the Greek text.

The genitive phrase ζυγῷ δουλείας *yoke of slavery* (Gal 5:1) is a good illustration for understanding the descriptive genitive. On one hand, it is not "Hebrew" or adjectival (e.g., *slavish yoke*); on the other hand, the writer does not qualify the yoke with any literal description that corresponds with its nature, like wood (e.g., *yoke of wood*). In this case it would be a qualitative genitive or genitive of material. The genitive in ζυγῷ δουλείας is descriptive. It describes metaphorically what kind of yoke it is. As we saw above, however, this phrase fits well also with the appositional epexegetic usage of the genitive (*a yoke which is slavery*).

There are many such descriptive genitives in Paul's letters. The following are some examples: ἐν λόγῳ ἀληθείας "truthful speech" (2 Cor 6:7 NIV ESV), ἐν εἰλικρινείᾳ τοῦ θεοῦ "godly sincerity" (2 Cor 1:12 REB ESV), ὁδὸν εἰρήνης *the way of peace* (Rom 3:17), ἡμέρᾳ ὀργῆς *the day of wrath* (Rom 2:5), τὰ ἔργα τοῦ σκότους ... τὰ ὅπλα τοῦ φωτός *the works of darkness ... the weapons of light* (Rom 13:12), τῇ πίστει τοῦ εὐαγγελίου *the faith of the Gospel* (Phil 1:27),[97] τῆς ἐξουσίας τοῦ σκότους *the authority of darkness* (Col 1:13), and πνεῦμα δειλίας "cowardly spirit" (2 Tim 1:7 REB).

Even the genitive of definition may be grouped with the descriptive genitive when the genitive indicates a value more than it indicates a definition. The phrase τὸ ποτήριον τοῦ κυρίου *the cup of the Lord* (1 Cor 11:27), illustrates this idea quite well. Here, the genitive defines not only whose cup it is, but gives to the cup a certain value because it is related to the Lord. Categorizing τὸ ποτήριον τοῦ κυρίου as

---

96 Wallace distinguishes "descriptive" (*ExSyn*, 79) from "attributive" (86) by defining the former as a generally broad category in which the relationship between head noun and its dependent genitive is difficult to establish precisely (the tongue-in-cheek title "aporetic" may apply).

97 Melick acknowledges the possibilities: descriptive, objective, subjective, or appositional. His first choice is the descriptive genitive (*Philippians, Colossians, Philemon*, 90n110). See also Hansen, *Philippians*, 98n213.

descriptive, however, does not nullify the possibility of considering it a genitive of identification. The nuances of both meanings are overlapping. We should understand βασιλείαν θεοῦ *the kingdom of God* (Gal 5:21), and ἡμέρα κυρίου *the day of the Lord* (1 Thess 5:2) in the same way. Also, ἡ εἰρήνη τοῦ θεοῦ "God's peace" (Phil 4:7 TEV),[98] and ἡ ὀργὴ τοῦ θεοῦ *God's wrath* (Eph 5:6), or "divine retribution" (REB), fit here under descriptive genitive.

Qualitative Genitive

The qualitative usage of the genitive refers to quality, substance, or content of which the head word in the genitive construction consists. There is a good illustration of the qualitative genitive in the phrase οἱ θησαυροὶ τῆς σοφίας καὶ γνώσεως *the treasures of wisdom and knowledge* (Col 2:3). Here, the treasures' substance and content, in figurative language, are wisdom and knowledge instead of precious metals. Another phrase is, ἐλπίδα σωτηρίας *the hope of salvation* (1 Thess 5:8); the substance of the hope is salvation.[99] Likewise λόγος σοφίας *word of wisdom* (1 Cor 12:8) is translated: "message full of wisdom" according to TEV. The phrase τὸν νόμον τῶν ἐντολῶν *the law of commandments* (Eph 2:15) is similarly rendered: "the law with its commandments and rules" (TEV), "the law with its rules and regulations" (NEB), and "the law with its commands and regulations" (NIV). The expression τοῦ εὐαγγελίου τῆς εἰρήνης *the gospel of peace* (Eph 6:15) also falls into this category.

There are some other genitive phrases that express quality. They must be put under a special section because the genitive in these constructions is related to specific words such as: form, fullness, and measurement. The following examples illustrate its usage: τὸ πλήρωμα τῶν ἐθνῶν *the fullness of the gentiles* (Rom 11:25), τὴν περισσείαν τῆς χάριτος *the abundance of the grace* (Rom 5:17), μέτρον πίστεως *measure of faith* (Rom 12:3), τὸ πλήρωμα τῆς θεότητος *the fullness of the Godhead* (Col 2:9), and τὴν ἀναλογίαν τῆς πίστεως *the analogy of the faith* (Rom 12:6). These genitives can also be classified with the reverse "adjectival" genitive or "attributed" genitive, as Wallace calls it.[100]

The genitive of quality is present also in phrases that contain words which refer to time. For example, ἡμέρα ὀργῆς *the day of wrath* (Rom 2:5), ἡμέρα σωτηρίας *the day of salvation* (2 Cor 6:2), and ἡμέραν ἀπολυτρώσεως *the day of redemption* (Eph

---

98 Melick describes the peace of God here as "divine peace" (*Philippians, Colossians, Philemon*, 149).

99 J. E. Frame calls it "objective gen." (*1 Thessalonians*, 187). Richard Lenski sees it as objective: "hope for the final rescue" (*The Interpretation of St. Paul's Epistles to the Colossians, to the Thessalonians, to Timothy, to Titus and to Philemon* [Minneapolis: Augsburg, 1937], 347).

100 Wallace, *ExSyn*, 89.

4:30). In such phrases, the genitive refers to the quality and nature of these times, and what they may contain. The genitive phrase τύπον διδαχῆς *pattern of teaching* (Rom 6:17) may fit here if it is considered qualitative: the teachings contained in the code of doctrine. These examples reveal the importance of the qualitative genitive as an aspect of the adjectival genitive.

Hebrew Genitive

This kind of adjectival genitive is called the "Hebrew" genitive, because it is rarely found in classical Greek. Its function and usage are almost exclusively Hebrew. Citing examples such as τὸ σῶμα τῆς ἁμαρτίας *the body of sin* (Rom 6:6), Blass and Debrunner note, "Hebrew usage is thus reflected, in that this construction compensates for the nearly non-existent adjective. Classical Greek exhibits very sparse parallels in poetry only."[101] Turner points to examples such as Exod 29:29 בגדי הקדש rendered by the LXX as ἡ στολὴ τοῦ ἁγίου *the robe of the holy* as evidence of Hebrew syntax on Greek usage.[102] Zerwick presents a similar view, but treats the matter from the Greek perspective: "The 'Hebrew' genitive, in as much as its scope and use in Biblical Greek is extended, owing to Semitic influence, to many expressions in which the Greeks used not a genitive but an adjective."[103] This is not to say that the usage is absolutely foreign to Greek: the usage is possible, but unusual in earlier periods of Greek until it is brought to the forefront in Hellenistic Greek by usage paralleled in Hebrew.

The Adjectival "Hebrew" Genitive in the OT

In order to appreciate well the use of the genitive as a "Hebrew" adjective in the NT, we must look to the OT, particularly to the Psalms. Many examples parallel to what we find in the NT appear, many of them adjectival genitives. Here are some examples: הר קדשי "the hill of the holiness-of-me" (Ps 2:6 [LXX has ὄρος τὸ ἅγιον αὐτοῦ, apparently from a *Vorlage* reading the 3ms suffix קדשו]). This phrase appears awkward in translation unless the genitive is read as adjective: *my holy hill* (KJV NET). Another similar phrase: אלהי צדקי *God of the righteousness-of-me* (Ps 4:1 LXX ὁ θεὸς τῆς δικαιοσύνης μου). The meaning becomes clear if "righteousness" is read as an adjective: *my righteous God* (NIV). Likewise, the following phrases: שפתי שקר *lips of lying* (Ps 31:19 MT) means, "lying/deceitful lips" (REB CSB NETS), איש שלום *man of peace* (Ps 37:37), rendered "peaceful people" (TEV), "peaceable person"

---

101 BDF §165 p. 91. cf. Turner (MHT₃ 213), "The adj. was nearly non-existent in Heb."
102 MHT₃ 213.
103 Zerwick, *Biblical Greek*, §40 p. 14.

(NETS); אלהי חסדי *the God of my mercy* (KJV; Ps 59:18), "my merciful God";[104] שם כבודו *the name of his glory* (Ps 72:19), "his glorious name" (most English versions); לבב חכמה *heart of wisdom* (Ps 90:12), "wise heart" (NRSV); and רקיע עזו "firmament of his power" (KJV ASV; Ps 150:1) "his mighty firmament" (NRSV).

The Adjectival "Hebrew" Genitive in the NT

The way many NT writers use the genitive as an adjective is evidence of influence of Semitic modes of expression. Paul is one of those NT writers who uses the adjectival genitive rather extensively, having been deeply influenced by the Hebrew Bible, probably mainly through the Septuagint. The following examples reveal Paul's use of the "Hebrew" genitive.

The phrase σοφίας λόγοις *words of wisdom* (1 Cor 2:4) is translated: "Wise ... words" (NIV), or "philosophical argument" (NJB); both renderings show an adjectival genitive. The genitive in λόγῳ κολακείας *word of flattery* (1 Thess 2:5) is rendered "words of flattery" (ESV). On the other hand, the KJV, often known for literal translation (followed by TEV NAB NEB NET CSB), renders it as "Hebrew" adjective: "flattering words."

Following the same pattern, the NRSV translates πάθη ἀτιμίας *passions of dishonor* (Rom 1:26) by "degrading passions" (cf. "dishonorable passions" ESV NET CSB). For τὸ σῶμα τῆς ἁμαρτίας *the body of sin* (Rom 6:6), the REB has "sinful self," and the RSV has "sinful body." For τῷ λίθῳ τοῦ προσκόμματος *the stone of stumbling* (Rom 9:32), the KJV and almost all versions have "stumbling stone." The phrase τὰ κρυπτὰ τῆς αἰσχύνης *the hidden things of shame* (2 Cor 4:2) "the hidden things of dishonesty" (KJV), appears as "shameful secrecy" in NJB, and "the shameful things that one hides" in NRSV (cf. ESV NET CSB). The translation of τὰς ἐπιθυμίας τῆς ἀπάτης *the desires of deceit* (Eph 4:22) should follow the same pattern: "deceitful lusts" (See KJV RSV NJB TEV REB NIV ESV NET). For ἐν δικαιοσύνῃ καὶ ὁσιότητι τῆς ἀληθείας *righteousness and holiness of the truth* (Eph 4:24), several English versions retain the literal translation "in righteousness and holiness ["purity" CSB] of the [- ASV] truth" (ASV NJB CSB). KJV translates the genitive as a "Hebrew" adjective: "in righteousness and true holiness." Other renderings let the "Hebrew" adjective govern the two substantives: "in true righteousness and holiness" (RSV NRSV NIV ESV).

More examples can be cited for this peculiar usage of the genitive as "Hebrew" adjectival. For ἄνθρακας πυρός *coals of fire* (Rom 12:20), REB has "live coals," and NJB has "red-hot coals." πρὸς οἰκοδομὴν τῆς χρείας *for the edification of the need*

---

104 "my gracious God" (REB), "my loving God" (NIV84), and "my faithful God" (CSB). These versions render the adjectival meaning of the genitive.

(Eph 4:29) fits in this category, interpreted as "for necessary edification" (NKJV). Lincoln, likewise, considers it a genitive of quality if not an objective genitive "for the needed building up."[105] The phrase ὀσμὴν εὐωδίας *fragrance of aroma* (Eph 5:2; Phil 4:18) is translated "a fragrance of sweet smell" by RV ASV, while the KJV renders the "Hebrew" genitive: "sweetsmelling savour" (NKJV "sweet-smelling aroma"). NASB renders, "fragrant aroma" and NRSV, "fragrant offering." The phrase τέρασιν ψεύδους *wonders of a lie* (2 Thess 2:9) is translated as "Hebrew" genitive "lying wonders" by KJV. Almost all other translations here use a synonymous adjective to bring forth the meaning of the "Hebrew" genitive. The phrase ἀπάτῃ ἀδικίας *deception of unrighteousness* (2 Thess 2:10) is also a "Hebrew" genitive and is translated in many versions "wicked/evil deception" (RSV NRSV TEV NET ESV). Also, ἐνέργειαν πλάνης *operation of deceit* (2 Thess 2:11) BDAG renders "a deluding influence."[106] The many examples in this section illustrate that Paul's extensive use of the genitive in an adjectival role.

There are multiple instances of the substantive "Hebrew" genitive as adjective modifying "spirit" in the Pauline corpus. For instance, πνεῦμα ἁγιωσύνης (Rom 1:4) "the spirit of holiness" (KJV RSV NRSV NIV ASV ESV CSB). Many versions translate the text literally. Other versions (e.g., NEB REB NET) and F. F. Bruce[107] have expressed the "Hebrew" usage by rendering the genitive adjectivally: "the Holy Spirit." Gordon Fee agrees with the "Hebrew" adjectival interpretation: "Most likely … Paul intends to refer to the Holy Spirit."[108] Paul again uses an adnominal genitive as an adjective in τῷ πνεύματι τῆς ἐπαγγελίας τῷ ἁγίῳ *the Spirit of promise, the holy* (Eph 1:13) "the Holy Spirit of promise" (KJV ASV). The "Hebrew" genitive here should appear in translation as an adjective: "the promised Holy Spirit" (RSV NEB WB NIV REB NRSV ESV NET CSB; cf. TEV).[109] The opposite phrase τὴν ἐπαγγελίαν τοῦ πνεύματος (Gal 3:14), the "promise of the Spirit" (KJV NIV NET), may be considered an attributed genitive: "the promised Spirit" (NEB NAB REB TEV NJB ESV CSB), or epexegetical genitive: "the promise, that is,

---

105 Lincoln, *Ephesians*, 306.
106 BDAG 335 s.v. ἐνέργεια. Frame renders it with an objective genitive, "an energy unto delusion" (*1 Thessalonians*, 272). Other versions translate "strong delusion" (RSV ESV) or "powerful delusion" (NRSV NIV), showing more an attributed genitive classification. See below.
107 Bruce notes, "Paul here reproduces the Hebrew idiom in Greek" (*Romans: An Introduction and Commentary*, TNTC 6 [Downers Grove: IVP, 1985], 79).
108 Gordon D. Fee, *God's Empowering Presence: The Holy Spirit in the Letters of Paul* (Peabody, MA: Hendrickson, 1994; repr., Grand Rapids: Baker, 2011), 483.
109 See also Hoehner, *Ephesians*, 240.

the Spirit."[110] A third example is πνεύματι πραΰτητος (1 Cor 4:21), translated literally by some versions "spirit of gentleness," (ASV NRSV NET ESV CSB). Other important versions render the genitive as an adjective: "a gentle spirit" (NAB NEB NIV REB). Another figurative Hebraic expression is ὁ πατὴρ τῆς δόξης (Eph 1:17; 2 Cor 1:3) "the Father of glory," literally rendered (KJV RSV NAB NJB ESV). Other leading translations have "the glorious Father" (TEV NEB REB NIV CSB). Bruce labels the genitive adjectival.[111]

The Plural "Hebrew" Genitive as Adjective

There is a phenomenon of Hebrew genitive usage in Paul's letters that deserves comment. It is the use of the plural genitive as "Hebrew" adjective. A few examples outside the Pauline corpus can be mentioned in this connection: ἐντάλματα ἀνθρώπων *the commands of men* (Matt 15:9) "man-made rules" (TEV), "human precepts as doctrines" (NRSV) τὴν παράδοσιν τῶν ἀνθρώπων *the tradition of men* (Mark 7:8) "human traditions" (NJB NET NIV). Accordingly, βαπτισμῶν διδαχῆς *teaching of baptisms* (Heb 6:2) with the head noun coming second, may mean "baptismal teaching."

This usage reflects the plural genitive as an adjective in many OT texts, expressing abstract ideas by using plural substantives. Waltke and O'Connor write about this phenomenon:

> An *abstract noun* is frequently expressed by a plural, which may have originally signified the diverse concrete manifestations of a quality or state. These plurals are frequently built on the adjectival *qātūl* and *qittūl* patterns. The singular of abstract plurals is rarely attested. Such plurals may refer to *qualities*.[112]

It seems that the force of this construction is founded upon the use of plural in order to intensify the idea.[113] The plural strengthens the description applied to the specified object; hence, the source of its relatedness to the adjective. The beginning of the Paternoster, Πάτερ ἡμῶν ὁ ἐν τοῖς οὐρανοῖς *our father, the one in the heavens* (Matt 6:9) is a good example of this phenomenon. The phrase "the One in the heavens," which is similar to the descriptions applied to God in Job 16:19;

---

110 By "This gift of the Spirit (who is the substance of the promise)," Ronald Fung indicates that this genitive is epexegetical, though he names it "genitive of definition" (*The Epistle to the Galatians*, NICNT [Grand Rapids: Eerdmans, 1988], 152n75).

111 Bruce, *Colossians, Philemon, Ephesians*, 269.

112 Bruce K. Waltke and Michael Patrick O'Connor, *An Introduction to Biblical Hebrew Syntax* (Winona Lake, IN: Eisenbrauns, 1990), 120. [bold type added; italic type original]

113 Paul Joüon and Takamitsu Muraoka, *A Grammar of Biblical Hebrew*, Rev. ed. (Rome: Pontifical Biblical Institute, 2006), §136f p. 470.

Isa 33:16; and Dan 7:18, is an intensive plural that idiomatically means "the Most High."[114] The tendency here is that every descriptive plural plays the role of the adjective, especially if it is used as a genitive.

The Plural "Hebrew" Genitive as Adjective in the OT

The following are some examples of plural genitives from the Hebrew Old Testament, quoted in order to constitute a basis for understanding such usage in the Pauline corpus:

The plural of דם "blood" The expressions איש דמים *man of blood(s)* (Ps 5:6), and אנשי דמים *men of blood[s]* (2 Sam 16:7–8; Pss 55:24; 59:3; 139:19; Prov 29:10) are translated "bloody" (KJV), "violent" (NJB REB NET), and "bloodthirsty," or "murderers" (NETS NIV TEV REB ESV HCSB). Likewise, בית הדמים "house of blood(s)" (2 Sam 21:1) is translated "bloody house" (KJV ASV) and "blood-stained house" (NIV). Also, עיר הדמים *city of blood(s)* (Ezek 22:2; 24:6, 9; Nah 3:1; Hab 2:12) is translated "bloody city" (KJV ASV ESV), "blood-stained city" (REB), and "murderous city" (TEV), "Une ville sanguinaire" (TOB).

The plural of עולם "age" The plural genitive תשועת עולמים *salvation of (for) ages* (Isa 45:17) appears as σωτηρίαν αἰώνιον in LXX, that is "everlasting salvation" (NETS; cf. KJV RSV NIV ESV CSB). The phrase צדק עלמים *righteousness of ages* (Dan 9:24) is translated δικαιοσύνην αἰώνιον in LXX, that is, "everlasting righteousness" (NETS; cf. KJV NJB NRSV NIV ESV HCSB). Also, צור עולמים *the rock of ages* (Isa 26:4) is translated "everlasting rock" (RSV ESV CSB), and "eternal rock" (REB). The expression שנות עולמים *years of ages* (Ps 77:5) is translated "times/years long past/ago" (NETS; cf. REB NJB ESV HCSB; דרות עולמים *generations of ages* Isa 51:9).

The plural of תהפוכה "perversion"[115] The expression לשון תהפכות *tongue of lies* (Prov 10:31) is translated "froward tongue" (KJV) and "perverse tongue" (RSV NIV ESV CSB). For פי תהפכות *mouth of lies* (Prov 8:13) the English versions render "lying mouth" (NJB), "false words" (TEV), have "perverted speech" (RSV ESV). For איש תהפכות *man of lies* (Prov 16:28) LXX reads ἀνὴρ σκολιός, and modern translators offer "a perverse man" (RSV NIV), "a slanderer" (NJB).

The following phrases are additional plural genitive examples: אל נקמות (Ps 94:1) *God of vengeance(s)* (NETS; LXX ὁ θεὸς ἐκδικήσεων) is translated "God who punishes" (TEV), or "God who avenges" (NIV). The familiar phrase יהוה צבאות (Ps 46:11; LXX κύριος τῶν δυνάμεων) in many versions appears as "Lord of hosts" (NETS; cf. KJV ASV REB NAB ESV), but others have "the Lord Almighty"

---

114 Joüon and Muraoka, *Biblical Hebrew*, §136d p. 470.
115 *HALOT* 1693 s.v.

(NIV TEV; "Le Seigneur, le tout-puissant" TOB). Likewise, לחם כזבים *bread of lies* (Prov 23:3) is translated "deceptive food" (RSV NIV NJB).

The Plural "Hebrew" Genitive as Adjective in the NT

The above examples clearly reveal that the Hebrew Bible extensively uses the plural genitive as a pure adjective. The adjectival plural genitive of Old Testament influenced Paul. There are several examples for the plural genitive used as "Hebrew" adjective in his letters. First of all, τὰ παθήματα τῶν ἁμαρτιῶν (Rom 7:5), which is translated "the motions of sins" in the KJV, is considered a plural genitive adjective "sinful passions" or "sinful desires" in almost all modern Bible versions (e.g., RSV NRSV NJB NAB TEV NIV NEB REB ESV). Even the most literal versions (RV ASV NASB) render it as adjective.[116] Moo argues for understanding the plural genitive (which makes a genitive of source unlikely, he says) as genitive of quality: "sinful passions."[117] A second example of the plural genitive in a Hebrew genitive construction is σοφίᾳ ἀνθρώπων *the wisdom of men* (1 Cor 2:5; so KJV RV RSV NAB TEV NIV ESV). There is a contrastive comparison here between "human wisdom" and "the power of God."[118] The plural genitive is likely to be adjectival: "human wisdom" or "human philosophy" (NJB NEB REB NRSV NIV). This last meaning is preferable not only because the genitive is plural, but also in view of the parallel ἀνθρωπίνης σοφίας λόγοις *words of human wisdom* in 1 Cor 2:13. A third example is ὁ πατὴρ τῶν οἰκτιρμῶν (2 Cor 1:3), rendered "the father of mercies" (KJV ASV RSV NASB NRSV NAB ESV CSB), and "the father of compassion" (NIV). Other versions emphasize the *plural* element in the genitive as intensive and translate the phrase by "all-merciful Father" (NJB TEV NEB REB). Barrett comments that "οἰκτιρμοί ... is a mainly Pauline word, used nearly always (Rom. 12:1; 2 Cor. 1:3; Phil. 2:1; Heb. 10:28; the exception is Col. 3:12) in the plural, probably because it is so used in the LXX as the translation of a Hebrew plural (*raḥᵃmim*)."[119] Harris characterizes τῶν οἰκτιρμῶν as qualitative, agreeing with Barrett about the Hebrew plural.[120] Using the adjective to describe the Father here correctly captures the meaning of this Semitic phrase.

---

116 Dunn translates it "sinful passions;" but classifes it as a "genitive of content" or of "direction" (*Romans 1–8*, WBC 38A [Dallas: Word, 1988], 358, 364). With the passions being sins, there is not much distance between appositive genitive (content as Dunn refers to it citing BDF §167) and a genitive of quality, "sinful passions."

117 Moo, *Romans*, 444n681.

118 See Barrett's treatment of vv. 4–5. Barrett, *1 Corinthians*, 65–66.

119 Barrett, *2 Corinthians*, 59.

120 Harris, *2 Corinthians*, 142.

Several more examples can be brought to bear here. The words πρόθεσιν τῶν αἰώνων *purpose of the ages* (Eph 3:11) the plural genitive is translated as an adjective "the eternal purpose" in the KJV and in leading modern Bible versions (RSV TEV NRSV NET ESV NIV CSB). The NEB and REB render it as "age-long purpose,"[121] Some of these versions use a verbal phrase to express clearly the adjectival meaning of the genitive. NJB stresses the eternal beginning of God's purpose: "according to the plan which he had formed from all eternity."[122] In the expression later in this chapter of Ephesians, τοῦ αἰῶνος τῶν αἰώνων *the age of ages* (Eph 3:21), the head word is singular and the genitive is plural. In other similar phrases in Paul's Epistles, the head words and genitives are plural (e. g., Gal 1:5; Phil 4:20; 1 Tim 1:17; 2 Tim 4:18).

The literal translation of τῷ βασιλεῖ τῶν αἰώνων (1 Tim 1:17),[123] "the king of the ages," retained by RSV NRSV ESV, and is close to "the king of all worlds" (NEB). But several versions follow KJV with an adjectival rendering "the king eternal" (REB ASV NASB NIV CSB; "the eternal king" in TEV NJB NET).[124] The adjectival meaning of the genitive should be followed here if the Hebraistic construction is taken into consideration.[125]

As the final example in this section, let us consider διδασκαλίαις δαιμονίων (1 Tim 4:1), "teachings of demons" (ESV). Following the conclusions of the examples given above, it is preferable, here too, to adopt the adjectival meaning of the plural genitive: "demonic teachings" (NET) as do Dibelius and Conzelmann,[126] or "demon-inspired doctrines" (REB). The subjective genitive shading off into source genitive is another possibility for this expression. Philip Towner opines that the "of demons" should probably be rendered to indicate the source of the doctrines.[127] William D. Mounce notes that subjective genitive emphasizes a

---

121 Markus Barth says: "the genitive, 'of the aeons,' may here be equivalent to the adjective, 'eternal' (*aionios*); cf. Rom 16:25. Then it points out that God's decision was made 'before all times' [1 Cor 2:7] and is 'eternal'" (*Ephesians*, 1:346).

122 A. T. Lincoln writes, "the expression is taken as a Hebraism in which the genitive functions as an adjective, here as an equivalent to αἰώνιος" (Lincoln, *Ephesians*, 189).

123 This expression occurs also in Rev 15:3 as a variant reading.

124 Wallace (*ExSyn*, 88) notes for English translation that, "the problem of taking this as attributive is that the gen. is plural." But if the singular were used, it would be misunderstood as "the king of the age ... a temporal king."

125 George W. Knight, pointing to the end of the verse (τοὺς αἰῶνας τῶν αἰώνων) says the preferred meaning is "eternal king" (*Pastoral Epistles*, 106).

126 Martin Dibelius and Hans Conzelmann, *The Pastoral Epistles*, ed. Helmut Koester, trans. Philip Buttolph and Adela Yarbro, Hermeneia (Philadelphia: Fortress, 1972), 64.

127 Philip H. Towner, *The Letters to Timothy and Titus*, NICNT (Grand Rapids: Eerdmans, 2006), 290.

"more direct and almost personal" nuance.[128] The objective genitive, although possible, is improbable.[129]

The plural genitive must be given the attention it deserves as an important idiomatic aspect of genitive usage. The roots of plural genitive adjectival meaning are firmly planted in the soil of the OT. The extensive use of the "Hebrew" genitive by Paul confirms the fact that he was influenced by OT idiom and that the study of the Hebrew Bible is imperative in order to understand the idioms of NT language, especially the genitive.

Attributed Genitive

The "attributed genitive"[130] is similar in function to the "Hebrew" adjectival genitive. In the "Hebrew genitive," the dependent genitive in the construction is adjectival. It describes the head word. The attributed genitive is the reverse: the *head word* describes the genitive, hence the name "attributed genitive," in contrast with "attributive genitive." In τοῦ σώματος τοῦ θανάτου *the body of death* (Rom 7:24) as an illustration, τοῦ θανάτου is adjectival, whereas in ἐπὶ πλούτου ἀδηλότητι *the uncertainty of riches* (1 Tim 6:17) the head word ἀδηλότητι is adjectival. Blass and Debrunner describe this kind of genitive as a "reverse"[131] to the customary form of the adjectival genitive. Their suggestion describes appropriately the nature of this usage of the genitive construction which Wallace calls "the attributed genitive." The use of the attributed genitive in Paul's writings is due to Semitic influence, although this usage is found also in Greek and Latin[132] and "has classical parallels."[133]

Attributed Genitive in the OT

The following examples of the attributed genitive selected from the OT demonstrate that this usage is not uncommon in the Hebrew Scriptures. The construct בְּיֹשֶׁר לֵבָב (Ps 119:7; LXX ἐν εὐθύτητι καρδίας), which literally means "with uprightness of heart" (NETS) is an attributed genitive. The translations: "upright heart" (NIV NRSV ESV CSB) and "sincere heart" (TNK HCSB) reveal the function

---

128 William D. Mounce, *Pastoral Epistles*, WBC 46 (Nashville: Nelson, 2000), 237.

129 Patrick Fairbairn, *Commentary on the Pastoral Epistles* (Edinbugh: T&T Clark, 1874), 169–70.

130 Wallace, *ExSyn*, 89.

131 BDF §165 p. 91.

132 Zerwick says this usage is "not specifically Semitic, but belongs to the style of many languages: 'newness of life' for 'new life', 'sublimity of speech' (1 Cor 2, 1) for 'sublime speech' might be cited as examples of Greek or Latin style" (Zerwick, *Biblical Greek*, §40 p. 16n6).

133 BDF §165 p. 91.

of this usage of genitive. Likewise, with בגבורת הסוס (Ps 147:10), the literal rendering "in the strength of the horse" (ESV) appears as an adjectival one "in strong horses" (TEV). The rest follow the same pattern: גדל לבב *arrogance of heart* (Isa 9:9; LXX ὑψηλῇ καρδίᾳ) becomes "arrogant" (TEV); ברע פנים *by sadness of faces* (Eccl 7:3; LXX ἐν κακίᾳ προσώπου), is rendered "bad countenance" (NETS) or "sad face" (NIV). The expression מגבה־רוח *more than pride of spirit* (Eccl 7:8), translates to "the proud in spirit" (NRSV), or "a haughty spirit" (TNK). The phrase עקשות פה ולזות שפתים *perversity of mouth and corruptness of lips* (Prov 4:24; LXX σκολιὸν στόμα καὶ ἄδικα χείλη), appears as "crooked speech and devious (deceitful) talk" in several English versions (TNK NRSV REB ESV). The phrase גדל חסדך *the greatness of your love* (Num 14:19; LXX τὸ μέγα ἔλεός σου) appears in translation as, "your great mercy" (NETS), "your great love" (NIV), "constant love" (REB), and "faithful love" (NJB HCSB).

Attributed Genitive in the NT

The attributed genitive is used frequently in Paul's writings, but the attributive genitive is more common.[134] But the "attributed genitive" and "the ascription-recipient genitive"[135] should not be confused, even though the two categories are similar. The focus in both of them is on the head word, yet they differ. In "the attributed genitive" the head word is adjectival. It describes the genitive. But in "the ascription-recipient genitive," the head word represents an attribute ascribed to the genitive.

Because the attributed genitive is rarely mentioned or treated in NT Greek grammars, Wallace comments this is an emerging need to explore, "for there are surely scores of texts in which this idiom is both a viable and unrecognized option."[136] The following examples represent the function and the quantity value of the attributed genitive. The items are listed successively each with a literal

---

134 Wallace, *ExSyn*, 89.

135 The "ascription-recipient" genitive differs from the genitive of definition. In the genitive of definition, the genitive is added in order to define the head word, while in the ascription-recipient genitive the head word is used to ascribe a certain value to the genitive. Examples of such a usage are: τὸ χρηστὸν τοῦ θεοῦ *the kindness of God* (Rom 2:4), τὴν πίστιν τοῦ θεοῦ *the faithfulness of God* (Rom 3:3), τῆς πραΰτητος καὶ ἐπιεικείας τοῦ Χριστοῦ "the meekness and gentleness of Christ" (2 Cor 10:1 ESV), τὸ πλοῦτος τοῦ Χριστοῦ *the wealth of Christ* (Eph 3:8), ἡ σοφία τοῦ θεοῦ *the wisdom of God* (Eph 3:10), δυνάμει θεοῦ *power of God* (2 Cor 6:7), ἡ δύναμις τοῦ Χριστοῦ *the power of Christ* (2 Cor 12:9), ἡ ἀγάπη τοῦ θεοῦ *the love of God* (2 Cor 13:13), τῆς δόξης τοῦ πατρός *the glory of the father* (Rom 6:4), and δυνάμει πνεύματος *power of the Spirit* (Rom 15:13). See the heading *Ascription-Recipient Genitive* above.

136 Wallace, *ExSyn*, 89n50.

translation accompanied by a functional translation selected from standard Bible versions for ready comparison.

- τὴν περισσείαν τῆς χάριτος (Rom 5:17) *the abundance of grace* "abundant grace" (TEV)
- ἐν καινότητι ζωῆς (Rom 6:4) *newness of life* "a new life" (REB NJB NIV NET)
- καινότητι πνεύματος (Rom 7:6) *newness of the Spirit* "new life of the Spirit" (NRSV NIV TEV NET)
- παλαιότητι γράμματος (Rom 7:6) *oldness of letter* "old written code (law)" (NRSV REB TEV NIV NET)
- ὑπὲρ ἀληθείας θεοῦ (Rom 15:8) *truthfulness of God* "to show that God is faithful" (TEV)
- σοφίᾳ λόγου (1 Cor 1:17) *wisdom of speech* "clever speech" (NET HCSB)
- τῆς μωρίας τοῦ κηρύγματος (1 Cor 1:21) *foolishness of preaching* "'foolish' message" (TEV)
- ὑπεροχὴν λόγου (1 Cor 2:1) *excellence of speech* "lofty words" (NRSV) "big words" (TEV) "Superior eloquence" (NET)
- συνοχῆς καρδίας (2 Cor 2:4) *distress of heart* "distressed heart" (TEV) "anguished heart" (HCSB)
- ὑπερβολὴ τῆς δυνάμεως (2 Cor 4:7) *excellence of the power* "extraordinary power" (NRSV) and "transcendent power" (REB) "surpassing power" (ESV)
- ἐλαφρὸν τῆς θλίψεως (2 Cor 4:17) *lightness of the affliction* "slight … affliction" (NRSV ESV) and with a predicate: "our troubles are slight" (REB)
- βάρος δόξης (2 Cor 4:17) *weight of glory* "a tremendous … glory" (TEV)
- ἁπλότητι τῆς κοινωνίας (2 Cor 9:13) *generosity of sharing* "liberal contribution" (REB)
- τῇ ὑπερβολῇ τῶν ἀποκαλύψεων (2 Cor 12:7) *the plenty of revelations* "surpassingly great revelations" (NIV) and with a paraphrase "the many wonderful things I saw" (TEV)
- ἐπαγγελίαν τοῦ πνεύματος (Gal 3:14)[137] "the promise of the Spirit" (NRSV NIV) "the promised Spirit" (NEB NAB REB TEV NJB).[138]
- καρπὸς ἔργου (Phil 1:22) *fruit of work* "fruitful labor (work)" (NRSV REB NIV) "productive work" (NET)

---

137 Cf. τῷ πνεύματι τῆς ἐπαγγελίας *the Spirit of the promise* (Eph 1:13), which is also a "Hebrew" adjectival genitive: "the promised Spirit."

138 Moule also considers it an attributed genitive (Moule, *Idiom Book*, 176).

- τὸ μυστήριον τῆς ἀνομίας (2 Thess 2:7) *the mystery of lawlessness* "the mysterious wickedness" (TEV)
- ἐνέργειαν πλάνης (2 Thess 2:11) *the work of delusion* the head word is translated "strong" (RSV ESV HCSB) "compelling" (REB) and "powerful delusion" (NIV NRSV). All these versions render an attributed genitive.[139]
- ἐν ὑποκρίσει ψευδολόγων (1 Tim 4:2) *hypocrisy of lies* "the plausible falsehoods" (REB)
- πλούτου ἀδηλότητι (1 Tim 6:17) *the uncertainty of riches* "uncertain riches" (KJV RSV REB).

Genitive of Manner

The genitive of manner is a title given to a usage of the genitive that expresses the *way* anything is done or happens. The genitive of manner answers questions that start with *how*.

An appropriate illustration of the genitive of manner occurs in Phil 2:8, with the expression θανάτου σταυροῦ. The context leaves no doubt that Paul wants here to describe the way Christ died. He *died on a cross*. This translation reveals the *manner* of Jesus' death (NIV REB NRSV ESV HCSB NET), the kind of death G. Walter Hansen contrasts as "not a heroic death, a noble death, but a shameful death, a disgraceful death."[140] In this example it is hard to distinguish between manner (the shame associated with crucifixion) and means (the torture instrument used to kill the victim) since they are so intertwined.

Another example of the genitive of manner is the phrase ἡ παρουσία τοῦ σώματος (2 Cor 10:10). Here, *the presence of the body* is to be compared with the phrase παρὼν δὲ τῷ πνεύματι (1 Cor 5:3), *present in spirit*, in order to identify this instance of the genitive of manner. Paul describes how he was present among the church people, either in body or in spirit. The *how* indicates the genitive of manner. Many versions (KJV ASV NRSV ESV NET CSB) have "his bodily/physical presence," which accords with the "Hebrew" genitive, which is discussed above. It does however justify categorizing the genitive of manner under the adjectival genitive. Meanwhile, TEV NJB NAB NIV have referred to the *manner of the presence* in 2 Cor 10:10 by using the phrase "in person."

The phrase σοφίᾳ λόγου *wisdom of speech* (1 Cor 1:17) may be located under the genitive of manner, since it indicates the skill (σοφίᾳ) and how it expresses itself in a rhetorical way (λόγου). Barrett says the expression reveals "both the content of the

---

139 NEB translates the genitive as subjective: "a delusion, which works upon them."
140 Hansen, *Philippians*, 157.

Gospel Paul preaches, and the manner in which he preaches it."[141] Although few, these examples are enough to illustrate the function of the genitive of manner, and the *manner* nature of the genitive fits appropriately the adjectival genitive.

Objective Genitive

One other main category under which a cluster of functions may be classified is the objective genitive. The genitive is identified as objective if it receives the action of the implicit verbal meaning of the head word of the genitive construction.[142] To say it in another way, when the first noun in a genitive construction has an inherent transitive verbal idea, the second noun (i.e., the genitive) takes the place of the accusative.[143] The objective genitive, as a construction, is in a way a complete sentence. It has a *subject* which is either implicit or explicit.[144] It has an *object* that is the genitive. Also, it has a *verb* implied in the first noun of the construction. This is the main reason for the extensive use of the objective genitive, in the NT in general, and in Paul's letters in particular.

Pure (Accusative) Objective Genitive

The "pure" objective genitive means that the second word in the genitive construction takes the place of the accusative merely because of the transitive verbal power implicit in the head word. It needs no preposition to govern the genitive. For example: τῆς παραβάσεως τοῦ νόμου *the transgression of the Law* (Rom 2:23). The transitive power of the verb "transgress" implied in the adnominal head word causes the genitive (i.e., the law) to receive the action, hence the title "objective genitive." Many new Bible translations have "breaking/transgressing the law" (NIV NRSV REB TEV NET HCSB ESV). Here, τοῦ νόμου stands for an accusative.

The following is a list of pure objective genitive constructions with their biblical references and an appropriate translation from Bible versions that reveal the accusative meaning of the genitive.

- τὴν πάρεσιν τῶν ἁμαρτημάτων (Rom 3:25) "overlooked the sins" (REB)
- ἐξουσίαν τοῦ πηλοῦ (Rom 9:21) "a right over the clay" (ASV)

---

141 Barrett, *1 Corinthians*, 49.
142 The "Objective genitive, i.e. the Genitive indicating the object of the verb represented by the word which governs it" (Moule, *Idiom Book*, 39–40).
143 See MHT₃ 210; Wallace, *ExSyn*, 116–18.
144 When the subject is explicit, it is not part of the genitive construction but implied in context.

- τῇ ἀναγνώσει τῆς παλαιᾶς διαθήκης (2 Cor 3:14) "they read ... the old Covenant" (TEV)
- καθαίρεσιν ὀχυρωμάτων (2 Cor 10:4) "to demolish strongholds" (NEB)
- ἀπολύτρωσιν τῆς περιποιήσεως (Eph 1:14) "redeemed what is his own." (REB)
- εἰς δόξαν καὶ ἔπαινον (Phil 1:11) "to glorify and praise God" (WB)
- τὴν ἀγάπην τῆς ἀληθείας (2 Thess 2:10) "to love the truth" (NRSV ESV)
- καταστροφῇ τῶν ἀκουόντων (2 Tim 2:14) "ruins those who listen" (NIV)

There are plenty of such examples in the letters of Paul. The use of the pure objective genitive is common in the whole NT.

Genitive of Advantage

The function of the genitive of advantage is to indicate what is done for the benefit of a person or thing. It has an implied "datival" meaning.[145] The genitive word fulfills the role of an indirect object or a datival object of the verbal idea that is expressed in the head word. The genitive of advantage is classified as a subheading under the objective genitive because its function fits well into this category. The above-noted examples indicate that Paul uses this function of the genitive not infrequently. Though this meaning is common, it is not frequently handled by grammars; only Brooks and Winbery take this meaning up.[146]

Translators express the force of the advantage meaning through the use of prepositions like *for* or *to*. We will list a few examples that represent the receiving (datival) function of the genitive:

- θύραν τοῦ λόγου *a door of the word* (Col 4:3)[147] "an opening for preaching" (REB)
- ἡ εὐλογία τοῦ Ἀβραάμ (Gal 3:14) "the blessing which God promised to Abraham" (TEV)
- ἡ εἰρήνη ἡμῶν (Eph 2:14) "Christ ... has brought us peace" (TEV)
- ἁμαρτίας διάκονος *a servant of sin* (Gal 2:17) "does that mean that Christ promotes sin?" (NIV), or "serving the cause of sin?" (TEV), or "encourages sin?" (NET)

With the example ζῆλον θεοῦ *zeal of God* (Rom 10:2), the genitive of advantage meaning is reflected in the following translations: "zeal(ous) for God" (ASV

---

145 See Books-Winbery, 17.
146 See Books-Winbery, 17.
147 This example comes from Books-Winbery, 17.

NASB REB NRSV NIV),[148] and "deeply devoted to God" (TEV). Similarly, the expression φῶς τῶν ἐν σκότει (Rom 2:19), appears in several versions as "a light for [or *to*] those who are in darkness" (TEV NRSV REB). These translations express the dative meaning of the genitive using the preposition *for* or *to*. For πλοῦτος κόσμου *riches of the world* (Rom 11:12), the meaning is well expressed by "riches for the world" (NIV NRSV), and "a great gain to the gentiles" (NJB). Barclay converts to a verbal clause, "enriched the world" (WB). This translation expresses the objective meaning of the genitive. For τῆς σαρκὸς πρόνοιαν *provision of the flesh* (Rom 13:14), KJV NRSV ESV have "provision for the flesh." In the phrase τὰς ἐπαγγελίας τῶν πατέρων *promises of the fathers* (Rom 15:8), the genitive reflects the advantage of the genitive noun: "the promises given to the fathers" (NJB NRSV ["patriarchs"]). The term τῆς βρώσεως τῶν εἰδωλοθύτων *the food of the idols* (1 Cor 8:4) means "food offered [sacrificed NIV CSB] to idols" (NRSV NIV HCSB CSB). For τῷ ἔργῳ τοῦ κυρίου *the work of the Lord* (1 Cor 15:58), REB TEV have "work for the Lord."

In this category it is worth pointing out the suggestion of Chiara Gianollo that the genitive overlaps the dative when the genitive is "extraposed," i.e., appears first in the construction,[149] as in Phil 2:2 πληρώσατέ μου τὴν χαρὰν *fulfill my joy*, where "the expression of events that affect the possessor" occurs, citing also ἐλέησόν μου τὸν υἱόν *have mercy on my son* (Matt 17:15) and οὐ διέλιπεν καταφιλοῦσά μου τοὺς πόδας *[she] has not stopped kissing my feet* (Luke 7:45). This last expression is somewhat paralleled by ὕδωρ μοι ἐπὶ πόδας οὐκ ἔδωκας *you did not give water to me for the feet* (Luke 7:44).[150] BDF observes, "The forward position of the gen. of the pron. often corresponds to the unemphatic Indo-European *dativus sympatheticus*."[151] This is especially true in the case of "body parts, psychological states, kinship or otherwise close personal relationships, other kinds of inalienable possession."[152] This is very much in line with a tendency, observed by Joanne Vera Stolk towards the replacement of the dative case by the genitive observable in the papyri.[153] Stolk observes that in this situation the most common word order involves situations in

---

148 This idea has been recognized for quite some time. Green, as far back as 1842, lists ζῆλον θεοῦ ἔχουσιν under the "genitive of object" and translates it "They have zeal for God." See Thomas Sheldon Green, *A Treatise on the Grammar of the New Testament* (London: Bagster, 1842), 261.

149 Gianollo, "External Possession," 104.

150 Gianollo, "External Possession," 110.

151 BDF §473 (1) p. 249.

152 Gianollo, "External Possession," 112.

153 Joanne Vera Stolk, "Dative by Genitive Replacement in the Greek Language of the Papyri: A Diachronic Account of Case Semantics," *JGL* 15.1 (2015): 91–121, doi:10.1163/15699846–01501001.

which the genitive pronoun occurs directly after a verbal form, and typically in a doubly transitive construction.[154]

Genitive of Destination

The function of the genitive of destination as a derivation of the objective genitive is to limit the target towards which the *nomen regens* is moving. Destination is the name given to this genitive because the destination may be spatial, or it may be metaphorical: purpose or result. The genitive of destination is best explained through appropriate illustrations. The following is a group of examples which illustrates the meaning of this kind of genitive.

The expression πρόβατα σφαγῆς *sheep of slaughter* (Rom 8:36) is an excellent example of this category: "sheep for [the] slaughter" (KJV NEB REB) or "sheep to be slaughtered" (ESV NET NIV CSB).[155] In τοῦ σώματος τοῦ θανάτου *the body of death* (Rom 7:24), some versions highlight the destination function of the genitive in an expressive way: TEV reads, "this body that is taking me to death," while NJB has "this body doomed to death." For τῆς δουλείας τῆς φθορᾶς *the bondage of decay* (Rom 8:21), TEV NRSV NIV ESV have "its bondage [TEV "slavery"] to decay [ESV "corruption"]." These translations indicate the destination function of the genitive.[156] Another example is σκεύη ὀργῆς *vessels of wrath* (Rom 9:22), which may mean "vessels destined for wrath." This meaning is supported by the parallel phrase κατηρτισμένα εἰς ἀπώλειαν "prepared for destruction."[157] The apparent meaning of νόμον δικαιοσύνης *law of righteousness* (Rom 9:31) is: "a law that *leads to* justification." It looks at righteousness as a result of keeping the law, "a law that would put them right with God" (TEV) or "the law as the way of righteousness" (NIV). "This phrase," Moo says, "has become a storm center of debate."[158] After sorting through various options he suggests the explanation of "law for righteousness" as the appropriate meaning of this phrase.[159] The phrase τὰ τῆς εἰρήνης *the things of peace* (Rom 14:19) means "things that are *for* peace." KJV ASV NRSV REB NET ESV have "the things which ..." or "what makes for peace." NJB has "the ways that

---

154 Stolk, "Dative by Genitive Replacement," 100, 102.

155 Wallace, *ExSyn*, 100.

156 Murray suggests that it is more natural to take τῆς φθορᾶς as appositive: "the bondage which consists in corruption" (*Romans*, 1:304n30). Turner lists this reference as a possible genitive of quality (e.g., slavery characterized by decay; MHT₃ 212–13). Moo concludes: "in light of the meaning of words, it is probably objective–'slavery to decay'" (*Romans*, 539n1095).

157 Wallace, *ExSyn*, 101.

158 Moo, *Romans*, 642.

159 Moo, *Romans*, 645.

lead to peace," and NIV reads "what leads to peace." For ζηλωταί πνεύματων *zealous of spiritual* [*things*] (1 Cor 14:12), REB NIV have "eager for gifts of the spirit." The NJB has "eager to have spiritual powers."[160] Some Bible versions translate the genitive τῇ διακονίᾳ τῆς κατακρίσεως *the service of condemnation* (2 Cor 3:9) in a way that indicates result: "the ministry which brings condemnation" or "the ministry that brought condemnation" (REB TEV NIV). Result is fairly close to the idea of destination. WB has "the dispensation which ends in man's condemnation."

The examples of the genitive of advantage or destination do not end here. The meaning of τὸ εὐαγγέλιον τῆς ἀκροβυστίας *the gospel of the uncircumcision* (Gal 2:7) is "the gospel to the uncircumcised" (NET) or "to take the gospel to the Gentiles" (REB; cf. TEV "preaching the gospel to the Gentiles"). For ἐλπίδα δικαιοσύνης *hope of righteousness* (Gal 5:5), REB has "we hope to attain that righteousness."[161] WB paraphrases, "the hoped-for right relationship with God." In this phrase, *righteousness* may be considered as an objective genitive—what we hope for. Ridderbos, however, maintains that hope here *is* righteousness, classifying δικαιοσύνης as a "genitive of explication."[162] The meaning of τὴν μεθοδείαν τῆς πλάνης *the scheming of deceit* (Eph 4:14) is that of result and destination. TEV draws out this meaning as, "who lead others into error by tricks," while WB has "craftily calculated to lead us astray." Also, ἐνέργειαν πλάνης *operation of deceit* (2 Thess 2:11) may belong in the destination category, though we have already seen it as an example of the attributed genitive. Frame suggests "an energy unto delusion" with the grounds that "πλάνης is a genitive of object, and denotes the goal of the active inward energy."[163] Concerning προφάσει πλεονεξίας *excuse of greed* (1 Thess 2:5), the meaning is clear in translation if *for*—a preposition indicating purpose—is rather than *of*. The motive here is toward greed, as the following versions indicate: "a pretext for greed" (NRSV ESV NET); "an excuse for greed" (NJB); or "a cloak for greed" (REB). Although Wallace says, "This is somewhat rare category,"[164] there are enough examples to demonstrate its occurrence in the Pauline corpus.

---

160 ζηλωταί πνεύματων may be considered as objective genitive in reference to 1 Cor 12:31; 14:1, however, including it under the genitive of destination does not exclude the accusative element because it is classified under the more general objective genitive category.

161 Burton says whether the genitive is objective or appositional, the effect is the same, "it is the righteousness which is the object both of hope and expectation" (Ernest De Witt Burton, *A Critical and Exegetical Commentary on the Epistle to the Galatians*, ICC [New York: Scribner, 1920]).

162 Herman N. Ridderbos, *The Epistle of Paul to the Churches of Galatia*, NICNT (Grand Rapids: Eerdmans, 1953), 189n14.

163 Frame, *1 Thessalonians*, 272.

164 Wallace, *ExSyn*, 100.

Genitive of Reference

The genitive of reference sees a construction in which the second substantive is *the central topic* of the head word in the genitive construction. The genitive of reference is best expressed by the preposition *about*.[165] It indicates engagement, regard and concern. Some grammarians speak about the genitive of reference as "a noun (or noun phrase) that acts as an adverb modifying an adjective."[166] Young says that this kind of genitive is "common with adjectives conveying (1) fullness, such as μεστός and πλήρης; (2) worthiness or unworthiness, such as ἄξιος and ἔνοχος; or (3) sharing or lacking, such as κοινωνός and μέτοχος."[167] The present treatment differs in form and function from Dana-Mantey's, Young's, and Wallace's description, although all use the same name. The following examples illustrate what is meant by the genitive of reference as used in the present work.

The phrase τὴν ἀλήθειαν τοῦ θεοῦ *the truth of God* (Rom 1:25) means in its context, "the truth about God" (NRSV TEV NIV ESV).[168] For τοῦ νόμου τοῦ ἀνδρός *law of the husband* (Rom 7:2), NRSV has "the law concerning the husband" and others translate similarly, "the law regarding the husband" (CSB; cf. "the law of the leper" [Lev 14:2] and "the law of Nazirites" [Num 6:13]). For τὸ εὐαγγέλιον τοῦ Χριστοῦ *the gospel of the Christ* (Rom 15:19; 1 Cor 9:12), NET translates, "the good news about the Messiah." For τὸ κήρυγμα τοῦ Ἰησοῦ (Rom 16:25), TEV reads "the Good News I preach about Jesus Christ." Bruce remarks, "Jesus Christ is its subject-matter and substance."[169] The TEV has "the good news I preach about Jesus." For the phrase τὸ μαρτύριαν τοῦ Χριστοῦ *the testimony of Christ* (1 Cor 1:6), TEV ESV NET NIV have "the message/witness/testimony about Christ."[170] The TEV translates the genitive of this phrase ὁ λόγος ὁ τοῦ σταυροῦ *the word of the cross* (1 Cor 1:18) as "the message about Christ's death on the cross." For ψευδομάρτυρες τοῦ θεοῦ *false witnesses of God* (1 Cor 15:15), the REB has "false evidence about God," and NIV NET CSB have "false witnesses about God." Similarly, NJB has

---

165 See Beekman-Callow, 256.

166 Young, *Intermediate Greek*, 38. See also Dana-Mantey, 78; Wallace, *ExSyn*, 127.

167 Young, *Intermediate Greek*, 38.

168 Ernst Käsemann's comment hints at a genitive of reference: "ἀλήθεια again means the self-disclosing reality of God, not an attribute of God nor his 'true nature'" (*Commentary on Romans*, trans. Geoffrey William Bromiley [Grand Rapids: Eerdmans, 1980], 48). Morris agrees (*Romans*, 90n261).

169 Bruce, *Romans*, 281.

170 The gospel's "content is indicated by the objective genitive τοῦ Χριστοῦ" Hans Conzelmann, *1 Corinthians*, ed. G. W. MacRae, trans. James W. Leitch (Philadelphia: Fortress, 1975), 27.

"false witnesses to God." Anthony Thiselton classifies this as an objective genitive.[171] The meaning of the phrase τὸν λόγον τῆς καταλλαγῆς *the word of reconciliation* (2 Cor 5:19) is "the message *concerning* reconciliation." For κατὰ τῆς γνώσεως τοῦ θεοῦ *against the knowledge of God* (2 Cor 10:5) WB has "to prevent men from knowing God," taking the genitive as objective, though since it is modified by the negative in context "against," the English-speaking reader does not have to work hard at coming to grips with the meaning. This construal, however, is in harmony with the genitive of reference "the knowledge *about* God."[172] The phrase τῷ μυστηρίῳ τοῦ Χριστοῦ *the mystery of Christ* (Eph 3:4; Col 4:3) may be a genitive of reference "the secret concerning Christ," or *the mystery whose central topic is Christ*. Bruce, however, thinks the genitive epexegetical.[173] For ὁ λόγος τοῦ κυρίου *the word of the Lord* (1 Thess 1:8), TEV has "the message about the Lord."[174] For τοῖς λόγοις τῆς πίστεως *the words of the faith* (1 Tim 4:6), one may suggest "the teachings *concerning* faith (in Christ)." For ἐπαγγελίαν ζωῆς *promise of life* (1 Tim 4:8), TEV indicates the objective force of the genitive: "it promises life." This translation demonstrates well the suitability of classifying ἐπαγγελίαν ζωῆς as a genitive of reference. The possible meaning of this construction could be "the promise *concerning* this present life." Several English translations have "promise for life" (NJB NIV REB HCSB NET ESV). Knight says that the genitive "signifies the thing promised," thus ζωῆς is the content of promise.[175] Similarly, τὴν ἐπαγγελίαν τοῦ πνεύματος *the promise of the Spirit* (Gal 3:14) may fit well here. For κατηγορίᾳ ἀσωτίας *accusation of dissipation* (Titus 1:6), NJB has "charged with disorderly conduct," catching the objective meaning of the genitive, which is in harmony with the category genitive of reference. It answers the question, "What is the charge *about?*" The usage of the genitive of reference is fairly common in the letters of Paul and deserves a subheading under the objective genitive.

---

171 Thiselton writes, "The objective genitive for τοῦ θεοῦ **concerning God** seems to fit the context better than a subjective genitive (*in God's service*)" (*The First Epistle to the Corinthians: A Commentary on the Greek Text*, NIGTC [Grand Rapids Eerdmans: 2000], 1219) [emphasis original].

172 As Furnish notes, "The genitive is objective, as in 2:14 ... 'knowledge about God'" (*II Corinthians*, 458).

173 Bruce, *Colossians, Philemon, Ephesians*, 313n19.

174 Bruce thinks this is a subjective genitive (*1 and 2 Thessalonians*, WBC [Dallas: Word, 1998], 17). But Gene Green notes that the word of the Lord "is a reference to the Gospel itself" (*The Letters to the Thessalonians*, PNTC [Grand Rapids: Eerdmans, 2002], 101). This would mean that the message would be *about* the Lord as well as *from* him.

175 Knight, *Pastoral Epistles*, 200. Knight cites 2 Tim 1:1; 2 Pet 3:4; Heb 9:15; 4:1; 1 John 2:25; Rom 4:13 as examples of parallel usage.

Genitive of Derivation

With the genitive of derivation, the head word is the *origin* or *source* of the second word in the construction. The genitive is derived from the head word, hence the genitive of derivation. Wallace calls this classification, "genitive of product."[176] Illustrations will clarify the genitive of derivation.

Paul regularly speaks about God as the giver of qualities or virtues that Christians need for their spiritual well-being. Several times he mentions God as the giver of peace: ὁ θεὸς τῆς εἰρήνης *the God of peace* (Rom 15:33; 16:20; 1 Cor 14:33; 2 Cor 13:11; Phil 4:9; 1 Thess 5:23). This phrase is synonymous with εἰρήνη ἀπὸ θεοῦ *peace from God* which occurs fairly commonly in the Pauline corpus, especially in epistolary greetings. In 2 Thess 3:16, it is the Lord of peace who gives peace: αὐτὸς ὁ κύριος τῆς εἰρήνης δῴη ὑμῖν τὴν εἰρήνην, "may the Lord of peace himself give you peace" (NET). God also is the God of comfort: ὁ θεὸς τῆς παρακλήσεως (Rom 15:5; 2 Cor 1:3); of hope: ὁ θεὸς τῆς ἐλπίδος (Rom 15:13); of love: ὁ θεὸς τῆς ἀγάπης (2 Cor 13:11); and of patience: ὁ θεὸς τῆς ὑπομονῆς (Rom 15:5). All these qualities derive from God, the source of all virtues. God is also called ὁ πατὴρ τῶν οἰκτιρμῶν *the Father of mercies* (2 Cor 1:3).

God is not the author of disorder: οὐ γάρ ἐστιν ἀκαταστασίας ὁ θεός (1 Cor 14:33). He does not give "a spirit of cowardice, but rather a spirit of power and of love and of self-discipline" (πνεῦμα δειλίας ἀλλὰ δυνάμεως καὶ ἀγάπης καὶ σωφρονισμοῦ 2 Tim 1:7 NRSV). These are derived from God and the Spirit. The importance of the derivation force noted in these examples makes gives the derivative genitive a place as a subheading under the objective genitive.

Superlative Genitive

The superlative genitive indicates the head word is supreme either as highest ("Lord of lords"), or as lowest (servant of servants). Usually the head word is in the singular and the genitive is in the plural. The words of the genitive construction in both positions have identical roots (e.g. Song of Songs).[177]

The superlative as description applies only to the head word in the genitive construction, not to the genitive itself. In the present work, however, the superlative is given to the genitive construction as a unit for convenience.

---

176 Wallace, *ExSyn*, 106.

177 Waltke and O'Connor define the superlative genitive: "A superlative may involve two instances of a single noun, the first a singular construct and the second a plural genitive" (*Biblical Hebrew Syntax*, 154). See also D. W. Thomas, "A Consideration of Some Unusual Ways of Expressing the Superlative in Hebrew," *VT* 3 (1953): 209–24, https://www.jstor.org/stable/1516347.

The superlative genitive in the NT is rooted in the language of the OT mediated perhaps through the LXX. In the examples that follow, only Gen 9:25 is not rendered literally by the LXX:

- Gen 9:25 עבד עבדים *slave of slaves* (LXX παῖς οἰκέτης) "servant of servants" (KJV ESV)[178]
- Exod 26:33 קדש הקדשים (LXX τοῦ ἁγίου τῶν ἁγίων) *holy of holies* "most holy place" (KJV NRSV NIV NET ESV CSB)
- Song 1:1 שיר השירים (LXX Ἆισμα ᾀσμάτων) "the Song of Songs" (ESV NIV), "Solomon's Finest Song" (HCSB)
- Deut 10:17 אלהי האלהים ואדני האדנים (LXX θεὸς τῶν θεῶν καὶ κύριος τῶν κυρίων) "the God of gods and the Lord of lords" (KJV NIV *et al.*), "God is supreme over all gods and over all powers" (TEV)
- Ps 148:4 שמי השמים *heaven of heavens* (LXX οἱ οὐρανοὶ τῶν οὐρανῶν), "highest heavens" (REB NIV ESV)
- Eccl 1:2 הבל הבלים (LXX ματαιότης ματαιοτήτων) "vanity of vanities" (KJV ESV) "utter futility" (REB).

The superlative genitive occurs rarely in the NT. Outside the Pauline corpus, mainly in the Apocalypse. The title of the victorious Christ βασιλεὺς βασιλέων καὶ κύριος κυρίων (Rev 19:16) "King of kings and Lord of lords" (HCSB) occurs once (cf. Rev 17:14). The conclusion to many NT doxologies εἰς τοὺς αἰῶνας τῶν αἰώνων *to the ages of ages* (Heb 13:21; 1 Pet 4:11; Rev 1:6, 18; 4:9, 10; 5:13; 7:12; 10:6; 11:15; 15:7; 19:3; 20:10; 22:5), is rendered in nearly all English versions as "forever and ever." Both head word and genitive are plural in all but one: τὸν αἰῶνα τοῦ αἰῶνος (Heb 1:8), where both are singular.

The superlative genitive occurs several times in the letters of Paul. It appears three times as singular head word and plural genitive in the following verses: τοῦ αἰῶνος τῶν αἰώνων *the age of the ages* (Eph 3:21) and ὁ βασιλεὺς τῶν βασιλευόντων καὶ κύριος τῶν κυριευόντων *the king of the ones who king and the lord of those who lord* (1 Tim 6:15). All the other occurrences are doxological superlatives: εἰς τοὺς αἰῶνας τῶν αἰώνων (Gal 1:5; Phil 4:20; 1 Tim 1:17; 2 Tim 4:18).

The singular head word superlative "the age of ages" (Eph 3:21) appears in the larger construction εἰς πάσας τὰς γενεὰς τοῦ αἰῶνος τῶν αἰώνων *to all the generations of the age of the ages*. Hoehner offers the explanation, "The repetition of αἰών in both singular and plural forms may be intended to emphasize longevity or, as in

---

178 See Allen P. Ross, "The Curse of Canaan: Studies in the Book of Genesis Part 1," *BSac* 137.547 (1980): 232.

this case, eternity."[179] We may offer in line with the superlative meaning, "to the last age (the supreme and most prosperous) of all the ages."

Subjective Genitive

The subjective genitive is one of the main meanings of the genitive. It functions as the subject of the implicit verb in the head noun. The subjective genitive governs the action implied in the noun attached to it. Usually in such genitive constructions where the head noun allows a verbal idea, the genitive may be the subject or the object.[180] In order to differentiate the subjective from the objective genitive one must ask whether the genitive noun *produces* the action inherent in the attached substantive (subjective genitive) or if the genitive noun *receives* the action (objective genitive). Transforming the construction into a verbal clause using a cognate verb is one of the chief ways of making such an identification (e.g., the king's decree = the king decreed). The subjective genitive is very common in the Pauline corpus and the rest of the NT. It is sufficient here to give some examples of this type of genitive before moving to some other distinctive meanings related to it.

The expression τῷ θελήματι τοῦ θεοῦ *the will of God* (Rom 1:10), illustrates well the verbal idea of a substantive attached to a genitive. The word θέλημα is a noun of action because there is a cognate verb θέλω. LB translates the phrase as "God willing," and NJB has "if it is God's will." The following examples show how the substantive head word in the genitive constructions was converted to a verbal statement:

- Rom 8:33 ἐκλεκτῶν θεοῦ *chosen ones of God*, "those whom God has chosen" (NJB REB)
- Rom 15:18 ὑπακοὴν ἐθνῶν *obedience of the Gentiles*, "to lead the gentiles to obey God" (TEV NIV)
- 1 Cor 7:22 ἀπελεύθερος κυρίου *a freedman of the Lord*, "a person the Lord has set free"
- 1 Cor 15:52 ῥιπῇ ὀφθαλμοῦ *a wink of an eye*, "the twinkling of an eye" (KJV ESV NIV), "the blink of an eye" (HCSB; cf. NET)

---

179 Hoehner, *Ephesians*, 495. Robertson (*Grammar*, 408), notes that the plural with "some words ... was felt to be more appropriate."

180 The key role of the verbal idea implicit in this kind of genitive leads Wallace to categorize both subjective and objective genitive under the broader category of "Verbal Genitive" (*ExSyn*, 112–19).

- Gal 4:2 τῆς προθεσμίας τοῦ πατρός *the date of the father*, "the date set by the father" (NRSV)
- Phil 1:20 ἐλπίδα μου *my hope*, "I ... hope" (NIV).
- Col 2:11 τῇ περιτομῇ τοῦ Χριστοῦ *the circumcision of Christ*, "the circumcision done by Christ" (NET), "you were circumcised by Christ" (NIV)
- 1 Thess 4:15 τὴν παρουσίαν τοῦ κυρίου *the coming of the Lord*, "when the Lord comes" (REB)
- 2 Tim 2:26 τῆς τοῦ διαβόλου παγίδος *the trap of the devil*, "the trap that the devil has laid," "the snare, set by the devil"[181]
- 2 Tim 2:19 θεμέλιος τοῦ θεοῦ *the foundation of God*, "God has laid a foundation-stone" (REB), "the solid foundation that God has laid" (TEV)

These examples are taken from the letters of Paul. They are selected from different letters with a variety of uses in order to show how common and diverse the subjective genitive is. There are several functions of the subjective genitive (as a broader category) that could be classified under the subjective genitive but with more specificity.

Genitive of Source

The title "genitive of source" describes the subjective genitive as "the source" of the related word in the genitive construction. Here are some examples of the genitive of source:

God is the source of righteousness: δικαιοσύνη θεοῦ *righteousness of God* (Rom 3:21). He is also the source of grace: τὴν χάριν τοῦ θεοῦ *the grace of God* (1 Cor 3:10). God gives promises: ἐπαγγελίαι θεοῦ *promises of God* (2 Cor 1:20), and honesty: ἁπλότητι ... τοῦ θεοῦ *sincerity of God* (2 Cor 1:12), "God-given frankness" (TEV), "sincerity ... from God" (NET). The Holy Spirit is the source of power δυνάμει πνεύματος ἁγίου *power of the Holy Spirit* (Rom 15:13). The Lord is the source of revelation: ἀποκαλύψεις κυρίου *revelation of the Lord* (2 Cor 12:1). Angels are sent from God: ἄγγελον θεοῦ *an angel of God* (Gal 4:14), "angel from heaven" (TEV). Churches send messengers: ἀπόστολοι ἐκκλησιῶν *apostles of churches* (2 Cor 8:23). The face of the Lord shines with glory: τὴν δόξαν κυρίου *the glory of the Lord* (2 Cor 3:18). God is the source of life τῆς ζωῆς τοῦ θεοῦ *the life of God* (Eph 4:18), "the life that God gives" (TEV). Christ gives peace: ἡ εἰρήνη τοῦ Χριστοῦ *the peace of Christ* (Col 3:15). God the Father raises Jesus διὰ τῆς δόξης τοῦ πατρός *through the glory of*

---

181 So Mounce, *Pastoral Epistles*, 537. See also Knight, *Pastoral Epistles*, 425

the Father (Rom 6:4) "by the Father's glorious power" (NJB), or "by the glorious power of the Father" (REB, TEV).

The controversial genitive phrase τύπον διδαχῆς *type of teaching* (Rom 6:17) deserves special treatment. This phrase may be an epexegetical genitive (e.g., the pattern that consists in teaching). Goppelt says: "διδαχῆς is to be taken as an appos. gen."[182] On the other hand, Robert Gagnon argues strongly for taking διδαχῆς as genitive of source and that τύπος should be understood here as "imprint," partly supporting his case from the literal "mark/imprint of the nails" (John 20:25) to mean "imprint from teaching."[183]

The phrase τὴν αὔξησιν τοῦ θεοῦ *growth of God* (Col 2:19) has engendered much discussion. While REB NEB take it as genitive of accordance "grows according to God's design"[184] and Lenski considers it a "characterizing genitive" (i.e., divine growth),[185] many other versions interpret it as merely a subjective genitive, more precisely a genitive of source. Examples of translations are these: "a growth ... from God" (RSV NJB NRSV ESV NET CSB), "grows as God causes it to grow" (NIV), or "it grows as God wants it to grow" (TEV). Many commentators also think it a subjective genitive. Zerwick and Grosvenor say: "*growth derived from* or *willed by God*."[186] Lohse, Dunn, Abbott, and Alford do the same.[187]

Genitive of Origin

The genitives of origin and source are very similar categories. In fact, some grammarians use both terms interchangeably.[188] Here, they are treated separately because both have their own distinctive nuance. Take for example χαρᾶς πνεύματος ἁγίου *joy of the Holy Spirit* (1 Thess 1:6) "joy inspired by the Holy Spirit" (RSV), meaning the Holy Spirit is the *source* of joy. Now, if the head noun indicates a deeper connection, e.g. σπέρμα Ἀβραάμ *seed of Abraham* (Rom 9:6), the genitive

---

182 Leonhard Goppelt *TDNT* 8:250n19 s.v. τύπος.

183 Robert A. J. Gagnon, "Heart of Wax and a Teaching that Stamps: ΤΥΠΟΣ ΔΙΔΑΧΗΣ (Rom 6:17b) Once More," *JBL* 112.4 (1993): 686–87.

184 See under the category *Genitive of Definition*.

185 Lenski, *Colossians-Philemon*, 136.

186 Max Zerwick and Mary Grosvenor, *A Grammatical Analysis of the Greek New Testament*, 5th ed. (Rome: Pontifical Biblical Institute, 1974), 608. [emphasis original]

187 Henry Alford, *The Greek Testament: An Exegetical and Critical Commentary*, 7th ed., 4 vols. (n.p.: 1874; repr., Grand Rapids: Guardian Press, 1976), 3:228; Abbott, *A Critical and Exegetical Commentary on the Epistles to the Ephesians and to the Colossians*, 272; Lohse, *Colossians and Philemon*, 114, 122; Dunn, *Colossians and Philemon*, 186.

188 See Wallace, *ExSyn*, 109.

would be a genitive of origin, because Abraham is considered as the origin of his descendants, the start of a new nation.[189]

The following are some other examples that illustrate the genitive of origin: God is the originator of creation: κτίσμα θεοῦ (1 Tim 4:4). Love is the originator of labor: τοῦ κόπου τῆς ἀγάπης *work of love* (1 Thess 1:3), "your love made you work so hard" (TEV). Faith motivates work: ἔργου πίστεως *work of faith* (2 Thess 1:11), "every act inspired by faith" (REB). The flesh is the originator of lust: ἐπιθυμίαν σαρκός *lust of the flesh* (Gal 5:16).[190] Jesse is the origin of the root: ἡ ῥίζα τοῦ Ἰεσσαί *the root of Jesse* (Rom 15:12). The devil is the originator of wicked schemes: τὰς μεθοδείας τοῦ διαβόλου *the schemes of the Devil* (Eph 6:11). The Holy Spirit is the originator of regeneration: ἀνακαινώσεως πνεύματος *regeneration of the Spirit* (Titus 3:5). Here, NIV CSB render it, "renewal by the Holy Spirit" (cf. TEV NJB).

Genitive of Authorship

The genitive of authorship is similar to the genitives of source and of origin. Despite the similarity of meaning among these titles of genitive, the genitive of authorship relates to the genitive constructions that imply the verb *to inspire*. This is a fine shade of nuance, and often difficult to clarify in translation.

Under the genitive of authorship fall many genitive phrases that occur in the Pauline corpus, such as εὐαγγέλιον θεοῦ *gospel of God* (Rom 1:1; 2 Cor 11:7). The genitive in this instance is not that of reference: "the gospel about God," but that of authorship: "the gospel that God initiated," "the gospel that comes from God." As Murray writes, "The stress falls upon the divine origin … of the gospel. It is a message of glad tidings from God."[191]

Other examples of the genitive of authorship may be noted: God is the author and giver of the law νόμῳ θεοῦ *the law of God* (Rom 7:25). Likewise, his word: τὸν λόγον τοῦ θεοῦ *the word of God* (Col 1:25), and his command ἐπιταγὴν τοῦ θεοῦ *the command of God* (Rom 16:26; cf. ἐπιταγὴν κυρίου *the command of the Lord* 1 Cor 7:25). Paul is the author of his prayers: τῶν προσευχῶν μου *my prayers* (Eph 1:16), his defense before the judge: μου ἀπολογίᾳ *my defense* (2 Tim 4:16), and also, the letter ἐπιστολῆς ἡμῶν *our letter* (2 Thess 2:15) he and his comrades sent to Thessalonica.

---

189 Blass and Debrunner group the genitive of origin with the genitive of relationship, including genetic relationships of father and son as well as relationships by marriage (BDF §162 p. 89).

190 Hans Dieter Betz says: "The flesh is active, a force which carries out intentions—of course, evil intentions. This is what the Apostle means by ἐπιθυμία σαρκός" (*Galatians: A Commentary on Paul's Letter to the Churches in Galatia*, Hermeneia [Philadelphia: Fortress, 1979], 278).

191 Murray, *Romans*, 1:3.

Genitive of Cause

The genitive of cause belongs to the family of the subjective genitive. The genitive of cause, being the subject, causes the effects the head word experiences. The function of the genitive of cause is similar to the subjective genitive, or that of source or origin, yet it differs from them. The subjective genitive represents the direct doer of the action, while the genitive of cause is just a "cause" or reason. The real doer of the action is an implied person or thing different from the *nomen rectum*. For example, ὁ δέσμιος τοῦ Χριστοῦ *the prisoner of Christ* (Eph 3:1; Phlm 1). The meaning here is not that Christ took Paul as prisoner, but that Roman authorities incarcerated Paul *because* he is proclaiming the gospel of Christ.

Here are some other examples which illustrate the function of the genitive of cause. For the expression τὰ τέκνα τῆς ἐπαγγελίας *the children of the promise* (Rom 9:8; anarthrous ἐπαγγελίας τέκνα in Gal 4:28), TEV renders, "the children born as a result of God's promise" (cf. NEB). The contextually implied subject is God, who made a promise to Abraham. The causal meaning of the genitive τὸ σκάνδαλον τοῦ σταυροῦ *the stumbling block of the cross* (Gal 5:11), is best rendered by TEV: "If that is true, then my preaching about the cross of Christ would cause no trouble." Faith in Christ is the causal force of believers' unity, as in τὴν ἑνότητα τῆς πίστεως *the unity of the faith* (Eph 4:13), "the unity inherent in our faith" (REB), implying that "our faith" is *the cause* of believers' oneness.[192] TEV renders τῆς ἐλπίδος τοῦ εὐαγγελίου *the hope of the gospel* (Col 1:23), "the hope you gained when you heard the gospel." It is clear that the gospel is *the factor-cause* by which God's hope is obtained. Similarly, TEV translates the phrase τῆς κατάρας τοῦ νόμου *the curse of the law* (Gal 3:13), "the curse that the Law brings." This translation excludes the defining aspect of the genitive and at the same time confirms the subjective aspect. The causal aspect is clear since, in the final conclusion, the curse is God's wrath on those who do not keep the Law. The Law is just a *cause*, but the curse is God's doing.[193] Another genitive of cause appears in παραμύθιον ἀγάπης *consolation of love* (Phil 2:1). Love is just a cause of comfort; the real actor is Christ. This relationship is rendered variously: "his love comforts you" (TEV), "comfort from his love" (NIV), "comfort provided by love" (NET). Melick says, "The NIV correctly translates this as affirming Christ's love for his people."[194]

---

192 Bruce comments, "It is by faith that the people of Christ are united to him, and in being united to him they realize their own unity one with another" (*Colossians, Philemon, Ephesians*, 350).

193 Büchsel notes "In [Gal] 3:13 the curse is the curse of the Law, since the Law expresses it ([Deut] 27:26; 21:23). Yet it is also the curse of God, for the Law is the revelation of God" (*TDNT* 1:450 s.v. κατάρα). Fung agrees (*Galatians*, 148n60).

194 Melick, *Philippians, Colossians, Philemon*, 93.

These examples are sufficient to establish that the genitive of cause has a special function that differs from other uses of the subjective genitive. This deserves an appropriate place under the subjective genitive.

Instrumental Genitive

We apply the term "instrumental" to the instrumental genitive because the head word is realized or performed *by means of* or *through the instrumentality of* the dependent genitive.[195] This is similar to the genitive of cause. But, the causal genitive gives the *basis* or *reason* for the action of the headword. With the instrumental genitive, by contrast, the agent of the verbal action is always *implicit*, to be found in the context outside the genitive construction. Sometimes it may look as if the genitive of instrument is a "pure" subjective genitive. A clear identification of the implied subject solves the ambiguity.

For the expression δικαιοσύνης πίστεως *righteousness of faith* (Rom 4:13), NIV has "the righteousness that comes by faith." REB offers, "through righteousness that came from faith." The source of righteousness, however, is God, not faith. Faith is just the instrument by which righteousness is received. The TEV paraphrases: "he believed and was accepted as righteous by God."

The phrase ἐκλογὴν χάριτος *election of grace* (Rom 11:5) is rendered, "chosen ["set aside" NJB] by grace" (NRSV NIV). REB expands to "chosen by the grace of God," adding "God" to specify the implicit subject. TEV does the same in a more explicit way: "God has chosen because of his grace." Morris says aptly, "Both *chosen* and *grace* speak of the priority of the divine and the love of God."[196] As a genitive, *grace* could be considered a subjective genitive (i.e., the doer of the election) if it were personified. Moo thinks that the genitive here may be descriptive: "an election characterized by grace."[197]

God gives comfort through Scriptures: διὰ τῆς παρακλήσεως τῶν γραφῶν *through the comfort of the scriptures* (Rom 15:4). The subject (God) is implicit, appearing in the context rather than in the genitive construction itself. The next verse (Rom 15:5) characterizes the comfort as from, "God who gives endurance and encouragement" (NIV). Without deeper consideration of context, the categorization appears at the surface to be a genitive of source,[198] but the instrumental genitive is the more precise designation in this instance.

---

195 Some grammarians call this category, "genitive of means." See Wallace, *ExSyn*, 125.
196 Morris, *Romans*, 401.
197 Moo, *Romans*, 695n593.
198 Moo, *Romans*, 886n707.

Christ's sanctifcation of the church, accomplished τῷ λουτρῷ τοῦ ὕδατος ἐν ῥήματι *by the washing of the water by the word* (Eph 5:26), involves an instrumental genitive. The washing is to be done "by water" (REB NEB; TEV "in water"; NIV "with water"). The implicit subject is Christ, who cleanses the church (Eph 5:25–26). The instrumental meaning of the genitive here is corroborated by the parallel phrase ἐν ῥήματι *by the word*.

Paul fully characterizes Jesus's obedient death by adding the phrase θανάτου δὲ σταυροῦ *even [the] death of [the] cross* (Phil 2:8), rendered by almost all English versions as "death on a cross" (e.g., NASB NET ESV NIV; only KJV has "death of a cross"). Besides its defining nature, this genitive phrase could be classified here in case it is considered a genitive of instrument "by means of the cross." The instrument of death is clear enough to an English reader, for being "on a cross" surely means death *by* it. These examples are scattered throughout the letters of Paul. Though Brooks and Winbery can find only one example, there are several, and clear enough to warrant a subheading under the subjective genitive.[199]

Genitive of Resemblance

The genitive of resemblance denotes similarity of character or action between the person(s) referred to and the one(s) represented by the genitive. The axis of resemblance between the two is the head word in the genitive construction. The genitive of resemblance falls naturally under the subjective genitive since the genitive in the construction is, most of the time, the subject of the related action or the owner of the related description or character. The nuance of resemblance would not be clear if the genitive construction were isolated from its wider context. For this reason, at first glance, the genitive would appear as a mere subjective; but if the wider context is considered, the resemblance element of this genitive may be clearly seen.

There are several examples of the genitive of resemblance in the Pauline corpus. One of them is πίστις Ἰησοῦ *faith of Jesus*, a phrase about which the intense debate is still ongoing. This debate includes the similar phrases διὰ πίστεως Ἰησοῦ Χριστοῦ *through faith of Jesus Christ* (Rom 3:22), ἐκ πίστεως Ἰησοῦ *from faith of Jesus* (Rom 3:26). Theories of interpretation of this phrase are many and diverse. The debate revolves mainly around the subjective (faith or faithfulness of Jesus)[200] and

---

199 Brooks and Winbery say that ἀνθρωπίνης σοφίας λόγοις *words of human wisdom* in 1 Cor 2:13 "is the only example known to the present writer of the substantive alone [i.e., without a preposition] being used to express means" (Books-Winbery, 24).

200 Melick writes, "In this context it is a quality of Jesus, and it should be understood as 'faithfulness of Jesus'" ("A Study in the Concept of Belief: A Comparison of the Gospel of John and the Epistle to the Romans" [Th.D. diss., Southern Baptist Theological Seminary, 1976], 202–3).

the objective genitive (faith in Jesus).[201] Some have emphasized the qualitative or adjectival aspect of the phrase by suggesting the term "Christic faith," as to correspond to "Abrahamic faith" based on Rom 4:12.[202] But others have emphasized a resemblance nuance of the subjective genitive, like L. T. Johnson:

> The final phrase, *ton ek pisteos Iesou* ([Rom] 3:26), is rendered by the *RSV*, "him who has faith in Jesus." This is the least likely of all the objective readings …. One would ordinarily … render this, "the one who shares the faith of Jesus," meaning, "one who has faith as Jesus had faith." The faith of the human being of Jesus is here clearly intended. In [Rom] 4:16, the same phrase occurs in reference to Abraham, *to ek pisteos Abraam*, The *RSV* does not there translate, "those who believe in Abraham," but (quite correctly) "those who share the faith of Abraham." So should we understand [Rom] 3:26.[203]

An echo to Johnson's viewpoint that the genitive in Rom 3:22 is genitive of resemblance is found in REB which reads: "it is effective through faith in Christ for all who have such faith."

Note also the resemblance nuance of the following genitives. The substantival phrase τῷ ἐκ πίστεως Ἀβραάμ *the one who is from the faith of Abraham* (Rom 4:16). This genitive denotes similarity in quality. It means "a faith *like* Abraham's." WB has "those who base their life on the same faith as Abraham had." TEV renders it as "who believe as Abraham did." The transformation of the noun πίστις into a verb and the addition of the comparative *as* bring out the genitive of resemblance. The ESV has, "who shares the faith of Abraham." All these translations attempt to elucidate this genitive construction, which points to resemblance between Abraham's faith and the faith of those who desire to be co-heirs of God's blessing. The key to interpreting this genitive is found in the same context, Rom 4:12, for people "who

---

201 See, for example, Barrett's translation of Rom 3:21–31 in which he supports the objective genitive interpretation (*Romans*, 2nd ed., BNTC [London: Hendrickson, 1991], 68). It is a daunting task to keep up with the vast array of secondary literature on this topic. See especially Fitzmyer, *Romans*, 345; Jewett, *Romans*, 275. And more recently, the collection of essays in *The Faith of Jesus Christ: Exegetical, Biblical, and Theological Studies*, ed. Michael F. Bird and Preston M. Sprinkle (Peabody, Mass: Hendrickson, 2010). Of particular interest are Debbie Hunn, "Debating the Faithfulness of Jesus Christ in Twentieth-Century Scholarship," 15–31; Stanley E. Porter and Andrew W. Pitts, "Πίστις with a Preposition and Genitive Modifier: Lexical, Semantic, and Syntactic Considerations in the Πίστις Χριστοῦ Discussion," 33–53.

202 Arland J. Hultgren, "The Pistis Christou Formulation in Paul," *NovT* 22.3 (1980): 256–57.

203 Luke Timothy Johnson, "Rom 3:21–26 and the Faith of Jesus," *CBQ* 44.1 (1982): 80. This article is also reprinted in Luke Timothy Johnson, "Romans 3:21–26 and the Faith of Jesus," in *Contested Issues in Christian Origins and the New Testament: Collected Essays* (Leiden: Brill, 2013), 241–54.

are not merely circumcised but also follow the example of the faith which our father Abraham had before he was circumcised" (RSV).

Another example of the genitive of resemblance is θεοῦ ζήλῳ *zeal of God* (2 Cor 11:2). Some Bible versions consider the phrase to be a descriptive genitive. Many have almost the same rendering: "I am jealous over you with godly jealousy" (KJV NET NIV CSB). NRSV has condensed the expression, "I feel a divine jealousy for you." Other versions translate the meaning as attributive, "the jealousy that I feel for you is, you see, God's own jealousy" (NJB). Furnish prefers genitive of origin over genitive of quality.[204] Plummer finds "unsatisfactory" taking θεοῦ here as superlative "very great zeal."[205] TEV captures the meaning of resemblance in translating the genitive phrase as follows: "I am jealous for you just as God is."

Commentators are divided about the genitive in θρησκείᾳ τῶν ἀγγέλων *worship of angels* (Col 2:18). The debate is whether it is an objective genitive: "worship offered to angels"[206] ("angel-worship" [NEB REB]), or subjective genitive: "angels offer worship to (God)."[207] The subjective genitive here fits appropriately the meaning of resemblance. If the subjective genitive is followed, Paul is saying that those people are insisting on humbling themselves falsely and are worshiping God *as* angels *do*. Dunn supports the subjective meaning in his treatment of this genitive expression.[208] Likewise, J. L. Sumney, pointing to the whole construction ταπεινοφροσύνη καὶ θρησκείᾳ τῶν ἀγγέλων argues that both nouns are related to the genitive. Since "angels" is subjective in relationship to "humility," likely "worship" is as well. Thus, both are descriptive angels' attitudes and acts as they worship God.[209] Thus, a more precise understanding of the value of the genitive of resemblance would mean *worship like the worship angels do*.

The genitive of resemblance also fits τὴν ὑπομονὴν τοῦ Χριστοῦ *the endurance of Christ* (2 Thess 3:5). Christ is the subject of the verb *endures* implicit in the substantive head word. Charles A. Wanamaker, pointing to the parallel τὴν ἀγάπην

---

204 Furnish, *II Corinthians*, 486.

205 Alfred Plummer, *The Second Epistle of St. Paul to the Corinthians* (Edinburgh: T&T Clark, 1915), 293.

206 Though Zerwick and Grosvenor favor objective genitive, "subjective gen. cannot be ruled out" (*Grammatical Analysis*, 607–08).

207 For Eduard Schweizer, the subjective genitive is ruled out by v. 23 "which speaks of an activity of the Colossians, not of the angels" ("Slaves of the Elements and Worshipers of Angels: Gal 4:3, 9 and Col 2:8, 18, 20," *JBL* 107.3 [1988]: 465n39).

208 Dunn, *Colossians and Philemon*, 180–82. The parallels adduced from first-century literature seem to support this idea as well.

209 Jerry L. Sumney, *Colossians: A Commentary*, NTL (London: Westminster John Knox, 2008), 154–55.

τοῦ θεοῦ (where the genitive is subjective), rightly takes the genitive as subjective, i.e., that it refers to taking Christ's endurance "as an example."[210] Classifying the genitive as subjective (the broader category) opens the way for a consideration of the genitive of resemblance (the narrower category). Ellingworth and Nida refer to this same meaning of the genitive: "endure even as Christ endured."[211]

There is also debate on whether one should take κρίμα τοῦ διαβόλου *the condemnation of the devil* (1 Tim 3:6) subjectively or objectively. Although these arguments are well known, a brief discussion will clarify the issues involved. Alford forcefully renders the genitive of resemblance: "the condemnation into which Satan fell through the same blinding effect of pride."[212] Dibelius and Conzelmann summarize the problem by presenting both interpretations:

> Here ... the meaning "devil" is to be assumed .... Therefore, we must take "condemnation of the devil" ... as referring either to the judgment which Satan, whose office it is to accuse or to tempt, speaks over the fallen neophyte, or to the judgment under which the devil himself once came. But perhaps we have no right to make the alternatives so distinct, since obviously one cannot differentiate clearly between "condemnation" ... and "snare of the devil."[213]

TEV paraphrases, "and be condemned, as the Devil was," while NJB renders "incur the same condemnation as the devil" (cf. NIV). NET translates it with the opposite view: "the punishment that the devil will exact." In the current examples that are mentioned under the resemblance meaning of the genitive, this is the only example that has an objective genitive. All other resemblance genitives are subjective. This is the rationale behind putting the genitive of resemblance under the subjective genitive, rather than the objective. The genitive, however, whether it is subjective or objective does not determine the resemblance function, but the head word and context do.

Ablatival Genitive

The ablatival genitive is a description given to genitives that bear the meaning of separation or departure.[214] The ablative expresses the "whence" meaning of the

210 Charles A. Wanamaker, *The Epistles to the Thessalonians: A Commentary on the Greek Text*, NIGTC (Grand Rapids: Eerdmans, 1990), 279.
211 Paul Ellingworth and Eugene Albert Nida, *A Handbook on Paul's Letters to the Thessalonians*, UBSHS (New York: United Bible Societies, 1976), 198.
212 Alford, *Greek Testament*, 3:325.
213 Dibelius and Conzelmann, *Pastoral Epistles*, 54.
214 Wallace, *ExSyn*, 107; MHT₃ 215.

genitive, as it is traditionally called, the sense of the genitive Winer so unreservedly proffered as its heart.[215] There are other similar uses of the genitive, like the genitive of comparison and partitive genitive. The notion of separation in the genitive is expressed by *from*, while other functions need the word *than*. Usually, all these functions of the genitive (i.e., separation, comparison, and partition) are categorized under the ablatival genitive.[216]

Wallace points out the semantic dimension of the ablatival genitive. Of the separation notion in the ablative, he observes, "This idea can be static (i.e., in a separated state) or progressive (movement away from, so as to become separated). The emphasis may be on either the state resulting from the separation or the cause of separation (in the latter, origin or source is emphasized)."[217] In differentiating source from separation, Wallace offers the helpful distinction, "separation stresses result while source stresses cause."[218]

Hellenistic Greek had mostly started expressing the separation idea using the prepositions ἐκ and ἀπό instead of the simple case usage. This is probably a factor in the decline of the ablative sense of the genitive.[219] The following classifications under the ablatival genitive illuminate the principles established in the present introduction.

Genitive of Separation

The genitive of separation implies the following meanings: *departing from, out of, away from*. The head word refers to the thing that is separated, while the dependent genitive refers to the source or place from which the head word departs.

As noted above, the genitive of separation is rare without prepositions, yet there are several examples of this kind of usage found in the letters of Paul. The first example of such meaning of the genitive is ἀναστάσεως νεκρῶν *resurrection of the dead* (Rom 1:4). It is abundantly clear that the reference is to a specific resurrection: that of Jesus *from among* the dead (cf. Rom 4:24; 8:11; 10:9).[220] The similar expression ἀνάστασις νεκρῶν *resurrection of the dead* in 1 Cor 15:12–13, is a

---

215 Robertson, *Grammar*, 514; Winer, *Grammar*, 230.

216 For example: Wallace, *ExSyn*, 107–112; Dana-Mantey, 81–83; Books-Winbery, 19–29. For these last two grammars, though, the ablative is a separate case.

217 Wallace, *ExSyn*, 107.

218 Wallace, *ExSyn*, 109.

219 See MHT₃ 235; Wallace, *ExSyn*, 107. See also Chrys C. Caragounis, *The Development of Greek and the New Testament: Morphology, Syntax, Phonology, and Textual Transmission* (Tübingen: Mohr Siebeck, 2004; repr., Grand Rapids: Baker, 2008), 143–44.

220 Fitzmyer, *Romans*, 236–37.

subjective genitive, where it refers generally to the resurrection of Christians from the dead (i.e., that dead Christians rise). The phrase τὴν τοῦ θεοῦ δικαιοσύνην *the righteousness of God* (Rom 10:3) denotes also the idea of separation (or source): "the righteousness that comes from God" (ESV NET).[221] A practical illustration of the genitive of separation is ἐπιστολὴ Χριστοῦ *letter of Christ* (2 Cor 3:3). The notion of ἐπιστολή as *letter* implies that it is intended *to be sent*. Therefore, ἐπιστολὴ Χριστοῦ is rendered: "a letter that has come from Christ" (REB), "letter from Christ" (NIV ESV). Barnett affirms: "The genitive Χριστοῦ is subjective, 'from Christ' (authorial), not objective 'about Christ.'"[222]

Paul uses other phrases that denote separation, such as ἐν λόγῳ κυρίου (1 Thess 4:15), "a word from the Lord" (REB WB). Alford understands the *word* as a "direct revelation."[223] NIV has a genitive of resemblance: "According the Lord's word." For the well-known expression θεοῦ τὸ δῶρον *the gift of God* (Eph 2:9), NJB has "a gift from God," rendering almost the same way ἄγγελος σατανᾶ *an angel of Satan* (2 Cor 12:7), "a messenger from Satan." Similarly, the expression ἐπιταγὴν κυρίου *command of the Lord* (1 Cor 7:25) comes across as "instructions from the Lord" (REB NJB). The word *from* in these translations denotes separation. Some genitive phrases mentioned here are similar to the subjective genitive. The difference is just a matter of where one puts the stress. Sometimes there is only a hair's breadth distance between nuances.

There are also some examples of the genitive of separation used with participles. Of course, this connection shades the discussion of the genitive off into the genitive with verbs. But we include it here in the discussion of adnominal genitives because participles can be used substantivally. The separation element in the construction is derived from the meaning of the verb that constitutes the root of the participle. Young suggests the title "genitive of disassociation" to describe the meaning of such genitive expressions.[224] Take, for example, ἀπηλλοτριωμένοι τῆς πολιτείας τοῦ Ἰσραήλ *alienated from the commonwealth of Israel* (Eph 2:12). The participle ἀπηλλοτριωμένοι has the meaning of "being aliens *from*," which confirms that "disassociation," or "separation," are integral part of the verb's meaning. Another example is ἀπεστερημένων τῆς ἀληθείας *deprived of the truth* (1 Tim 6:5).[225]

---

221 Wallace categorizes this instance under genitive of source (*ExSyn*, 110), but Fitzmyer believes that the RSV's meaning here is imported from Phil 3:9. He prefers "God's uprightness." (*Romans*, 583). TEV's translation speaks to the method of justification: "the way in which God puts people right with himself."

222 Barnett, *2 Corinthians*, 167n37. See also Furnish, *II Corinthians*, 182.

223 Alford, *Greek Testament*, 3:274.

224 Young, *Intermediate Greek*, 35.

225 See Moule, *Idiom Book*, 41.

The Partitive Genitive

The partitive genitive indicates the head word constitutes a part of the dependent genitive which constitutes the whole. In fact, the genitive here is not strictly "partitive," but refers to the whole of which the head word is just a portion. It was Winer who titled it "the genitive of the whole."[226] Brooks and Winbery suggest for it the name "the ablative of the whole or the ablative of the divided whole."[227] Not satisfied with "divided whole," Wallace suggests the term "wholative."[228] Here, the traditional title "partitive genitive" will be used for the genitive construction as a unit, with full awareness that the head word represents the part and the genitive represents the whole.

There is really no fixed border to differentiate between the possessive genitive and the partitive genitive. Therefore, the question persists: where to categorize such phrases as "the hand of the man," "the tip of the finger," "a tenth of the city," and "blood of Jesus"? Are they to be considered under possessive or partitive genitive? The way forward is to ask whether the head word is of the same nature or class of the genitive. If it were of the same nature or class it would be partitive, if not, it would be possessive. For example: "the *tip* of the *finger*" and "the *tenth* of the *city*." These two parts are of the same class as the whole, so they are partitive genitives; but "the *hand* of the *man*" and "the *blood* of *Jesus*" are not, so they are possessive genitives. The atmosphere of the partitive is "sameness," whereas the atmosphere of the possessive is "belonging." Wallace helpfully suggests:

> "The tail of the dog" is possessive, while "the bumper of the car" is partitive. As can be seen, the difference between these two has to do with animateness. One *crude* way to test whether a genitive is partitive or possessive is to ask whether the genitive substantive would object to the head noun's departure. A dog would (possession); a car would not (partitive).[229]

Samuel Green presents a practical guide for identifying the genitive of partition: "this genitive is most commonly found after (1) partitive adjectives, (2) the indefinite and interrogative pronouns, (3) the numerals, and (4) adjectives in the superlative degree."[230] Wallace says, "This usage is relatively common in the NT."[231]

---

226 Winer, *Grammar*, 244.

227 Books-Winbery, 28.

228 Wallace, *ExSyn*, 84.

229 Wallace, *ExSyn*, 84.

230 Samuel G. Green, *Handbook to the Grammar of the Greek Testament*, Rev. ed. (London: Religious Tract Society, 1907), 215.

231 Wallace, *ExSyn*, 84.

The following examples illustrate the usage of this kind of genitive in the Pauline corpus.

The "poor" in τοὺς πτωχοὺς τῶν ἁγίων *the poor of the saints* (Rom 15:26) are part of the saints, a group identified within a larger group. Epaenetus was the first convert, ἀπαρχή τῆς Ἀσίας *the firstfruits of Asia* (Rom 16:5), of those who believed in Asia. A synonymous phrase ἀπαρχὴ τῶν κεκοιμημένων *the firstfruits of those who have fallen asleep* (1 Cor 15:20), Christ is the first portion *out of* the people who have died.[232] Another example is μείζων δὲ τούτων ἡ ἀγάπη *the greatest of these is love* (1 Cor 13:13). Love is greater than faith and hope; "nevertheless, it is one of the three."[233] Therefore, it is a partitive genitive.

Head words in genitive constructions that naturally lend themselves to a partitive idea, like *one, some, most, any*, etc., make for easy identification of the partitive genitive. For example: τινες τῶν κλάδων *some of the branches* (Rom 11:17); τις ὑμῶν *any of you* (1 Cor 6:1); τινος τῶν λοιπῶν *some of the other(s)* (1 Cor 15:37), ἑνὶ ἡμῶν *one of us* (Eph 4:7), and τοὺς πλείονας τῶν ἀδελφῶν *most of the brothers* (Phil 1:14).

The disputed example τὸν ἀρραβῶνα τοῦ πνεύματος *earnest of the Spirit* (2 Cor 1:22; cf. Eph 1:14), is to be taken as partitive if "first installment" is a portion of the whole spirit. Gordon Fee analyzes this metaphor: "this metaphor also (especially) suggests that what is given is part of the whole. For Paul the gift of the spirit is the first part of the redemption of the whole person."[234] Barrett thinks that this sense seems improbable because "Paul does not think of the Spirit as given in parts."[235]

Genitive of Comparison

The genitive that follows a comparative adjective, as one would expect, usually indicates comparison. In this case, the genitive "is the standard against which the comparison is made."[236] The genitive of comparison is related to the ablative idea, a kind of mental separation. The genitive of comparison is used several times in the letters of Paul and is best expressed by using *than* in translation.

Paul is a master in using comparative rhetorical expressions. For instance, τὸ μωρὸν τοῦ θεοῦ σοφώτερον τῶν ἀνθρώπων ἐστὶν *the foolishness of God is wiser than men* (1 Cor 1:25). Paul calls himself the least among God's saints: ἐμοὶ τῷ ἐλαχιστοτέρῳ πάντων ἁγίων *to me the least of all saints* (Eph 3:8), though in this example, if the

232 See BDAG 98 s.v. ἀπαρχή 2bα.
233 Green, *Grammar*, 212.
234 Fee, *Empowering Presence*, 293.
235 Barrett, *2 Corinthians*, 80. See also Furnish, *II Corinthians*, 137. Robertson, *Grammar*, 498, and MHT₃ 214.
236 Wallace, *ExSyn*, 110.

superlative form implies a comparison to other people, the genitive could be partitive: "I am the least [person] from among the saints." Concerning the criteria for widows to be enrolled (for special service or support),[237] Paul says that they should not be less *than* sixty μὴ ἔλαττον ἐτῶν ἑξήκοντα (1 Tim 5:9).

We have already seen classified under the epexegetic genitive the phrase εἰς τὰ κατώτερα μέρη τῆς γῆς *to the lower parts of the earth* (Eph 4:9), but it could be a genitive of comparison (i.e., "parts lower than the earth"), for which F. Büchsel points to the context: "Το κατέβη εἰς τὰ κατώτερα μέρη τῆς γῆς there obviously corresponds ὁ ἀναβὰς ὑπεράνω πάντων τῶν οὐρανῶν. If He mounted up above all heavens, the obvious antithesis is that He descended under the earth, not to the earth."[238] But Wallace raises to a key reason comparison is unlikely in this example: the comparative adjective modifies μέρη.[239]

Conclusion

In this chapter the nuances of the two-word genitive constructions have been investigated. the meanings of the genitives fall into five main categories: genitive of definition, adjectival genitive, objective genitive, subjective genitive, and ablatival genitive. The nuances of the genitive usage that have been classified under these main categories are both numerous and diverse. They testify in a remarkable way to the wealth of Paul's usage of the genitive and to its versatility.

Yet, investigating the two-word genitive constructions alone does not demonstrate all the faculty of Paul's diverse usage of the genitive case. Paul also uses three-word genitive constructions in a very versatile way. Studying both of these kinds of constructions throws light on each of them and leads to deeper understanding of the genitive phenomena in Paul's writings. Investigating the semantics of the two-word genitive (and of genitives in general) has laid the foundation in order to proceed to understanding the multi-word genitive constructions in the following chapters.

---

237 Knight, *Pastoral Epistles*, 222–23.
238 F. Büchsel, *TDNT* 3:641 s.v. κάτω, κατωτέρω, κατώτερος.
239 Wallace, *ExSyn*, 112.

Bibliography

Abbott, Thomas Kingsmill. *A Critical and Exegetical Commentary on the Epistles to the Ephesians and to the Colossians*. Edinburgh: T&T Clark, 1897. Reprint, 1964.

Abbott, Thomas Kingsmill. *A Critical and Exegetical Commentary on the Epistles to the Ephesians and to the Colossians*. International Critical Commentary 36. New York: Scribner, 1903.

Alford, Henry. *The Greek Testament: An Exegetical and Critical Commentary*. 4 vols. 7th ed. n.p., 1874. Reprint, Grand Rapids: Guardian, 1976.

Arichea, Daniel C. and Eugene Albert Nida. *A Handbook on Paul's Letter to the Galatians*. UBS Handbook Series. New York: United Bible Societies, 1976.

Barnett, Paul. *The Second Epistle to the Corinthians*. New International Commentary on the New Testament. Grand Rapids: Eerdmans, 1997.

Barrett, C. K. *The Second Epistle to the Corinthians*. Black's New Testament Commentaries. London: Continuum, 1973.

Barrett, Charles Kingsley. *The First Epistle to the Corinthians*. Black's New Testament Commentary. Peabody, MA: Hendrickson, 1968.

Barrett, Charles Kingsley. *The Epistle to the Romans*. 2nd ed. Black's New Testament Commentaries. London: Hendrickson, 1991.

Barth, Markus. *Ephesians*. 2 vols. Anchor Yale Bible 34–34A. New Haven: Yale University Press, 1974.

Beale, Gregory K. *The Book of Revelation: A Commentary on the Greek Text*. New International Greek Testament Commentary. Grand Rapids: Eerdmans, 1999.

Betz, Hans Dieter. *Galatians: A Commentary on Paul's Letter to the Churches in Galatia*. Hermeneia. Philadelphia: Fortress, 1979.

Bockmuehl, Markus. *The Epistle to the Philippians*. Black's New Testament Commentary. London: Black, 1997.

Bratcher, Robert G. and Eugene Albert Nida. *A Handbook on Paul's Letter to the Ephesians*. UBS Handbook Series. New York: United Bible Societies, 1982.

Bruce, F. F. *The Epistle to the Galatians: A Commentary on the Greek Text*. New International Greek Testament Commentary. Grand Rapids: Eerdmans, 1982.

Bruce, F. F. *The Epistles to the Colossians, to Philemon, and to the Ephesians*. New International Commentary on the New Testament. Grand Rapids: Eerdmans, 1984.

Bruce, F. F. *Romans: An Introduction and Commentary*. Tyndale New Testament Commentaries 6. Downers Grove: IVP, 1985.

Bruce, F. F. *1 and 2 Thessalonians*. Word Biblical Commentary. Dallas: Word, 1998.

Büchsel, Friedrich. "κατάρα." Pages 1:449–51 in *Theological Dictionary of the New Testament*. Edited by Gerhard Kittel. Translated by Geoffrey W. Bromiley. vol. 1. Grand Rapids: Eerdmans, 1963.

Büchsel, Friedrich. "κάτω, κατωτέρω, κατώτερος." Pages 640–42 in *Theological Dictionary of the New Testament*. Edited by Gerhard Kittel. Translated by Geoffrey W. Bromiley. vol. 3. Grand Rapids: Eerdmans, 1965.

Burton, Ernest De Witt. *A Critical and Exegetical Commentary on the Epistle to the Galatians.* International Critical Commentary. New York: Scribner, 1920.

Caragounis, Chrys C. *The Development of Greek and the New Testament: Morphology, Syntax, Phonology, and Textual Transmission.* Tübingen: Mohr Siebeck, 2004. Reprint, Grand Rapids: Baker, 2008.

Conzelmann, Hans. *1 Corinthians.* Edited by G. W. MacRae. Translated by James W. Leitch. Philadelphia: Fortress, 1975.

Dibelius, Martin and Hans Conzelmann. *The Pastoral Epistles.* Edited by Helmut Koester. Translated by Philip Buttolph and Adela Yarbro. Hermeneia. Philadelphia: Fortress, 1972. https://muse.jhu.edu/book/45992.

Downs, David J. "'The Offering of the Gentiles' in Romans 15.16," *Journal for the Study of the New Testament* 29.2 (2006): 173–86. doi:10.1177/0142064x06072837.

Downs, David J. *The Offering of the Gentiles: Paul's Collection for Jerusalem in Its Chronological, Cultural, and Cultic Contexts.* Wissenschaftliche Untersuchungen zum Neuen Testament 2/248. Tübingen: Mohr Siebeck, 2008.

Dunn, James D. G. *Romans 1–8.* Word Biblical Commentary 38A. Dallas: Word, 1988.

Dunn, James D. G. *The Epistles to the Colossians and to Philemon: A Commentary on the Greek Text.* New International Greek Testament Commentary. Grand Rapids: Eerdmans, 1996.

Ellingworth, Paul. *The Epistle to the Hebrews: A Commentary on the Greek Text.* New International Greek Testament Commentary. Grand Rapids: Eerdmans, 1993.

Ellingworth, Paul and Eugene Albert Nida. *A Handbook on Paul's Letters to the Thessalonians.* UBS Handbook Series. New York: United Bible Societies, 1976.

Fairbairn, Patrick. *Commentary on the Pastoral Epistles.* Edinburgh: T&T Clark, 1874.

Fee, Gordon D. *God's Empowering Presence: The Holy Spirit in the Letters of Paul.* Peabody, MA: Hendrickson, 1994. Reprint, Grand Rapids: Baker, 2011.

Fee, Gordon D. *Paul's Letter to the Philippians.* New International Commentary on the New Testament. Grand Rapids: Eerdmans, 1995.

Fee, Gordon D. *Philippians.* IVP New Testament Commentary 11. Downers Grove: IVP, 1999.

Fee, Gordon D. *The First Epistle to the Corinthians.* Rev. ed. New International Commentary on the New Testament. Grand Rapids: Eerdmans, 2014.

Fitzmyer, Joseph A. *Romans: A New Translation with Introduction and Commentary.* Anchor Yale Bible 33. New York: Doubleday, 1993.

Frame, James Everett. *A Critical and Exegetical Commentary on the Epistles of St. Paul to the Thessalonians.* International Critical Commentary. New York: Scribner, 1912.

Fung, Ronald Y. K. *The Epistle to the Galatians.* New International Commentary on the New Testament. Grand Rapids: Eerdmans, 1988.

Furnish, Victor Paul. *II Corinthians.* Anchor Bible 32A. Garden City, NY: Doubleday, 1984. Reprint, New Haven: Yale University Press, 2008.

Gagnon, Robert A. J. "Heart of Wax and a Teaching that Stamps: ΤΥΠΟΣ ΔΙΔΑΧΗΣ (Rom 6:17b) Once More," *Journal of Biblical Literature* 112.4 (1993): 667–87.

Garland, David E. *1 Corinthians.* Baker Exegetical Commentary on the New Testament. Grand Rapids, MI: Baker Academic, 2003.

Gianollo, Chiara. "External Possession in New Testament Greek," *Journal of Latin Linguistics* 11.1 (2010): 101–30. doi:10.1515/joll.2010.11.1.101.

Goppelt, Leonhard. "τύπος, ἀντίτυπος, τυπικός, ὑποτύπωσις." Pages 8:246–60 in *Theological Dictionary of the New Testament*. Edited by Gerhard Friedrich. Translated by Geoffrey W. Bromiley. vol. 8. Grand Rapids: Eerdmans, 1972.

Green, Gene L. *The Letters to the Thessalonians*. Pillar New Testament Commentary. Grand Rapids: Eerdmans, 2002.

Green, Samuel G. *Handbook to the Grammar of the Greek Testament*. rev. and imp. ed. New York: Revell, 1904.

Green, Samuel G. *Handbook to the Grammar of the Greek Testament*. Rev. ed. London: Religious Tract Society, 1907. https://archive.org/details/handbooktogramm00gree/page/n5.

Green, Thomas Sheldon. *A Treatise on the Grammar of the New Testament*. London: Bagster, 1842.

Hansen, G. Walter. *The Letter to the Philippians*. Pillar New Testament Commentary. Grand Rapids: Eerdmans, 2009.

Harris, Murray J. *The Second Epistle to the Corinthians: A Commentary on the Greek Text*. New International Greek Testament Commentary. Grand Rapids: Eerdmans, 2005.

Hoehner, Harold W. *Ephesians: An Exegetical Commentary*. Grand Rapids: Baker Academic, 2002.

Hultgren, Arland J. "The *Pistis Christou* Formulation in Paul," *Novum Testamentum* 22.3 (1980): 248–63.

Hunn, Debbie. "Debating the Faithfulness of Jesus Christ in Twentieth-Century Scholarship." Pages 15–31 in *The Faith of Jesus Christ: Exegetical, Biblical, and Theological Studies*. Edited by Michael F. Bird and Preston M. Sprinkle. Peabody, MA: Hendrickson, 2010.

Jewett, Robert, with the assistance of Roy David Kotansky. *Romans: A Commentary*. Edited by Eldon Jay Epp. Hermeneia. Minneapolis: Fortress, 2007.

Johnson, Luke Timothy. "Rom 3:21–26 and the Faith of Jesus," *Catholic Biblical Quarterly* 44.1 (1982): 77–90.

Joüon, Paul and Takamitsu Muraoka. *A Grammar of Biblical Hebrew*. Rev. ed. Rome: Pontifical Biblical Institute, 2006.

Käsemann, Ernst. *Commentary on Romans*. Translated by Geoffrey W. Bromiley. Grand Rapids: Eerdmans, 1980.

Knight, George W. *The Pastoral Epistles: A Commentary on the Greek Text*. New International Greek Testament Commentary. Grand Rapids: Eerdmans, 1992.

Lenski, Richard C. H. *The Interpretation of St. Paul's Epistles to the Colossians, to the Thessalonians, to Timothy, to Titus and to Philemon*. Minneapolis: Augsburg, 1937.

Lenski, Richard C. H. *The Interpretation of St. Paul's First and Second Epistles to the Corinthians*. Minneapolis: Augsburg, 1937.

Lincoln, Andrew T. *Ephesians*. Word Biblical Commentary 42. Dallas: Word, 1990.

Lohse, Edward. *Colossians and Philemon*. Edited by Helmut Koester. Translated by William R. Poehlmann and Robert J. Karris. Hermeneia. Philadelphia: Fortress, 1971.

Martin, Ralph P. *2 Corinthians*. Word Biblical Commentary 40. Dallas: Word, 1986.

Melick, Richard R. "A Study in the Concept of Belief: A Comparison of the Gospel of John and the Epistle to the Romans." Th.D. diss., Southern Baptist Theological Seminary, 1976.

Melick, Richard R., Jr. *Philippians, Colossians, Philemon*. New American Commentary 32. Nashville: Broadman, 1991.

Merriam-Webster's Collegiate Dictionary. Edited by Frederick C. Mish. 11th ed. Springfield, MA: Merriam-Webster, 2003.

Moo, Douglas J. *The Epistle to the Romans*. 2nd ed. New International Commentary on the New Testament. Grand Rapids: Eerdmans, 2018.

Morris, Leon. *The Epistle to the Romans*. Pillar New Testament Commentary. Grand Rapids: IVP, 1988.

Mounce, William D. *Pastoral Epistles*. Word Biblical Commentary 46. Nashville: Nelson, 2000.

Murray, John. *The Epistle to the Romans*. 2 vols. New International Commentary on the New Testament. Grand Rapids: Eerdmans, 1968.

Nikiforidou, Kiki. "The Meanings of the Genitive: A Case Study in Semantic Structure and Semantic Change," *Cognitive Linguistics* 2.2 (1991): 149–205. https://doi.org/10.1515/cogl.1991.2.2.149.

Plummer, Alfred. *The Second Epistle of St Paul to the Corinthians*. Edinburgh: T&T Clark, 1915.

Porter, Stanley E. and Andrew W. Pitts. "Πίστις with a Preposition and Genitive Modifier: Lexical, Semantic, and Syntactic Considerations in the Πίστις Χριστοῦ Discussion." Pages 33–53 in *The Faith of Jesus Christ: Exegetical, Biblical, and Theological Studies*. Edited by Michael F. Bird and Preston M. Sprinkle. Peabody, MA: Hendrickson, 2010.

Rengstorf, Karl Heinrich. "δοῦλος, σύνδουλος, δούλη, δουλεύω, δουλεία, δουλόω, καταδουλόω, δουλαγωγέω, ὀφθαλμοδουλία." Pages 261–80 in *Theological Dictionary of the New Testament*. Edited by Gerhard Kittel. Translated by Geoffrey W. Bromiley. vol. 2. Grand Rapids, MI: Eerdmans, 1964.

Ridderbos, Herman N. *The Epistle of Paul to the Churches of Galatia*. New International Commentary on the New Testament. Grand Rapids: Eerdmans, 1953.

Robertson, A. T. *Word Pictures in the New Testament*. Nashville: Broadman, 1930.

Robinson, John A. T. *Commentary on Ephesians: The Greek Text with Introduction Notes and Indexes*. 2nd ed. London: Macmillan, 1904. Reprint, 1909. https://archive.org/details/stp aulsepistleto00robiuoft/page/n7/mode/2up.

Ross, Allen P. "The Curse of Canaan: Studies in the Book of Genesis Part 1," *Bibliotheca Sacra* 137.547 (1980): 223–40.

Ruef, John S. *Paul's First Letter to Corinth*. Westminster Pelican Commentaries. Philadelphia: Westminster John Knox, 1977.

Sanday, W. and Arthur C. Headlam. *A Critical and Exegetical Commentary on the Epistle to the Romans*. 5th ed. International Critical Commentary. Edinburgh: T&T Clark, 1902.

Schweizer, Eduard. "Slaves of the Elements and Worshipers of Angels: Gal 4:3, 9 and Col 2:8, 18, 20," *Journal of Biblical Literature* 107.3 (1988): 455–68.

Stolk, Joanne Vera. "Dative by Genitive Replacement in the Greek Language of the Papyri: A Diachronic Account of Case Semantics," *Journal of Greek Linguistics* 15.1 (2015): 91–121. doi:10.1163/15699846-01501001.

Strachan, R. H. *The Second Epistle of Paul to the Corinthians*. Moffat New Testament Commentary. London: Hodder & Stoughton, 1935. Reprint, Eugene, OR: Wipf & Stock, 2008.

Sumney, Jerry L. *Colossians: A Commentary*. New Testament Library. London: Westminster John Knox, 2008.

Thielman, Frank. *Ephesians*. Baker Exegetical Commentary on the New Testament. Grand Rapids: Baker Academic, 2010.

Thiselton, Anthony C. *The First Epistle to the Corinthians: A Commentary on the Greek Text*. New International Greek Testament Commentary. Grand Rapids: Eerdmans, 2000.

Thomas, D. W. "A Consideration of Some Unusual Ways of Expressing the Superlative in Hebrew," *Vetus Testamentum* 3 (1953): 209–24. https://www.jstor.org/stable/1516347.

Towner, Philip H. *The Letters to Timothy and Titus*. New International Commentary on the New Testament. Grand Rapids: Eerdmans, 2006.

Turner, Nigel. *Grammatical Insights into the New Testament*. Edinburgh: T&T Clark, 1966.

Waltke, Bruce K. and Michael Patrick O'Connor. *An Introduction to Biblical Hebrew Syntax*. Winona Lake, IN: Eisenbrauns, 1990.

Wanamaker, Charles A. *The Epistles to the Thessalonians: A Commentary on the Greek Text*. New International Greek Testament Commentary. Grand Rapids: Eerdmans, 1990.

Wuest, Kenneth Samuel. *The Pastoral Epistles in the Greek New Testament*. Grand Rapids: Eerdmans, 1953.

Young, Richard A. *Intermediate New Testament Greek: A Linguistic and Exegetical Approach*. Nashville: Broadman & Holman, 1994.

Zerwick, Max and Mary Grosvenor. *A Grammatical Analysis of the Greek New Testament*. 5th ed. Rome: Pontifical Biblical Institute, 1974.

CHAPTER FIVE

Adnominal Three-Word Genitive Constructions

After investigating the two-word genitive constructions in Chapter Four and establishing the basic meanings and categories with all the involved nuances, we come now to analyzing and examining the three-word genitive constructions of the Pauline corpus. A full list of these constructions appears at the end of the chapter.

Though genitive usage is frequent in Paul's writing, usage of the genitive in clusters is less frequent. But in many instances, Paul is not satisfied with adding one genitive to the head word in a phrase; but he adds two or three genitives successively.[1] Besides the approximately 1,800 hundred two-word genitive constructions in the entire Pauline corpus, the number of three-word genitive constructions is 181. This figure includes also the genitive constructions connected by καί. This is thinking about the constructions as wholes, mostly in terms of noun phrases, counting in terms of the head noun in the construction, so ὁ θεὸς καὶ πατὴρ τοῦ κυρίου ἡμῶν (2 Cor 1:3) will count as a three-word genitive construction. But in this instance, our accounting excludes the simple appositive Ἰησοῦ Χριστοῦ. When the head word unit forms a TSKS (see Wallace, *ExSyn*, 270) kind of construction, we count them as a single head. There is one example, πᾶσαν ἀσέβειαν καὶ ἀδικίαν ἀνθρώπων *all ungodliness and unrighteousness of men* (Rom 1:18) that may also be

---

1   See, for instance, Robertson, *Grammar*, 503.

considered three-word, since the determiner πᾶσαν functions somewhat like an article. On the other end of the construction, if there are multiple genitives connected to a headword by καί, these do not count as three-word genitives, but resolve to multiple two-word genitives. This, too, is sometimes fraught with difficulty. For instance, στῦλος καὶ ἑδραίωμα τῆς ἀληθείας *pillar and base of the truth* (1 Tim 3:15) seems more like a double head, since it is an appositive to ἐκκλησία. But to keep the analysis as much as possible at the purely structural level, this will not count as a three-word genitive construction. ἐν ἁπλότητι καὶ εἰλικρινείᾳ τοῦ θεοῦ *in sincerity and purity of God* (2 Cor 1:12) is also slightly problematic for double-head consideration in view of the preposition and the hendiadys-like quality of this head. Other examples are clearer. The construction ὁ ξένος μου καὶ ὅλης τῆς ἐκκλησίας (Rom 16:23) resolves to two two-word constructions, with the καί distributing the head word into the two constructions: (1) ὁ ξένος μου καὶ (2) [ὁ ξένος] ὅλης τῆς ἐκκλησίας.

Other examples, e.g., τῶν λοιπῶν συνεργῶν μου *the rest of my co-workers* (Phil 4:3), could be disputed. In the instance of Phil 4:3, λοιπῶν can be taken as a substantival adjective (in which case, a three-word construction), or as an attributive adjective (in which case a two-word construction). The difference would be hard to bring out in English translation, and there is no real difference in sense. Naturally, there are other ambiguities which may lead to come of these constructions' counting being subject to dispute. For instance, Rom 2:4 reads ἢ τοῦ πλούτου τῆς χρηστότητος αὐτοῦ καὶ τῆς ἀνοχῆς καὶ τῆς μακροθυμίας καταφρονεῖς, ἀγνοῶν ὅτι τὸ χρηστὸν τοῦ θεοῦ εἰς μετάνοιάν σε ἄγει; It is abundantly clear that τοῦ πλούτου, the head noun of the construction, is the genitive direct object of καταφρονεῖς. So, we read at least one three-word construction τοῦ πλούτου τῆς χρηστότητος αὐτοῦ. But it is harder to know what to make of the words καὶ τῆς ἀνοχῆς καὶ τῆς μακροθυμίας. They could be seen as additional genitives dependent on πλούτου (in which case we possibly have a five-word construction: "the wealth of his kindness and [wealth of his] forbearance and [wealth of his] patience"), or they could be additional objects of the verb ("do you despise the wealth of his kindness and [despise his] forbearance and [despise his] patience"). This kind of broad ambiguity, however, is very rare—this is probably the only instance in which such a chain of genitives appears.

As observed in Chapter Two, the leading NT grammars tend to treat three-word and four-word genitive constructions under the title "Multiplicity of genitives" or "Concatenation of genitives," and in this fashion are not given the attention they deserve. Our survey revealed that there is a serious need for a thorough study of three-word and four-word genitive constructions. This task is the aim of this chapter and the one following. After introducing the nature, scope and limits of this investigation of the genitive in its three-word construction usage in the letters of Paul, a demonstration of some linguistic aspects is needed in order to understand the structural elements of the three-word genitive fully.

The Grammatical Aspect

Structural Elements

The three-word genitive construction consists of two genitives attached to a head word, regardless of the case of the head word. The head word as an integral part of the genitive construction becomes the link between the dependent genitives and the rest of the clause. This conception must be clear before any analysis is done to explore the meaning of the three-word genitive, or any other genitive construction.

Winer only counts the *genitive* nouns but not their head nouns. Under the three-genitive category, he refers to 2 Cor 4:4 τὸν φωτισμὸν τοῦ εὐαγγελίου τῆς δόξης τοῦ Χριστοῦ, and also cites Eph 1:6, and 4:13 (all these have three genitives but are four-word genitive constructions with non-genitive head words). Under the same category, he refers to Rom 2:4 τοῦ πλούτου τῆς χρηστότητος αὐτοῦ, Col 1:20 διὰ τοῦ αἵματος τοῦ σταυροῦ αὐτοῦ, and to 2 Thess 1:9 ἀπὸ τῆς δόξης τῆς ἰσχύος αὐτοῦ. These last two phrases have two genitives added to head words that are genitives because of prepositions. He does the same with the four-genitive category (citing, e.g., Rev 14:8; 16:19; 19:15). He mixes what we are calling four-word and five-word genitive constructions together, again counting only the nouns or substantives that are in the genitive case.[2] Buttmann is more consistent and systematized than Winer is in categorizing the two-, three-, and four-word genitives, clearly distinguishing that these clusters of genitives depend "on one and the same substantive."[3]

Pure Nouns

The nominal form structure of the three-word genitive construction appears in different formulae. Sometimes all words in the construction are anarthrous (N-N$_g$-N$_g$), for example, πληρώματι εὐλογίας Χριστοῦ *fullness of the blessing of Christ* (Rom 15:29), and πίστιν ἐκλεκτῶν θεοῦ *faith of the elect of God* (Titus 1:1). At other times, all words of the three-word genitive construction appear with the article (A-N-A-N$_g$-A-N$_g$), for example: ὁ νόμος τοῦ πνεύματος τῆς ζωῆς *the law of the Spirit of life*

---

2 Winer, *Grammar*, 238.
3 Buttmann, *Grammar*, 155.

(Rom 8:2) and τῷ λόγῳ τῆς ἀληθείας τοῦ εὐαγγελίου *the word of the truth of the gospel* (Col 1:5). This is the normal expectation in line with Apollonius' Canon.[4]

At times, the head words in the three-word genitive constructions are anarthrous (N-A-N$_g$-A-N$_g$), like ἐπ' ἐλπίδι τῆς δόξης τοῦ θεοῦ *on the hope of the glory of God* (Rom 5:2), εἰς οἰκοδομὴν τοῦ σώματος τοῦ Χριστοῦ *to the edification of the body of Christ* (Eph 4:12). This is not unexpected, since often in such situations the head word is the object of a preposition. Sometimes the head word and middle word are anarthrous λόγον ἀκοῆς παρ' ἡμῶν τοῦ θεοῦ ἐδέξασθε *you received the word of God of hearing from us* (1 Thess 2:13).

Some constructions involve proper names that do not take the article (A-N-A-N$_g$-N$_g$), like τὴν νέκρωσιν τῆς μήτρας Σάρρας *the deadness of the womb of Sarah* (Rom 4:19), ὁ ἀριθμὸς τῶν υἱῶν Ἰσραήλ *the number of the sons of Israel* (Rom 9:27), and ἐπιχορηγίας τοῦ πνεύματος Ἰησοῦ *the supply of the Spirit of Jesus* (Phil 1:19), in this last reference the head word also is anarthrous (N-A-N$_g$-N$_g$).

Noun-Pronoun

There are very few three-word genitives with pronouns where the head is *anarthrous* (N-N$_g$-P$_g$), like ἐκ κοιλίας μητρός μου *from the womb of my mother* (Gal 1:15), εἰς ἔπαινον δόξης αὐτοῦ *to the praise of his glory* (Eph 1:12) and μετ' ἀγγέλων δυνάμεως αὐτοῦ *with angels of his strength* (2 Thess 1:7). For emphasis, or perhaps to distribute the genitive, the writer may change the position of the pronoun from last to first, like τίς γὰρ **ἡμῶν** ἐλπὶς ἢ χαρὰ ἢ **στέφανος καυχήσεως** *for who is **our** hope or joy or crown of boasting* (1 Thess 2:19).[5]

As one would expect, the lion's share of three-word genitives has the two first nouns used with the definite article with final pronouns (A-N-A-N$_g$-P$_g$). The following examples contain samples of all kinds of pronouns used in this category: τῷ εὐαγγελίῳ τοῦ υἱοῦ αὐτοῦ *the gospel of his son* (Rom 1:9), τῇ δυνάμει τοῦ κυρίου ἡμῶν Ἰησοῦ *the power of our Lord Jesus* (1 Cor 5:4), τὰ ὑστερήματα τῆς πίστεως ὑμῶν *the things lacking of your faith* (1 Thess 3:10), ἡ κοινωνία τῆς πίστεώς σου *the fellowship of your faith* (Phlm 6), τὴν πώρωσιν τῆς καρδίας αὐτῶν *the hardness of their hearts* (Eph 4:18), and τῷ νόμῳ τοῦ νοός μου *the law of my mind* (Rom 7:23). Sometimes the head noun is followed by an article that puts the genitive phrase into third attributive position[6] (N-A-A-N$_g$-P$_g$), like λόγοις τοῖς τοῦ κυρίου ἡμῶν Ἰησοῦ *words*

---

4   Apollonius Dyscolus, *Syntax* 1.140. For translation and commentary on the formulation of the rule, see Householder, *Apollonius*, 78. The rule is cited by MHT$_3$ 180. For discussion, see Wallace, *ExSyn*, 239–40.

5   BDF §168(1) p. 93.

6   Wallace, *ExSyn*, 239.

of our Lord Jesus (1 Tim 6:3), or there is a change to the position of a pronoun (A-P$_g$-N-A-N$_g$), like εἰς τὴν ὑμῶν προκοπὴν ... τῆς πίστεως *for your advance ... of faith* (Phil 1:25), and τὸ ὑμῶν ὑστέρημα τῆς πρός με λειτουργίας *your lack of service toward me* (Phil 2:30); or (P$_g$-A-N-A-N$_g$): ὑμῶν τοῦ ἔργου τῆς πίστεως *your work of faith* (1 Thess 1:3).

Some noun-pronoun three-word genitives have the article only with the dependent genitive (N-A-N$_g$-P$_g$). For examples: μιᾷ ἐλπίδι τῆς κλήσεως ὑμῶν *one hope of your calling* (Eph 4:4), κατ' ἐπιταγὴν τοῦ σωτῆρος ἡμῶν θεοῦ *according to the command of our savior, God* (Titus 1:3). In this category sometimes for emphasis the pronoun comes second (N-P$_g$-A-N$_g$): συγκοινωνούς μου τῆς χάριτος *partakers of mine of grace* (Phil 1:7) and ἡ σφραγίς μου τῆς ἀποστολῆς *the seal of my apostleship* (1 Cor 9:2); or the pronoun comes first (A-P$_g$-N-A-N$_g$): ἡ ἐπίγειος ἡμῶν οἰκία τοῦ σκήνους *our earthly home of the tent* (2 Cor 5:1). This last word-order reconfiguration may be because the possessive sense of the pronoun ἡμῶν is different from the epexegetic sense of τοῦ σκήνους.

Noun-Pronoun-Adjective

There are few three-word genitives in the Pauline corpus that have a substantival adjective (A-N[Adj]-A-N$_g$-P$_g$), like τὸ ... ἐλαφρὸν τῆς θλίψεως ἡμῶν *the ... lightness of our affliction* (2 Cor 4:17), and τὰ κρυπτὰ τῆς καρδίας αὐτοῦ *the hidden things of his heart* (1 Cor 14:25). Also appearing occasionally, are (1) an adjective as head word with final noun (N[Adj]-A-N$_g$-A-N$_g$) in καὶ ξένοι τῶν διαθηκῶν τῆς ἐπαγγελίας *strangers to the covenants of the promise* (Eph 2:12), or (2) adjective as head word with final pronoun (N[Adj]-A-N$_g$-P$_g$) like συνεργοί ἐσμεν τῆς χαρᾶς ὑμῶν *we are fellow workers of your joy* (2 Cor 1:24), and Ἄξιος ὁ ἐργάτης τοῦ μισθοῦ αὐτοῦ *the worker is worthy of his wage* (1 Tim 5:18).

Noun-Participle

Participles appear infrequently as the head noun in three-word genitive constructions in the pattern: N[Participle]-N$_g$-A-N$_g$. Examples include ἀπηλλοτριωμένοι τῆς πολιτείας τοῦ Ἰσραήλ *alienated from the commonwealth of Israel* (Eph 2:12), and ἀπηλλοτριωμένοι τῆς ζωῆς τοῦ θεοῦ *alienated from the life of God* (Eph 4:18).

Article-Implicit Substantives

There are two examples of three-word genitives where the head noun is the article acting as a "substantiver" with genitive phrases.[7] These instances are: τὰ τοῦ

---

7   Wallace, *ExSyn*, 231, 235.

πνεύματος τοῦ θεοῦ *the things of the Spirit of God* (1 Cor 2:14), τὰ τῆς ἀσθενείας μου *the things of my weakness* (2 Cor 11:30).

Three-Word Genitives Connected by καί

There are several instances in the New Testament where the substantives in three-word genitive constructions are connected by the conjunction καί, and the examples can be encountered outside the Pauline corpus.[8] Paul's letters contain the higher number of three-word genitives in this configuration. There are three ways of connecting the genitives with καί.

Additional Head Word

Surveying the words in genitive constructions connected with καί reveals that καί add additional head words. These examples are worth noting:

- ὁ θεὸς καὶ πατὴρ τοῦ κυρίου ἡμῶν *the God and Father of our Lord* (Eph 1:3)
- εἰς τὴν ὑμῶν προκοπὴν καὶ χαρὰν τῆς πίστεως, *for your joy and progress of faith* (Phil 1:25)
- ἐπὶ τῇ θυσίᾳ καὶ λειτουργίᾳ τῆς πίστεως ὑμῶν *upon the sacrifice and service of your faith* (Phil 2:17)

These three examples constitute a double head word because of the dynamics of a single article governing substantives connected by καί, what Wallace calls the "TSKS construction."[9] We will consider this a single head for the purposes of counting three-word genitive constructions.

The situation with τοῦ κυρίου γὰρ ἡ γῆ καὶ τὸ πλήρωμα αὐτῆς. *for the earth [is] of the Lord and its fullness [is of the Lord]* (1 Cor 10:26) is somewhat different. In this instance καί joins two verbless clauses where the implied verb is ἐστίν, so that the construction resolves to τοῦ κυρίου [ἐστιν] ἡ γῆ καὶ τὸ πλήρωμα αὐτῆς [ἐστιν τοῦ κυρίου]: *the earth is of the Lord and its fullness is of the Lord.*

Connecting a Middle-Word with an Additional Middle-Word

The second word may also be connected by καί with an additional second word(s) as the following constructions show: Ὦ **βάθος πλούτου** καὶ σοφίας καὶ **γνώσεως θεοῦ**

---

8   For example, ἡ σωτηρία καὶ ἡ δόξα καὶ ἡ δύναμις τοῦ θεοῦ ἡμῶν (Rev 19:1), and τὸν ποιμένα καὶ ἐπίσκοπον τῶν ψυχῶν ὑμῶν (1 Pet 2:25).

9   Wallace, *ExSyn*, 270. For a monograph-length treatment, see Wallace, *Sharp's Canon*. [bibliographic data in the abbreviations list]

*O the depth of the wealth and of the wisdom and **knowledge of God*** (Rom 11:33). This example has three three-word genitives, resolving thus: (1) βάθος πλούτου θεοῦ *the depth of the wealth of God* (2) βάθος σοφίας θεοῦ *the depth of the wisdom of God*, and (3) βάθος γνώσεως θεοῦ *the depth of the knowledge of God*.

The dynamics are slightly different with ἔνοχος ἔσται τοῦ σώματος καὶ τοῦ αἵματος τοῦ κυρίου *he will be guilty of the body and of the blood of the Lord* (1 Cor 11:27) because ἔσται is implied by the connective. This resolves as two three-word genitives: (1) ἔνοχος ἔσται τοῦ σώματος τοῦ κυρίου, and (2) [ἔνοχος ἔσται] τοῦ αἵματος τοῦ κυρίου.

The situation is more complicated with τὴν ἔνδειξιν τῆς ἀγάπης ὑμῶν καὶ ἡμῶν καυχήσεως ὑπὲρ ὑμῶν (2 Cor 8:24). The construction resolves to two three-word genitives: (1) τὴν ἔνδειξιν τῆς ἀγάπης ὑμῶν and (2) [τὴν ἔνδειξιν τῆς] ... ἡμῶν καυχήσεως. The alternation of the pronouns ὑμῶν and ἡμῶν make for an impressive rhetorical flourish.

Connecting a Third-Word with an Additional Third-Word

The third word in a three-word genitive construction may occasionally be connected with an additional third word(s) as in the following examples: διὰ τῶν ὅπλων τῆς δικαιοσύνης τῶν δεξιῶν καὶ ἀριστερῶν *through the weapons of righteousness of the right and the left* (2 Cor 6:7), which again resolves to two three-word genitive constructions: (1) τῶν ὅπλων τῆς δικαιοσύνης τῶν δεξιῶν, and (2) τῶν ὅπλων τῆς δικαιοσύνης τῶν ... ἀριστερῶν.

Finally, there is a question as to when genitive word-units connected by καί should or should not be considered part of the genitive construction. Though it is outside the Pauline corpus, the construction ὁ συμπρεσβύτερος καὶ μάρτυς τῶν τοῦ Χριστοῦ παθημάτων *the co-elder and witness of the sufferings of Christ* (1 Pet 5:1) presents a conundrum worthy of comment. This is a situation in which structure and semantics both need consideration. The TSKS construction ὁ συμπρεσβύτερος καὶ μάρτυς fits all the structural criteria and semantics for Sharp's rule to apply (singular, personal, and non-proper).[10] Thus, these two words describe one and same person, Peter. There is real semantic relationship between μάρτυς and τῶν τοῦ Χριστοῦ παθημάτων. Logically, though, it is difficult to connect ὁ συμπρεσβύτερος with the genitive τῶν τοῦ Χριστοῦ παθημάτων, so συμπρεσβύτερος is not a head to the genitive in this instance. Largely, though, when the TSKS construction stands as the head with a dependent genitive, the semantics fit distributing the genitive to the united two head nouns of the construction.

---

10   Wallace, *ExSyn*, 272; Wallace, *Sharp's Canon*, 132.

The Semantic Aspect

The three-word genitive is a cluster of words unified in one construction. This unified construction is a block of substantives strung together, usually without conjunctions. The result is in Turner's estimation "a clumsy accumulation."[11] The interpreter in this situation must analyze and discover the relationships between the pieces of the construction. In the sections that follow, the semantics of three-word genitive constructions may be approached from different angles.

Sentence Approach

Many three-word (even two-word) genitive constructions can in fact be resolved as complete sentences. Despite lacking the traditional structural elements of a sentence, they can be understood as such. The role of semantics in such constructions is to identify the subject, the verb, and the object from among each of the substantives of the three-word genitive. This may be achieved in translation by using the transformational grammar approach. Here are some examples:

- ἡ σφραγίς μου τῆς ἀποστολῆς ὑμεῖς ἐστε (1 Cor 9:2): You are **the seal** that proves my **apostleship**.
- τήρησις ἐντολῶν θεοῦ. (1 Cor 7:19): **Observing the commandments** which **God** has given
- διὰ τοῦ αἵματος τοῦ σταυροῦ αὐτοῦ (Col 1:20): through the shedding of **his blood** on **the cross**
- τὸ βραβεῖον τῆς ἄνω κλήσεως τοῦ θεοῦ (Phil 3:14): **the prize** that **God** gives to those who respond to his high **call**

Subject-Predicate Approach

Sometimes the head word in a genitive three-word construction stands as subject, controller or as key word to the rest of the construction. Some other times the first two words stand as the subject to the third. The following illustrations will explain this approach:

- οἰκονόμους μυστηρίων θεοῦ (1 Cor 4:1): We are stewards over the mysteries of God.

---

11 MHT₃ 218.

- τὸν ἄρχοντα τῆς ἐξουσίας τοῦ ἀέρος (Eph 2:2): He is the ruler of the power of the air.
- ὁ θεὸς τοῦ κυρίου ἡμῶν Ἰησοῦ Χριστοῦ (Eph 1:17): God is the God of our Lord Jesus Christ.
- τὴν ἀποκάλυψιν τῶν υἱῶν τοῦ θεοῦ (Rom 8:19): The sons of God will be revealed.
- τῆς ἐπιγνώσεως τοῦ υἱοῦ τοῦ θεοῦ (Eph 4:13): The Son of God is known.

At other times the first two words in a three-word genitive construction stand as the subject to the third word, i.e. the predicate. For example:

- τῶν ὅπλων τῆς δικαιοσύνης τῶν δεξιῶν καὶ ἀριστερῶν (2 Cor 6:7): The weapons of righteousness are for the right hand and the left hand.
- συγκοινωνούς μου τῆς χάριτος (Phil 1:7): You partake with me in grace.
- ἐπιθέσεως τῶν χειρῶν τοῦ πρεσβυτερίου. (1 Tim 4:14): The hands of the presbytery are laid on you.

Inter-relational Approach

As grammarians have pointed out before, the default way to decode the three-word genitive construction is to consider the relationship of its words in any construction successively.[12] For example:

- χάρις τοῦ κυρίου ἡμῶν (Rom 16:20): the grace of the Lord of us
- ἐν τῷ πνεύματι τοῦ θεοῦ ἡμῶν (1 Cor 6:11): in the Spirit of the God of us
- εἰς οἰκοδομὴν τοῦ σώματος τοῦ Χριστοῦ (Eph 4:12): to the edification of the body of Christ
- κατὰ πίστιν ἐκλεκτῶν θεοῦ (Titus 1:1): according to the faith of the chosen ones of God
- διὰ τοῦ θανάτου τοῦ υἱοῦ αὐτοῦ (Rom 5:10): through the death of the son of him

However, the relationship between the words of a three-word genitive must be analyzed more carefully beyond simple word order.[13] Paul's versatility allows for a wide range of word order and inter-constructional relationships. In the phrase τοῦ

---

12 BDF §168(2) p. 93.
13 Wallace wrestles with this dynamic in Rom 8:21 (a four-word genitive construction): τὴν ἐλευθερίαν τῆς δόξης τῶν τέκνων τοῦ θεοῦ "when an attributive gen. [τῆς δόξης] is in the mix, matters are a bit more complicated. Since an attributive gen. is by nature strongly adjectival, it is best to convert it into an adjective and take it 'out of the loop' of the gen. chain." Wallace, *ExSyn*, 87–88.

αἵματος τοῦ σταυροῦ αὐτοῦ *the blood of the cross of him* (Col 1:20), the pronoun αὐτοῦ *his* is not related to τοῦ σταυροῦ but to τοῦ αἵματος. The meaning of this phrase is not "the blood of his cross," but "*his* blood of [i.e., shed on] the cross."

Meanings of the Three-Word Genitive

After discussing the grammatical and semantic aspects of the three-word genitive in the Pauline corpus, attention is directed now to analyzing the syntactic meanings of this phase of genitive construction. In Chapter Four we categorized the meanings of genitives in two-word constructions. In this chapter we will use the same principles to handle the distinctive features of the three-word genitive.

Cumulative Genitive

The three-word genitive construction is a language phenomenon that deserves attention. The mere nominal nature of the three-word genitive makes it very fertile in producing a diversity of meanings. Paul prefers to pile up synonymous substantives without conjunctions in genitive constructions. I am naming this kind of genitive usage "cumulative genitive," because it grows by successive additions.

The translation of ὁ νόμος τοῦ πνεύματος τῆς ζωῆς *the law of the Spirit of the life* (Rom 8:2) varies widely. Some say: "the life-giving law of the Spirit" (NEB REB), or "the law of the Spirit, which brings us life" (TEV NJB "gives us life"). Barclay renders, "the law of the life-giving Spirit" (WB). It seems cumulative effect of the genitives adds more: "the law of Spirit *and* life." This becomes even clearer in the opposite parallel genitival phrase τοῦ νόμου τῆς ἁμαρτίας καὶ τοῦ θανάτου *the law of sin and death*, for there καὶ appears.[14] Instead of the literal "the purpose/counsel of his will" for τὴν βουλὴν τοῦ θελήματος αὐτοῦ (Eph 1:11; KJV RSV NIV), the NRSV has "his counsel and will."

Another example of the cumulative genitive appears twice in the first chapter of Ephesians: εἰς ἔπαινον δόξης αὐτοῦ (Eph 1:12, 14). Usually this three-word genitive is rendered "to the praise of his glory." But REB translates the second phrase that of Eph 1:14 by "to his glory and praise." The justification for such translation is founded on that *praise* and *glory* are synonymous. A similar phrase, εἰς δόξαν καὶ ἔπαινον θεοῦ, appears in Phil 1:11, where it is explicitly accumulated using καὶ.

---

14 J. D. G. Dunn complains that NEB NJB "move too far from the parallelism with 'the law of sin and death'" (*Romans 1–8*, WBC 38A [Dallas: Word, 1988], 416).

NEB REB render the expression τῷ πνεύματι τοῦ νοὸς ὑμῶν *the Spirit of your mind* (Eph 4:23), "in your mind and spirit."[15] TEV which is usually conservative to accumulate in similar phrases, takes liberty when it translates τὸ πλοῦτος τῆς δόξης τοῦ μυστηρίου τούτου (Col 1:27) "this rich and glorious secret."

The similar phrases τῷ κράτει τῆς ἰσχύος αὐτοῦ *the might of his strength* (Eph 6:10) and τὸ κράτος τῆς δόξης αὐτοῦ *the might of his glory* (Col 1:11) are two three-word constructions which could be put in the cumulative genitive category. So instead of translating—as attributive genitives—the first "his mighty power" (REB), and the second "his glorious might" (RSV), one may consider a synony-mous wording of these phrases: "in his power and might," and "according to his power and glory." Edward Lohse points out that κράτος and δόξα frequently occur together in ascriptions of praise (citing 1 Pet 4:11; 5:11; Jude 25; Rev 1:6; 5:13).[16] Such a translation would add forcefulness to the addition of terms.

Since ἐπιφάνεια and παρουσία in the expression τῇ ἐπιφανείᾳ τῆς παρουσίας αὐτοῦ *the appearing of his coming* (2 Thess 2:8), are synonyms in the terminology of the second coming of Christ,[17] RSV translates the accumulation, "his appearing and his coming." It is precisely that the two words appear so close in meaning that prompts F. F. Bruce to say, "If ἐπιφάνεια ('manifestation') were synonymous with παρουσία here, the construction would be pleonastic."[18]

There is some division among English versions as to where "glory" belongs in the expression **τὸ εὐαγγέλιον τῆς δόξης** τοῦ μακαρίου **θεοῦ** *the gospel of the glory of the blessed **God*** (1 Tim 1:11). It is clear that μακαρίου modifies θεοῦ as an at-tributive adjective. Many English versions take δόξης as a "Hebrew" genitive, "the glorious gospel of the blessed God" (KJV NRSV NET NIV). TEV renders the construction a cumulative genitive, "the Good News from the glorious and blessed God," relating δόξης to "God." But, in a similar phrase to 1 Tim 1:11, the TEV in **ἐπιφάνειαν τῆς δόξης** τοῦ **μεγάλου θεοῦ καὶ σωτῆρος ἡμῶν** *the appearing of the glory of our great God and savior* (Titus 2:13) inconsistently translates noun and the

---

15 Gordon Fee questions whether this rendering is permissible, preferring instead an epexe-getical genitive (*God's Empowering Presence: The Holy Spirit in the Letters of Paul* [Peabody, MA: Hendrickson, 1994; repr., Grand Rapids: Baker, 2011], 710n162).

16 Edward Lohse, *Colossians and Philemon*, ed. Helmut Koester, trans. William R. Poehlmann and Robert J. Karris, Hermeneia (Philadelphia: Fortress, 1971), 30.

17 Charles Wanamaker notes, "ἐπιφάνεια and παρουσία are both used in the literature of the time as technical terms for the manifestation of a divine figure" (*The Epistles to the Thessalonians: A Commentary on the Greek Text*, NIGTC [Grand Rapids: Eerdmans, 1990], 258). BDAG 386 s.v. ἐπιφάνεια 1b points out, "the combination is not overly redundant, for ἐ. refers to the salvation that goes into effect when the π. takes place."

18 F. F. Bruce, *1 and 2 Thessalonians*, WBC 45 (Dallas: Word, 1998), 172.

adjective, "when the glory of our great God and Savior … will appear." We will take this passage up in greater detail in Chapter Six, for it is likely part of a four-word instead of a three-word construction. It is possible that for English style the redundancy of "and" in "our glorious and great God and Savior" occasioned the difference in translation.

Adjectival Genitive

The adjectival genitive is another feature of the three-word genitive construction. A quick survey shows that about a quarter of the three-word genitive constructions in Paul contain an adjectival element. This is in line with Winer's dictum that "one of the substantives often represents an adjectival notion."[19] This phenomenon deserves some comment.

The adjectival element appears in different locations. Sometimes the adjectival element appears at the beginning of the three-word genitive construction as head word; at other times in the middle, and in a few instances, it appears at the end.

Adjectival Head Word

There are many three-word genitive constructions in the Pauline corpus that have adjectival head words, meaning the lexical domain of the word is adjectival. Using a nominal adjective instead of a regular one strengthens the meaning intended by the author and makes it more expressive. This is different than using a genitive as an adjective (as we have already seen).

The following examples will illustrate. In Rom 2:4 τοῦ πλούτου τῆς χρηστότητος αὐτοῦ *the wealth of his kindness* (Rom 2:4) *wealth* is used in place of *wealthy* ("his great kindness," TEV "his abundant goodness" NJB). For the expression τὴν νέκρωσιν τῆς μήτρας Σάρρας (Rom 4:19), "the deadness of Sarah's womb" (KJV NET), NIV has "Sarah's womb was also dead" (cf. NJB), replacing the noun with a predicate adjective. TEV reads "his abundant glory" for τὸν πλοῦτον τῆς δόξης αὐτοῦ (Rom 9:23 "the riches of his glory" [ESV]), using an adjective. NJB takes the second word as an adjectival genitive, "glorious riches."

This examination leads to the rule: when an adjectival element stands as the head words in three-word genitive constructions, the head word always describes the second word, but not the third. The following references illustrate this principle:

- Rom 11:33 Ὦ βάθος πλούτου καὶ σοφίας καὶ γνώσεως θεοῦ (Rom 11:33): "Oh, the depth of the riches of the wisdom and knowledge of God" (NIV)

19 Winer, *Grammar*, 238.

- 2 Cor 3:7 τὴν δόξαν τοῦ προσώπου αὐτοῦ "the glory of his face" (NET)
- 2 Cor 4:17 τὸ παραυτίκα ἐλαφρὸν τῆς θλίψεως ἡμῶν "our momentary light affliction" (CSB)
- 2 Cor 8:2 ἡ περισσεία τῆς χαρᾶς αὐτῶν "their overflowing joy" (NIV)
- 2 Cor 8:24 τὴν ἔνδειξιν τῆς ἀγάπης ὑμῶν "clear evidence of your love" (REB)
- Eph 1:19 τὸ ὑπερβάλλον μέγεθος τῆς δυνάμεως αὐτοῦ "his incomparably great power" (NIV)
- Eph 4:17 ματαιότητι τοῦ νοὸς αὐτῶν "their futile notions" (REB)
- Col 2:5 τὸ στερέωμα τῆς εἰς Χριστὸν πίστεως ὑμῶν "how firm your faith in Christ is" (NIV)
- Col 2:13 τῇ ἀκροβυστίᾳ τῆς σαρκὸς ὑμῶν "the uncircumcision of your flesh" (NET)
- 2 Thess 2:8 τῇ ἐπιφανείᾳ τῆς παρουσίας αὐτοῦ "glorious appearance" (NJB), or "dazzling presence" (TEV)

Adjectival Middle-Word

The adjectival middle word in three-word genitive constructions is a phenomenon that deserves attention, for there is a diversity of meaning to be discovered. It is also a fairly frequent genitive expression used by Paul in his letters, but not so much so in the rest of the books of the New Testament where the adjectival middle-word of three-word genitive constructions rarely occurs.

Careful attention must be given to the semantics of the adjectival middle word in three-word genitive. The semantic structure should be decoded in order to catch the meaning of the construction. An adjectival middle-word three-word construction like θρόνου δόξης αὐτοῦ *the throne of the glory of him* (Matt 25:31) should be reconstituted to make sense. The "throne + glory + him" formula should be changed to "glorious + throne + him", or in a better English style "his + glorious + throne" (NIV NET ESV). Here is the real meaning of the construction, not that the glory of Christ has a throne, but that his throne is glorious. Of course, this is what most translations and interpreters do instinctively. It helps to observe that in over half of three-word genitive constructions, a genitive pronoun appears as the last term, so frequently the possessive genitive at the end of the sequence applies to the first two in the chain.

Paul's three-word genitive usage can be ascribed to the influence of the OT, whether bearing linguistic the imprint of Hebrew or mediated through the LXX. In fact, the "adjectival genitive" used in the NT is called "Hebrew genitive" because they are related. Structurally, both the adjectival and "Hebrew" genitive appear in are adnominal three-word genitives. The middle or second word in both constructions is always used as an adjective, and almost always to describe the head word. We have already presented examples to illustrate this phenomenon (See the examples under *The Adjectival Hebrew Genitive in the Old Testament* in Chapter Four). One would naturally expect Paul's Semitic heritage to make an impression on his writing (Gal 1:10; Phil 3:4–6; Acts 22:3; 23:6; 24:14; 26:4). So, it stands to reason many such adjectival middle-word constructions would occur, and they do. An adjectival middle word may describe the head word or the third word in its construction.

The Adjectival Middle-Word Describing the Head Word

The adjectival middle word in τὴν ἀσθένειαν τῆς σαρκὸς ὑμῶν *the weakness of your flesh* (Rom 6:19) is recognized as "your human weakness" in REB (cf. ESV NIV). Likewise in τοὺς ὀφθαλμοὺς τῆς καρδίας ὑμῶν (Eph 1:18), instead of "the eyes of your heart/understanding" (NIV KJV), REB has "your inward eyes."[20] In translating ταῖς ἐπιθυμίαις τῆς σαρκὸς ἡμῶν (Eph 2:3), "the lusts of our flesh" (KJV), TEV has "our natural desires" (cf. NIV NJB REB CSB). The meaning of κατὰ τὴν ἐνέργειαν τῆς δυνάμεως αὐτοῦ (Eph 3:7) "the working of his power" (ESV NIV), may be rendered as "according to his powerful action" (REB "powerfully at work"). To translate κατὰ τὸ πλοῦτος τῆς δόξης αὐτοῦ *according to the wealth of his glory* (Eph 3:16), NIV has "out of his glorious riches" (cf. Phil 4:19). Similarly, the adjectival meaning of the expression τῷ κράτει τῆς ἰσχύος αὐτοῦ (Eph 6:10), "the power of his might" (KJV) is rendered as "his mighty power" (REB NIV TEV), or "his vast strength" (CSB). Similarly, for τὸ κράτος τῆς δόξης αὐτοῦ *the power of his might* (Col 1:11), several versions translate "his glorious might/strength/power" (REB NIV NJB NRSV TEV NET CSB).

In Phil 3:21, two parallel three-word genitives appear: ὃς μετασχηματίσει τὸ σῶμα τῆς ταπεινώσεως ἡμῶν σύμμορφον τῷ σώματι τῆς δόξης αὐτοῦ. ASV's literal rendering "the body of our humiliation ... the body of his glory" is a step backwards in the dynamics of translation's art (followed by NRSV's departure from RSV), from KJV's "our vile body ... his glorious body." NASB takes a half step towards KJV from ASV, "the body of our humble state ... the body of His glory" Most recent versions, however, have correctly rendered this three-word genitive pair "our humble bodies/condition ... his glorious body" (REB NIV NAB NET CSB), "our lowly body ... his glorious body" (ESV), or "the wretched body of ours ... his glorious body" (NJB).

---

20 Marcus Barth interprets "the eyes of your hearts" as "inner eyes" (*Ephesians*, 2 vols., AB 34–34A [New Haven: Yale University Press, 1974], 1:150).

Another example of the adjectival middle-word is the following awkward construction: τῷ σώματι τῆς σαρκὸς αὐτοῦ (Col 1:22), "the body of his flesh" (KJV), which is translated "his fleshly body" (NRSV) "Christ's physical body" (NIV NET CSB) and "mortal body" (NJB). The middle term δόξης in τὸ πλοῦτος τῆς δόξης τοῦ μυστηρίου τούτου (Col 1:27), "the riches of the glory of this mystery" (ESV), is also adjectival: "the glorious riches/wealth of this mystery" (NIV NET CSB). TEV accumulates the head word with the middle-word and lets both of them describe the third word "this rich and glorious secret." The phrase τοῦ νοὸς τῆς σαρκὸς αὐτοῦ *the mind of his flesh* (Col 2:18) is translated "his fleshly mind" (KJV NET), "a human way of thinking" (NRSV NJB), and "his sensuous notions/mind" (ESV) or even the more interpretive "their unspiritual mind" (NIV). All these translations see the middle-word as adjectival describing the head word. The literal rendering of ἀγγέλων δυνάμεως αὐτοῦ (2 Thess 1:7) "the angels of his power" (ASV, NJB), is improved by seeing an adjectival middle word, "his mighty/powerful angels" (KJV NRSV REB NIV TEV NET ESV CSB).

Paul uses τὸ πνεῦμα τοῦ υἱοῦ αὐτοῦ *the spirit of his son* (Gal 4:6) in almost a technical way. The context of Gal 4:1–7 contrasts slavery and sonship: God sends the spirit of his son to into believers' hearts, allowing them to address God as Father. So, by relating sonship to God with receiving "the Spirit of his son," believers can perceive that Paul is using this three-word genitive with an adjectival middle word describing the head word "the Spirit." Therefore, the expression can be fully explained: "the sonship Spirit of His own He sends to our hearts."[21]

In the phrase ἀπὸ προσώπου τοῦ κυρίου καὶ ἀπὸ τῆς δόξης τῆς ἰσχύος αὐτοῦ (2 Thess 1:9), "from the presence of the Lord, and from the glory/splendor of his power/might" (KJV REB NRSV NIV NJB ESV), some versions consider the head word τῆς δόξης in the second construction adjectival, describing the middle word τῆς ἰσχύος "his glorious might/strength" (TEV HCSB). There is good reason to agree with this interpretation. The phrase consists of two parallel synonymous members where ἀπὸ προσώπου stands opposite to ἀπὸ τῆς δόξης.[22] The parallelism may be laid out thus:

ἀπὸ προσώπου [lacking τοῦ φόβου from Isa 2:10, 19, 21 LXX] τοῦ κυρίου

καὶ

ἀπὸ τῆς δόξης τῆς ἰσχύος αὐτοῦ.

---

21 See also Martinus C. de Boer, *Galatians: A Commentary*, NTL (Louisville: Westminster John Knox, 2011), 266.

22 See the analysis of this parallelism in James Everett Frame, *A Critical and Exegetical Commentary on the Epistles of St. Paul to the Thessalonians*, ICC (New York: Scribner, 1912), 234–35.

If τοῦ φόβου (LXX) describes ἀπὸ προσώπου "the dread presence" (REB) in the first half of the parallelism, τῆς ἰσχύος should describe τῆς δόξης in the second half: "the powerful radiance." According to this analysis "the glory" in the second half of the parallel is a synonym to "face." In this instance, τῆς ἰσχύος should be an adjective describing τῆς δόξης: "from the face of the Lord and from his powerful radiance," or " ... his strong brightness."

Adjectival Middle Word Describing the Third Word

As we have seen, usually the adjectival middle word describes the head word that precedes. However, there are few instances where the middle word describes the third word that follows, as in the phrase τὸ πλοῦτος τῆς δόξης τοῦ μυστηρίου τούτου (Col 1:27), "the riches of the glory of this mystery" (ESV). While the NET NIV CSB let the middle-word describe the head-word translating the phrase: "the glorious riches/wealth of this mystery," TEV turns both the head word and the middle word into adjectives describing the third word "this rich and glorious secret."

It is difficult to decide sometimes whether to relate the adjectival middle-word in a three-word genitive construction to the head word or to the third word, as with τῷ λόγῳ τῆς ἀληθείας τοῦ εὐαγγελίου *the word of the truth of the gospel* (Col 1:5). Some take the middle word τῆς ἀληθείας as an adjective that describes the final term: "the message of the true gospel" (NEB REB), but if our rule about the middle word almost always describing the head word, the meaning should be "the true message of the gospel" (NIV).[23] Many other versions have used an appositional translation of the third term: "the true message, the gospel" (NRSV TEV NJB NET CSB). Their conclusion is on fairly strong footing since in light of the synonymous phrase in Eph 1:13: τὸν λόγον τῆς ἀληθείας, τὸ εὐαγγέλιον τῆς σωτηρίας ὑμῶν, "the message of truth, the gospel of your salvation" (NIV) that enlightens the meaning of this genitive construction.

Another example of how the middle-word *may* describe the third word occurs in the phrase πλοῦτος τῆς πληροφορίας τῆς συνέσεως *wealth of certainty of knowledge* (Col 2:2). Here NRSV HCSB have "the riches of assured understanding." NIV reads "the full riches of complete understanding."[24] Still, the phrase might be taken

---

23   This translation has a potential weak point since "there is no evidence that Paul would call a non-Christian message a 'false gospel.' It is not a gospel at all, real or counterfeit" (Richard R. Melick, Jr., *Philippians, Colossians, Philemon*, NAC 32 [Nashville: Broadman, 1991], 197). Dunn points to a similar phrase τὴν ἀλήθειαν τοῦ εὐαγγελίου in Gal 2:5, 14 as support for the more literal translation (*The Epistles to the Colossians and to Philemon: A Commentary on the Greek Text*, NIGTC [Grand Rapids: Eerdmans, 1996], 61).

24   BDAG 827 s.v. πληροφορία allows for the possibility that the word means "fullness."

with a different relationship between the component parts: "all the riches that assurance brings in their understanding of the knowledge" (NET).

Adjectival Third Word

The adjectival third word in three-word genitive constructions in the Pauline corpus is very rare if compared with the frequency of the adjectival head word and middle-word. Semantically an adjectival third word is unlikely, not impossible. There are few examples of such usage.

The first of these examples is ἐλπίδι τῆς δόξης τοῦ θεοῦ *the hope of the glory of God* (Rom 5:2) where τοῦ θεοῦ is translated "divine splendor" (NEB) or "divine glory" (REB). Fitzmyer explains the expression thus: "Christians should boast of a share in *the glorious life of God himself.*"[25] The second example is ὁ νόμος τοῦ πνεύματος τῆς ζωῆς (Rom 8:2), "the law of the Spirit of life" (KJV). REB translates the phrase, "the life-giving law of the Spirit," taking τῆς ζωῆς an adjective that describes the law of the Spirit. Others have "the law of the life-giving Spirit" (NET), or "the law of the Spirit who gives life" (NIV). This translation relates τῆς ζωῆς with the Spirit the word that precedes it rather than the law. All these translations have in common that they take the third word as an adjective. In the next verse, there is another example to consider. Many versions render ὁμοιώματι σαρκὸς ἁμαρτίας *the likeness of the flesh of sin* (Rom 8:3) as "the likeness of sinful flesh" (KJV NIV NRSV ESV NET; cf. REB TEV). Likewise, the third word τῆς σαρκός in ἐν τῇ ἀπεκδύσει τοῦ σώματος τῆς σαρκός (Col 2:11), "by putting off the body of the flesh" (ESV) which is translated "lower nature" (REB), "sinful nature" (NIV84), "natural self" (NJB), "fleshly body" (NET). All these adjectives are used to describe τοῦ σώματος which stands for "self", "nature" or "body." In the adjectival third word examples above, the third word describes the middle word that precedes it. However, the third-word in Rom 8:2 is disputed and may describe both the head word and the middle word as a unit.

Multivalent Functions of the Middle Word

Under this section, which is a much-disputed area in the syntax of the three-word genitive, care is directed towards discovering some new dimensions in the use of the middle word. There is merit in noticing situations in which the middle word in the construction is not adjectival, even though an adjectival flavor can never be

---

25 Joseph A. Fitzmyer, *Romans: A New Translation with Introduction and Commentary,* AB 33 (New York: Doubleday, 1993), 396. [emphasis added].

fully ruled out. The middle word is free to function in other almost non-genitive ways, like datival, some other times as locative, or instrumental.

The discovery of such development in the function of the middle word in three-word genitive constructions lies in the language of Paul himself. Comparing Paul's expressions reveals certain clues that provide the key to decoding some difficult passages. For example, in the phrase τὸ πλοῦτος τῆς δόξης αὐτοῦ (Eph 3:16), "the wealth of his glory" (NET), the middle word τῆς δόξης is difficult to define: it may mean "the wealth of his glory" or "his glorious riches." But help is found in the synonymous phrase κατὰ τὸ πλοῦτος αὐτοῦ **ἐν δόξῃ** ἐν Χριστῷ Ἰησοῦ (Phil 4:19), "according to his riches **in glory.**" The head noun τὸ πλοῦτος relates to αὐτοῦ and the prepositional phrase ἐν δόξῃ does here what the phrase τῆς δόξης did in Eph 3:16. Observing this pattern of linguistic variation in Paul could show us the way forward in some problematic genitive expressions.

It seems that the following versions have followed this pattern in translating ἡ κοινωνία τῆς πίστεώς σου (Phlm 6), "the sharing of your faith" (NRSV NIV84 ESV), "your fellowship in faith" (NJB), "your partnership with us in the faith" (NIV), and "your participation in the faith" (CSB). In the same way, συγκοινωνούς μου τῆς χάριτος (Phil 1:7), "partakers of my grace" (KJV), REB renders "you all share in the privilege that is mine" (cf. TEV NIV NRSV NJB NET CSB).

The phrase διὰ τοῦ αἵματος τοῦ σταυροῦ αὐτοῦ (Col 1:20) is also another example of the multiple function of the middle-word (σταυροῦ) of the three-word genitive. Thus, instead of the more literal rendering "through the blood of his cross" (KJV ASV NASB RSV NRSV NAB ESV NET HCSB), the following translations relate τοῦ αἵματος with αὐτοῦ and give to τοῦ σταυροῦ an instrumental meaning "the shedding of his blood *on the cross*" (REB TEV NIV CSB; "upon" NEB "his death" NJB).

The middle word of a three-word genitive construction can act in a kind of datival or instrumental capacity. For instance, **ἡμῶν** ἐλπὶς ἢ χαρὰ ἢ **στέφανος καυχήσεως** (1 Thess 2:19), "crown of boasting" (ESV) can be more fully rendered as "our reason *for* boasting" (TEV) or "*in* which we will boast/glory" (NIV) or "crown to boast of" (NAB NET).

There is an abundance of three-word genitive expressions in the Hebrew Bible—approximating the situation of the constructions we are considering—in which the middle words are instrumental, such as מִשְׁפְּטֵי־פִיךָ (Ps 119:13; LXX τὰ κρίματα τοῦ στόματός σου), "the ordinances of your mouth" (NRSV), that is, "your ordinances given through (your) mouth." NIV renders "the laws that come from your mouth." Another example is מַעֲשֵׂי יָדָיו (Ps 111:7), "the works of his hands" (NRSV), which means "his works done through [his] hands" (cf. "the words of my mouth" Ps 54:2).

Understanding the potential for the middle word to act in an instrumental sense may shed light on two ambiguous three-word genitive constructions that appear in reference to the eucharistic context in 1 Cor 10:16: τὸ ποτήριον τῆς εὐλογίας ὃ εὐλογοῦμεν, οὐχὶ [1] κοινωνία ἐστὶν τοῦ αἵματος τοῦ Χριστοῦ; τὸν ἄρτον ὃν κλῶμεν, οὐχὶ [2] κοινωνία τοῦ σώματος τοῦ Χριστοῦ ἐστιν;

It is clear from the traditional material in the larger context that the cup refers to the blood and the bread refers to the body (1 Cor 11:23–25). Now if the middle words of the two three-word genitives—τοῦ αἵματος in (1) and τοῦ σώματος in (2)— were considered instrumental, the thrust of meaning would move from the *means* to the *person*. Then the text would be interpreted, "the cup of blessing that we bless, is it not a sharing in [a fellowship with] Christ through the instrument of his blood [through drinking from the cup]? The bread that we break, is it not a sharing in [a fellowship with] Christ through his body [through eating from the bread]?" Paul underscores the personal relationship through the instrumental idea because he wants to contrast Christian from pagan practice. Those who eat from animals sacrificed to idols are partakers with demons; offering sacrifices to idols is the same thing as sacrificing to demons. He warns his readers with an emphatic genitive construction: οὐ θέλω δὲ ὑμᾶς κοινωνοὺς τῶν δαιμονίων γίνεσθαι *I do not want you to be partakers of demons* (1 Cor 10:20). Along the same line of thought Paul asks, "are not those who eat the sacrifices partners in the altar?" (κοινωνοὶ τοῦ θυσιαστηρίου 1 Cor 10:18). So, those who eat from sacrifices are related to what stands behind them such as altar, demons, God, or Christ.

Appendix: List of Three-Word Genitive Constructions

This is a list of the 181 three-word genitive constructions in the main text of NA28 for the *corpus Paulinum*. Words in square brackets represent those words required by context or ellipsis. Instances marked with a dagger (†), e.g., τῶν λοιπῶν συνεργῶν μου (Phil 4:3), could be disputed on the grounds of differing syntactical analysis, but have been included in the list for completeness (and are included in the count). In the instance of Phil 4:3, for example, λοιπῶν can be taken as a substantival adjective (in which case, a three-word construction), or as an attributive adjective (in which case a two-word construction).

Romans: 32†

Rom 1:9	τῷ εὐαγγελίῳ τοῦ υἱοῦ αὐτοῦ
Rom 1:23	ὁμοιώματι εἰκόνος φθαρτοῦ ἀνθρώπου

Rom 1:24	ταῖς ἐπιθυμίαις τῶν καρδιῶν αὐτῶν
Rom 1:27	τὴν ἀντιμισθίαν … τῆς πλάνης αὐτῶν
Rom 2:4	τοῦ πλούτου τῆς χρηστότητος αὐτοῦ
Rom 2:5	ἀποκαλύψεως δικαιοκρισίας τοῦ θεοῦ
Rom 3:25	εἰς ἔνδειξιν τῆς δικαιοσύνης αὐτοῦ
Rom 3:26	πρὸς τὴν ἔνδειξιν τῆς δικαιοσύνης αὐτοῦ
Rom 4:11	σφραγῖδα τῆς δικαιοσύνης τῆς πίστεως
Rom 4:19	τὴν νέκρωσιν τῆς μήτρας Σάρρας
Rom 5:2	ἐλπίδι τῆς δόξης τοῦ θεοῦ
Rom 5:10	τοῦ θανάτου τοῦ υἱοῦ αὐτοῦ
Rom 5:14	τῷ ὁμοιώματι τῆς παραβάσεως Ἀδάμ
Rom 5:17†	**τὴν περισσείαν** τῆς χάριτος καὶ **τῆς δωρεᾶς τῆς δικαιοσύνης**
Rom 6:5	τῷ ὁμοιώματι τοῦ θανάτου αὐτοῦ
Rom 6:5	[τῷ ὁμοιώματι] τῆς ἀναστάσεως [αὐτοῦ]
Rom 6:19	τὴν ἀσθένειαν τῆς σαρκὸς ὑμῶν
Rom 7:23	τῷ νόμῳ τοῦ νοός μου
Rom 8:2	ὁ νόμος τοῦ πνεύματος τῆς ζωῆς
Rom 8:3	ὁμοιώματι σαρκὸς ἁμαρτίας
Rom 8:19	τὴν ἀποκάλυψιν τῶν υἱῶν τοῦ θεοῦ
Rom 8:23	τὴν ἀπολύτρωσιν τοῦ σώματος ἡμῶν
Rom 9:23	τὸν πλοῦτον τῆς δόξης αὐτοῦ
Rom 9:27	ὁ ἀριθμὸς τῶν υἱῶν Ἰσραηλ
Rom 11:22	χρηστότητα καὶ ἀποτομίαν θεοῦ
Rom 11:33	βάθος πλούτου … θεοῦ
Rom 11:33	βάθος … σοφίας … θεοῦ
Rom 11:33	βάθος … γνώσεως … θεοῦ
Rom 15:6	τὸν θεὸν καὶ πατέρα τοῦ κυρίου ἡμῶν
Rom 15:19	δυνάμει πνεύματος θεοῦ
Rom 15:29	πληρώματι εὐλογίας Χριστοῦ
Rom 16:20	ἡ χάρις τοῦ κυρίου ἡμῶν

1 Corinthians: 18

1 Cor 1:2	τὸ ὄνομα τοῦ κυρίου ἡμῶν
1 Cor 1:7	τὴν ἀποκάλυψιν τοῦ κυρίου ἡμῶν
1 Cor 1:8	τῇ ἡμέρᾳ τοῦ κυρίου ἡμῶν
1 Cor 1:9	κοινωνίαν τοῦ υἱοῦ αὐτοῦ

1 Cor 1:10	τοῦ ὀνόματος τοῦ κυρίου ἡμῶν
1 Cor 2:14	τὰ τοῦ πνεύματος τοῦ θεοῦ
1 Cor 4:1	οἰκονόμους μυστηρίων θεοῦ
1 Cor 5:4	τῷ ὀνόματι τοῦ κυρίου ἡμῶν
1 Cor 5:4	τῇ δυνάμει τοῦ κυρίου ἡμῶν
1 Cor 6:11	τῷ πνεύματι τοῦ θεοῦ ἡμῶν
1 Cor 7:19	τήρησις ἐντολῶν θεοῦ
1 Cor 9:2	ἡ σφραγίς μου τῆς ἀποστολῆς
1 Cor 10:16	κοινωνία ἐστὶν τοῦ αἵματος τοῦ Χριστοῦ
1 Cor 10:16	κοινωνία τοῦ σώματος τοῦ Χριστοῦ
1 Cor 10:26	τὸ πλήρωμα αὐτῆς [τοῦ κυρίου]
1 Cor 11:27	ἔνοχος ἔσται τοῦ σώματος
1 Cor 11:27	[ἔνοχος ἔσται] τοῦ αἵματος τοῦ κυρίου
1 Cor 14:25	τὰ κρυπτὰ τῆς καρδίας αὐτοῦ

2 Corinthians: 20

2 Cor 1:3	ὁ θεὸς καὶ πατὴρ τοῦ κυρίου ἡμῶν
2 Cor 1:12	τὸ μαρτύριον τῆς συνειδήσεως ἡμῶν
2 Cor 1:14	τῇ ἡμέρᾳ τοῦ κυρίου ἡμῶν
2 Cor 1:24	συνεργοί ἐσμεν τῆς χαρᾶς ὑμῶν
2 Cor 2:14	τὴν ὀσμὴν τῆς γνώσεως αὐτοῦ
2 Cor 3:7	τὴν δόξαν τοῦ προσώπου αὐτοῦ
2 Cor 4:17	ἐλαφρὸν τῆς θλίψεως ἡμῶν
2 Cor 5:1	ἡ ἐπίγειος ἡμῶν οἰκία τοῦ σκήνους
2 Cor 6:7	διὰ τῶν ὅπλων τῆς δικαιοσύνης τῶν δεξιῶν
2 Cor 6:7	διὰ τῶν ὅπλων τῆς δικαιοσύνης [τῶν] ἀριστερῶν
2 Cor 8:2	ἡ περισσεία τῆς χαρᾶς αὐτῶν
2 Cor 8:2	τὸ πλοῦτος τῆς ἁπλότητος αὐτῶν
2 Cor 8:9	τὴν χάριν τοῦ κυρίου ἡμῶν
2 Cor 8:24	τὴν ἔνδειξιν τῆς ἀγάπης ὑμῶν
2 Cor 8:24	[τὴν ἔνδειξιν τῆς] ἡμῶν καυχήσεως
2 Cor 9:10	τὰ γενήματα τῆς δικαιοσύνης ὑμῶν
2 Cor 9:13	τῇ ὑποταγῇ τῆς ὁμολογίας ὑμῶν
2 Cor 10:1	τῆς πραΰτητος καὶ ἐπιεικείας τοῦ Χριστοῦ
2 Cor 10:4	τὰ ὅπλα τῆς στρατείας ἡμῶν
2 Cor 11:30	τὰ τῆς ἀσθενείας μου

Gal: 6†

Gal 1:14†	**ζηλωτὴς** ὑπάρχων **τῶν** πατρικῶν **μου παραδόσεων** [taking πατρικῶν as an attributive adjective]
Gal 1:15	κοιλίας μητρός μου
Gal 2:20	πίστει ζῶ τῇ τοῦ υἱοῦ τοῦ θεοῦ
Gal 4:6	τὸ πνεῦμα τοῦ υἱοῦ αὐτοῦ
Gal 6:14	τῷ σταυρῷ τοῦ κυρίου ἡμῶν
Gal 6:18	ἡ χάρις τοῦ κυρίου ἡμῶν

Eph: 38

Eph 1:3	πατὴρ τοῦ κυρίου ἡμῶν
Eph 1:5	τὴν εὐδοκίαν τοῦ θελήματος αὐτοῦ
Eph 1:7	τὸ πλοῦτος τῆς χάριτος αὐτοῦ
Eph 1:9	τὸ μυστήριον τοῦ θελήματος αὐτοῦ
Eph 1:10	οἰκονομίαν τοῦ πληρώματος τῶν καιρῶν
Eph 1:11	τὴν βουλὴν τοῦ θελήματος αὐτοῦ
Eph 1:12	ἔπαινον δόξης αὐτοῦ
Eph 1:13	τὸ εὐαγγέλιον τῆς σωτηρίας ὑμῶν
Eph 1:14	ἀρραβὼν τῆς κληρονομίας ἡμῶν
Eph 1:14	ἔπαινον τῆς δόξης αὐτοῦ
Eph 1:17	ὁ θεὸς τοῦ κυρίου ἡμῶν
Eph 1:18	τοὺς ὀφθαλμοὺς τῆς καρδίας ὑμῶν
Eph 1:18	ἡ ἐλπὶς τῆς κλήσεως αὐτοῦ
Eph 1:19	τὸ ὑπερβάλλον μέγεθος τῆς δυνάμεως αὐτοῦ
Eph 2:2	τὸν ἄρχοντα τῆς ἐξουσίας τοῦ ἀέρος
Eph 2:3	ταῖς ἐπιθυμίαις τῆς σαρκὸς ἡμῶν
Eph 2:7	τὸ ὑπερβάλλον πλοῦτος τῆς χάριτος αὐτοῦ
Eph 2:12	ἀπηλλοτριωμένοι τῆς πολιτείας τοῦ Ἰσραὴλ
Eph 2:12	ξένοι τῶν διαθηκῶν τῆς ἐπαγγελίας
Eph 3:2	τὴν οἰκονομίαν τῆς χάριτος τοῦ θεοῦ
Eph 3:7	τὴν ἐνέργειαν τῆς δυνάμεως αὐτοῦ
Eph 3:16	τὸ πλοῦτος τῆς δόξης αὐτοῦ
Eph 3:19	τὴν ὑπερβάλλουσαν τῆς γνώσεως ἀγάπην τοῦ Χριστοῦ
Eph 3:21	πάσας τὰς γενεὰς τοῦ αἰῶνος τῶν αἰώνων
Eph 4:4	ἐλπίδι τῆς κλήσεως ὑμῶν
Eph 4:7	τὸ μέτρον τῆς δωρεᾶς τοῦ Χριστοῦ
Eph 4:12	οἰκοδομὴν τοῦ σώματος τοῦ Χριστοῦ

Eph 4:13	τῆς ἐπιγνώσεως τοῦ υἱοῦ τοῦ θεοῦ
Eph 4:17	ματαιότητι τοῦ νοὸς αὐτῶν
Eph 4:18	ἀπηλλοτριωμένοι τῆς ζωῆς τοῦ θεοῦ
Eph 4:18	τὴν πώρωσιν τῆς καρδίας αὐτῶν
Eph 4:23	τῷ πνεύματι τοῦ νοὸς ὑμῶν
Eph 5:20	ὀνόματι τοῦ κυρίου ἡμῶν
Eph 5:30	μέλη ἐσμὲν τοῦ σώματος αὐτοῦ
Eph 6:5	ἁπλότητι τῆς καρδίας ὑμῶν
Eph 6:10	τῷ κράτει τῆς ἰσχύος αὐτοῦ
Eph 6:15	ἑτοιμασίᾳ τοῦ εὐαγγελίου τῆς εἰρήνης
Eph 6:19	ἀνοίξει τοῦ στόματός μου

Phil: 13†

Phil 1:7	συγκοινωνούς μου τῆς χάριτος
Phil 1:19	ἐπιχορηγίας τοῦ πνεύματος Ἰησοῦ Χριστοῦ
Phil 1:25	τὴν ὑμῶν προκοπὴν καὶ χαρὰν τῆς πίστεως
Phil 2:17	τῇ θυσίᾳ καὶ λειτουργίᾳ τῆς πίστεως ὑμῶν
Phil 2:25	λειτουργὸν τῆς χρείας μου
Phil 2:30	τὸ ὑμῶν ὑστέρημα τῆς πρός με λειτουργίας
Phil 3:8†	τὸ ὑπερέχον τῆς γνώσεως Χριστοῦ Ἰησοῦ
Phil 3:10	τὴν δύναμιν τῆς ἀναστάσεως αὐτοῦ
Phil 3:10	τὴν κοινωνίαν τῶν παθημάτων αὐτοῦ
Phil 3:14	τὸ βραβεῖον τῆς ἄνω κλήσεως τοῦ θεοῦ
Phil 3:18	τοὺς ἐχθροὺς τοῦ σταυροῦ τοῦ Χριστοῦ
Phil 3:21	τῷ σώματι τῆς δόξης αὐτοῦ
Phil 4:3†	τῶν λοιπῶν συνεργῶν μου

Colossians: 18

Col 1:3	πατρὶ τοῦ κυρίου ἡμῶν
Col 1:5	τῷ λόγῳ τῆς ἀληθείας τοῦ εὐαγγελίου
Col 1:9	τὴν ἐπίγνωσιν τοῦ θελήματος αὐτοῦ
Col 1:11	τὸ κράτος τῆς δόξης αὐτοῦ
Col 1:12	τὴν μερίδα τοῦ κλήρου τῶν ἁγίων
Col 1:18	ἡ κεφαλὴ τοῦ σώματος τῆς ἐκκλησίας
Col 1:20	τοῦ αἵματος τοῦ σταυροῦ αὐτοῦ
Col 1:22	τῷ σώματι τῆς σαρκὸς αὐτοῦ
Col 1:24	τὰ ὑστερήματα τῶν θλίψεων τοῦ Χριστοῦ

Col 1:27   τὸ πλοῦτος τῆς δόξης τοῦ μυστηρίου τούτου
Col 2:2   πᾶν πλοῦτος τῆς πληροφορίας τῆς συνέσεως
Col 2:2   ἐπίγνωσιν τοῦ μυστηρίου τοῦ θεοῦ
Col 2:5   τὸ στερέωμα τῆς εἰς Χριστὸν πίστεως ὑμῶν
Col 2:11   τῇ ἀπεκδύσει τοῦ σώματος τῆς σαρκός
Col 2:12   τῆς πίστεως τῆς ἐνεργείας τοῦ θεοῦ
Col 2:13   τῇ ἀκροβυστίᾳ τῆς σαρκὸς ὑμῶν
Col 2:18   τοῦ νοὸς τῆς σαρκὸς αὐτοῦ
Col 2:22   τὰ ἐντάλματα καὶ διδασκαλίας τῶν ἀνθρώπων

1 Thessalonians: 8†

1 Thess 1:3   ὑμῶν τοῦ ἔργου τῆς πίστεως
1 Thess 1:3†   [ὑμῶν] τοῦ κόπου τῆς ἀγάπης
1 Thess 2:13   λόγον ἀκοῆς ... τοῦ θεοῦ
1 Thess 2:19†   ἡμῶν ... στέφανος καυχήσεως
1 Thess 3:10   τὰ ὑστερήματα τῆς πίστεως ὑμῶν
1 Thess 3:13   τῇ παρουσίᾳ τοῦ κυρίου ἡμῶν
1 Thess 5:23   τῇ παρουσίᾳ τοῦ κυρίου ἡμῶν
1 Thess 5:28   ἡ χάρις τοῦ κυρίου ἡμῶν

2 Thessalonians: 11

2 Thess 1:5   ἔνδειγμα τῆς δικαίας κρίσεως τοῦ θεοῦ
2 Thess 1:7   ἀγγέλων δυνάμεως αὐτοῦ
2 Thess 1:8   τῷ εὐαγγελίῳ τοῦ κυρίου ἡμῶν
2 Thess 1:9   τῆς δόξης τῆς ἰσχύος αὐτοῦ
2 Thess 1:12   τὸ ὄνομα τοῦ κυρίου ἡμῶν
2 Thess 1:12   τὴν χάριν τοῦ θεοῦ ἡμῶν
2 Thess 2:1   τῆς παρουσίας τοῦ κυρίου ἡμῶν
2 Thess 2:8   τῷ πνεύματι τοῦ στόματος αὐτοῦ
2 Thess 2:8   τῇ ἐπιφανείᾳ τῆς παρουσίας αὐτοῦ
2 Thess 3:6   ἐν ὀνόματι τοῦ κυρίου ἡμῶν
2 Thess 3:18   ἡ χάρις τοῦ κυρίου ἡμῶν

1 Timothy: 6

1 Tim 1:11   τὸ εὐαγγέλιον τῆς δόξης τοῦ μακαρίου θεοῦ
1 Tim 1:14   ἡ χάρις τοῦ κυρίου ἡμῶν

1 Tim 4:14	ἐπιθέσεως τῶν χειρῶν τοῦ πρεσβυτερίου
1 Tim 5:18	ἄξιος … τοῦ μισθοῦ αὐτοῦ
1 Tim 6:3	λόγοις τοῖς τοῦ κυρίου ἡμῶν
1 Tim 6:14	τῆς ἐπιφανείας τοῦ κυρίου ἡμῶν

2 Timothy: 4

2 Tim 1:6	τῆς ἐπιθέσεως τῶν χειρῶν μου
2 Tim 1:8	τὸ μαρτύριον τοῦ κυρίου ἡμῶν
2 Tim 1:10	τῆς ἐπιφανείας τοῦ σωτῆρος ἡμῶν
2 Tim 4:6	ὁ καιρὸς τῆς ἀναλύσεώς μου

Titus: 6†

Titus 1:1	πίστιν ἐκλεκτῶν θεοῦ
Titus 1:3	ἐπιταγὴν τοῦ σωτῆρος ἡμῶν
Titus 2:10	τὴν διδασκαλίαν τὴν τοῦ σωτῆρος ἡμῶν
Titus 2:13†	**τὴν** μακαρίαν **ἐλπίδα καὶ ἐπιφάνειαν τῆς δόξης τοῦ** μεγάλου **θεοῦ** καὶ σωτῆρος ἡμῶν
Titus 3:4†	ἡ χρηστότης … τοῦ σωτῆρος ἡμῶν θεοῦ,
Titus 3:4	ἡ φιλανθρωπία … τοῦ σωτῆρος ἡμῶν

Philemon

Phlm 6	ἡ κοινωνία τῆς πίστεώς σου

Bibliography

Barth, Markus. *Ephesians.* 2 vols. Anchor Yale Bible 34–34A. New Haven: Yale University Press, 1974.

Boer, Martinus C. de. *Galatians: A Commentary.* New Testament Library. Louisville: Westminster John Knox, 2011.

Bruce, F. F. *1 and 2 Thessalonians.* Word Biblical Commentary 45. Dallas: Word, 1998.

Dunn, James D. G. *Romans 1–8.* Word Biblical Commentary 38A. Dallas: Word, 1988.

Fee, Gordon D. *God's Empowering Presence: The Holy Spirit in the Letters of Paul.* Peabody, MA: Hendrickson, 1994. Reprint, Grand Rapids: Baker, 2011.

Fitzmyer, Joseph A. *Romans: A New Translation with Introduction and Commentary.* Anchor Yale Bible 33. New York: Doubleday, 1993.

Frame, James Everett. *A Critical and Exegetical Commentary on the Epistles of St. Paul to the Thessalonians.* International Critical Commentary. New York: Scribner, 1912.

Lohse, Edward. *Colossians and Philemon.* Edited by Helmut Koester. Translated by William R. Poehlmann and Robert J. Karris. Hermeneia. Philadelphia: Fortress, 1971.

Melick, Richard R., Jr. *Philippians, Colossians, Philemon.* New American Commentary 32. Nashville: Broadman, 1991.

Wanamaker, Charles A. *The Epistles to the Thessalonians: A Commentary on the Greek Text.* New International Greek Testament Commentary. Grand Rapids: Eerdmans, 1990.

CHAPTER SIX

Adnominal Four-Word Genitive Constructions

In Chapter Five the three-word adnominal genitive was fully treated. In this chapter the investigation will concentrate on four-word genitive constructions. This kind of construction is rare in the New Testament. It occurs 29 times in the New Testament books altogether, 17 of them in the Pauline corpus. A list of these constructions appears at the end of the chapter.

Structural Elements

The four-word genitive is a construction consisting of four words (substantives): a headword and three genitives that are attached to each other successively. This kind of construction contains a diversity of substantival elements in its fabric. The following analysis will illustrate the matter:

Pure Nouns

Some of these four-word genitives are pure nouns like: τὴν ἐλευθερίαν τῆς δόξης τῶν τέκνων τοῦ θεοῦ *the freedom of the glory of the children of God* (Rom 8:21), συγκοινωνὸς τῆς ῥίζης τῆς πιότητος τῆς ἐλαίας *co-partakers of the root of fatness of the olive tree* (Rom 11:17), τὸν φωτισμὸν τοῦ εὐαγγελίου τῆς δόξης τοῦ Χριστοῦ *the enlightenment of the gospel of the glory of Christ* (2 Cor 4:4), φωτισμὸν τῆς γνώσεως τῆς δόξης τοῦ θεοῦ *the enlightenment of the knowledge of the glory of God* (2 Cor 4:6), and μέτρον ἡλικίας τοῦ πληρώματος τοῦ Χριστοῦ *the measure of the stature of the fullness of Christ* (Eph 4:13).

Pronoun Involved

Noun-Pronoun

In addition to nouns some of the four-word genitives appear with pronouns like: τοῖς ἴχνεσιν τῆς ἐν ἀκροβυστίᾳ πίστεως τοῦ πατρὸς ἡμῶν *the footsteps of the faith in uncircumcision of our father* (Rom 4:12); **ζηλωτὴς** ὑπάρχων **τῶν πατρικῶν μου παραδόσεων** *being a zealot for the traditions of my fathers* (Gal 1:14);[1] εἰς ἔπαινον δόξης τῆς χάριτος αὐτοῦ *to the praise of the glory of his grace* (Eph 1:6); ὁ πλοῦτος τῆς δόξης τῆς κληρονομίας αὐτοῦ *the wealth of the glory of his inheritance* (Eph 1:18); τὴν ἐνέργειαν τοῦ κράτους τῆς ἰσχύος αὐτοῦ *the operation of the strength of his power* (Eph 1:19); τὴν βασιλείαν τοῦ υἱοῦ τῆς ἀγάπης αὐτοῦ *the kingdom of the son of his love* (Col 1:13); and περιποίησιν δόξης τοῦ κυρίου ἡμῶν *the gaining of the glory of our Lord* (2 Thess 2:14).

Adjective-Noun-Pronoun

There is one four-word genitive with an adjective head word with a noun and pronoun in the construction: σύμμορφους τῆς εἰκόνος τοῦ υἱοῦ αὐτοῦ *conformed to the image of his son* (Rom 8:29).

Participle-Noun-Pronoun

One other construction has a participle in addition to noun and pronoun: τὸ ὑπερέχον τῆς γνώσεως Χριστοῦ Ἰησοῦ τοῦ κυρίου μου *the surpassing knowledge of Christ Jesus my Lord* (Phil 3:8).

Four-Word Genitives Connected by καί

There are three four-word genitives in the Pauline corpus connected by καί (Rom 2:5; Eph 4:13; Titus 2:13). These will be treated individually below.

---

1 This genitive cluster is considered four-word if the adjective πατρικῶν is used substantivally. The genitive pronoun μου may be a strengthening factor for this consideration: *traditions of my ancestors* or *fathers* (see NRSV REB NJB ESV NIV NET), rather than *my ancestral traditions*. The difference is subtle, but in this instance, important for classification.

Rom 2:5

There is some doubt about identifying ἐν ἡμέρᾳ ὀργῆς καὶ ἀποκαλύψεως δικαιοκρισίας τοῦ θεοῦ (Rom 2:5) as a four-word construction. It is possible to read καὶ ἀποκαλύψεως κτλ. as a genitive of apposition: *the day of wrath, even the revelation of the just judgments of God.* But if we take ἡμέρᾳ as a single head with two main dependent genitives ὀργῆς and ἀποκαλύψεως joined by καί, then the second construct can be seen as a complete example of the four-word genitive construction. It is also worth pointing out that ὀργῆς and ἀποκαλύψεως are both anarthrous, lending further support to the idea they are connected at an equal level. So, there is a simple two-word construction ἡμέρᾳ ὀργῆς, followed by the four-word construction with the head noun implied by καί: (1) [ἡμέρᾳ] (2) ἀποκαλύψεως (3) δικαιοκρισίας (4) τοῦ θεοῦ.

There is nothing in the context here that would contradict the conclusion. Almost all leading versions of the NT link "the day of wrath" with "the revelation of the righteous judgment" by translating the Greek phrase as "the day of wrath, when God's righteous judgment is/will be revealed" (NIV REB NRSV NET ESV CSB; cf. NJB).[2] TEV combines "wrath" and "revelation" with "the day" in an expressive way: "the Day when God's anger and righteous judgment will be revealed." Beekman and Callow declare "day" governs both genitives: "There are really two genitive constructions ... fused into a single complex expression."[3] This one complicated turn of phrase is surprising, since, as Jewett says, "The two concepts [wrath and God's righteous character] are ordinarily kept separate .... [Paul] balances it with a unique expression that lifts up the standard of divine righteousness by which sinners as well as the righteous are measured."[4]

Eph 4:13

Another four-word genitive construction with the head word connected by καί is τὴν ἑνότητα τῆς πίστεως καὶ τῆς ἐπιγνώσεως τοῦ υἱοῦ τοῦ θεοῦ *the unity of the faith and of the knowledge of the son of God* (Eph 4:13). The question rises whether the connections of τὴν ἑνότητα are confined to τῆς πίστεως or whether the link should extend to τῆς ἐπιγνώσεως. If τὴν ἑνότητα is connected with τῆς ἐπιγνώσεως, then we have a full four-word genitive τὴν ἑνότητα τῆς ἐπιγνώσεως τοῦ υἱοῦ τοῦ θεοῦ.

---

2   Joseph A. Fitzmyer offers the literal translation "(and on the day) of the revelation of God's just judgement" (*Romans: A New Translation with Introduction and Commentary*, AB 33 [New York: Doubleday, 1993], 301). See also Richard N. Longenecker, *The Epistle to the Romans*, NIGTC (Grand Rapids: Eerdmans, 2016), 250.

3   Beekman-Callow, 359.

4   Robert Jewett, with the assistance of Roy David Kotansky, *Romans: A Commentary*, ed. Eldon Jay Epp, Hermeneia (Minneapolis: Fortress, 2007), 203.

The majority of English NT versions take both "faith" and "knowledge" in connection with "unity." They have either "unity of the faith and of the knowledge" (RSV NASB NRSV ESV NET) or "unity in the faith and in the knowledge" (NIV CSB; NJB lacks "the"), or "unity of faith and knowledge" (NAB), or "unity inherent in our faith and in our knowledge of the Son of God" (REB). Other language versions follow suit: "à l'unité dans la foi et dans la connaissance du Fils de Dieu" (TOB), "zur Einheit des Glaubens und der Erkenntnis des Sohnes Gottes" (LUT). Commentators generally agree on this connection as well.[5]

Titus 2:13

The third and final four-word genitive in this category is a theologically significant passage: προσδεχόμενοι τὴν μακαρίαν ἐλπίδα καὶ ἐπιφάνειαν τῆς δόξης τοῦ μεγάλου θεοῦ καὶ σωτῆρος ἡμῶν Ἰησοῦ Χριστοῦ *waiting for the blessed hope and appearing of the glory of our great God and Savior Jesus Christ* (Titus 2:13). The syntactical issues surrounding τοῦ μεγάλου θεοῦ καὶ σωτῆρος are, of course, well known because of the Christological implications raised by Granville Sharp at the close of the eighteenth century.[6] If Sharp and later scholars who support the identification of "God" and "savior" (especially Wallace) are correct (i.e., *our great God and Savior*), then the construction will be classified as a four-word genitive. If, on the other hand, τοῦ μεγάλου θεοῦ refers only to God the Father ("of the great God and [separately, of] our Saviour" KJV), we would have a three-word genitive τὴν μακαρίαν ἐλπίδα καὶ ἐπιφάνειαν τῆς δόξης τοῦ μεγάλου θεοῦ, if counting the head as τὴν μακαρίαν ἐλπίδα καὶ ἐπιφάνειαν.

Titus 2:13 contains two instances of what Wallace calls the "TSKS construction,"[7] two (or more) substantives headed by one article and joined by καὶ: (1) τὴν

---

5 Thomas Kingsmill Abbott, *A Critical and Exegetical Commentary on the Epistles to the Ephesians and to the Colossians*, ICC 36 (New York: Scribner, 1903), 120; Ernest Best, *A Critical and Exegetical Commentary on Ephesians*, ICC (Edinburgh: T&T Clark, 1998), 400; R. C. H. Lenski, *The Interpretation of St Paul's Epistles to the Galatians, to the Ephesians, and to the Philippians* (Columbus, OH: Lutheran Book Concern, 1937; repr., Minneapolis, MN: Augsburg, 1961), 533; Robert G. Bratcher and Eugene Albert Nida, *A Handbook on Paul's Letter to the Ephesians*, UBSHS (New York: United Bible Societies, 1982), 103; Andrew T. Lincoln, *Ephesians*, WBC 42 (Dallas: Word, 1990), 255–56; Harold W. Hoehner, *Ephesians: An Exegetical Commentary* (Grand Rapids: Baker Academic, 2002), 553.

6 Granville Sharp, *Remarks on the Uses of the Definitive Article in the Greek Text of the New Testament, Containing Many New Proofs of the Divinity of Christ, from Passages Which Are Wrongly Translated in the Common English Version* (London: n.p., 1798).

7 Wallace, *ExSyn*, 270. For a monograph length treatment, see Wallace, *Sharp's Canon*. [bibliographic data can be found in the abbreviations list]

... ἐλπίδα καὶ ἐπιφάνειαν, and (2) τοῦ ... θεοῦ καὶ σωτῆρος. This purposely leaves out of the construction the simple appositive Ἰησοῦ Χριστοῦ, and does not count attributive adjectives. Both these constructions fit the *structural* criteria for the TSKS. The upshot of this is that the whole cluster should be considered a four-word adnominal genitive construction, even though only the second unit fits the *semantic* criteria to consider θεοῦ and σωτῆρος the same person. The construction counts, then thus as (1) τὴν ... ἐλπίδα καὶ ἐπιφάνειαν (2) τῆς δόξης (3) τοῦ ... θεοῦ καὶ σωτῆρος (4) ἡμῶν. We will explain how (1) and (3) relate in reverse order.

Regarding τοῦ ... θεοῦ καὶ σωτῆρος, Moule says that if the two descriptions "God" and "savior" are for two separate persons, that sense would be assured if "the article were repeated with σωτῆρος,"[8] making it more probable that one person is described. Robertson, says, "it is almost certain that one person is ... described."[9] Wallace has virtually settled the case in his exhaustive study of this kind of construction: "when both substantives are (1) singular (both grammatically and semantically), (2) personal, (3) and common nouns (not proper names or ordinals), they have the same referent. This rule as stated, covers *all* the so-called exceptions."[10] Exegetically, Knight brings, *inter alia*, other contextual arguments in favor of taking τοῦ μεγάλου θεοῦ καὶ σωτῆρος ἡμῶν as referring to one person: (1) ἐπιφάνεια in the New Testament always refers to Christ's appearing (cf. 2 Thess 2:8; 1 Tim 6:14; 2 Tim 1:10; 4:1; 4:8). (2) Christian hope revolves around Christ and his return. (3) The next verse, Titus 2:14, continues with "who gave himself on behalf of us," strongly implying one person rather than two.[11]

Having said that the genitive fits the criteria for reference to one person in the dependent genitive, we now turn to the head of the construction. We count the first of these as the head of the construction as a hendiadys, without claiming that ἐλπίδα and ἐπιφάνειαν are the same thing. The two nouns, semantically speaking, are impersonal, and thus fall outside of the semantic criteria for identification, obviously, as the same *person*. But the TSKS construction allows for, and almost requires, semantic overlap between the nouns,[12] and they can refer to the same

---

8   Moule, *Idiom Book*, 109.

9   Robertson, *Grammar*, 786.

10 Wallace, *Sharp's Canon*, 132. [emphasis original]; see also Wallace, *ExSyn*, 270, 272. For a discussion of Titus 2:13, see Wallace, *Sharp's Canon*, 255–64.

11 George W. Knight, *The Pastoral Epistles: A Commentary on the Greek Text*, NIGTC (Grand Rapids: Eerdmans, 1992), 23. Not everyone agrees that Sharp's rule is enough to show that "God" and "Savior" refer to Jesus. See J. Christopher Edwards, "The Christology of Titus 2:13 and 1 Timothy 2:5," *TynBul* 62.1 (2011): 141–47. See, however, the response from Murray J. Harris, "A Brief Response to: 'The Christology of Titus 2:13 and 1 Tim. 2:5' by J. Christopher Edwards," *TynBul* 62.1 (2011):149–50.

12 Of particular help here is Wallace, *Sharp's Canon*, 163–77.

event. Glory and hope are tied together in Paul (cf. Rom 5:2; Col 1:27), so that the hope is or consists of the appearing.[13] All of this makes it likely that the appearing is not described as glorious (a Hebrew genitive), but that the revelation will be an unveiling and public manifestation of the glorious character of Jesus Christ when he returns.

The OT Roots of Paul's Genitive Clusters

In addition to the four-word genitives noted, there two five-word genitive constructions in Rev 16:19; 19:15.[14] Outside Paul, genitive clusters of any length are rare; Paul uses genitives in clusters much more than any other New Testament writer.[15] Thus, the question arises as to what influence accounts for Paul's use of multiple genitive constructions.

According to Robertson the concatenation of genitives is "common in earlier Greek."[16] Winer points out a genitive cluster from Plato: μετοίκησις τῇ ψυχῇ τοῦ τόπου τοῦ ἐνθένδε *the migration of the soul away from this place* (*Apol.* 40c), calling it "a very harsh instance."[17] Even then, the repetition of the article after τόπου makes the adverb ἐνθένδε work like an attributive adjective. So, the example from Plato really does not qualify as an *adnominal* genitive cluster. On the other hand, Turner—without giving examples—says that several different genitives are joined together "more commonly, especially in Paul, but also in the papyri."[18]

The influence of the Greek literature on Paul's style is undeniable, since Paul is a Hellenized Jew. But there seems not to be much evidence that Greek literature had an influence on the genitive cluster phenomena we observe in Paul. On the other hand, for Paul, since his writings are about what Israel's God has done in Jesus Christ, it would stand to reason the Hebrew Bible and its translation into Greek are a closer influence than other Greek sources. Buttmann follows his NT genitive cluster examples—drawn mostly from Paul—with the opaque statement that the OT "also offers examples of the sort,"[19] regrettably without references.

---

13   Knight, *Pastoral Epistles*, 322.

14   Rev 16:19 τὸ ποτήριον τοῦ οἴνου τοῦ θυμοῦ τῆς ὀργῆς αὐτοῦ. Similar wording appears also in Rev 19:15: τὴν ληνὸν τοῦ οἴνου τοῦ θυμοῦ τῆς ὀργῆς τοῦ θεοῦ with an additional genitive in simple apposition: τοῦ παντοκράτορος.

15   "Paul in particular is fond of piling up genitives" (Robertson, *Grammar*, 503).

16   Robertson, *Grammar*, 503.

17   Winer, *Grammar*, 239.

18   MHT₃ 218.

19   Buttmann, *Grammar*, 155.

But following Buttmann's lead, we can look to the OT to find evidence of influence on Paul when it comes to genitives in concatenation. The translations of the examples below are *of the Hebrew text* taken from literal English Bible translations and the author's own translation. These passages demonstrate possible sources for multiple genitives, especially the four-word genitive construction. For the parallel to Greek usage, the pronominal suffixes count as words in the construction. The LXX text is given for comparison. Many of these examples the LXX renders literally, others more periphrastically.

- Gen 6:5 כל־יצר מחשבת לבו πᾶς τις διανοεῖται ἐν τῇ καρδίᾳ αὐτοῦ "every intention of the thoughts of his heart" (ESV)
- Gen 49:26 לקדקד נזיר אחיו ἐπὶ κορυφῆς ὧν ἡγήσατο ἀδελφῶν "on the brow of the prince among his brothers" (NIV)
- Job 12:24 לב ראשי עם־הארץ καρδίας ἀρχόντων γῆς *the heart of the heads of the people of the earth*
- Job 37:15 הופיע אור עננו φῶς ποιήσας ἐκ σκότους *the shining of the lightning of his cloud*
- Ps 18:15 מנשמת רוח אפך ἀπὸ ἐμπνεύσεως πνεύματος ὀργῆς σου "at the blast of the breath of thy nostrils" (KJV)
- Ps 20:6 בגברות ישע ימינו ἡ σωτηρία τῆς δεξιᾶς αὐτοῦ "with the saving strength of his right hand" (KJV)
- Ps 26:8 מקום משכן כבודך τόπον σκηνώματος δόξης σου *the place of the dwelling of your glory*
- Ps 79:10 נקמת דם־עבדיך ἡ ἐκδίκησις τοῦ αἵματος τῶν δούλων σου *the vengeance of the blood of your servants*
- Ps 135:2 בחצרות בית אלהינו ἐν αὐλαῖς οἴκου θεοῦ ἡμῶν "in the courts of the house of our God" (NRSV)
- Isa 10:12 על־פרי־גדל לבב מלך־אשור ἐπὶ τὸν νοῦν τὸν μέγαν, τὸν ἄρχοντα τῶν Ἀσσυρίων "on the fruit of the great heart of the king of Assyria" [five-word construction in Hebrew text]
- Isa 10:12 ועל־תפארת רום עיניו καὶ ἐπὶ τὸ ὕψος τῆς δόξης τῶν ὀφθαλμῶν αὐτοῦ "and the glory of his high looks" (KJV)
- Isa 13:13 בעברת יהוה צבאות וביום חרון אפו διὰ θυμὸν ὀργῆς κυρίου σαβαωθ τῇ ἡμέρᾳ, ᾗ ἂν ἐπέλθῃ ὁ θυμὸς αὐτοῦ *on account of the Lord Sabaoth and on the day of the burning of his anger*
- Isa 28:3 עטרת גאות שכורי אפרים ὁ στέφανος τῆς ὕβρεως, οἱ μισθωτοὶ τοῦ Ἐφραίμ "the crown of pride of the drunkards of Ephraim" (KJV)
- Isa 50:1 ספר כריתות אמכם τὸ βιβλίον τοῦ ἀποστασίου τῆς μητρὸς ὑμῶν "the bill of your mother's divorcement" (KJV)

- Isa 51:22 קבעת כוס חמתי τὸ κόνδυ τοῦ θυμοῦ *the bowl of the cup of my wrath*
- Jer 3:19 נחלת צבי צבאות גוים κληρονομίαν θεοῦ παντοκράτορος ἐθνῶν *inheritance of the beauty of the hosts of the nations*
- Jer 8:11 את־שבר בת־עמי [no LXX translation] "the hurt of the daughter of my people" (KJV)
- Ezek 24:27 בשברי את־מטות עלם ἐν τῷ συντρῖψαί με τὸν ζυγὸν αὐτῶν *by my breaking of the bars of their yoke*

Usually when the four-word construct chain of the Hebrew text is easy to grasp, the LXX is often literal and clear. Ambiguities usually lead the LXX translator(s) to disconnect the construction and translate more freely. In other instances, the translator adds a genitive or two from the context, often constructing four- or five-word genitives as in the second example from Isa 10:12. At other times, like the first example from Isa 10:12 above a five-word genitive construction in Hebrew is translated by only two words in LXX. Compare the Hebrew text with LXX in Jer 3:19 is rendered rather literally. Job 37:15, on the other hand is transformed without any adnominal genitives. The LXX has rendered Gen 49:26 more freely. Isa 13:13 appears in the LXX with its own genitive chain somewhat displaced from that of the Hebrew text. In Isa 28:3 the problem is simply confusion of letters. It would appear the LXX translator, in an ironic fit of Ephraimite pronunciation (Jud 12:6), has probably read *śin* for *šin*, שָׂכִיר (*laborer*)[20] for MT's שֹׁכְרֵי (*drunkards*)[21] to arrive at its rendering οἱ μισθωτοί *wage earners*.

In addition to the examples given above, there are two purely Greek examples to note from the LXX:

- Job 3:10 πύλας γαστρὸς μητρός μου *the gates of my mother's womb*
- Is 30:23 ὁ ἄρτος τοῦ γενήματος τῆς γῆς σου *the bread of the produce of your land.*

Genitive clusters can also be found in the Apocrypha of the LXX. In some cases, we have only Greek texts, though the original language of some of these works is still debated. The examples Winer cites from Judith are helpful:[22]

- Jdt 9:8 τὸ σκήνωμα τῆς καταπαύσεως τοῦ ὀνόματος τῆς δόξης σου "the covert of the resting place of the name of your glory" (NETS) [five-word]
- Jdt 10:3 ἐν ταῖς ἡμέραις τῆς ζωῆς τοῦ ἀνδρὸς αὐτῆς "in the days of the life of her husband" (NETS) [four-word]

20 *HALOT* 1327 s.v.
21 *HALOT* 1429 s.v.
22 Winer, *Grammar*, 238.

- Jdt 13:18 εἰς τραῦμα κεφαλῆς ἄρχοντος ἐχθρῶν ἡμῶν "for a wound to the head of our enemies' commander" (NETS) [five-word].

The Hebrew OT contains not only clusters of four-word genitive constructions, but also clusters of five- and six-word genitive constructions. The following examples (in addition to Isa 10:12 cited above) are five-word genitives:

- Is 28:1 עַל־רֹאשׁ גֵּיא־שְׁמָנִים הֲלוּמֵי יָיִן ἐπὶ τῆς κορυφῆς τοῦ ὄρους τοῦ παχέος, οἱ μεθύοντες ἄνευ οἴνου "on the head of the fat valley of them that are overcome with wine" (ASV)
- Jer 8:19 הִנֵּה־קוֹל שַׁוְעַת בַּת־עַמִּי ἰδοὺ φωνὴ κραυγῆς θυγατρὸς λαοῦ μου "Behold, the voice of the cry of the daughter of my people" (ASV)

In this last example the Septuagint translates the five-word construction of the Hebrew text with a five-word construction in Greek.

There is at least one six-word genitive construction, probably a unique Biblical expression. It is a rare concatenate and a long substantival sentence, yet very clear:

- Isa 21:17 וּשְׁאָר מִסְפַּר־קֶשֶׁת גִּבּוֹרֵי בְנֵי־קֵדָר καὶ τὸ κατάλοιπον τῶν τοξευμάτων τῶν ἰσχυρῶν υἱῶν Κηδαρ *and the rest of the number of bows of the warriors of the children of Kedar*

The LXX translator reduced the six-word genitive to a five-word genitive.

Meanings of the Four-Word Genitive

The four-word genitive, as a construction, can be divided into smaller constructional units. A four-word construction usually contains three two-word and two three-word units. These units correlate and interrelate with each other by virtue of being parts of the same construction. In a four-word construction like τὴν ἐλευθερίαν τῆς δόξης τῶν τέκνων τοῦ θεοῦ *the freedom of the glory of the sons of God* (Rom 8:21), the first two words τὴν ἐλευθερίαν τῆς δόξης are related by virtue of order, likewise the second and third τῆς δόξης τῶν τέκνων, and the third and fourth τῶν τέκνων τοῦ θεοῦ; but some of these two-word units are interrelated by virtue of syntax. For example, τῆς δόξης syntactically can be related either to τὴν ἐλευθερίαν or to τῶν τέκνων. Since we have already explored some of the more regular features of genitive concatenations, the following section focuses on some syntactical peculiarities of the four-word genitive construction.

Cumulative Genitive

The four-word genitive construction makes it easy for the writer to use synonymous words in the same construction cumulatively. The following examples illustrate the conjunctional usage of successive genitives.

A good illustration of the cumulative genitive occurs in εἰς τὴν ἐλευθερίαν τῆς δόξης τῶν τέκνων τοῦ θεοῦ (Rom 8:21), "the freedom of the glory of the children of God" (ESV). Whereas NIV84 CSB NET have taken the second word in the construction τῆς δόξης adjectivally to describe the head word, "the glorious freedom," NIV has made both words a cumulative genitive by rendering them successively "the freedom and glory of the children of God."

Another example of the cumulative genitive occurs in Rom 11:17, συγκοινωνὸς τῆς ῥίζης τῆς πιότητος τῆς ἐλαίας, "partaker ... of the root of the fatness of the olive tree" (ASV), which also contains a textual variation. τῆς ῥίζης, which stood likely in the Alexandrian archetype (ℵ* B C 1175. 1506), is missing from 𝔓⁴⁶ and the Western archetype (D F G). A host of secondary witnesses and the Byzantine majority, while retaining τῆς ῥίζης, add καί, presumably because the chain of genitives is rather ponderous.[23] Some versions (NIV NJB NAB CSB ESV) and commentators, such as Barrett, and Murray, see τῆς πιότητος *fatness* as an adjectival genitive describing τῆς ῥίζης, as "rich," or "nourishing."[24] Some other versions ("to share the same root and sap as the olive" NEB REB) prefer to accumulate the two genitives τῆς ῥίζης τῆς πιότητος using *and* which, like the Byzantine reading, gives the four-word construction a clearer meaning in English. Whether these versions follow the Byzantine reading in this instance, or whether they are just clarifying the English meaning is unclear. Jewett classifies the genitive as appositive " 'the root of the olive with its fatness," which "seems more consistent with Paul's stress on the extraordinary privileges of wealth, holiness, and nourishment."[25]

There is a disputed example in Eph 1:6 εἰς ἔπαινον δόξης τῆς χάριτος αὐτοῦ. While many versions render this phrase "the praise of the glory of His grace" (KJV NASB NJB NRSV ESV NET), implying an objective genitive, other versions take δόξης as an adjectival genitive describing grace "to the praise of his glorious grace" (NRSV NIV; cf. NAB TEV). F. F. Bruce, however sees δόξης qualifying ἔπαινον

---

23 Bruce M. Metzger notes that the "introduction of καί and the omission of τῆς ῥίζης ... are suspicious as ameliorating emendations" (*A Textual Commentary on the Greek New Testament*, 2nd ed. [Stuttgart: Deutsche Bibelgesellschaft, 1994], 464).

24 C. K. Barrett, *The Epistle to the Romans*, 2nd ed., BNTC (London: Hendrickson, 1991), 196n1, 201; John Murray, *The Epistle to the Romans*, 2 vols., NICNT (Grand Rapids: Eerdmans, 1968), 2:86n34.

25 Jewett, *Romans*, 685.

as a "Hebraic qualifying genitive," thus translating it "to the glorious praise of His grace."[26] But Bruce's interpretation is unlikely. This particular turn of phrase cannot be found elsewhere in the undisputed letters of Paul, but a similar phrase occurs in Phil 1:11 εἰς δόξαν καὶ ἔπαινον θεοῦ,[27] "to the glory and praise of God" (ESV). Turner says that ἔπαινον and δόξης are "to be taken very closely together."[28] It is more natural to accumulate "praise *and* glory" and take both ἔπαινον and δόξης as verbal nouns governing τῆς χάριτος αὐτοῦ "praising and glorifying His grace."

In the four-word phrase ὁ πλοῦτος τῆς δόξης τῆς κληρονομίας αὐτοῦ *the wealth of the glory of his inheritance* (Eph 1:18), "wealth" and "glory" may be considered as two adjectival phrases describing "his inheritance." Instead of a literal rendering, REB describes the inheritance as "rich and glorious," accumulating ὁ πλοῦτος τῆς δόξης with *and*. In Rom 8:21 τὴν ἐλευθερίαν τῆς δόξης τῶν τέκνων τοῦ θεοῦ, the NEB follows a similar procedure: "the liberty and splendour of the children of God."

Epexegetical Genitive

The concatenate nature of the four-word genitive makes words that occur in appositive succession possible. The apposition treated here is not merely simple apposition but the epexegetical genitive, providing additional explanation. This is one rationale we used to classify the appositive genitive is under the genitive of definition.[29] The appositive genitive is not frequent in four-word genitive constructions in Paul, but there are three instances worth comment and consideration for this label.

Though we have already mentioned Rom 11:17 under the cumulative genitive (above), συγκοινωνὸς τῆς ῥίζης τῆς πιότητος τῆς ἐλαίας (Rom 11:17) might involve an epexegetical genitive. Fitzmyer offers an interpretive translation alongside a literal one: "*and have come to share in the rich sap of the olive root.* Lit., 'have become sharer of the root, of the richness of the olive tree.'"[30] Fitzmyer here puts τῆς πιότητος in apposition to τῆς ῥίζης. He identifies the two words "root" and "sap" as having one intention, or that the second gives an additional explanation of its function. This is in line, Fitzmyer says, with what Paul affirms about Abraham and his descendants sharing the same root of faith (cf. Gal 3:29).[31] The NIV has "share the nourishing sap from the olive root." Cranfield brings out his preference for the appositive

---

26 F. F. Bruce, *The Epistles to the Colossians, to Philemon, and to the Ephesians*, NICNT (Grand Rapids: Eerdmans, 1984), 258n46. Citing Col 1:11, 27 as parallels.

27 Lincoln, *Ephesians*, 26.

28 MHT₃ 218.

29 See *Appositive Genitive* under *Genitive of Definition* in Chapter Four.

30 Fitzmyer, *Romans*, 615. [emphasis original]

31 Fitzmyer, *Romans*, 610.

sense with his translation, "in the root, that is to say, in the fatness (of the root)."[32] A final decision on the categorization of this genitive cluster is difficult.

Another example is εἰς μέτρον ἡλικίας τοῦ πληρώματος τοῦ Χριστοῦ (Eph 4:13), "to the measure of the stature of the fullness of Christ" (ESV). Both μέτρον and ἡλικίας are anarthrous, the main head term being the object of the preposition εἰς and probably definite.[33] Since μέτρον and ἡλικίας are synonymous terms,[34] it is more probable that ἡλικίας is an appositional term to μέτρον. The next pair of genitive terms, then, are even further explanation: "to the measure, namely, the maturity of the fullness of Christ"[35] (cf. TEV NET CSB).

One more example is φωτισμὸν τῆς γνώσεως τῆς δόξης τοῦ θεοῦ (2 Cor 4:6), "the light of the knowledge of the glory of God" (ESV). In this phrase the genitive τῆς γνώσεως may be considered instrumental "to enlighten them with the knowledge of God's glory" (NJB), or objective genitive, looking to a causative sense of ἔλαμψεν,[36] "to bring to light the knowledge," or genitive of source "*the enlightenment coming from the knowledge.*"[37] But C. K. Barrett has another viewpoint, taking the genitive as appositive "illumination that consists in the knowledge,"[38] and the REB shares in this view: "the light which is knowledge of the glory of God."

Adjectival Genitive

The adjectival genitive is a common feature in the four-word genitive constructions in the Pauline corpus. It resembles the way it is used in the three-word genitive construction, both being concatenate constructions. As the adjectival genitive in the three-word construction appears at the middle of the construction,[39] the adjectival genitive in the four-word construction follows the same pattern.

In the following four-word examples, the adjectival genitive describes the word that precedes it. Notice that in εἰς τὴν ἐλευθερίαν τῆς δόξης τῶν τέκνων τοῦ θεοῦ (Rom 8:21), the adjectival τῆς δόξης describes τὴν ἐλευθερίαν. Thus, instead of "the

---

32   C. E. B. Cranfield, *A Critical and Exegetical Commentary on the Epistle to the Romans*, 6th ed., 2 vols., ICC (Edinburgh: T&T Clark, 1975–79), 2:567. See also James D. G. Dunn, *Romans 9–16*, WBC 38B (Dallas: Word, 1988), 661.

33   See, for instance, Wallace, *ExSyn*, 115n117, 247.

34   LN §81.1 and §81.4 respectively.

35   Hoehner, *Ephesians*, 557.

36   Ralph P. Martin, *2 Corinthians*, WBC 40 (Dallas: Word, 1986), 80.

37   Victor Paul Furnish, *II Corinthians*, AB 32A (Garden City, N.Y.: Doubleday, 1984; repr., New Haven: Yale University Press, 2008), 224.

38   C. K. Barrett, *The Second Epistle to the Corinthians*, BNTC (London: Continuum, 1973), 134.

39   See under the heading *Adjectival Genitive* in Chapter Five.

freedom of the glory of the children of God" (ESV) it is better to translate "the glorious freedom of the children of God/of God's children" (NIV84 TEV REB NJB NET CSB).

Likewise, in the following examples a literal translation of each genitive structure appears after the Greek text, followed by a more dynamic translation bringing out the adjectival sense [emphasis added in all examples]:

- φωτισμὸν τῆς γνώσεως τῆς δόξης τοῦ θεοῦ (2 Cor 4:6). "the light of the knowledge of the glory of God" (ESV). "the light of *the glorious* knowledge of God" (NET)
- τὴν ἐνέργειαν τοῦ κράτους τῆς ἰσχύος αὐτοῦ (Eph 1:19). "the working of the strength of His might" (NASB). "his *great* power/might" (NRSV ESV), "his *immense* strength" (NET)
- μέτρον ἡλικίας τοῦ πληρώματος τοῦ Χριστοῦ (Eph 4:13) "the measure of the stature of the fullness of Christ" (ESV) "the measure of Christ's *full* stature" (NET)
- τὴν βασιλείαν τοῦ υἱοῦ τῆς ἀγάπης αὐτοῦ (Col 1:13). *the kingdom of the son of his love* (literal trans.) "the kingdom of his *dear/beloved* Son" (TEV NRSV ESV).

Some Enigmatic Four-Word Adjectival Constructions

Some four-word genitives present significant challenges for interpretation. In 2 Cor 4:4, 6 there are two four-word genitives as such. The following treatment of these two constructions is an attempt to solve these problematic genitives.

The first of our examples is τὸν φωτισμὸν τοῦ εὐαγγελίου τῆς δόξης τοῦ Χριστοῦ (2 Cor 4:4). The diversity of renderings among Bible versions is testimony to the enigma. Several versions avoid the problem by translating the phrase literally, "the light of the gospel of the glory of Christ" (NRSV NJB NIV84 NASB ESV CSB), with which C. K. Barrett, P. Barnett, and R. P. Martin agree.[40] Other versions try to explain the syntax and relation among the units of the genitive cluster; some consider τοῦ εὐαγγελίου a genitive of source, the source of light. For example, TEV has "the light that comes from the Good News about the glory of Christ." REB somewhat more periphrastically renders "the gospel of the glory of Christ … cannot dawn upon them and bring them light."

On the other hand, KJV NET have "the light of the glorious gospel of Christ." It is a highly probable translation for this phrase, harmonizing very well with the

---

40 Barrett, *2 Corinthians*, 131–32; Paul Barnett, *The Second Epistle to the Corinthians*, NICNT (Grand Rapids: Eerdmans, 1997), 218–20; Martin, *2 Corinthians*, 79.

majority of the three-word genitive uses of the Hebrew adjectival genitives.[41] Relating τῆς δόξης with τοῦ εὐαγγελίου syntactically is more appropriate than any other solution. Furnish says: "it is not impossible that this genitive phrase [i.e. of Christ] should be taken more closely with *the gospel* than with what immediately precedes. In such a case, *of the splendor* and *of Christ* would be parallel descriptions of *the gospel*."[42]

There is a structurally similar expression in τὸ εὐαγγέλιον τῆς δόξης τοῦ μακαρίου θεοῦ *the gospel of the glory of the blessed God* (1 Tim 1:11). Here also τῆς δόξης is related to τὸ εὐαγγέλιον more than to τοῦ μακαρίου θεοῦ. Almost all major English versions that render the phrase dynamically translate "glorious gospel." Only TEV NIV (*contra* NIV84) relate "glory" to "God."

The second of our challenging four-word examples occurs in the same context: φωτισμὸν τῆς γνώσεως τῆς δόξης τοῦ θεοῦ (2 Cor 4:6), "the light of the knowledge of the glory of God" (ESV). In this instance, almost all versions and commentaries avoid relating τῆς δόξης to τῆς γνώσεως. They prefer to relate τῆς δόξης to τοῦ θεοῦ. But following the same syntactic analysis of 2 Cor 4:4, it is quite possible to take τῆς δόξης as adjectival genitive describing τῆς γνώσεως "the light of the glorious knowledge of God" (NET). This translation is in harmony with the nature of the "Hebrew" adjectival genitive as expressed in the three-word genitive constructions.[43] Describing the knowledge of God as glorious does not eliminate the meaning of Paul's conclusion here. The knowledge of God is glorious because God is known through the face of Jesus Christ. Describing the knowledge as glorious, then, would emphasize the value of such knowledge that a believer recognizes, in contrast to those blinded by "the god of this age" who are unable to appreciate the treasure Christians carry through suffering into the world.

Six-Word and Five-Word Genitive Construction

One construction—depending on one's analysis of the syntax—actually forms a six-word group in the Pauline corpus. Having no other place to categorize it, we will note it here: μεστοὺς φθόνου φόνου ἔριδος δόλου κακοηθείας (Rom 1:29). If the head word μεστοὺς (parallel to the participle πεπληρωμένους) is a taken as a substantival adjective, then the following set of five genitives, describing depraved humanity as full of "envy, murder, strife, deceit, hostility" (NET) can be taken as a six-word adnominal genitive. The head word is distributed to each of the dependent genitives. Since each is related to the head, and not to any of the others,

---

41 See under the heading *Adjectival Middle-Word* in Chapter Five.

42 Furnish, *II Corinthians*, 222.

43 See under the heading *Adjectival Middle-Word* in Chapter Five.

structurally it becomes an interesting point of trivia; it does not fit the genitive cluster formation we have been describing in Chapters Five to Six. Jewett points out that the asyndetic arrangement is for rhetorical effect: "the vices have completely crowded out any virtues."[44]

There is only one five-word genitive construction, found in the longest chain of genitives in the Pauline corpus:[45] μνημονεύοντες ὑμῶν τοῦ ἔργου τῆς πίστεως καὶ τοῦ κόπου τῆς ἀγάπης καὶ τῆς ὑπομονῆς τῆς ἐλπίδος τοῦ κυρίου ἡμῶν (1 Thess 1:3). The analysis is daunting. First of all, there are three nouns acting as genitive objects of the participle μνημονεύοντες *remembering* which frequently takes a genitive object:[46] τοῦ ἔργου, τοῦ κόπου, and τῆς ὑπομονῆς. The third of these, as we have noted, is actually the head of a *four-word* genitive construction. The last object of μνημονεύοντες, τῆς ὑπομονῆς, has the pronoun ἡμῶν at the end of its construction, so we will not count it as part of the five-word construction established here.

So, this five-word construction resolves thus: (1) ὑμῶν (2) τοῦ ἔργου (3) τῆς πίστεως, and—because of καὶ—(4) τοῦ κόπου (5) τῆς ἀγάπης. The leading position of the pronoun ὑμῶν with the conjunction καὶ distributes the pronoun, making it modify both (4) τοῦ κόπου and (5) τῆς ἀγάπης. This is likely because the actions implied by (2) τοῦ ἔργου and (4) τοῦ κόπου can be ascribed to the letter's recipients. The same could be said of τῆς ὑπομονῆς. Thus, the distribution of ὑμῶν likely also extends to the complete four-word construction τῆς ὑπομονῆς τῆς ἐλπίδος τοῦ κυρίου ἡμῶν. James Everett Frame says, "The most favoured solution is that which joins ὑμῶν with ἔργου, κόπου, ὑπομονῆς, and which explains τῆς πίστεως, τῆς ἀγάπης, and τῆς ἐλπίδος as subjective genitives, and τοῦ κυρίου as an objective genitive qualifying ἐλπίδος."[47] The structural parallelism of the constructions lends weight to the semantic parallelism; Frame's analysis is correct.

List of Four-, Five-, and Six-Word Genitives

The following lists lay out the remaining adnominal genitives in the main text of NA[28]. Instances marked with a dagger (†) could be disputed on the grounds of

---

44 Jewett, *Romans*, 185.

45 Lenski comments on the concatenation of genitives. He says: "The striking feature is this series of ten genitives with not a single other word breaking the line. Even the last phrase adds more genitives" (*The Interpretation of St. Paul's Epistles to the Colossians, to the Thessalonians, to Timothy, to Titus and to Philemon* [Minneapolis: Augsburg, 1937], 221).

46 BDAG 655 s.v. μνημονεύω 1a.

47 James Everett Frame, *A Critical and Exegetical Commentary on the Epistles of St. Paul to the Thessalonians*, ICC (New York: Scribner, 1912), 76.

differing syntactical analysis, but have been included in the list for completeness. It is important to note that simple appositives are excluded from the count of terms in the construction—as are personal names—on the grounds they are simple appositives (e.g., Phil 3:8). When it is more probable that τοῦ Χριστοῦ is a title rather than a proper name in collocation with Ἰησοῦ, it is included in the count of main terms in the construction.

List of Four-Word Genitives in Paul

Rom 2:5	ἐν ἡμέρᾳ ὀργῆς καὶ ἀποκαλύψεως δικαιοκρισίας τοῦ θεοῦ
Rom 4:12	τοῖς ἴχνεσιν τῆς ἐν ἀκροβυστίᾳ πίστεως τοῦ πατρὸς ἡμῶν
Rom 8:21	τὴν ἐλευθερίαν τῆς δόξης τῶν τέκνων τοῦ θεοῦ
Rom 8:29	συμμόρφους τῆς εἰκόνος τοῦ υἱοῦ αὐτοῦ
Rom 11:17	συγκοινωνὸς τῆς ῥίζης τῆς πιότητος τῆς ἐλαίας
2 Cor 4:4	τὸν φωτισμὸν τοῦ εὐαγγελίου τῆς δόξης τοῦ Χριστοῦ
2 Cor 4:6	φωτισμὸν τῆς γνώσεως τῆς δόξης τοῦ θεοῦ
Gal 1:14†	**ζηλωτὴς** ὑπάρχων **τῶν πατρικῶν μου παραδόσεων** [taking πατρικῶν as a substantival adjective]
Eph 1:6	ἔπαινον δόξης τῆς χάριτος αὐτοῦ
Eph 1:18	ὁ πλοῦτος τῆς δόξης τῆς κληρονομίας αὐτοῦ
Eph 1:19	τὴν ἐνέργειαν τοῦ κράτους τῆς ἰσχύος αὐτοῦ
Eph 4:13	τὴν ἑνότητα τῆς πίστεως καὶ τῆς ἐπιγνώσεως τοῦ υἱοῦ τοῦ θεοῦ [2 constructions]
Eph 4:13	μέτρον ἡλικίας τοῦ πληρώματος τοῦ Χριστοῦ
Phil 3:8†	**τὸ ὑπερέχον τῆς γνώσεως** Χριστοῦ Ἰησοῦ **τοῦ κυρίου μου**
Phil 3:21	σύμμορφον τῷ σώματι τῆς δόξης αὐτοῦ
Col 1:13	τὴν βασιλείαν τοῦ υἱοῦ τῆς ἀγάπης αὐτοῦ
2 Thess 2:14	περιποίησιν δόξης τοῦ κυρίου ἡμῶν
Titus 2:13	τὴν μακαρίαν ἐλπίδα καὶ ἐπιφάνειαν τῆς δόξης τοῦ μεγάλου θεοῦ καὶ σωτῆρος ἡμῶν

List of Four-Word Genitives in the NT

Matt 1:1†	Βίβλος γενέσεως ... υἱοῦ Δαυὶδ
Mark 1:1	Ἀρχὴ τοῦ εὐαγγελίου ... υἱοῦ θεοῦ.
Luke 1:78	σπλάγχνα ἐλέους θεοῦ ἡμῶν
Acts 4:25†	πνεύματος ἁγίου στόματος ... παιδός σου
Acts 23:9	τινὲς τῶν γραμματέων τοῦ μέρους τῶν Φαρισαίων
Heb 5:12	τὰ στοιχεῖα τῆς ἀρχῆς τῶν λογίων τοῦ θεοῦ

Jas 2:1	τὴν πίστιν τοῦ κυρίου ἡμῶν ... τῆς δόξης.
Rev 3:12	τὸ ὄνομα τῆς πόλεως τοῦ θεοῦ μου
Rev 11:15	ἡ βασιλεία τοῦ κόσμου τοῦ κυρίου ἡμῶν καὶ τοῦ χριστοῦ αὐτοῦ
Rev 14:8	τοῦ οἴνου τοῦ θυμοῦ τῆς πορνείας αὐτῆς
Rev 18:3	τοῦ οἴνου τοῦ θυμοῦ τῆς πορνείας αὐτῆς
Rev 18:14	ἡ ὀπώρα σου τῆς ἐπιθυμίας τῆς ψυχῆς
Rev 21:12	τὰ ὀνόματα τῶν δώδεκα φυλῶν υἱῶν Ἰσραήλ

Bibliography

Abbott, Thomas Kingsmill. *A Critical and Exegetical Commentary on the Epistles to the Ephesians and to the Colossians.* International Critical Commentary 36. New York: Scribner, 1903.

Barnett, Paul. *The Second Epistle to the Corinthians.* New International Commentary on the New Testament. Grand Rapids: Eerdmans, 1997.

Barrett, C. K. *The Second Epistle to the Corinthians.* Black's New Testament Commentaries. London: Continuum, 1973.

Barrett, Charles Kingsley. *The Epistle to the Romans.* 2nd ed. Black's New Testament Commentaries. London: Hendrickson, 1991.

Best, Ernest. *A Critical and Exegetical Commentary on Ephesians.* International Critical Commentary. Edinburgh: T&T Clark, 1998.

Bratcher, Robert G. and Eugene Albert Nida. *A Handbook on Paul's Letter to the Ephesians.* UBS Handbook Series. New York: United Bible Societies, 1982.

Bruce, F. F. *The Epistles to the Colossians, to Philemon, and to the Ephesians.* New International Commentary on the New Testament. Grand Rapids: Eerdmans, 1984.

Cranfield, C. E. B. *A Critical and Exegetical Commentary on the Epistle to the Romans.* 2 vols. 6th ed. International Critical Commentary. Edinburgh: T&T Clark, 1975–79.

Dunn, James D. G. *Romans 9–16.* Word Biblical Commentary 38B. Dallas: Word, 1988.

Edwards, J. Christopher. "The Christology of Titus 2:13 and 1 Timothy 2:5," *Tyndale Bulletin* 62.1 (2011): 141–47.

Fitzmyer, Joseph A. *Romans: A New Translation with Introduction and Commentary.* Anchor Yale Bible 33. New York: Doubleday, 1993.

Frame, James Everett. *A Critical and Exegetical Commentary on the Epistles of St. Paul to the Thessalonians.* International Critical Commentary. New York: Scribner, 1912.

Furnish, Victor Paul. *II Corinthians.* Anchor Bible 32A. Garden City, NY: Doubleday, 1984. Reprint, New Haven: Yale University Press, 2008.

Harris, Murray J. "A Brief Response to: 'The Christology of Titus 2:13 and 1 Tim. 2:5' by J. Christopher Edwards," *Tyndale Bulletin* 62.1 (2011): 149–50.

Hoehner, Harold W. *Ephesians: An Exegetical Commentary.* Grand Rapids: Baker Academic, 2002.

Jewett, Robert, with the assistance of Roy David Kotansky. *Romans: A Commentary.* Edited by Eldon Jay Epp. Hermeneia. Minneapolis: Fortress, 2007.

Knight, George W. *The Pastoral Epistles: A Commentary on the Greek Text.* New International Greek Testament Commentary. Grand Rapids: Eerdmans, 1992.

Lenski, R. C. H. *The Interpretation of St Paul's Epistles to the Galatians, to the Ephesians, and to the Philippians.* Columbus, OH: Lutheran Book Concern, 1937. Reprint, Minneapolis, MN: Augsburg, 1961.

Lenski, Richard C. H. *The Interpretation of St. Paul's Epistles to the Colossians, to the Thessalonians, to Timothy, to Titus and to Philemon.* Minneapolis: Augsburg, 1937.

Lincoln, Andrew T. *Ephesians.* Word Biblical Commentary 42. Dallas: Word, 1990.

Longenecker, Richard N. *The Epistle to the Romans.* New International Greek Testament Commentary. Grand Rapids: Eerdmans, 2016.

Martin, Ralph P. *2 Corinthians.* Word Biblical Commentary 40. Dallas: Word, 1986.

Metzger, Bruce M. *A Textual Commentary on the Greek New Testament.* 2nd ed. Stuttgart: Deutsche Bibelgesellschaft, 1994.

Murray, John. *The Epistle to the Romans.* 2 vols. New International Commentary on the New Testament. Grand Rapids: Eerdmans, 1968.

Sharp, Granville. *Remarks on the Uses of the Definitive Article in the Greek Text of the New Testament, Containing Many New Proofs of the Divinity of Christ, from Passages Which Are Wrongly Translated in the Common English Version.* London: n.p., 1798.

CHAPTER SEVEN

Interpretive Principles

In Chapter Two we investigated the main NT grammars for uses of the genitive case in the Pauline corpus. In Chapter Three the results and conclusions of the semantic era have been analyzed, showing that semantics as a discipline has greatly influenced how scholars encounter the syntax of the genitive case. In Chapter Four the two-word genitive constructions have been surveyed. Each of the meanings deduced for the two-word genitive constructions in Paul's letters are classified under five main title headings: (1) genitive of definition, (2) adjectival genitive, (3) objective genitive, (4) subjective genitive, and (5) ablatival genitive. The three-word genitive constructions in Chapter Five and the four-word genitive constructions in Chapter Six have been given due consideration and have been analyzed syntactically. The stage is now prepared for drawing some conclusions as to how Paul's adnominal genitive constructions should be analyzed.

Syntactical Aspects of the Genitive

The Article

The surface structure of adnominal genitive constructions is concerned at first with the presence or absence of the article. When present, the article governs the meaning of the genitive and the stress is on "identity,"[1] but if the genitive is anarthrous the meaning in certain cases may become descriptive or adjectival.[2] Turner remarks that the "omission of the article tends to emphasize the inherent qualities of abstract nouns while the article makes them more concrete, unified and individual."[3]

Sometimes Paul uses the article twice, as in ὁ λόγος ὁ τοῦ σταυροῦ (1 Cor 1:18), and τὴν διδασκαλίαν τὴν τοῦ σωτῆρος ἡμῶν θεοῦ (Titus 2:10). The repetition of the article has the effect of putting the genitive phrase into the second attributive position.[4] He does that "for more emphasis or prominence."[5] In other places the article puts the genitive phrase into the rarer third attributive position[6] following an anarthrous noun, as in λόγοις τοῖς τοῦ κυρίου ἡμῶν (1 Tim 6:3), and ἡ δωρεὰ ἐν χάριτι τῇ τοῦ ἑνὸς ἀνθρώπου Ἰησοῦ (Rom 5:15).[7]

Article as Substantive

Paul uses the article as a substantive with dependent genitives in a few places.[8] He uses the masculine plural twice to refer to those who belong to Christ whether they are male or female, οἱ τοῦ Χριστοῦ the [people] of Christ (1 Cor 15:23; Gal 5:24). The neuter singular is found four times: τὸ ἑαυτοῦ ... τὸ τοῦ ἑτέρου the [things] of one's own ... the [things] of the other [person] (1 Cor 10:24), and τὸ ἐμαυτοῦ ... τὸ τῶν πολλῶν the [thing] of my own ... the [thing] of the many (1 Cor 10:33). These idiomatic uses, of course, must be rendered clearer from context. All other uses of the article as substantive in Paul's letters appear in the neuter plural, such as τὰ τοῦ νηπίου in 1 Cor 13:11, τὰ τοῦ πνεύματος τοῦ θεοῦ the [things] of the Spirit of God in 1 Cor 2:14, and οὐ γὰρ ζητῶ τὰ ὑμῶν ἀλλὰ ὑμᾶς for I do not seek your [things] but you in 2 Cor 12:14.

---

1   Dana and Mantey observe "An object of thought may be conceived of from two points of view: as to *identity* or *quality*. To convey the first point of view the Greek use the article; for the second the anarthrous construction is used" (Dana-Mantey, 149). See also Wallace, *ExSyn*, 209–10.

2   See for example, τῆς ὀργῆς τοῦ ἀρνίου (Rev 6:16) and τῆς ὀργῆς τοῦ θεοῦ (Rev 19:15), but anarthrous ὀργὴ θεοῦ (Rom 1:18) may have a descriptive meaning "divine wrath." See also Ray Summers, *Essentials of New Testament Greek*, Revised ed. by Thomas Sawyer (Grand Rapids: B&H Academic, 1995), k.l. 5785. [Kindle ed.] Compare also ἡ ἀγάπη τοῦ θεοῦ (2 Cor 13:13) and ἐν ἀγάπη θεοῦ (Jude 21).

3   MHT₃ 176. See also Wallace, *ExSyn*, 244.

4   Such a use makes the genitive phrase "prominent." See Wallace, *ExSyn*, 238, 306.

5   Winer, *Grammar*, 163. See also Wallace, *ExSyn*, 239–40.

6   Wallace, *ExSyn*, 238, 307.

7   See also τὸ πλήρωμα τοῦ τὰ πάντα ἐν πᾶσιν πληρουμένου (Eph 1:23), and πρόθεσιν τοῦ τὰ πάντα ἐνεργοῦντος (Eph 1:11), and outside the Pauline corpus τὸ αἷμά μου τῆς διαθήκης (Matt 26:28).

8   This particular usage appears in only in five of the Pauline epistles; e.g., Rom 8:24, 1 Cor 15:23, 2 Cor 12:14, Gal 5:24 and Phil 2:21.

Remarkably, Paul almost always uses the substantival article in juxtaposed antitheses such as τὰ τῆς σαρκὸς / τὰ τοῦ πνεύματος (Rom 8:5), τὰ τοῦ ἀνθρώπου / τὰ τοῦ θεοῦ (1 Cor 2:11), τὰ τοῦ κυρίου (1 Cor 7:32) / τὰ τοῦ κόσμου (1 Cor 7:33), and τὰ τοῦ κυρίου / τὰ τοῦ κόσμου (1 Cor 7:34), τὸ ἑαυτοῦ / τὸ τοῦ ἑτέρου (1 Cor 10:24), τὸ ἐμαυτοῦ / τὸ τῶν πολλῶν (1 Cor 10:33) and τὰ ἑαυτῶν / τὰ Ἰησοῦ Χριστοῦ (Phil 2:21). Again, Paul says, "if I must boast I will boast of *the things that show my weakness*" (τὰ τῆς ἀσθενείας μου 2 Cor 11:30 ESV [emphasis added]), and later, οὐ γὰρ ζητῶ τὰ ὑμῶν ἀλλὰ ὑμᾶς "For I do not seek your things, but [I seek] you" (2 Cor 12:14). The phrase οἱ τοῦ Χριστοῦ (Gal 5:24), "those who belong to Christ" is an antithesis to οἱ τὰ τοιαῦτα πράσσοντες (Gal 5:21), "those who practice such [evil] things" (NET).

In contrast with the use of the substantive article phrases in antitheses, there are only two incidents where substantival article-headed phrases are used synthetically: οἱ ποιηταὶ νόμου *the doers of the law* (Rom 2:13) with τὰ τοῦ νόμου ποιῶσιν [*Gentiles*] *do the* [*things*] *of the law* (Rom 2:14); and τὰ τῆς εἰρήνης ... τὰ τῆς οἰκοδομῆς *the* [*things*] *of peace ... the* [*things*] *of edification* (Rom 14:19). The only phrase that is not so juxtaposed is τὰ ἑαυτῆς *its own* [*things*] in 1 Cor 13:5. Perhaps there Paul is putting what love does antithetically alongside what selfishness may do, or perhaps alongside another's concerns (as in 1 Cor 10:24).

To put a definition to the conclusion derived from the substantival use of the article that arises from the investigation done above would be: *Genitive phrases headed by a substantival article in the Pauline corpus appear almost exclusively in juxtaposition of thesis and antithesis. The relation between the thesis and the antithesis is almost always antithetic, though it may be synthetic.*

One should bear in mind two things in the interpretation of genitives following a substantival article: (1) the need to provide an adnominal periphrasis to the article used substantivally; and (2) the need to identify the syntactical relationship between the articular periphrasis *nomen regens* and the genitive *nomen rectum*.

For instance, the periphrasis for οἱ τοῦ Χριστοῦ (1 Cor 15:23) could be "*those who belong* to Christ" (ESV) for a possessive genitive. τὰ τοῦ πνεύματος τοῦ θεοῦ (1 Cor 2:14), perhaps genitive of source or a subjective genitive, could mean "*what comes from God's Spirit*" (CSB); τὰ τοῦ κυρίου (1 Cor 7:32) "the Lord's *business*" (REB); τὰ τοῦ κόσμου (1 Cor 7:33) "worldly *affairs*" (REB). For τὰ τοῦ νηπίου (1 Cor 13:11) "childish *things*" (REB) or "childish *ways*" (TEV); τὰ Ἰησοῦ Χριστοῦ (Phil 2:21), "*the cause* of Christ" (TEV) or "*those of* Jesus Christ" (NET) [emphasis added].[9]

---

9 Examples of such periphrasis include συνείδησιν δὲ λέγω οὐχὶ τὴν ἑαυτοῦ ἀλλὰ τὴν τοῦ ἑτέρου *but I mean not one's own conscience but the other person's* (1 Cor 10:29) and τὸ ἐμὸν πνεῦμα καὶ τὸ ὑμῶν *my own spirit and yours* (1 Cor 16:18).

Likewise, τὰ τῆς εἰρήνης (Rom 14:19) could be an objective genitive, "the things that make for peace" (REB), "what promotes peace" (CSB) or "bring peace" (TEV).[10]

Emphatic Position of the *Nomen Rectum*

It is well known that word order often plays a role in emphasis.[11] The typical order for nouns in a genitive construction is that the genitive follows the head word, *nomen regens* comes first, then *nomen rectum*. Each occurs with its respective article, such as τῇ ἐκκλησίᾳ τοῦ θεοῦ *the church of God* (1 Cor 10:32), τὴν δόξαν τοῦ θεοῦ *the glory of God* (2 Cor 4:15), and τοῖς υἱοῖς τῶν ἀνθρώπων *the sons of men* (Eph 3:5), or if anarthrous, like ἐλπίδα δικαιοσύνης *hope of righteousness* (Gal 5:5), and διὰ θελήματος θεοῦ *by the will of God* (2 Tim 1:1).[12]

Moving the *nomen rectum* to a position preceding the *nomen regens* puts the weight on the genitive word, whether in articular or anarthrous constructions. A writer like Paul may rearrange the position of the substantives in the construction in order to emphasize a genitive.[13] We will describe such constructions below using Wallace's notation N-N$_g$ to denote the head noun (N) and the noun in the genitive (N$_g$).[14]

---

10 To list all occurrences of genitives that are used with substantival articles in Paul: τὰ τοῦ νόμου (Rom 2:14); τὰ τῆς σαρκὸς (Rom 8:5); τὰ τῆς εἰρήνης ... τὰ τῆς οἰκοδομῆς (Rom 14:19); τὰ τοῦ ἀνθρώπου ... τὰ τοῦ θεοῦ (1 Cor 2:11); τὰ τοῦ πνεύματος τοῦ θεοῦ (1 Cor 2:14); τὰ τοῦ κυρίου (1 Cor 7:32); τὰ τοῦ κόσμου (1 Cor 7:33); τὰ τοῦ κυρίου ... τὰ τοῦ κόσμου (1 Cor 7:34); τὸ ἑαυτοῦ ... τὸ τοῦ ἑτέρου (1 Cor 10:24); τὰ ἑαυτῆς (1 Cor 13:5); τὰ τοῦ νηπίου (1 Cor 13:11); οἱ τοῦ Χριστοῦ (1 Cor 15:23); τὰ τῆς ἀσθενείας μου (2 Cor 11:30); οὐ γὰρ ζητῶ τὰ ὑμῶν ἀλλ' ὑμᾶς (2 Cor 12:14); οἱ ... τοῦ Χριστοῦ (Gal 5:24); τὰ ἑαυτῶν ... τὰ ἑτέρων (Phil 2:4); τὰ ἑαυτῶν ... τὰ Ἰησοῦ Χριστοῦ (Phil 2:21). One example involves a specific ellipsis of σύμφορον in context, which allows the reader to supply it from the parallel: τὸ ἐμαυτοῦ σύμφορον ἀλλὰ τὸ τῶν πολλῶν [σύμφορον] (1 Cor 10:33).

11 Stanley E. Porter, "The Adjectival Attributive Genitive in the New Testament: A Grammatical Study," *TrinJ* 4.1 (1983): 4, 7–8. See also MHT₃ 217; Herbert Weir Smyth, *Greek Grammar*, Revised ed. by Gordon M. Messing (Cambridge: Harvard University Press, 1956), §§1154–83 pp. 293–97, and Antonius N. Jannaris, *An Historical Greek Grammar* (London: Macmillan, 1897), 323–24.

12 The concern here is directed towards nominal substantives. If the *nomen rectum* were a pronoun the article would not appear.

13 For a treatment of word order, see Moule, *Idiom Book*, 166–70, and Friedrich Blass, *Grammar of New Testament Greek*, 2nd ed., trans. Henry St. John Thackeray (London: Macmillan, 1905; repr., 1911), 287–88.

14 Wallace, *ExSyn*, 75.

Article + Article$_g$ + N$_g$ + N

In this syntactical category the articular *nomen rectum* stands in attributive position between the article and its head noun, such as τῷ τοῦ ἑνὸς παραπτώματι in Rom 5:15, and ὁ τῆς δικαιοσύνης στέφανος in 2 Tim 4:8. This position seems adopted for emphasis in NT Greek, since the attributive position seems to have been the unemphatic position in classical Greek.[15] For instance, the example from Rom 5:17 (cf. 5:14) puts the weight on Adam's sin as contrasted to Christ's obedience.[16] There are fifteen such genitive constructions in the Pauline corpus, each consisting of two nouns.[17]

Article + N$_g$ + N

Here the anarthrous *nomen rectum* is placed between the *nomen regens* and its article. This type of emphatic order occurs six times in Paul, five of them with proper nouns, for example, τὸν Στεφανᾶ οἶκον (1 Cor 1:16), τῷ Μωϋσέως νόμῳ (1 Cor 9:9), and τήν τινων πίστιν (2 Tim 2:18).[18] This category is similar to the previous one since the article with proper nouns varies in its usage overall.

Article + N$_g$ (Pronoun) + N

This category has the same order as the one before, but differs in that the *nomen rectum* is a personal pronoun or demonstrative. This type occurs 49 times in the Pauline corpus, five of them using demonstrative pronouns, for example, τοῦ ἐμοῦ πνεύματος (1 Cor 5:4), τῆς ὑμῶν οἰκοδομῆς (2 Cor 12:19), and τῇ ἐκείνου χάριτι (Titus

---

15 MHT₃ 217.

16 C. E. B. Cranfield (*A Critical and Exegetical Commentary on the Epistle to the Romans*, 6th ed., 2 vols., ICC [Edinburgh: T&T Clark, 1975–79], 1:284) notes the contrast, but does not comment on the grammar. Commentators are usually silent on the position of the phrase, since there is much more to discuss in the context.

17 This is the list of such constructions in the Pauline corpus: τῷ τοῦ ἑνὸς παραπτώματι (Rom 5:15); τῷ τοῦ ἑνὸς παραπτώματι (Rom 5:17); τὴν τοῦ θεοῦ δικαιοσύνην (Rom 10:3); τῇ τοῦ θεοῦ διαταγῇ (Rom 13:2); ἡ τῶν ἐπουρανίων δόξα (1 Cor 15:40 [there is also the ellipsis of this construction at the end of the verse with ἡ τῶν ἐπιγείων]); ὁ τοῦ θεοῦ υἱὸς (2 Cor 1:19); ἡ τοῦ κόσμου λύπη (2 Cor 7:10); τὸ τῆς ὑμετέρας ἀγάπης γνήσιον (2 Cor 8:8); πρὸς τὴν αὐτοῦ τοῦ κυρίου δόξαν (2 Cor 8:19); τὸ τοῦ θεοῦ εὐαγγέλιον (2 Cor 11:7); τὸ τῆς εὐσεβείας μυστήριον (1 Tim 3:16); ταῖς τοῦ βίου πραγματείαις (2 Tim 2:4); ἐκ τῆς τοῦ διαβόλου παγίδος (2 Tim 2:26); ὁ τοῦ θεοῦ ἄνθρωπος (2 Tim 3:17); ὁ τῆς δικαιοσύνης στέφανος (2 Tim 4:8). This construction is not unique to Paul, e.g., τὸν τῆς ἀρχῆς τοῦ Χριστοῦ λόγον (Heb 6:1) and τῇ τῶν ἀθέσμων πλάνῃ (2 Peter 3:17)

18 These constructions appear in1 Cor 1:16, 9:9; Phil 4:22; 2 Tim 1:16, 2:18, 4:19.

3:7).[19] This category is similar in form to the one above, since definite articles drop before pronouns.

N_g (Pronoun) + Article + N

When the N_g is a pronoun (including personal pronouns, relative pronouns, and the indefinite adjective τις functioning pronominally), its appearance in predicate position gives an emphasis to the pronoun. For example, ἡμῶν ἡ σωτηρία (Rom 13:11), τινος τὸ ἔργον (1 Cor 3:15), ὧν τὸ τέλος (2 Cor 11:15), μου τὴν χαρὰν (Phil 2:2), and αὐτῶν τὰς ἁμαρτίας (1 Thess 2:16). This type of repositioned emphatic pronoun appears forty times in the Pauline corpus.[20]

N_g + N

This type consists of two anarthrous noun-words genitive construction, but changes the natural order of genitive construction from *nomen regens + nomen rectum*, to *nomen rectum + nomen regens* for the purpose of emphasis, for example, θεοῦ διάκονός (Rom 13:4), θεοῦ βασιλείαν (1 Cor 6:9; cf. with βασιλείαν θεοῦ 1 Cor 6:10), μιᾶς γυναικὸς ἄνδρες (1 Tim 3:12), πλούτου ἀδηλότητι (1 Tim 6:17) and Χριστοῦ δοῦλος (Gal 1:10). Brian J. Dodd comments on Gal 1:10, "The word order ... is emphatic, unique in Paul .... Thus we should understand it as, '*Christ* is my master and I am controlled by no one or nothing else.'"[21] Such nominal genitive phrases occur about twenty-five times in Paul's writings.[22]

N_g (Pronoun) + N

This category consists of two anarthrous substantives, with a pronoun as the *nomen rectum*. For the purpose of emphasis, the pronoun comes first, for example: μου

---

19   Rom 3:24, 25; 4:19 (*bis*), 10:1; 11:11, 30; 16: 4, 18, 19; 1 Cor 5:4; 7:2, 35, 37, 38; 9:12; 2 Cor 1:6 (twice), 4:16; 7:7; 8:14 (4x); 9:2; 11:8; 12:19; 13:9; Eph 5:28 (*bis*), 33; Phil 1:19, 25, 26; 2:12, 30 (a three-word construction); Gal 1:8; 1 Thess 2:7, 8, 12; 3:7; 4:4; 2 Thess 2:6; 3:12; 1 Tim 5:23; 2 Tim 2:26; Titus 3:5, 7; Phlm 10, 14.

20   Rom 11:14; 13:11; 14:16; 1 Cor 3:13 (*bis*); 3:14, 15; 8:12; 9:2, 11, 18, 27; 10:33; 11:24; 2 Cor 1:24; 2:11; 10:6; 11:15; Gal 2:13; 6:2; Phil 2:2; 3:19 (*bis*); 3:20; 4:3, 14; Col 2:5; 4:18; 1 Thess 1:3; 2:16; 3:10, 13; 5:23; 2 Thess 2:17; 3:5; 1 Tim 4:12; 4:15; 2 Tim 1:4; 3:10; Titus 1:15; Phlm 5; 20.

21   Brian J. Dodd, "Christ's Slave, People Pleasers and Galatians 1.10," *NTS* 42.1 (1996): 98.

22   Rom 11:13; 13:4 (*bis*); 1 Cor 1:24 (*bis*); 2:4, 7; 3:9 (3x); 6:9; 6:15; 14:37; 2 Cor 2:15; 6:4; 8:24 [ἡμῶν καυχήσεως? though there are significant construal issues with this verse]; 11:2; Gal 1:10; 2:17; 3:15; 4:28, 31; 1 Thess 2:7; 1 Tim 3:2, 12; 5:9; 6:17; Titus 1:7

τέκνον (1 Cor 4:17) and ὑμῶν ἀπόστολον (Phil 2:25). This construction is used ten times in the Pauline corpus.[23] The function of the word order change is emphasis or contrast. For instance, in Phil 2:25 ὑμῶν δὲ ἀπόστολον (*your apostle*) contrasts Epaphroditus's relationship to the Philippian churches to his relationship to Paul as συστρατιώτην μου (*my comrade*).[24]

Article + N$_g$ + N

An anarthrous head noun preceded by an articular *nomen rectum* is extremely rare. There are only two instances like this in the Paul's writings: τῆς σαρκὸς πρόνοιαν (Rom 13:14) and τοῦ Ἀβραὰμ σπέρμα (Gal 3:29). In the first instance, this may be ascribed to the emphatic beginning of the sentence, καὶ τῆς σαρκὸς πρόνοιαν μὴ ποιεῖσθε εἰς ἐπιθυμίας "and make no provision for the flesh, to gratify its desires" (ESV). This thorough investigation of the emphatic usage of the genitive establishes a good foundation for interpreting Pauline genitive constructions.

Prepositions

The use of prepositions with genitive constructions contributes to their interpretation by limiting the range of meanings for the genitive. By this we do not mean the genitive as the object of a preposition; we refer here to situations where the head noun is the object of a preposition. But prepositional phrases are an element of the language that shows that the meaning of genitive constructions is not determined by syntax alone. The following examples will illustrate this point.

In Rom 3:7 εἰ δὲ ἡ ἀλήθεια τοῦ θεοῦ ἐν τῷ ἐμῷ ψεύσματι ἐπερίσσευσεν εἰς τὴν δόξαν αὐτοῦ, the preposition εἰς drives the identification of the genitive αὐτοῦ towards the objective category because the whole structure should be taken together. The semantic idea of goal or result inherent in the preposition εἰς limits the meaning of N-N$_g$ unit. Thus, "to his glory" would mean "that God would be glorified" or "that people would glorify God." This would be true of many εἰς δόξαν (τοῦ) θεοῦ (πατρός) examples (Rom 15:7; Phil 2:11; 1 Cor 10:31).[25]

The preposition διὰ also limits the meaning of the genitive construction by constraining its head noun. In Rom 6:4 ἠγέρθη Χριστὸς ἐκ νεκρῶν διὰ τῆς δόξης τοῦ

---

23 Rom 12:5; 1 Cor 4:17; 2 Cor 6:16 (*bis*: αὐτῶν θεὸς and μου λαός, a modification of LXX Ezek 37:27); Eph 2:10; 4:25; Phil 1:28; 2:25; 1 Thess 2:19; 2 Thess 2:1.

24 Gerald F. Hawthorne, *Philippians*, WBC 43 (Dallas: Word, 2004), 163.

25 τὸ ἀμὴν τῷ θεῷ πρὸς δόξαν δι' ἡμῶν (2 Cor 1:20) and δοὺς δόξαν τῷ θεῷ (Rom 4:20) illustrate the semantic parallel with the dative case. In these examples the genitive is objective.

πατρός the preposition διά determines the function of the *nomen regens* τῆς δόξης an instrumental one: "as Christ was raised from the dead *by the glorious power* of the Father" (REB [emphasis added]). This means the *nomen rectum* (πατρός) is a subjective genitive. Likewise, in Rom 4:25, ὃς παραδόθη διὰ τὰ παραπτώματα ἡμῶν "He was given over *because* of our transgressions" (NET [emphasis added]).[26]

The preposition ἀπό functions in the same way as in 2 Thess 1:9, ἀπὸ προσώπου τοῦ κυρίου καὶ ἀπὸ τῆς δόξης τῆς ἰσχύος αὐτοῦ, rendered "separated from" and "cut off from" by NRSV and REB respectively. The phrase "the penalty of eternal destruction" has a role in determining the meaning of the "separating" or "cutting off," but that insight is gained from the context not from grammar. Milligan is precise in saying that, "The words are borrowed … from [Isa 2:10, 19, 21], and hence ἀπό is best understood neither temporarily nor causally but locally in the sense of *separation from* the face of the Lord. For this pregnant use of the preposition cf. [2 Thess 2:2; Rom 9:3; 2 Cor. 11:3; Gal 5:4]."[27]

Conjunctions in Genitive Constructions

As one might expect, conjunctions—most often καί (sometimes joined by τε)—extend the use of one head noun to cover multiple genitives. In the expression τοῦ νόμου τῆς ἁμαρτίας καὶ τοῦ θανάτου *the law of sin and death* (Rom 8:2), the conjunction extends the headship of νόμου over both ἁμαρτίας and θανάτου; likewise with θώρακα πίστεως καὶ ἀγάπης *shield of faith and love* (1 Thess 5:8). Instead of repetition of τοῦ νόμου before τοῦ θανάτου, or θώρακα before ἀγάπης, the conjunction καί achieves the same effect with an economy of words. The conjunction connects the nominal parts of genitive constructions, such as τὰ θελήματα τῆς σαρκὸς καὶ τῶν διανοιῶν *the desires of the flesh and of the thoughts* (Eph 2:3), and ἡ κεφαλὴ πάσης ἀρχῆς καὶ ἐξουσίας *the head over every ruler and authority* (Col 2:10); and connects pronominal compounds, such as τὴν μητέρα αὐτοῦ καὶ ἐμοῦ *his mother and mine* (Rom 16:13). Such constructions involve both articular and anarthrous genitive nouns. Examples of articular constructions include τὰ κλίματα τῆς Συρίας καὶ τῆς Κιλικίας *the regions of Syria and Cilicia* (Gal 1:21), and ταῖς γλώσσαις τῶν ἀνθρώπων … καὶ τῶν ἀγγέλων *with the tongues of men and angels* (1 Cor 13:1). Anarthrous examples are

---

26   For a discussion of the genitive of cause see Chrys C. Caragounis, *The Development of Greek and the New Testament: Morphology, Syntax, Phonology, and Textual Transmission* (Tübingen: Mohr Siebeck, 2004; repr., Grand Rapids: Baker, 2008), 144.

27   George Milligan, *St. Paul's Epistles to the Thessalonians: The Greek Text, with Introduction and Notes* (New York: Macmillan, 1908), 91.

εἷς … μεσίτης θεοῦ καὶ ἀνθρώπων *one mediator between God and men* (1 Tim 2:5), and δυνάμει σημείων καὶ τεράτων *power of signs and wonders* (Rom 15:19).

Two nouns joined by καί (occasionally other conjunctions) generate some of the three- and four-word constructions. For example, τοῦ πλούτου τῆς χρηστότητος αὐτοῦ καὶ τῆς ἀνοχῆς καὶ τῆς μακροθυμίας *the wealth of his kindness and forbearance and patience* (Rom 2:4), καὶ ὑμῶν τὸ πνεῦμα καὶ ἡ ψυχὴ καὶ τὸ σῶμα *your spirit and soul and body* (1 Thess 5:23). At times, the dependent genitives are in a mixed situation, some connected by καί and others in simple dependence. For instance, in the long phrase οἱ τὴν περισσείαν τῆς χάριτος καὶ τῆς δωρεᾶς τῆς δικαιοσύνης λαμβάνοντες (Rom 5:17), the head noun περισσείαν is followed by two articular genitives, the second of which, τῆς δωρεᾶς, which itself has a dependent genitive. There are forty-two passages with these kind of constructions in Paul.[28]

We have already raised the issue of Sharp's constructions in connection to Titus 2:13 (see that heading in Chapter Six). Such constructions where Sharp's construction appears (i.e., a multi-word head) with dependent genitives appear in the following verses: Rom 15:6; 2 Cor 1:3 (*bis*); 10:1; 11:31; Gal 1:4; Eph 1:3; 2:20; Phil 1:7, 25; 2:17, 25; 4:20; Col 2:22; 1 Thess 1:3; 2:12; 3:2, 11, 13; 1 Tim 6:15; Titus 2:13; Phlm 1.

The majority of these instances are constructions referring to God as Father (Rom 15:6; 2 Cor 1:3; 2 Cor 11:31; Gal 1:4; Eph 1:3; Phil 4:20; 1 Thess 3:2, 11, 13) or the christologically significant passage proclaiming Jesus as God and Savior (Titus 2:13). The others involve some plural nouns (τῷ θεμελίῳ τῶν ἀποστόλων καὶ προφητῶν *the foundation of the apostles and prophets* Eph 2:20), or impersonal nouns. For instance, in the phrase τῆς πραΰτητος καὶ ἐπιεικείας τοῦ Χριστοῦ *the gentleness and meekness of Christ* (2 Cor 10:1), the head noun is a compound τῆς πραΰτητος καὶ ἐπιεικείας with a dependent genitive, τοῦ Χριστοῦ. Because the head compound consists of two impersonal nouns, it cannot be said that the two nouns are the same. There is lexical overlap between the concepts, though, as Murray Harris points out "they are not synonyms."[29] The single article indicates a general overlap between the two concepts without them being identical.[30] At any rate, both of these qualities belong to Christ and are the model for Paul's approach in his appeal to his audience. Two other examples are in this impersonal noun category. The expression

28 Rom 1:12; 1:23; 2:4; 2:20; 5:17; 6:5; 6:16; 8:2; 10:12; 11:33; 15:5; 15:19; 16:13; 1 Cor 1:2; 2:1, 4; 5:8; 10:26; 11:27; 13:1; 16:17; 2 Cor 1:6; 2 Cor 6:7; 7:1; 8:24; 13:1, 11; Gal 1:4, 21; Eph 2:3, 20; 4:13; 5:5; 6:9; Phil 4:15; Col 2:3, 10; 1 Thess 1:6, 5:8; 1 Tim 1:1; 2:5; Titus 3:5
29 Murray J. Harris, *The Second Epistle to the Corinthians: A Commentary on the Greek Text*, NIGTC (Grand Rapids: Eerdmans, 2005), 667.
30 Wallace hints at this. See *Sharp's Canon*, 170.

τὴν μακαρίαν ἐλπίδα καὶ ἐπιφάνειαν τῆς δόξης as part of the longer cluster already noted in Titus 2:13. Another instance is the TSKS construction of the phrase ἐν τῇ ἀπολογίᾳ καὶ βεβαιώσει τοῦ εὐαγγελίου *the defense and confirmation of the gospel* (Phil 1:7), which joins *defense* and *confirmation*[31] as the double head noun with the single dependent genitive. Another example of this kind of construction includes τὴν ἑαυτοῦ βασιλείαν καὶ δόξαν *his own kingdom and glory* (1 Thess 2:12). The glory is not the kingdom, but it is a characterization of it. The expression τὰ ἐντάλματα καὶ διδασκαλίας τῶν ἀνθρώπων *the commandments and teachings of men* (Col 2:22) joins commandments with the teachings of humans; not that they are identical, but that there is a close relationship between these legalistic requirements and the vehicle of teaching by which they are conveyed.

Other examples involving TSKS personal constructions include τὸν ἀδελφὸν καὶ συνεργὸν καὶ συστρατιώτην μου (Phil 2:25), and Φιλήμονι τῷ ἀγαπητῷ καὶ συνεργῷ ἡμῶν (Phlm 1). These serve to join the terms to strengthen the descriptions of Timothy and Philemon.

The example of 1 Tim 1:1 requires comment: κατ᾽ ἐπιταγὴν θεοῦ σωτῆρος ἡμῶν καὶ Χριστοῦ Ἰησοῦ τῆς ἐλπίδος ἡμῶν *according to the commandment of God our savior and of Jesus Christ* (cf. Rom 16:26; Titus 1:3) shows two different persons. This expression lacks the article, so it is not a structural fit for TSKS syntax. Because the head noun in this construction is anarthrous, one would expect anarthrous *nomen rectum*, which is what we have, at least with θεοῦ σωτῆρος. Thus, two different persons—both the Father and Jesus Christ—are the source of the command. But this occurrence needs more explanation from the standpoint of Apollonius's Canon.

Following Apollonius' Canon,[32] we should expect ὁ τοῦ ἀνθρώπου υἱός or ὁ υἱός τοῦ ἀνθρώπου or υἱός ἀνθρώπου, but usually not other configurations such as ὁ υἱός ἀνθρώπου. Apollonius himself recognized, too, that proper names are exempt from the rule. There are other exceptions to this rule, in "five configurations" identified by Sanford a

> The first configuration features an anarthrous *nomen regens* followed by an articular *nomen rectum*, e.g., υἱὲ τοῦ θεοῦ (Luke 8:28). In the second, the articular nomen regens precedes the anarthrous *nomen rectum*, e.g. τοῦ πνεύματος Ἰησοῦ (Phil 1:19). In the third configuration, the anarthrous *nomen rectum* precedes the articular *nomen regens*, e.g., θεοῦ τὸ δῶρον (Eph 2:8). The fourth features an articular *nomen rectum* preceding an

---

31 Gerald Hawthorne (*Philippians*, 28) points out that the terms "are technical, legal terms common in the law courts of the first century."

32 Apollonius Dyscolus, *Syntax* 1.140. For translation and commentary on the formulation of the rule, see Householder, *Apollonius*, 78. The rule is cited in most NT grammars: e.g., MHT₃ 180; BDF §259 p.135; Wallace *ExSyn* 239.

anarthrous *nomen regens*, e.g., τῆς ἀναστάσεως υἱοὶ (Luke 20:36). In the fifth, the article and *nomen regens* with which it agrees bracket the anarthrous *nomen rectum*, e.g., τὸ Ἰωάννου βάπτισμα (Acts 19:3).[33]

In many of the instances of adnominal genitives where anarthrous head nouns appear with articular dependent genitives, the head noun is the object of a preposition. For instance, εἰς ἔνδειξιν τῆς δικαιοσύνης αὐτοῦ (Rom 3:25), ἐν δεξιᾷ τοῦ θεοῦ (Rom 8:34), εἰς ἀπολύτρωσιν τῆς περιποιήσεως (Eph 1:14). NT grammars have noted this exception.[34] In 105 instances of anarthrous *nomen regens* with an articular *nomen rectum*, 47 of them are objects of a preposition. In the remaining examples, many are in regimen with a pronominal head noun such as τινες τῶν κλάδων (Rom 11:17), οὐδεὶς τῶν ἀρχόντων τοῦ αἰῶνος τούτου (1 Cor 2:8), and ἕτερον τῶν ἀποστόλων (Gal 1:19). In these examples, the pronoun cannot take the article.

Many of the other examples involve the regimen being part of a complement— whether a subject or an object complement. Examples of the subject complement are fairly straightforward: τοῦ Ἀβραὰμ σπέρμα ἐστέ (Gal 3:29), θεοῦ τὸ δῶρον (Eph 2:8). This is hardly surprising, because anarthrous pre-verbal predicate nominatives are a commonplace. In these situations where the articular *nomen rectum* appears with an anarthrous *nomen regens*, they are all to be considered definite.[35] Wallace demonstrates that the semantics of subject-complement and object-complement constructions are parallel,[36] so examples of the object complement are like them. For instance, in Rom 4:11 σημεῖον ἔλαβεν περιτομῆς **σφραγῖδα** τῆς δικαιοσύνης τῆς πίστεως "he received the sign of circumcision **as a seal** of the righteousness" (NET; cf. 1 Cor 12:23), σημεῖον is the object and σφραγῖδα the object complement. Perhaps we should translate, "he received the sign of circumcision as *the* seal of the righteousness," but this is perhaps too subtle a difference for English translation.

In some cases, the *nomen rectum* occurs in the predicate of the sentence, and *nomen regens* should be supplied with each additional *nomen rectum*: γεγόναμεν τῷ ὁμοιώματι τοῦ θανάτου αὐτοῦ, ἀλλὰ καὶ τῆς ἀναστάσεως ἐσόμεθα *we have become in likeness to his death; we shall also be [in likeness] of his resurrection* (Rom 6:5); ὡς κοινωνοί ἐστε τῶν παθημάτων, οὕτως καὶ τῆς παρακλήσεως *as you are partakers of the sufferings,*

---

33 Sanford D. Hull, "Exceptions to Apollonius' Canon in the New Testament: A Grammatical Study," *TrinJ* 7 (1986): 4–5.

34 Robertson (*Grammar*, 780) explicitly so, Moule (*Idiom Book*, 115), too, but without mentioning prepositions, though one might infer such from his examples comparing Rom 3:25, 26.

35 Cf. John 1:49 σὺ βασιλεὺς εἶ τοῦ Ἰσραήλ ("you are *the* king of Israel"). See Wallace, *ExSyn* 263–64. For a wider discussion of the significance of the anarthrous pre-verbal predicate nominative, see Wallace, *ExSyn* 256–70.

36 Wallace, *ExSyn* 184. See also Daniel B. Wallace, "The Semantics and Exegetical Significance of the Object-Complement Construction in the New Testament," *GTJ* 6.1 (1985): 101–5.

so also [*you are partakers*] *of the encouragement* (2 Cor 1:7); and καύχημα ὑμῶν ἐσμεν καθάπερ καὶ ὑμεῖς ἡμῶν *we are your boast just as also you* [*are*] *our* [*boast*] (2 Cor 1:14). In these examples the head noun is elided in the second member of the parallelism, so that in Rom 6:5 καὶ τῆς ἀναστάσεως is construed as καὶ [τῷ ὁμοιώματι] τῆς ἀναστάσεως ἐσόμεθα. In 2 Cor 1:14 καὶ ὑμεῖς ἡμῶν is construed as καύχημα ὑμῶν ἐσμεν καθάπερ καὶ ὑμεῖς [καύχημα ἐστε] ἡμῶν.

In the phrase ἐν ἡμέρᾳ ὀργῆς καὶ ἀποκαλύψεως δικαιοκρισίας τοῦ θεοῦ (Rom 2:5), ἡμέρα should govern ἀποκαλύψεως in addition to ὀργῆς. Likewise, in the phrase ἐν δυνάμει σημείων καὶ τεράτων (Rom 15:19), δυνάμει should also govern τεράτων. Similarly, the καί distributes the genitives under the same head in ποιοῦντες τὰ θελήματα τῆς σαρκὸς καὶ τῶν διανοιῶν (Eph 2:3), effectively making a construal like τὰ θελήματα τῆς σαρκὸς καὶ τὰ θελήματα τῶν διανοιῶν. In Phil 1:25, εἰς τὴν ὑμῶν προκοπὴν καὶ χαρὰν τῆς πίστεως *for your progress and joy of the faith*, the pronoun ὑμῶν appearing early in the construction makes for potential ambiguity. Is it to be understood as *your progress and joy* or *your faith*? The parallel three-word genitive construction in ἐπὶ τῇ θυσίᾳ καὶ λειτουργίᾳ τῆς πίστεως ὑμῶν *on the sacrifice and service of your faith* (Phil 2:17) helps solve the ambiguity: ὑμῶν is clearly construed with τῆς πίστεως in Phil 2:17, and so should be treated the same way in Phil 1:25.[37] Seen in this light, one can also see a rhetorical flourish in which the genitives form a sort of *inclusio*.

In τὴν ἑνότητα τῆς πίστεως καὶ τῆς ἐπιγνώσεως τοῦ υἱοῦ τοῦ θεοῦ (Eph 4:13), ἑνότητα *unity* should be linked not only with πίστεως *faith* but also with ἐπιγνώσεως *knowledge*. In τοῦ πλούτου τῆς χρηστότητος αὐτοῦ καὶ τῆς ἀνοχῆς καὶ τῆς μακροθυμίας (Rom 2:4), both τοῦ πλούτου and αὐτοῦ should probably be supplied with every new compound created by καί.[38]

The conjunctions ἤ and τε appear in a few of our genitive constructions. One of the more interesting is: καί in τίς γὰρ ἡμῶν ἐλπὶς ἢ χαρὰ ἢ στέφανος καυχήσεως ἢ οὐχὶ καὶ ὑμεῖς ἔμπροσθεν τοῦ κυρίου ἡμῶν (1 Thess 2:19).[39] This conglomeration extends the relationship between the fronted ἡμῶν and the nouns connected by ἤ ("*our* hope or *our* joy or *our* crown of boasting") Other similar alternation of the conjunctions appears in these passages:

---

37 Perhaps because of the already complicated syntax, many commentators do not address the value of ὑμῶν in this context. See, for instance, G. Walter Hansen, *The Letter to the Philippians*, PNTC (Grand Rapids: Eerdmans, 2009), 90–91; Hawthorne, *Philippians*, 63; Mark J. Keown, *Philippians*, EEC (Bellingham, WA: Lexham Press, 2017), 265–66.

38 See also Ὦ βάθος πλούτου καὶ σοφίας καὶ γνώσεως θεοῦ (Rom 11:33).

39 Winer allows that on occasion ἤ and καί come close to each other in meaning, citing 1 Cor 13:1 and 2 Cor 13:1 as examples (Winer, *Grammar*, 550).

- Rom 1:12 διὰ τῆς ἐν ἀλλήλοις πίστεως ὑμῶν τε καὶ ἐμοῦ
- Rom 6:16 δοῦλοί ἤτοι ἁμαρτίας [εἰς θάνατον] ἢ ὑπακοῆς [εἰς δικαιοσύνην]
- Rom 10:12 διαστολὴ Ἰουδαίου τε καὶ Ἕλληνος
- 1 Cor 2:1 καθ᾽ ὑπεροχὴν λόγου ἢ σοφίας
- Col 2:16 ἐν μέρει ἑορτῆς ἢ νεομηνίας ἢ σαββάτων

Exegetical Principles for Genitive Interpretation

Grammarians have often repeated Winer's contention that, "the decision between the subjective and the objective genitive belongs to exegesis, not to grammar."[40] Gerald Stevens plays on words when he opines, "A decision about a subjective or objective genitive is *subjective*. Each case has to be decided by the interpreter on the basis of context and exegesis."[41] Exegesis involves explaining contextually the relation between the genitive and its noun. Turner remarks:

> The sole question which the translator and exegete need ask is whether the relationship is directed outwards from the noun in the genitive to some other person or from some other person to the noun in the genitive; or, to put it differently, whether or not the action implied by the independent noun is carried out by the noun in the genitive.[42]

Buttmann's observation concerning interpreting the genitive is remarkable:

> As the subject, however, is one of the weighty importance for the understanding of Scripture, and the decision in all disputed cases necessarily presumes thorough investigation of the usage of individual writers, exposition of the internal connection in every passage, comparison of parallel expressions, and the like, it well deserves a separate and systematic treatment of its own. [43]

Appealing to context, wider considerations and general usage are necessary in determining the meaning of the genitive constructions.[44] Moulton's advice to

---

40 Winer, *Grammar*, 232. This is a thought echoed by Moulton ("It is as well to remember that in Greek this question [subjective/objective genitive] is entirely one of exegesis, not of grammar." MHT$_1$ 72) and Chamberlain (*An Exegetical Grammar of the Greek New Testament* [New York: Macmillan, 1941; repr., Grand Rapids: Baker, 1979], 31).

41 Gerald L. Stevens, *New Testament Greek* (Lanham: University Press of America, 1997), 187.

42 MHT$_3$ 207.

43 Buttmann, *Grammar*, 154–55.

44 "The immediate context and general usage must be called in to decide the [subjective-objective] point" (Chamberlain, *Grammar*, 31). "The relationship expressed by the genitive is so vague that it is only by means of the context and wider considerations that it can be made definite." MHT$_3$ 207.

Bible translators forms a suitable conclusion here, "Here is the translator's eternal problem, to which there is no dogmatic answer. He must see what is involved, consult with others as best he can, and make in each case what seems the wisest decision."[45]

But there is more to say than simply to advise the interpreter to look to the context for the resolution for conundrums of the genitive case. There are helps for the interpreter derived from this study which can now be brought to bear, with the hope that more satisfactory and more securely validated solutions can be reached.

Thus, an understanding of the basic meaning, nature, and grammatical aspects of adnominal genitive constructions are essential in interpreting the genitive. The foregoing discussion provides the basis now for the task of presenting certain principles or guidelines for interpreting the genitive as it is used in adnominal constructions. Moving from the narrowest to the widest context, treatment of the subject involves consideration of the following exegetical aspects.

Relationships Between Substantives

Identifying the relationship between nouns in a genitive construction is vital for understanding genitival phrases. Syntactically the head noun is the main term, and the substantive in the genitive is subordinate to it. Any genitives that occur after the headword depend on it as the basis for the whole construction. But the surface structure does not always correspond to the semantics. The central or most prominent substantive in a genitive construction may or may not appear first in the word group. Some instances are fairly easily handled. For example, in the phrase τῷ Μωϋσέως νόμῳ *the law of Moses* (1 Cor 9:9) the base-noun is νόμῳ. This is the head-word and the central word in the construction, and the genitive Μωϋσέως is added to modify it. The genitive θεοῦ in νόμῳ θεοῦ *law of God* (Rom 7:25) or Χριστοῦ in τὸν νόμον τοῦ Χριστοῦ *law of Christ* (Gal 6:2) may be added to modify the central word. But in other genitive constructions like ἡμέρᾳ ὀργῆς καὶ ἀποκαλύψεως δικαιοκρισίας τοῦ θεοῦ (Rom 2:5), the weight of the construction lies on ὀργῆς καὶ ἀποκαλύψεως δικαιοκρισίας not ἡμέρᾳ, even though the latter is syntactically the head noun in the construction. ἡμέρᾳ appears only to refer to the *time* of the judgment, but the prominence is placed on its intensity. Another example is the four-word genitive φωτισμὸν τῆς γνώσεως τῆς δόξης τοῦ θεοῦ *enlightenment of the knowledge of the glory of God* (2 Cor 4:6). The head noun φωτισμὸν is the anchor of the construction, but syntactically the central word is γνώσεως. The role of the head word, so to speak, is

---

45 Harold K. Moulton, "Of," *Bible Translator* 19.1 (1968): 25, doi:10.1177/000608446801900105.

to illuminate the second, while the third and fourth words provide the content of the knowledge.

Figures of Speech

Considerations above those of simple grammar must weigh in to any interpretation; sensitivity to figures of speech, such as "metonymy, synecdoche, metaphor, and euphemism"[46] is of particular importance because they challenge ordinary boundaries of usage in rich and unexpected ways. It is easy enough to interpret genitive constructions involving *non-figurative* terms such as ὁ οἰκονόμος τῆς πόλεως *the treasurer of the city* (Rom 16:23), ταῖς ἐκκλησίαις τῆς Γαλατίας *the churches of Galatia* (1 Cor 16:1), or τὴν πόλιν Δαμασκηνῶν *the city of the Damascenes* (2 Cor 11:32). Literal terms (or terms with literal referents) are usually concrete, plain and simple and involve little ambiguity.

But nouns in genitive constructions may be *abstract* conceptions that cannot be fully expressed if each word is taken literally. This requires lexical semantics be brought to bear, since a decision about what kind of head noun is involved is a preliminary consideration. Genitive expressions such as τὸ τῆς εὐσεβείας μυστήριον *the mystery of godliness* (1 Tim 3:16), πλοῦτος τῆς πληροφορίας τῆς συνέσεως *wealth of the certainty of knowledge* (Col 2:2), τῆς ὑπομονῆς τῆς ἐλπίδος *the endurance of hope* (1 Thess 1:3), πνεῦμα σοφίας *spirit of wisdom* (Eph 1:17), τὴν ἑνότητα τῆς πίστεως *unity of the faith* (Eph 4:13), τῆς δόξης τῆς ἰσχύος *glory of the might* (2 Thess 1:9), and τῆς μωρίας τοῦ κηρύγματος *foolishness of the preaching* (1 Cor 1: 21), are expressions with clearly abstract head nouns. Small wonder, then, that many of this category involve an ambiguous *nomen regens* clarified by a less ambiguous *nomen rectum*.[47]

Personifications of abstract expressions like grace, righteousness and sin alter how we read genitive constructions. In the phrase λεῖμμα κατ᾽ ἐκλογὴν χάριτος *remnant according to the selection of grace* (Rom 11:5), "a remnant chosen by grace" (NET), grace is "a quasi-personified power."[48] In light of the personification, perhaps it should be read as a subjective genitive rather than simply as an adjectival genitive: "the election God's grace accomplishes" rather than simply "gracious election." Likewise, in τὰ ὀψώνια τῆς ἁμαρτίας θάνατος *the wages of sin [is] death* (Rom 6:23), sin, like a ghastly quartermaster, pays out deadly wages.

---

46 Beekman-Callow, 360.
47 On this point, see especially Wallace, *ExSyn* 96.
48 Neil Richardson, *Paul's Language About God,* JSNTSS 99 (Sheffield, England: Sheffield Academic Press, 1994), 75.

The abundance of figurative expressions in genitive constructions such as ἀνέμῳ τῆς διδασκαλίας *wind of teaching* (Eph 4:14), υἱοὶ φωτός *sons of light* (1 Thess 5:5), ὁ καρπὸς τοῦ φωτός *the fruit of the light* (Eph 5:9) and σκεύη ὀργῆς *vessels of wrath* (Rom 9:22) are always ambiguous, requiring additional analysis. Disambiguation is required in a verse like ἐπὶ τῇ θυσίᾳ καὶ λειτουργίᾳ τῆς πίστεως ὑμῶν (Phil 2:17), "on the sacrifice and service of your faith" (NET).[49] Recognition of the head nouns' figurative referent along with their meaning in the sphere of action ("sacrifice and service") narrows the field of likely candidates for the categorization of τῆς πίστεως. Combined with the main verb σπένδομαι *I am poured*, "sacrifice and service" represent actions Paul is taking to strengthen the faith of his audience. Euodia, Syntyche, and Clement are described as believers *whose names are in the book of life* (Phil 4:3). The metaphorical phrase ἐν βίβλῳ ζωῆς calls to mind OT antecedents such as Exod 32:32 and Ps 69:28, pointing to the divine "register of God's covenant people"[50] The head noun relates to its dependent genitive figuratively: the book in which God keeps the names of those destined for (eternal) life. Another metaphorical example is ζυγῷ δουλείας *the yoke of slavery* (Gal 5:1; cf. Acts 15:10). As Richard N. Longenecker points out, the yoke of Torah is seen in a positive light in Rabbinic literature (m. Pirqe ʾAbot 3:5; m. Ber. 2:2), and Jesus's yoke has a positive connotation (Matt 11:29–30), but also negatively in Greek literature (Plato, *Leg.* 6.770E; Demosthenes 18.289), where "yoke of slavery" appears.[51] Thus, a yoke that, though it seems good at first, ironically leads to slavery.

Much of the figurative language used in the NT, including the Pauline corpus, has been influenced by Semitic idioms that display somewhat wooden Greek translations of Hebrew Bible. Expressions translating אלהים are good examples, ζῆλον θεοῦ (Rom 10:2) could mean "great zeal," κιθάρας τοῦ θεοῦ (Rev 15:2) "large harps." These seem to operate along the lines of Job 1:16 as "great fire" ("A lightning storm" [HCSB] cf. "God's fire" [CSB]), and in Ps 68:15 as "mighty mountain" (NRSV), "majestic mountain" (NIV).[52]

Other frequent Semitisms appear in the Pauline corpus: expressions such as "son"[53] (τοῖς υἱοῖς τῆς ἀπειθείας Eph 2:2), "father" (ὁ πατὴρ τῆς δόξης Eph 1:17, ὁ

---

49 The picture likely comes from OT passages like Num 28:7, but the idea is broadly known in pagan religious contexts, from which many in Philippi might have come (See Hansen, *Philippians*, 187).

50 Hawthorne, *Philippians*, 181. See also Joseph Barber Lightfoot, *Saint Paul's Epistle to the Philippians* (London: Macmillan, 1913), 158.

51 Richard N. Longenecker, *Galatians*, WBC 41 (Dallas: Word, 1990), 224–25.

52 On this idea, see especially D. W. Thomas, "A Consideration of Some Unusual Ways of Expressing the Superlative in Hebrew," *VT* 3 (1953): 210, https://www.jstor.org/stable/1516347.

53 "The use of υἱός in a figurative sense (often) is predominantly a Hebraism" (BDF §162, p. 89). "The acknowledged 'Semitism' by which *son of* = *belong to, destined for*" Moule, *Idiom Book*, 38.

πατὴρ τῶν οἰκτιρμῶν 2 Cor 1:3; cf. ἀπὸ τοῦ πατρὸς τῶν φώτων Jas 1:17), "bowels of mercies" (KJV σπλάγχνα οἰκτιρμοῦ Col 3:12), and "glory" (τὸν κύριον τῆς δόξης 1 Cor 2:8) come to mind. For Moule, this is "[t]he Semitic idiom whereby *sons of light, of darkness, of life, of death,* etc. means simply *people worthy of,* or *associated with light,* etc."[54] As de Waard and Nida observe, "distinctive Hebrew meanings have come into the Greek New Testament by way of the Septuagint."[55]

Verbal Head Nouns

Unlike concrete expressions like *the pinnacle of the temple* (Matt 4:5), *the hairs of head* (Luke 12:7), *the parts of the body* (1 Cor 12:22), or *the lions mouth* (2 Tim 4:17), constructions in which the *nomen regens* has a verbal component, such as *the foundation of the world* (Eph 1:4), *the will of God* (1 Thess 4:3), *the obedience of faith* (Rom 1:5), or *the promise of the Spirit* (Gal 3:14), require more interpretive work. Each of these genitive constructions contains substantives that have an inherent verbal power. In order to make sense out of such expressions, a transformation of the verbal-inherent adnominals into explicit verbal sentences, such as "God founded the world," "God wills," "the faith that inspires obedience," and "God promised to send the Spirit," helps clarify the ambiguity created by English *of.* These verbal meanings are inherent in adnominals. But when transformed according to Chomsky's method, they become clear.[56]

G. Henry Waterman, applying Chomsky's transformational grammar to noun-noun constructions, helpfully sets out a list of functions for the genitive case:

> The genitive in a noun-noun phrase may, then, function as (1) the subject of the idea expressed in the noun on which it depends; (2) the object of the idea expressed in the noun on which it depends; (3) a predicate nominative adjective describing or characterizing the noun on which it depends; (4) a predicate nominative noun in apposition with the noun on which it depends; (5) a noun denoting someone to whom the noun on which it depends is related (in a familial sense); (6) a noun denoting someone who possesses the noun on which it depends; and (7) a verb indicating the action or state of the noun on which it depends. In other words, this kind of genitive construction may be regarded as a "transform" from "kernel" sentences, in which the

---

54 Moule, *Idiom Book,* 174.

55 Jan de Waard and Eugene A. Nida, *From One Language to Another: Functional Equivalence in Bible Translating* (Nashville: Nelson, 1986), 174.

56 See Nida's treatment of this in Eugene A. Nida, *Toward a Science of Translating: With Special Reference to Principles and Procedures Involved in Bible Translating* (Leiden: Brill, 1964), 207–08. See also Eugene A. Nida and Charles R. Taber, *The Theory and Practice of Translation,* HFT 8 (Leiden: Brill, 1969; repr., 1982), 33–55.

genitive replaces any of the basic parts of the sentence: subject, object, predicate nominative adjective, predicate nominative noun, object of the verb *echei* (both to express relationship and possession), and even the verb itself.[57]

Many obscure genitive adnominal phrases can be better understood by transforming them into verbal expressions, as much as one is able to transform the verbal ideas into adnominal genitive constructions. Verb and noun in generative grammar are compatible, and meaning under their respective forms is transferable. As Jan de Waard remarks, "In terms of the underlying semantic relationship, there is a coordinate structure which reflects a nominal transformation of a sequence that occurs commonly enough in its corresponding verb structure."[58]

Concerning these verbal-inherent subjective-objective genitive constructions it is appropriate to conclude that in solving the problem of a genitive ambiguity, the use of Chomsky's transformational method as a mechanical tool to switch from noun to verb and vice versa is insufficient. In each case the context of each construction must be considered to determine the meaning of problematic genitives.

Often deciding whether a genitive is subjective or objective requires careful examination of the context and interpretive outcomes for validation. Ian H. Thomson offers an example of such an endeavor in handing "the circumcision of Christ" (Col 2:11):

> At the risk of doing injustice to the various views, they may be condensed into two main approaches .... The first sees the introduction of a baptismal metaphor in which the stripping off of the body of the flesh becomes a spiritual 'Christian' equivalent of Jewish circumcision, but now accomplished by baptism. The genitive in the phrase ἐν τῇ περιτομῇ τοῦ Χριστοῦ [Col 2:11] becomes subjective, and is interpreted as 'the circumcision which Christ gave', that is baptism. The second approach sees a figurative, but vivid, allusion to the death of Christ, and the believer's sharing in it .... In this the genitive in the phrase ἐν τῇ περιτομῇ τοῦ Χριστοῦ is objective, and Christ's circumcision is seen, not as 'the stripping off of a small portion of flesh, but the violent removal of the whole body in death'.[59]

57 G. Henry Waterman, "The Greek 'Verbal Genitive'," in *Current Issues in Biblical and Patristic Interpretation*, ed. Gerald F. Hawthorne (Grand Rapids: Eerdmans, 1975), 292.

58 Waard and Nida, *One Language to Another*, 135.

59 Ian H. Thomson, *Chiasmus in the Pauline Letters*, JSNTSS 111 (Sheffield: Sheffield Academic Press, 1995), 164–65.

Immediate Context

In order to investigate the meaning of the genitive one should also look to the immediate context to see what it suggests. This step should be made after one has defined the interrelation between the substantives that constitute a genitive construction as above.

The noun πλησμονή, derived from the verb πίμπλημι[60] in the construction πλησμονὴν τῆς σαρκός *gratification*[?] *of the flesh* (Col 2:23) signals the need for thorough investigation of context (i.e. verses 21–23), since it can be taken as (1) subjective *the flesh indulges*, or (2) objective *to indulge the flesh*, or, if the verbal idea in the head noun is not important, (3) adjectival *physical passions*. The context of vv. 21–22 is important: the string of commands espoused by the opponents are dismissed as "human commands and teachings … with no true value" (NET). This drives the identification in the direction of subjective genitive. If the "indulgence" is of the flesh or human desires whose operation is supposed—ineffectually as it turns out—to be curbed by these human commands. Thus, the meaning of the preposition πρός in v. 23b turns out to have an adversarial role: "against."[61] Finally, there is a contrast between the internal πλησμονὴν τῆς σαρκός and the external ἀφειδίᾳ σώματος "unsparing treatment of the body" (NET) intended to deal with it. This contrast, James Dunn points out, "needs to be given more weight."[62] This is the way most English versions have handled it (e.g., NRSV TEV REB CSB).

Another example of a contextually validated subjective genitive appears in Rom 8:39. The expression in question is ἀπὸ τῆς ἀγάπης τοῦ θεοῦ τῆς ἐν Χριστῷ Ἰησοῦ *from the love of God which is in Christ*. In this instance, the head noun is ἀγάπης (itself genitive because it is the object of a preposition) and the dependent genitive is θεοῦ. The addition of the adjectival phrase τῆς ἐν Χριστῷ Ἰησοῦ with the addition of the appositive τῷ κυρίῳ ἡμῶν, points to a *subjective* genitive "God's love *towards us*," since it is expressed in Christ to believers (cf. ὑπὲρ ἡμῶν in Rom 8:31). With the overwhelming emphasis on God's sovereign providence for believers, it would be hard to think that believers' love for God (an objective genitive) were in view.

---

60 BDAG 830 s.v. πλησμονή.

61 BDAG 874 s.v. πρός lists Col 2:23 under 3eδ "in accordance with." But 3e, "with reference/regard to," 3d, "against, for," and particularly 3dα, "hostile *against*" seems more appropriate.

62 James D. G. Dunn, *The Epistles to the Colossians and to Philemon: A Commentary on the Greek Text*, NIGTC (Grand Rapids: Eerdmans, 1996), 197. See also Edward Lohse, *Colossians and Philemon*, ed. Helmut Koester, trans. William R. Poehlmann and Robert J. Karris, Hermeneia (Philadelphia: Fortress, 1971), 124–31; R. McL. Wilson, *A Critical and Exegetical Commentary on Colossians and Philemon*, ICC (London: T&T Clark, 2005), 231; Douglas J. Moo, *The Letters to the Colossians and to Philemon*, PNTC (Grand Rapids: Eerdmans, 2008), 242.

Yet another example showing the significance of context for interpreting a genitive is ἡ προσφορὰ τῶν ἐθνῶν *the offering of the Gentiles* (Rom 15:16), an expression that can be taken as (1) subjective genitive ("the offering the Gentiles make to the Jews"), or (2) appositional/epexegetical ("the offering that Paul makes, namely the Gentiles"). Paul announces the purpose of his travel to Jerusalem to advance the Gospel is "that the offering of the Gentiles might become acceptable" (cf. Rom 15:31 where prayers are offered to this effect). The head noun is a verbal (from προσφέρω) idea,[63] opening the door to subjective and objective senses. A subjective genitive ("the offering the Gentiles make") would make good sense: the collection of the Gentile churches for the Jerusalem church is the subject of discussion from Paul with several early Christian groups (Gal 2:1–10 cf. Acts 11:27–30; 12:25; 2 Cor 8–9). David J. Downs strongly defends the subjective genitive in contrast to the appositional.[64] Downs points to Phil 2:17 ἐπὶ τῇ θυσίᾳ καὶ λειτουργίᾳ τῆς πίστεως ὑμῶν for support of the subjective genitive, with the referent being the Philippian church's offering for Paul (Phil 4:10–20).[65]

Yet in spite of the prominence of the collection for the Judean church in Paul's writings, the immediate context of Romans affirms an objective (Paul is offering the Gentiles to God) or epexegetical sense. Several commentators take ἡ προσφορὰ τῶν ἐθνῶν as an epexegetical (appositive), with objective sense.[66] Robert Jewett supports this view, basing his judgment on the phrase ἡγιασμένη ἐν πνεύματι ἁγίῳ "made holy by the Holy Spirit" as a description "of the purity of God's chosen people." In Paul's thinking money offerings cannot be sanctified by the Holy Spirit, but God's people are.[67]

---

63 BDAG 887 s.v. προσφορά

64 David J. Downs, "'The Offering of the Gentiles' in Romans 15.16,"*JSNT* 29.2 (2006): 173–86, doi:10.1177/0142064x06072837. Also covered in Downs' revision of his Ph.D. thesis: David J. Downs, *The Offering of the Gentiles: Paul's Collection for Jerusalem in Its Chronological, Cultural, and Cultic Contexts*, WUNT 2/248 (Tübingen: Mohr Siebeck, 2008).

65 Downs, "Offering," 178.

66 Charles Kingsley Barrett, *The Epistle to the Romans*, 2nd ed., BNTC (London: Hendrickson, 1991), 275; Joseph A. Fitzmyer, *Romans: A New Translation with Introduction and Commentary*, AB 33 (New York: Doubleday, 1993), 712; Douglas J. Moo, *The Epistle to the Romans*, 2nd ed., NICNT (Grand Rapids: Eerdmans, 2018), 907.

67 Robert Jewett, with the assistance of Roy David Kotansky, *Romans: A Commentary*, ed. Eldon Jay Epp, Hermeneia (Minneapolis: Fortress, 2007), 906–10, esp. 908.

Wider Context

After considering the immediate context the wider context should be considered next. A good practical example is found in Margaret Thrall's analysis of ἀπὸ κυρίου πνεύματος *from the Lord, the Spirit* (2 Cor 3:18). Thrall appeals to both the immediate and wider contexts, also considering similar passages outside the book. The phrase κυρίου πνεύματος could well be regarded as one of the most difficult genitive expressions in the Pauline corpus. Her treatment provides a good model to be followed in any serious analysis. She says the phrase:

> has been given numerous explanations. Disagreement centres not on the meaning of the preposition but on the force of κυρίου πνεύματος, which has been interpreted in at least seven ways. (i) 'A sovereign Spirit', with κυρίου seen as an adjective. Elsewhere in the NT, however, κύριος is nowhere used adjectivally. (ii) 'The Lord of the Spirit'. This is grammatically simple, but the phrase would have no NT parallels. (iii) 'The Spirit which is the Lord'. This reverses the word order, and, more importantly, the sense of v. 17a. (iv) 'The Lord who is Spirit'. This does not fit v.17, Which speaks of 'the Spirit' as an entity rather than as a mode of being. (v) 'The Lord the Spirit', or 'The Lord who is the Spirit'. This is a likely possibility. (vi) 'A Yahweh who is (now with us as) Spirit'. The point would be that the Lord of the Moses story is no longer remote, but 'present as the Spirit among his people'. This translation (though not the comment?) fits the anarthrous state of the nouns. But Paul could scarcely have meant 'a Yahweh', as though there could be more than one .... (vii) 'The Spirit of the Lord'. The word order might count against this, but πνεύματος might be placed last because it carries the emphasis. Paul would wish to stress yet once more that life in the sphere of the covenant is life inspired and directed by the Spirit. There is not much to choose between this interpretation and (v) above. But since in Rom 8:11, 13–15, it is the Spirit, not 'the Lord', that is the transformative agent, the rendering 'The Spirit of the Lord' is preferable.[68]

Same Wording but Different Meanings

Although several genitive constructions may have the same wording, they may differ in meaning when used in different contexts. A subjective genitive in one context may be an objective in another context. The terms *the glory of God* in καὶ ὑστεροῦνται τῆς δόξης τοῦ θεοῦ (Rom 3:23) and in καὶ καυχώμεθα ἐπ' ἐλπίδι τῆς δόξης τοῦ θεοῦ (Rom 5:2) are subjective genitive. But the same terms in καθὼς καὶ ὁ Χριστὸς προσελάβετο ὑμᾶς εἰς δόξαν τοῦ θεοῦ (Rom 15:7), and in πάντα εἰς δόξαν θεοῦ

---

68 Margaret E. Thrall, *A Critical and Exegetical Commentary on the Second Epistle of the Corinthians*, 2 vols., ICC (London: T&T Clark, 1994), 1:287.

ποιεῖτε (1 Cor 10:31), also in τὴν εὐχαριστίαν περισσεύσῃ εἰς τὴν δόξαν τοῦ θεοῦ (2 Cor 4:15) are objective genitive. This underscores the vital importance of context for interpretation.

Likewise, the genitive phrase δικαιοσύνη θεοῦ *the righteousness of God* in Rom 1:17; 3:21–22 needs careful consideration. This phrase occurs in a context that speaks about the way God bestows his righteousness to those who believe, whereas the same phrase in Jas 1:20, speaks about the righteousness required by God in order to fulfill his will through believers, which is "what God is accomplishing in this world."[69]

Taking another example from this category, the phrase ἡ ἀγάπη τοῦ θεοῦ *the love of God* may be considered. It seems that the meaning of this genitive construction in Paul's writings is always subjective, thus Rom 5:5; 8:39; 2 Cor 13:13; and 2 Thess 3:5. But TEV renders the expression in 1 John with an objective meaning in 1 John 2:5; 3:17; 5:3, and subjective meaning in 1 John 4:9.[70]

Parallel Genitive Expressions

The interpreter of genitive constructions should also take into consideration parallel genitive expressions that occur in the same verse or passage, whether they are used synthetically or antithetically. The genitive constructions in ἡ χάρις τοῦ κυρίου Ἰησοῦ Χριστοῦ καὶ ἡ ἀγάπη τοῦ θεοῦ καὶ ἡ κοινωνία τοῦ ἁγίου πνεύματος μετὰ πάντων ὑμῶν (2 Cor 13:13) provides an ideal example of this proposition. There are three parallel genitive expressions in this verse: (1) ἡ χάρις τοῦ κυρίου Ἰησοῦ, (2) ἡ ἀγάπη τοῦ θεοῦ, and (3) ἡ κοινωνία τοῦ ἁγίου πνεύματος. Jeffrey Weima provides an explanation in his treatment of Pauline letter endings:

> Virtually all scholars agreed in taking the first two phrases ('The grace of the Lord Jesus Christ' and 'the love of God') as subjective genitives. There is much disagreement, however, over whether the third phrase ('the fellowship of the Holy Spirit') is subjective (the fellowship with other believers brought about by the Holy Spirit) …. Since the first two phrases use a subjective genitive, and a similar reading of the third phrase fits well with the rest of the closing which emphasizes peace and unity within the Corinthian church, it would seem best to take 'the fellowship of the Holy Spirit' as a subjective genitive.[71]

---

69   Scot McKnight, *The Letter of James*, NICNT (Grand Rapids: Eerdmans, 2011), 139.

70   TEV interprets "the love of God" according to context. Other versions offer little help.

71   Jeffrey A. D. Weima, *Neglected Endings: The Significance of the Pauline Letter Closings*, JSNTSS 101 (Sheffield, England: JSOT Press, 1994), 213–14n3.

Another example is found in 1 Cor 15:20: νυνὶ δὲ Χριστὸς ἐγήγερται ἐκ νεκρῶν ἀπαρχὴ τῶν κεκοιμημένων. The second part of the verse, ἀπαρχὴ τῶν κεκοιμημένων *firstfruits of those who have fallen asleep*, is *synthetic* to the first part, ἐγήγερται ἐκ νεκρῶν *he has been raised from the dead*, with the first part shedding light on the second. If the second genitive expression ἀπαρχὴ τῶν κεκοιμημένων were read apart from its context, it would mean that Christ was the first of those who were fallen asleep (i.e., the first person to die). But since ἀπαρχὴ τῶν κεκοιμημένων is preceded by ἐγήγερται ἐκ νεκρῶν, the preposition ἐκ extends its meaning to the second construction "the first to rise from those who were fallen asleep."

A similar synthetic parallel is εἴτε ἀδελφοὶ ἡμῶν, ἀπόστολοι ἐκκλησιῶν, δόξα Χριστοῦ (2 Cor 8:23). Here the genitives are genitives of separation, "messengers sent from the churches [and glory] reflected from Christ." This translation is based on the fact that the word ἀπόστολοι carries an inherent meaning of sending, hence a genitive of separation, "sent by/from the churches."[72] The juxtaposition of ἀπόστολοι ἐκκλησιῶν and δόξα Χριστοῦ strongly supports regarding δόξα Χριστοῦ as a genitive of separation also: "messengers reflecting the glory and honor of Christ."

Antithetic parallel constructions also need to be compared in order to determine the meaning of the genitive. In 1 Cor 2:12 there are two parallel antithetic expressions: τὸ πνεῦμα τοῦ κόσμου ... τὸ πνεῦμα τὸ ἐκ τοῦ θεοῦ. Each is an interpretive key to the other. Likewise, in ἡ γὰρ κατὰ θεὸν λύπη μετάνοιαν εἰς σωτηρίαν ἀμεταμέλητον ἐργάζεται· ἡ δὲ τοῦ κόσμου λύπη θάνατον κατεργάζεται (2 Cor 7:10), the preposition κατὰ in the first part should be supplied in the second to give the appropriate meaning. The phrase ἡ κατὰ θεὸν λύπη *sorrow according to God* informs how to take ἡ τοῦ κόσμου λύπη: "sorrow of the world's viewpoint."

Different Passages by the Same Author

To ensure a sound interpretative procedure, similar genitive expressions should be compared, and all the better if they come from the same author. The following expressions provide a case in point: τὴν ἀλήθειαν τοῦ εὐαγγελίου (Gal 2:14), ἐν τῷ λόγῳ τῆς ἀληθείας τοῦ εὐαγγελίου (Col 1:5), and τὸν λόγον τῆς ἀληθείας, τὸ εὐαγγέλιον τῆς σωτηρίας ὑμῶν (Eph 1:13). Comparing these genitive constructions helps solve the ambiguity: *the truth of the gospel* or *the word of truth*. The second part of the phrase in Col 1:5, for example, has a middle adjectival noun, τῆς ἀληθείας. Is this adjectival genitive a description for τῷ λόγῳ or for τοῦ εὐαγγελίου? The need for

---

72 Hans Dieter Betz translates ἀπόστολοι ἐκκλησιῶν as "envoys representing the churches" with a cross reference to Acts 15:22, 27 (*2 Corinthians 8 and 9: A Commentary on Two Administrative Letters of the Apostle Paul*, Hermeneia [Philadelphia: Fortress, 1985], 81n343).

analysis of the three-word genitive construction, the interrelation of words in the construction and comparison with synthetic parallels, all these steps are crucial for reaching a solution. It seems here that τῆς ἀληθείας describes τῷ λόγῳ, and that both words translated as "the truthful word" stand in apposition to the "Gospel," following the example of Eph 1:13.

Often parallel structures signal parallel semantics, and comparing them can provide good illumination. Richard B. Hays insightfully compares the genitive constructions in Gal 2:20 and Rom 5:15:

Rom 5:15: ἐν χάριτι τῇ [τοῦ ἑνὸς ἀνθρώπου Ἰησοῦ Χριστοῦ.]

Gal 2:20: ἐν πίστει τῇ [τοῦ υἱοῦ τοῦ θεοῦ.]

Both of these involve the repetition of the article to put a genitive in second attributive position; the difference being only that in one χάρις is the head noun, where in the other πίστις is the *nomen regens*. "It would never occur to anyone to translate τοῦ ἑνὸς ἀνθρώπου Ἰησοῦ Χριστοῦ [Rom 5:15] here as an objective genitive." That is, the grace comes from Jesus Christ. So, it follows on this reasoning that the structure in Gal 2:20 is also a subjective or source genitive: "'by the faith of the Son of God ...' or '... by the faith which comes from the Son of God.'" For Hays, both meanings are possible; the operative point is that neither is an objective genitive.[73]

Along similar lines of investigation one should take note of a phenomenon in Paul's writings in which similar genitive constructions are used with converse word order. Each of these genitive constructions has almost the same meaning, despite the difference in order. A phrase like ὁ δὲ θεὸς τῆς εἰρήνης (Rom 15:33; 16:20), which means "the God who gives peace," is quite similar in meaning to ἡ εἰρήνη τοῦ θεοῦ (Phil 4:7), "the peace given by God." Likewise, the phrases τὴν ἐπαγγελίαν τοῦ πνεύματος *the promise of the Spirit* (Gal 3:14) and τῷ πνεύματι τῆς ἐπαγγελίας *the Spirit of the promise* (Eph 1:13), are also similar in meaning. So, too ἐν δυνάμει πνεύματος ἁγίου *by the power of the Holy Spirit* (Rom 15:13, 19) and πνεῦμα ... δυνάμεως *Spirit ... of power* (2 Tim 1:7); and ὁ θεὸς τῆς ἀγάπης *the God of love* (2 Cor 13:11), and ἡ ἀγάπη τοῦ θεοῦ *the love of God* (2 Cor 13:13).

---

73 Richard B. Hays, *The Faith of Jesus Christ: The Narrative Substructure of Galatians 3:1–4:11*, 2nd ed. (Grand Rapids: Eerdmans, 2002), 154. See also J. Louis Martyn, *Galatians: A New Translation with Introduction and Commentary*, AB 33A (New Haven: Yale University Press, 2010), 259, who cites this argument favorably from the 1st ed.

Genitive and Non-genitive Expressions

To comprehend the meaning of genitive constructions the interpreter needs also to compare them with phrases that are similar in wording, even if non-genitival. Such non-genitive phrases may provide a clue for decoding enigmatic genitive constructions. For example, a possible key to understanding δικαιοσύνη θεοῦ (Rom 3:22) is found in τὴν ἐκ θεοῦ δικαιοσύνην (Phil 3:9). Similarly, the phrase τῆς δικαιοσύνης τῆς πίστεως (Rom 4:11) may be explained by comparison with δικαιοσύνην τὴν ἐκ πίστεως (Rom 9:30), or with ἡ ἐκ πίστεως δικαιοσύνη (Rom 10:6). Likewise, the meaning of εἰς τὴν ὑμῶν προκοπὴν καὶ χαρὰν τῆς πίστεως (Phil 1:25) is made clear by comparison with πάσης χαρᾶς καὶ εἰρήνης ἐν τῷ πιστεύειν (Rom 15:13). So also, the following phrases throw light on each other: τὸν πλοῦτον τῆς δόξης αὐτοῦ (Rom 9:23) and κατὰ τὸ πλοῦτος αὐτοῦ ἐν δόξῃ ἐν Χριστῷ Ἰησοῦ (Phil 4:19). In 1 Thess 1:6 the genitive μετὰ χαρᾶς πνεύματος ἁγίου may be interpreted by the prepositional phrase in χαρὰ ἐν πνεύματι ἁγίῳ of Rom 14:17. The phrase ἡ πίστις ὑμῶν (Rom 1:8) is synonymous with τὴν καθ᾽ ὑμᾶς πίστιν (Eph 1:15).

Understanding a genitive construction can be enhanced by gathering and comparing related references with similar wording. We can get a better picture of what ἐν χάριτι Χριστοῦ *in the grace of Christ* (Gal 1:6) means by comparing it to ἐν τῇ χάριτι τῇ ἐν Χριστῷ *the grace which is in Christ* (2 Tim 2:1). The latter lends more weight to a genitive of source in the former. When Paul writes that each Christian is given grace *according to the measure of the gift of Christ* ἡ χάρις κατὰ τὸ μέτρον τῆς δωρεᾶς τοῦ Χριστοῦ (Eph 4:7), the similar expression describing *the grace of God* as *given to you in Christ Jesus* τῇ χάριτι τοῦ θεοῦ τῇ δοθείσῃ ὑμῖν ἐν Χριστῷ Ἰησοῦ (1 Cor 1:4) helps identify Christ as the agent of God's activity among Christians, the source of the grace given to them.

It is appropriate now to examine that famous and most-debated genitive construction πίστεως Ἰησοῦ Χριστοῦ *the faith/faithfulness of Jesus Christ*. The theological implications related to the phrase and its similar expression πίστεως Ἰησοῦ have somewhat clouded the debate. Porter summarizes the debate as follows:

> Rom. 3.22: πίστεως Ἰησοῦ Χριστοῦ ... has been an item of recurring debate. The debate is often put in terms of whether the genitive is subjective (or source or origin) and rendered 'faith of Jesus Christ', 'faith given by Jesus Christ', or even 'Jesus Christ's faithfulness', or (b) objective and rendered 'faith in Jesus Christ', or (c) both. Semantic or syntactical analysis alone will not solve the problem; context must decide. Commentators weigh such factors as whether suitable parallels are found in Romans 4 with reference to Abraham's faith, whether reference to "to all who believe" (v. 22) is

redundant, whether Christ's faithfulness is an issue for Paul in Romans, and whether and in what way Paul's emphasis is on God's righteousness.[74]

If the principle set out above about the need to compare genitive with non-genitive expressions, especially those with the same wording, were applied to the phrase πίστεως Ἰησοῦ Χριστοῦ, the debate could perhaps be settled. The problematic phrases are πίστεως Ἰησοῦ Χριστοῦ (Rom 3:22; Gal 2:16; 3:22);[75] πίστεως Ἰησοῦ (Rom 2:26); πίστεως Χριστοῦ (Gal 2:16; Phil 3:9); ἐν πίστει ζῶ τῇ τοῦ υἱοῦ τοῦ θεοῦ (Gal 2:20);[76] ἐν ἀκροβυστίᾳ πίστεως τοῦ πατρὸς ἡμῶν Ἀβραάμ (Rom 4:12); πίστεως Ἀβραάμ (Rom 4:16); διὰ τῆς πίστεως αὐτοῦ (Eph 3:12); διὰ τῆς πίστεως τῆς ἐνεργείας τοῦ θεοῦ (Col 2:12). These phrases relate "faith" to "Jesus," to "Christ," to "him," to "the Son of God," to "Abraham," even to "the action of God" without using any connecting preposition.

A number of phrases have almost the same wording as the genitive phrases above, but in them faith is related to Jesus Christ through the use of prepositions. Relevant verses are: Πάντες γὰρ υἱοὶ θεοῦ ἐστε διὰ τῆς πίστεως ἐν Χριστῷ Ἰησοῦ (Gal 3:26); ἀκούσαντες τὴν πίστιν ὑμῶν ἐν Χριστῷ Ἰησοῦ (Col 1:4); τὸ στερέωμα τῆς εἰς Χριστὸν πίστεως ὑμῶν (Col 2:5); ἀκούσας τὴν καθ᾽ ὑμᾶς πίστιν ἐν τῷ κυρίῳ Ἰησοῦ (Eph 1:15); ἐν πίστει τῇ ἐν Χριστῷ Ἰησοῦ (1 Tim 3:13); and εἰς σωτηρίαν διὰ πίστεως τῆς ἐν Χριστῷ Ἰησοῦ (2 Tim 3:15). These phrases using prepositions constitute a clue to understand the problematic genitives that are used without prepositions.[77]

Authorial Usage

A consideration not to be ignored is an author's usage in similar contexts or similar constructions. Certain patterns emerge in an author's habits that can be observed to the advantage of the interpreter. As we have seen before the term "the love of God" is a subjective genitive wherever it appears in Paul's writings. So, the natural frame of reference in reading Paul's use "the love of God" views love as an act directed from God to man. The interpreter, accordingly, when meeting a difficult genitive

---

74 Porter, *Idioms*, 95.

75 Hays remarks: "Just as in Gal 3:22, there is a ponderous redundancy in Rom 3:22 if πίστις Ἰησοῦ Χριστοῦ means 'faith in Jesus Christ.' Why then would Paul need to add εἰς πάντας τοὺς πιστεύοντας?" (*Faith of Jesus Christ*, 158).

76 Dunn, on the other hand, interprets the opposite way: "The latter phrase is more cumbersome than usual ('faith which is in … ') and again makes a better sense as 'faith in the Son of God' than 'by the faith(fulness) which is of the Son of God'" (*The Epistle to the Galatians*, BNTC [London: Continuum, 1993], 146).

77 There is no attempt here to solve the theological problems of the πίστις Χριστοῦ debate. The aim of this section is only to direct attention to exegetical possibilities.

phrase should search for parallel constructions and study them in their contexts in order to discover the author's frame of reference. Take, for instance, κατὰ τὸ εὐαγγέλιόν μου καὶ τὸ κήρυγμα Ἰησοῦ Χριστοῦ *according to my gospel and the preaching of Jesus Christ* (Rom 16:25). Should the second genitive Ἰησοῦ be considered subjective (Christ's preaching) as the genitive μου must be (Paul's preaching), or a genitive of reference or substance (the preaching *about* Jesus Christ)? Both give a satisfactory sense. If the genitives here are subjective, then the verse speaks about Paul's and Jesus' proclamation, but if the second genitive τὸ κήρυγμα Ἰησου is a genitive of substance, then it refers to the proclamation of Paul and of the other apostles, and in both cases the content of the proclamation (Jesus) is the same. However, further considerations are necessary at this point. Thorough examination of these two genitive phrases and parallel expressions should guide our understanding of "his gospel" and of τὸ κήρυγμα Ἰησου. Examination of texts such as 1 Cor 1:21; 2:4; 15:14; 2 Tim 4:17; and Titus 1:3 leaves one with the impression that the κήρυγμα is *about* Jesus. Thus, the genitive is one of reference (i.e., an objective genitive).[78]

Beneath the Surface

Surface grammatical structures are not enough in determining the meaning of certain genitives. To illustrate this proposition, it is bewildering at first sight to encounter εἰς ὑπακοὴν πίστεως *to obedience of faith* (Rom 1:5). Usually the head noun in a genitive construction governs the following noun. But applying grammatical rules to this phrase does not help here. A deeper semantic study is necessary to explore the cause-effect relationship between obedience and faith. Thus, NIV has "the obedience that comes from faith."

Richard Hays, however, argues on the basis of ἡ πίστις ἐξ ἀκοῆς (Rom 10:17), ἐξ ἀκοῆς πίστεως (Gal 3:2), and τοὺς οἰκείους τῆς πίστεως (Gal 6:10), that the meaning of "faith" in Rom 1:5—rather than being the act of believing—stands for what is believed, i.e., the name of the Christian movement. According to the use of "faith" in Galatians, Hays suggests that ἀκοῆς πίστεως should be translated as: "the message of faith" or "the gospel-message."[79] In this case, we should prefer the epexegetical sense of the genitive: "the message which is the faith."

The endeavors for deeper investigation do not stop here. Don B. Garlington's monograph handles the concept of obedience in Paul's letter to the Romans. After an examination of "obedience" in intertestamental Greek literature, he concludes that Paul coined this phrase, "The obedience of faith" to show that the motive

---

78 James D. G. Dunn, *Romans 9–16*, WBC 38B (Dallas: Word, 1988), 914.

79 Hays, *Faith of Jesus Christ*, 131.

behind his missionary work was to make people of all nations faithful covenant-keepers by virtue of their trust in Christ, and that is in contrast with "The obedience to the law."[80]

Septuagintal Influence

Sometimes the interpreter of genitive constructions faces a problematic text such as ἀπὸ προσώπου τοῦ κυρίου καὶ ἀπὸ τῆς δόξης τῆς ἰσχύος αὐτοῦ *away from the face of the Lord and from the glory of his strength* (2 Thess 1:9). In this verse there is a three-word genitive with two nouns, τῆς δόξης τῆς ἰσχύος. Either of the two could be an "adjective" describing the other: *glorious strength* or *strong glory*. Precision as to which is the "adjective" may be achieved by examination of the LXX. Verse 9b is a direct quotation from a thrice repeated verse in the Septuagint: ἀπὸ προσώπου τοῦ φοβου τοῦ κυρίου καὶ ἀπὸ τῆς δόξης τῆς ἰσχύος αὐτοῦ (Isa 2:10, 19, 21), "from before the fear of the Lord and from the glory of his strength" (NETS). In this verse there are two juxtaposed three-word genitives each with a set of three substantives that contrast each other successively:

ἀπὸ προσώπου τοῦ φόβου τοῦ κυρίου

ἀπὸ τῆς δόξης τῆς ἰσχύος αὐτου

According to the common rule of identifying the relatedness of the adjectival genitive in three-word constructions τοῦ φόβου here describes προσώπου, and τῆς ἰσχύος describes τῆς δόξης. In this case the translation would be "from the dread face [presence] of the Lord and from his strong radiance." This reading of the Septuagint-influenced expression can be applied to the text of 2 Thess 1:9. Therefore instead of translating the two genitives as "his glorious might/strength" (TEV CSB) or as "the splendor of his might" (REB NRSV NIV NJB) the more satisfactory rendering is "his powerful splendor."[81]

Contemporary Texts

Early grammarians were aware of the fact that historical data have a role in discovering the meaning of the genitive. Winer's treatment of the "genitive of

---

80   Don B. Garlington, *Faith, Obedience, and Perseverance: Aspects of Paul's Letter to the Romans*, WUNT 79 (Tübingen: Mohr, 1994; repr., Eugene, OR: Wipf & Stock, 2009), 145–46.

81   James Everett Frame, *A Critical and Exegetical Commentary on the Epistles of St. Paul to the Thessalonians*, ICC (New York: Scribner, 1912), 234–36.

kindred" discusses the importance of history in order to explain obscure genitive constructions:

> οἱ Χλόης [sic], [1 Cor 1:11], are *those who are connected with Chloe*, like οἱ Ἀριστοβούλου, οἱ Ναρκίσσου, [Rom 16:10–11]; a more definite explanation the history alone could supply. Perhaps, with most interpreters, we should understand the *households* of these persons: others suppose the slaves to be referred to. To the original readers of the Epistles the expression was clear.[82]

Robertson similarly points to history as an interpretive tool, "in [Matt 1:12] we have μετοικεσίαν Βαβυλῶνος. It is translated 'removal to Babylon.' Now the genitive does not mean 'to,' but that is the correct translation of the total idea obtained by knowledge of the O. T."[83] In accordance with this principle the phrase ἐν ταπεινοφροσύνῃ καὶ θρησκείᾳ τῶν ἀγγέλων (Col 2:18) is chosen for application. The problem here is that the genitive τῶν ἀγγέλων could be either subjective or objective. The genitive phrase could mean "worship that humans offer to angels" (objective), for there are hints to such an attitude in Rev 19:10 and 22:8. Or it could mean (subjective) "the worship that angels offer to God" (e.g., Isa 6:2, 3; Rev 5:11, 12). In order to decide which of the two meanings the author intended, context and historical data should be investigated. Markus Barth and Helmut Blanke set a good example:

> Paul does not use this occurrence of "worship of angels," which characterizes the piety of his "adversaries," to point out that only God is to be revered .... If veneration of angels were meant, it would be very astonishing that such worship would escape comment from Paul. A reverence for angels would raise questions concerning the supremacy of Christ over all things, which is so broadly detailed in Col. Thus it is more likely that we have a *genitivus subjectivus* in the verse.[84]

Contemporary Jewish literature, examples of which F. O. Francis gathers, shows this fascination with "the motif of participation in the heavenly worship service of angels was widely distributed in the Jewish apocalyptic literature."[85] There is another grammatical factor that supports Barth and Blanke's subjective genitive

---

82 Winer, *Grammar*, 238.

83 Robertson, *Grammar*, 494.

84 Markus Barth and Helmut Blanke, *Colossians: A New Translation With Introduction and Commentary*, trans. Astrid B. Beck, AB 34B (New York: Doubleday, 1994), 345.

85 Barth and Blanke, *Colossians: A New Translation With Introduction and Commentary*, 345. J. D. G. Dunn lists Isa 6:2–3; Dan 7:10; and a host of Second Temple literature: 1 Enoch 14:18–23 36:4, 39–40; 61:10–12; 2 Enoch 20–21; Apoc. Ab. 17–18; T. Levi 3:3–8; T. of Job 48–50 (*Colossians and Philemon*, 180–81). This literature is the subject of detailed discussion in Fred O. Francis, "Humility and Angelic Worship in Col 2:18," *Studia Theologica: Nordic Journal of Theology* 16.2 (1962): 109–34, doi:10.1080/00393386208599828.

interpretation: the phrase contains a copulative καὶ that connects ταπεινοφροσύνη with θρησκείᾳ. The verbal power of ταπεινοφροσύνη, "self-abasement," is intransitive, while θρησκείᾳ "worship" could be either transitive or intransitive. Now, if this is the case, then the intransitive meaning of "worship" should follow that of "self-abasement"; this would make the phrase a subjective genitive. Though it is possible that this is an objective genitive (John is warned against this in Rev 19:10; 22:8–9 as is Isaiah in Ascen. Isa. 7:21), the interpretation of τῶν ἀγγέλων as subjective genitive, "is confirmed and not contradicted by the derivative possibility of worship directed to angels."[86]

Another example that may be mentioned in this category is the phrase τὸ ἑαυτοῦ σκεῦος κτᾶσθαι ἐν ἁγιασμῷ καὶ τιμῇ in 1 Thess 4:4. There are a variety of possible meanings for the problematic use of σκεῦος, "vessel," in the genitive construction τὸ ἑαυτοῦ σκεῦος: (1) *Wife*: "that each one of you know how to take a wife for himself in holiness and honor" (RSV); (2) *Body*: "each one of you must learn to gain mastery over his body, to hallow and honour it" (REB NIV NRSV NJB NET ESV); or (3) *Member*: "each of you guarding his member in sanctity and honor" (NAB). For Raymond Collins, the σκεῦος-wife option is somewhat stronger. His arguments appeal to *grammar*: the use of ἑαυτοῦ; to *semantics*: the use of the related verb κτᾶσθαι: to procure for oneself, to acquire, get; to *Bible parallels*: 1 Pet 3:7; to *extra-biblical parallels*: a number of rabbinic texts use *keli*, the equivalent of σκεῦος, to indicate a woman.[87]

Torleif Elgvin argues against the σκεῦος-wife interpretation, citing the emended wording כלי חיקכה "the vessel of your bosom," from *Sapiential Work A*, a fragmentary second century BCE text from Qumran (1Q26 4Q415/416/417/418a/418b/423). Hoping to elucidate the meaning of σκεῦος of 1 Thess 4:4, Elgvin says חיק (Gen 16:5; Deut 13:7, 28:54, 56; 2 Sam 12:8; 1 Kings 1:2; Micah 7:5; Prov 5:20; 6:27) appears in OT texts with connotations of reference to sexual organs, but כלי חיקכה finds no parallel in the OT or in second temple texts with the referent of *wife*. Instead, Elgvin points to 1 Sam 21:6, where כלי refers to male sexual organs.[88] The oddly worded expression in Sap. Work A probably owes its influence to "the wife of your bosom" (Deut 13:7; 28:54; cf. Deut 28:56 for a parallel expression "the man of her bosom").[89] This reasoning leads to the conclusion that τὸ

---

86 Francis, "Angelic Worship," 129.

87 Raymond F. Collins, *Studies on the First Letter to the Thessalonians*, BETL 66 (Leuven, Belgium: Leuven University Press, 1984), 313.

88 Torleif Elgvin, "'To Master His Own Vessel': 1 Thess 4.4 in Light of New Qumran Evidence,"*NTS* 43 (1997): 607, doi:10.1017/S0028688500023419.

89 Elgvin, "Vessel," 608.

ἑαυτοῦ σκεῦος κτᾶσθαι in 1 Thess 4:4, "guarding his member" (NAB), is a reference to the protection of the male sexual organ from sexual immorality.[90]

Genitive in Concatenation

What have been considered thus far are aspects of investigation deemed necessary for setting principles of interpretation for genitive constructions in general. Now it is appropriate to discuss rules that may guide the interpreter in genitive-in-concatenation exposition. The first step toward that goal should be to examine the history and progress of interpretation of the genitive in concatenation.

History of Interpretation

Here we will draw together what we found about the discussion of genitive clusters in the NT grammars surveyed in Chapter Two. In the nineteenth century, Winer introduced a rule to interpret genitives in concatenation: "Not unfrequently, especially in Paul's style, *three* genitives are found connected together, one governed grammatically by the other. In this case one of the substantives often represents an adjectival notion."[91] Alexander Buttmann, a contemporary of Winer's, offers more systematic handling of the genitive in clusters:

(a) If the Genitives depend one on another, they stand, as far as possible, in the order in which they depend on one another;

(b) If, however, two Genitives depend on one and the same substantive, this fact is also, at least as a rule, indicated by the position (before and after the governing substantive).[92]

Blass and Debrunner do not bring any new principles for interpreting genitive in concatenation, they only reverse the order of Buttmann's rules:

(1) Two genitives dependent on the same noun – which then usually stands between them – do not occur often: [2 Cor 5:1] ἡ ἐπίγειος ἡμῶν οἰκία τοῦ σκήνους (possessive and appositive genitives). (2) Generally one genitive is dependent on another, whereby an author, particularly Paul, occasionally produces a quite cumbersome accumulation of genitives; to facilitate clarity in such cases, the governing genitive must always precede

---

90 Elgvin, "Vessel," 604, 617–19. See also Jay E. Smith, "1 Thessalonians 4:4: Breaking the Impasse," *BBR* 11.1 (2001): 65–105.

91 Winer, *Grammar*, 238.

92 Buttmann, *Grammar*, 155.

the dependent genitive ... [2 Cor 4:4] τὸν φωτισμὸν τοῦ εὐαγγελίου ('the light emanating from the Gospel') τῆς δόξης (content) τοῦ Χριστοῦ.[93]

A. T. Robertson mentions only one general rule for interpreting genitives in concatenation: "The governing genitive comes before the dependent genitive," though he does comment on exceptions to the general rule (cf. 2 Pet 3:2).[94] Nigel Turner notices Paul sometimes uses two genitives that "depend on the same noun, which then usually stands between them," citing 2 Cor 5:1, and Phil 2:30. Beyond this, he says what Blass and Debrunner to the effect that successive genitives usually depend on the one before them, which "sometimes [creates] a clumsy accumulation."[95]

Beekman and Callow offer rules for the genitive in concatenation with the Bible translator in mind. Applying a transformational grammar, they hold that each two-word genitive construction contains one or two propositions depending on how the two words in the construction relate to each other. Concerning three- and four-word genitives, they write:

> The simple form A of B may represent one or two propositions. The same observation applies to chains of genitives. The presence of three or four nominals does not imply that three or four propositions are represented; each genitive construction has to be considered individually in its context to see how it can be restated.[96]

Beekman and Callow offer three examples: Col 1:9, 13, 22. In Col 1:9 τὴν ἐπίγνωσιν τοῦ θελήματος αὐτοῦ which is a simple concatenation: the translation "knowledge of his will" works well enough, but implies "he wills" (subjective genitive) and "to know" (where the second chain in the cluster is the object of the verbal head noun).[97] The example of Col 1:13 εἰς τὴν βασιλείαν τοῦ υἱοῦ τῆς ἀγάπης αὐτοῦ *into the kingdom of the Son of the love of him* is more difficult:

> with four nominals ... "the love of him" is a Subjective genitive, equivalent to "he loves." "The kingdom of the Son" is also a Subjective genitive, representing the proposition "the Son rules (us)." ... In this case, then, although there are four nominals, there are only two propositions .... [thus:] "He loves his Son who rules us" [or] "(we) are ruled by his Son whom he loves."[98]

93 BDF §168 p. 93.
94 Robertson, *Grammar*, 503.
95 MHT₃ 218.
96 Beekman-Callow, 358.
97 Beekman-Callow, 358.
98 Beekman-Callow, 358–59.

More complicated genitive constructions, they suggest, require a step-by-step analysis. Romans 2:5 (ἡμέρᾳ ὀργῆς καὶ ἀποκαλύψεως δικαιοκρισίας τοῦ θεοῦ) is just such an example, designating the nominals ABCD, " [A] a day [B] of revelation [C] of righteous-judgment [D] of God" The best way to handle it, they propose, "to proceed backwards along the genitive construction working out each relation in turn, and this may well be a procedure that can be used to elucidate this type of complex chained genitive."[99] The C-D unit expands to "God judges (people) righteously," with God as agent (a subjective genitive). The B nominal is a verbal "it will be revealed that God judges (people) righteously." Adding headword A to this, the chain resolves to, "a day when it will be revealed that God judges (people) righteously."[100] The only shortcoming of this analysis is that the anarthrous head noun should be taken as definite: *the* day instead of *a* day. As we have already seen, it is not uncommon when the head noun is the object of a preposition for it to be anarthrous. On the corollary to Apollonius' Canon, the chain is made definite by the definiteness of the final nominal in the chain τοῦ θεοῦ.[101]

Daniel B. Wallace observes an important modification to BDF in interpreting the genitive in concatenation:

> Normally in gen. chains … each successive gen. modifies the one that precedes it. But when an attributive gen. is in the mix, matters are a bit more complicated. Since an attributive gen. is by nature strongly adjectival, it is best to convert it into an adjective and take it "out of the loop" of the gen. chain …. an attributive gen. does not normally, if ever, take a modifier.[102]

In conclusion to this survey of the history of interpretation of concatenative genitive, it seems that only a few rules were set for genitive interpretation and only a few observations made. Thus far, there has been no really comprehensive investigation into the genitive in clusters.

Interpretive Principles

In Chapters Five to Six, we proposed several principles of interpretation for genitives in clusters. These principles were deduced from the analyses made of cluster genitive constructions so that one may comprehend fully all the nuances

---

99   Beekman-Callow, 359
100 Beekman-Callow, 360.
101 For Apollonius' corollary see Wallace, *ExSyn* 250–51.
102 Wallace, *ExSyn* 87–88.

of such a sophisticated grammatical structure. So as not to repeat what has been written in full in those chapters, a short summary is presented here.

Interpretation of the Three-Word Genitive

Since two- and three-word genitive constructions have the same problem of ambiguity, and very similar solutions, attention is directed here to the distinctive interrelation of words and grammatical and semantic features of the three-word genitive. Because by definition a two-word genitive is contained within three-word genitive structure, both genitive constructions deserve discussion and interpretation. However, the following will be confined to analyzing the syntactic aspects of the three-word genitive.

Attention needs to be given to the form of a three-word genitive. The construction may contain only nouns such as πληρώματι εὐλογίας Χριστοῦ (Rom 15:29), a pronoun as in τῇ δυνάμει τοῦ κυρίου ἡμῶν (1 Cor 5:4), an adjective as in ξένοι τῶν διαθηκῶν τῆς ἐπαγγελίας (Eph 2:12).

The words in three-word genitive constructions are sometimes connected by the conjunction καί, such as the headwords in ὁ θεὸς καὶ πατὴρ τοῦ κυρίου ἡμῶν Ἰησοῦ Χριστοῦ (Eph 1:3), the middle words in ἔνοχος ἔσται τοῦ σώματος καὶ τοῦ αἵματος τοῦ κυρίου (1 Cor 11:27), or the final words in διὰ τῶν ὅπλων τῆς δικαιοσύνης τῶν δεξιῶν καὶ ἀριστερῶν (2 Cor 6:7).

In order to understand the three-word genitive it is crucial to consider also the semantics of such constructions. The three-word construction is a block of words with inter-relational links. Despite the lack of verbs or prepositions, the unifying factors are present and need to be discovered. Semantically, the three-word genitive construction may be approached from different angles: (1) the *sentence approach* as seen in τὸ βραβεῖον τῆς ἄνω κλήσεως τοῦ θεοῦ ἐν Χριστῷ Ἰησοῦ (Phil 3:14) "the prize that God gives to those who respond to his call," (2) *the subject-predicate approach*, which is concerned with identifying the subject or controller of the rest of the construction. Sometimes it consists of the headword of the construction, but other times it consists of the first two words in the construction. Similarly, the predicate may consist of the second and third words, or just the third word. Here are some examples that represent these two categories: οἰκονόμου / μυστηρίων θεοῦ (1 Cor 4:1), τὸν ἄρχοντα / τῆς ἐξουσίας τοῦ ἀέρος (Eph 2:2), τῶν ὅπλων τῆς δικαιοσύνης / τῶν δεξιῶν καὶ ἀριστερῶν (2 Cor 6:7), and ἐπιθέσεως / τῶν χειρῶν τοῦ πρεσβυτερίου or ἐπιθέσεως τῶν χειρῶν / τοῦ πρεσβυτερίου (1 Tim 4:14). Another approach one can take is (3) *the inter-relational three-word genitive approach*: grammarians agree that each genitive is dependent on the noun that precedes it, or to put it in another way, that the headword governs the second word and the second word governs the third word. Such successive relations between words in genitive concatenation are not the only possibilities, however. Any word in the construction can relate to any other word, as we shall see below.

Syntactical Categories to Add

After discussing the grammatical and semantic aspects of the three-word genitive, it is fitting to suggest some changes to classification schemes for the genitive. The following is an analysis of the syntactic meanings of three-word constructions.

Cumulative Genitive

Adding genitives successively to each other, especially when they are synonymous, opens the opportunity to use a cumulative genitive. The phrase εἰς ἔπαινον δόξης αὐτοῦ (Eph 1:12), "to the praise of his glory," (NET) could mean, "for his praise and glory." This is suggested by the parallel phrase εἰς δόξαν καὶ ἔπαινον θεοῦ (Phil 1:11), "to the glory and praise of God" (NET). In Rom 8:2, ὁ γὰρ νόμος τοῦ πνεύματος τῆς ζωῆς ἐν Χριστῷ Ἰησοῦ ἠλευθέρωσέν σε ἀπὸ τοῦ νόμου τῆς ἁμαρτίας καὶ τοῦ θανάτου, the phrase "the law of the spirit of life" is parallel to "the law of the sin and death." The parallel suggests that the meaning of τοῦ πνεύματος τῆς ζωῆς is "the spirit and life."

Adjectival Genitive

Analyzing the adjectival feature of the three-word genitive is important to understand its structure. There are about 40 adjectival three-word genitive constructions among the 181 three-word genitives found in the Pauline corpus. The adjectival noun in the three-word genitive may appear at the beginning of the construction, in the middle, or, in few cases at the end.

The Adjectival Headword The adjectival headword appears in the following phrases: τοῦ πλούτου τῆς χρηστότητος αὐτοῦ (Rom 2:4), τὴν νέκρωσιν τῆς μήτρας Σάρρας (Rom 4:19), and τὴν ἔνδειξιν τῆς ἀγάπης ὑμῶν (2 Cor 8:24).

The Adjectival Middle Word This type of three-word form, with a middle adjectival noun, is common in the LXX especially in poetic books like the Psalms and Isaiah. Paul was influenced by this type of expression and used it fairly extensively. For example, "the mountain of the holiness of me" (Ps 2:6), means "my holy mountain." The re-forming of the three-word phrase is done by changing the middle noun into an adjective, and then, by reading the words of the construction in reverse order. The adjectival middle-word may describe the headword. To illustrate, NIV renders κατὰ τὸ πλοῦτος τῆς δόξης αὐτοῦ (Eph 3:16) "his glorious riches" rather than "the wealth of his glory," which better corresponds with the parallel κατὰ τὸ πλοῦτος αὐτοῦ ἐν δόξῃ ἐν Χριστῷ Ἰησοῦ (Phil 4:19). Having the middle word act as an adjective to the headword is the most common rule for this type of adjectival three-word genitive. On the other hand, the adjectival middle word may describe the third word in the construction. There are few examples of this kind of adjectival three-word genitive, such as the phrase τὸ πλοῦτος τῆς δόξης τοῦ μυστηρίου τούτου (Col 1:27), which the TEV treats by turning both the headword and the middle-word into adjectives describing the third word thus, "this rich and glorious secret." Using the middle-word to describe the third word is far less common than using it to describe the headword.

The Adjectival Third Word The adjectival use of third words is very rare in the Pauline corpus. Semantically, it is difficult for an adjectival genitive to appear at the end of a three-word construction, but it is not impossible. In the phrase ἐλπίδι τῆς δόξης τοῦ θεοῦ (Rom 5:2), the end-word τοῦ θεοῦ is translated as "divine" ("divine splendour," or "divine glory") in the NEB and REB, and the phrase ὁ γὰρ νόμος τοῦ πνεύματος τῆς ζωῆς ἐν Χριστῷ Ἰησοῦ (Rom 8:2) is translated by the REB as "the life-giving law of the Spirit."

Multivalence of the Middle Word

The term *multivalent* describes the situation of the middle word in a cluster of genitives, which may suggest an adjectival genitive, but at the same time allows for other simultaneous possibilities. Concerning structure, the middle word could be used adjectivally to describe either the headword or the third word. Concerning semantics, the middle-word could be datival, locative or instrumental.

Some examples illustrate this matter: the phrase κατὰ τὸ πλοῦτος τῆς δόξης αὐτοῦ (Eph 3:16), could be translated, "according to his riches *in glory*," in parallel with the phrase κατὰ τὸ πλοῦτος αὐτοῦ ἐν δόξῃ ἐν Χριστῷ Ἰησοῦ (Phil 4:19). The NJB has followed this method in translating ἡ κοινωνία τῆς πίστεώς σου (Phlm 6) with "your fellowship in faith." Similarly, the phrase τοῦ αἵματος τοῦ σταυροῦ αὐτοῦ (Col 1:20), probably does not mean "the blood of his cross," but rather "his blood shed on the cross."

The Four-Word Genitive

The four-word genitive construction appears in the NT rarely (only 14 times) outside the Pauline corpus. It is more common in the Pauline corpus (17 times). There is also one five-word genitive construction in the Pauline corpus in 1 Thess 1:3, and possibly a six-word construction in Rom 1:29. Two other five-word constructions appear in the Apocalypse (see the list at the end of Chapter Six).

The construction of a four-word genitive consists of a headword and three substantival genitives, which are added to it successively. The construction may include pronouns, adjectives and participles in addition to nouns.[103] The phenomenon of four- and five-word genitive construction is not confined to the New Testament alone. As we demonstrated from examples in Chapter Six, it has its roots Septuagintal renderings of the Hebrew text.

Additional Categories for the Four-Word Genitive

The four-word genitive construction can be divided into smaller units. It contains two two-word units and three three-word units. These units correlate and interrelate with each other by virtue of being parts of the same construction. The phrase τὴν ἐλευθερίαν τῆς δόξης τῶν τέκνων τοῦ θεοῦ (Rom 8:21), for example, consists of three two-word units: τὴν ἐλευθερίαν τῆς δόξης / τῆς δόξης τῶν τέκνων / τῶν τέκνων τοῦ θεοῦ. It also contains two three-word units: τὴν ἐλευθερίαν τῆς δόξης τῶν τέκνων / τῆς δόξης τῶν τέκνων τοῦ θεοῦ. The interpreter should investigate these units of genitives in clusters. The principles of interpretation and exegesis of the two- and three-word genitives can be applied to the units of four-word genitives in order to reach adequate solutions.

Analyzing four-word genitive constructions is similar in categorization to that of the three-word genitive and involves the treatment of the same problems. There are three main types of additional categories needed to describe these concatenate four-word genitives. These additional categories are the cumulative, the appositive, and the adjectival genitive, and were treated fully in Chapter Six.

Conclusion

In this chapter rules and principles for genitive interpretation were demonstrated starting with the basic meaning of the genitive to the treatment of genitive in concatenation. The nature of the genitive was discussed, considering the factors that constitute its genesis and development, such as appurtenance, concatenation, construction, and propagation. In terms of the grammatical aspects of the genitive the relationship between the genitive and the use of the article was discussed, as well as prepositions and their role in identifying the meaning of the genitive. Here, the repositioning of the *nomen rectum* was observed, as also the use of the conjunction

---

103 Adjectives and participles are considered "adnominal" parts of the genitive constructions when they function substantivally.

καὶ in liking genitive constructions. Each of these items when considered together provides a foundation for understanding the genitive in all its adnominal modifications. These introductory discussions now set the stage for further considerations in interpreting the meaning of a genitive construction. Then, after showing the value of exegesis for understanding the genitive constructions, principles of genitive interpretation were demonstrated, discussed, and illustrated, one by one. Finally, a summary of Chapters Five to Six concerning interpretation of the genitive when used in clusters was presented. Taken together, these principles provide help for interpreters grappling with the genitive case in the Pauline corpus.

Bibliography

Barrett, Charles Kingsley. *The Epistle to the Romans.* 2nd ed. Black's New Testament Commentaries. London: Hendrickson, 1991.

Barth, Markus and Helmut Blanke. *Colossians: A New Translation with Introduction and Commentary.* Translated by Astrid B. Beck. Anchor Bible 34B. New York: Doubleday, 1994.

Betz, Hans Dieter. *2 Corinthians 8 and 9: A Commentary on Two Administrative Letters of the Apostle Paul.* Edited by George W. MacRae. Hermeneia. Philadelphia: Fortress, 1985.

Blass, Friedrich. *Grammar of New Testament Greek.* Translated by Henry St. John Thackeray. 2nd ed. London: Macmillan, 1905. Reprint, 1911.

Caragounis, Chrys C. *The Development of Greek and the New Testament: Morphology, Syntax, Phonology, and Textual Transmission.* Tübingen: Mohr Siebeck, 2004. Reprint, Grand Rapids: Baker, 2008.

Chamberlain, William Douglas. *An Exegetical Grammar of the Greek New Testament.* New York: Macmillan, 1941. Reprint, Grand Rapids: Baker, 1979.

Collins, Raymond F. *Studies on the First Letter to the Thessalonians.* Bibliotheca Ephemeridum Theologicarum Lovaniensium 66. Leuven, Belgium: Leuven University Press, 1984.

Cranfield, C. E. B. *A Critical and Exegetical Commentary on the Epistle to the Romans.* 2 vols. 6th ed. International Critical Commentary. Edinburgh: T&T Clark, 1975–79.

Dodd, Brian J. "Christ's Slave, People Pleasers and Galatians 1.10," *New Testament Studies* 42.1 (1996): 90–104.

Downs, David J. "'The Offering of the Gentiles' in Romans 15.16," *Journal for the Study of the New Testament* 29.2 (2006): 173–86. doi:10.1177/0142064x06072837.

Downs, David J. *The Offering of the Gentiles: Paul's Collection for Jerusalem in Its Chronological, Cultural, and Cultic Contexts.* Wissenschaftliche Untersuchungen zum Neuen Testament 2/248. Tübingen: Mohr Siebeck, 2008.

Dunn, James D. G. *Romans 9–16.* Word Biblical Commentary 38B. Dallas: Word, 1988.

Dunn, James D. G. *The Epistle to the Galatians.* Black's New Testament Commentary. London: Continuum, 1993.

Dunn, James D. G. *The Epistles to the Colossians and to Philemon: A Commentary on the Greek Text*. New International Greek Testament Commentary. Grand Rapids: Eerdmans, 1996.

Elgvin, Torleif. "'To Master His Own Vessel': 1 Thess 4.4 in Light of New Qumran Evidence," *New Testament Studies* 43 (1997): 604–19. doi:10.1017/S0028688500023419.

Fitzmyer, Joseph A. *Romans: A New Translation with Introduction and Commentary*. Anchor Yale Bible 33. New York: Doubleday, 1993.

Frame, James Everett. *A Critical and Exegetical Commentary on the Epistles of St. Paul to the Thessalonians*. International Critical Commentary. New York: Scribner, 1912.

Francis, Fred O. "Humility and Angelic Worship in Col 2:18," *Studia Theologica: Nordic Journal of Theology* 16.2 (1962): 109–34. doi:10.1080/00393386208599828.

Garlington, Don B. *Faith, Obedience, and Perseverance: Aspects of Paul's Letter to the Romans*. Wissenschaftliche Untersuchungen zum Neuen Testament 79. Tübingen: Mohr, 1994. Reprint, Eugene, OR: Wipf & Stock, 2009.

Hansen, G. Walter. *The Letter to the Philippians*. Pillar New Testament Commentary. Grand Rapids: Eerdmans, 2009.

Harris, Murray J. *The Second Epistle to the Corinthians: A Commentary on the Greek Text*. New International Greek Testament Commentary. Grand Rapids: Eerdmans, 2005.

Hawthorne, Gerald F. *Philippians*. Word Biblical Commentary 43. Dallas: Word, 2004.

Hays, Richard B. *The Faith of Jesus Christ: The Narrative Substructure of Galatians 3:1–4:11*. 2nd ed. Grand Rapids: Eerdmans, 2002.

Hull, Sanford D. "Exceptions to Apollonius' Canon in the New Testament: A Grammatical Study," *Trinity Journal* 7 (1986): 3–16.

Jannaris, Antonius N. *An Historical Greek Grammar*. London: Macmillan, 1897.

Jewett, Robert, with the assistance of Roy David Kotansky. *Romans: A Commentary*. Edited by Eldon Jay Epp. Hermeneia. Minneapolis: Fortress, 2007.

Keown, Mark J. *Philippians*. Evangelical Exegetical Commentary. Bellingham, WA: Lexham Press, 2017.

Lightfoot, Joseph Barber. *Saint Paul's Epistle to the Philippians*. London: Macmillan, 1913.

Lohse, Edward. *Colossians and Philemon*. Edited by Helmut Koester. Translated by William R. Poehlmann and Robert J. Karris. Hermeneia. Philadelphia: Fortress, 1971.

Longenecker, Richard N. *Galatians*. Word Biblical Commentary 41. Dallas: Word, 1990.

Martyn, J. Louis. *Galatians: A New Translation with Introduction and Commentary*. Anchor Yale Bible 33A. New Haven: Yale University Press, 2010.

McKnight, Scot. *The Letter of James*. New International Commentary on the New Testament. Grand Rapids: Eerdmans, 2011.

Milligan, George. *St. Paul's Epistles to the Thessalonians: The Greek Text, with Introduction and Notes*. New York: Macmillan, 1908.

Moo, Douglas J. *The Letters to the Colossians and to Philemon*. Pillar New Testament Commentary. Grand Rapids: Eerdmans, 2008.

Moo, Douglas J. *The Epistle to the Romans*. 2nd ed. New International Commentary on the New Testament. Grand Rapids: Eerdmans, 2018.

Moulton, Harold K. "Of," *Bible Translator* 19.1 (1968): 18–25. doi:10.1177/000608446801900105.

Nida, Eugene A. *Toward a Science of Translating: With Special Reference to Principles and Procedures Involved in Bible Translating.* Leiden: Brill, 1964.

Nida, Eugene A. and Charles R. Taber. *The Theory and Practice of Translation.* Helps for Translators 8. Leiden: Brill, 1969. Reprint, 1982.

Porter, Stanley E. "The Adjectival Attributive Genitive in the New Testament: A Grammatical Study," *Trinity Journal* 4.1 (1983): 3–17.

Richardson, Neil. *Paul's Language About God.* Journal for the Study of the New Testament Supplement Series 99. Sheffield, England: Sheffield Academic Press, 1994.

Smith, Jay E. "1 Thessalonians 4:4: Breaking the Impasse," *Bulletin for Biblical Research* 11.1 (2001): 65–105.

Smyth, Herbert Weir. *Greek Grammar.* Revised ed. by Gordon M. Messing. Cambridge: Harvard University Press, 1956.

Stevens, Gerald L. *New Testament Greek.* Lanham: University Press of America, 1997.

Summers, Ray. *Essentials of New Testament Greek.* Revised ed. by Thomas Sawyer. Grand Rapids: B&H Academic, 1995.

Thomas, D. W. "A Consideration of Some Unusual Ways of Expressing the Superlative in Hebrew," *Vetus Testamentum* 3 (1953): 209–24. https://www.jstor.org/stable/1516347.

Thomson, Ian H. *Chiasmus in the Pauline Letters.* Journal for the Study of the New Testament Supplement Series 111. Sheffield: Sheffield Academic Press, 1995.

Thrall, Margaret E. *A Critical and Exegetical Commentary on the Second Epistle of the Corinthians.* 2 vols. International Critical Commentary. London: T&T Clark, 1994.

Waard, Jan de and Eugene A. Nida. *From One Language to Another: Functional Equivalence in Bible Translating.* Nashville: Nelson, 1986.

Wallace, Daniel B. "The Semantics and Exegetical Significance of the Object-Complement Construction in the New Testament," *Grace Theological Journal* 6.1 (1985): 91–112.

Waterman, G. Henry. "The Greek 'Verbal Genitive'." Pages 289–93 in *Current Issues in Biblical and Patristic Interpretation.* Edited by Gerald F. Hawthorne. Grand Rapids: Eerdmans, 1975.

Weima, Jeffrey A. D. *Neglected Endings: The Significance of the Pauline Letter Closings.* Journal for the Study of the New Testament Supplement Series 101. Sheffield, England: JSOT Press, 1994.

Wilson, R. McL. *A Critical and Exegetical Commentary on Colossians and Philemon.* International Critical Commentary. London: T&T Clark, 2005.

CHAPTER EIGHT

Conclusion

Summaries

The central focus of this study has been on adnominal genitive constructions in the Pauline corpus. The adnominal genitive was chosen for investigation for three main reasons: (1) the ambiguous and problematic nature of adnominal constructions involving multiple successive genitive words, (2) the lack of comprehensive studies of this aspect of the genitive, especially in its clusters; and (3) Paul's usage of adnominal genitive constructions is both peculiar and versatile. These factors mean that the adnominal genitive deserves special examination.

Problematic Genitive Interpretation

That adnominal genitive constructions are often challenging to interpret is well recognized by grammarians and has been mentioned extensively. Words such as *ambiguous*, *vague*, *difficult*, *clumsy*, *enigmatic*, and *problematic* are regularly used to describe the adnominal genitive in concatenation. This fact itself highlighted the need for a comprehensive investigation of this aspect of the genitive case, in each of its structures, in order to determine a set of principles that would help in interpreting it and understanding its various meanings.

Method

The method followed in this present work to establish a solid basis for adnominal genitive interpretation has been to concentrate firstly on the grammatical, syntactic, and semantic dimensions of the genitive structures. Then, after identifying the adnominal genitive by isolating it from other aspects such as "genitive with prepositions" and "genitive with verbs," the stage was set for investigating the grammatical and syntactical dimensions of the genitive.

Traditional Grammars

For that purpose, we laid a groundwork in Chapter Two by examining major NT Greek grammars. These grammars embrace a variety of opinions for they represent a broad variety of scholarship. Each of the grammars was chosen for its own merit as a reference or manual volume for NT Greek, provided it had contributed to this field of knowledge. Introductory grammars designed for undergraduate work were typically excluded. In each of the grammars consulted, a critical evaluation of the grammar's adnominal genitive case and its meanings was made, also giving particular attention to the grammarians' suggestions about genitive interpretation. The result of that evaluation was classified under two categories: a cumulative outline of "true" and "ablatival" genitive uses, and a cumulative outline of principles of interpretation.

Semantics and Structuralism

After investigating the grammatical structures and meanings of the genitive, Chapter Three examined the semantic dimension of the adnominal genitive. Semantics as a field of linguistic discipline has been applied to biblical studies and interpretation since the beginning of the 1950s. The beginning of Chapter Three offered a short history of linguistic theories. This review showed how, in the modern era, the study of grammar has been influenced by the successive development of linguistics of grammatical study, and how these theories in turn have affected the study of NT Greek grammar. The rationalistic period comes first, represented by Winer. This was followed by the comparative-historical period with Blass, Debrunner, Moulton and Robertson as foremost names in applying comparative and historical linguistics to the NT. Third in line is the structuralist period. The process of finding the units in sentences (i.e. groups of words), called "immediate constituent analysis," is a first step to deriving structural meaning. David A. Black observes that *structural meaning* is associated with word-combinations as opposed to *lexical meaning*, which is associated with separate words.[1] Eventually scholars such as Funk, Cotterell, Turner, Black, Patte, and Fee applied structuralism to NT studies.

Transformational Grammar

Noam Chomsky launched the transformational-generative theory, which has had far reaching effect on modern science of grammar. This theory is concerned with kernels, the basic structural elements from which language builds its elaborate surface structures. When kernels consisting of nouns represent events, the implicit verbal sense within nouns should be identified as a first step to disambiguating the construction. This transformation generates the starting point for interpretation, lending the description "transformational-generative" to this theory.

Linguists who apply their tools to the study of the language of the NT (such as Nida, Taber, Wonderly, Beekman, Callow, and Louw) have found in Chomsky's theory of "transformational grammar" a solution for the structural problem of the genitive. Pure-noun combinations often create ambiguity. The application of transformational theory to genitive constructions in the NT renders implicit meanings explicit. Thus, "the condemnation of the devil" (1 Tim 3:6) becomes "be condemned as the devil was," and "before the foundation of the world" (Eph 1:4) becomes "before the world was founded." Such linguistic processing has proven useful in the commonly encountered subjective-objective genitive dilemma. However, transformational theory does not solve all structural problems. As Cotterell and Turner helpfully observe, clarifying the questions is not equivalent to finding proper solutions.[2] Each genitive construction requires serious exegetical work for it to be adequately interpreted.

Levels of Investigation

Methodologically, the review of the treatment of genitive adnominal constructions completed thus far has laid a foundation for a thorough investigation of the syntactic meanings of genitive expressions in Paul's usage. Investigating syntactical meanings of genitive constructions in the Pauline corpus is not an easy task. It

---

1 David Alan Black, *Linguistics for Students of NT Greek: A Survey of Basic Concepts and Applications*, 2nd ed. (Grand Rapids: Baker, 1995), 97.
2 Peter Cotterell and Max Turner, *Linguistics and Biblical Interpretation* (Downers Grove: IVP, 1989), 196.

involves working on three levels: (1) *the level of meaning*, that is, identifying all possible syntactic meanings of genitive constructions; (2) *the level of categorization*, that is, classifying the meanings of the genitive under headings that represent the main functions of genitive adnominal constructions; (3) *the level of combination*, that is, dividing the adnominal genitive phrases into their natural accumulate constituencies, namely two-, three-, and four-word constructions.

Meaning

In examining *the level of meaning*, hundreds of two-word genitive constructions that occur in the Pauline corpus were located, analyzed, and identified with regard to meaning. Examining the two-word genitive phrases resulted in the identification of approximately thirty categories of adnominal genitive constructions.

Categorization

As to the second level, *the level of categorization*, the difficulty was in recognizing which are the main themes of genitive adnominal meanings. Grammarians are used to observing two main themes: the genitive and the ablative, or the true genitive and the ablatival genitive, according to their view of the number of cases of the Greek language. These main categories need expansion to five: (1) the genitive of definition; (2) the adjectival genitive; (3) the objective genitive; (4) the subjective genitive; and (5) the ablatival genitive.[3]

Genitives in Concatenation

In treating *the level of combination*, genitive adnominal constructions were divided according to the number of substantives in the combination. Genitive combinations can be divided into three divisions: two-word, three-word, and four-word (and rarely five- and six-word) genitive constructions. Each of these combinations was treated in turn in Chapters Four to Six. In Chapter Four every two-word genitive construction in the Pauline corpus was scrutinized and categorized according to its

---

3 To this scheme, one can compare Richard A. Young's four main categories ("genitives functioning as adjectival phrases," "in deep structure event clauses," "as adverbial phrases," and "as noun phrases"; *Intermediate NT Greek: A Linguistic and Exegetical Approach* [Nashville: Broadman & Holman, 1994], 23–41), and Daniel B. Wallace's four categories (adjectival genitive, ablatival genitive, "verbal genitive," and adverbial genitive; *ExSyn*, 72).

main theme. No statistics for the two-word genitives were provided because they are very common.

The Three-Word Genitive

Chapter Five took up the three-word genitive constructions for a comprehensive treatment, since traditional NT Greek grammars have not thoroughly investigated this construction. The 181 three-word genitive constructions appearing in the Pauline corpus were selected and arranged according to their canonical order. They were divided according to the kind of substantives they contain, whether pronouns, adjectives, or participles; or whether they were articular or anarthrous. Three-word genitives that are connected internally with the conjunction καὶ were organized as connecting headwords with additional headwords, the same with middle-words or third-words. Adjectival genitives were examined and categorized according to a threefold division: the adjectival headword, the adjectival middle-word, and the adjectival third-word. The adjectival middle-word can also be split into two subgroups: the adjectival middle-word describing the headword, and the adjectival middle-word describing the third word.

The Four-Word Genitive

Chapter Six took up the four-word genitive constructions. Although the number of four-word genitives was limited, it was worthy of thorough investigation. These four-word cluster genitives have features similar to those of the three-word constructions. Both have been influenced by OT usage, both Hebrew usage and in translation into Greek. Both have features occasioned by their multivalent nature, such as accumulation, apposition, and adjectival elements. The principles for analyzing three-word genitives were found to be equally applicable to their four-word counterparts, since both are concatenate constructions. The review of genitive case adnominal structures their investigation Chapters Four to Six set the stage for presenting criteria of interpretation for adnominal genitive constructions.

Criteria for Genitive Interpretation

Chapter Seven explains principles of interpreting adnominal genitives in the Pauline corpus. In this chapter various opinions about the basic meaning of the genitive were analyzed,[4] and factors of the genitive's nature were discussed.[5]

4   Such as ablatival, possessive, restrictive, adjectival and defining meaning.
5   These factors are: appurtenant, concatenate, constructional, propagate, and problematic.

Grammatical aspects were discussed next, showing how either the article or prepositions could affect the meaning of a genitive construction. Two important aspects were considered: the repositioning of the *nomen rectum* for emphasis, and the use of the conjunction καί in connecting substantives within genitive constructions. Investigating these grammatical and semantic aspects of the genitive was essential preparation to deal with the next issue: the principles of interpreting genitive adnominal constructions.

The task of genitive interpretation involves consideration of the following aspects: the figures of speech used in genitive constructions, internal relations between substantives, the verbal power inherent in nominals, the immediate and wider context, parallel genitive expressions occurring synthetically or antithetically, comparing genitive and non-genitive expressions that have similar wording, investigating the writer's frame of reference, searching for embedded sentences beneath the surface forms, checking Hebrew and Greek OT backgrounds, and, finally an appeal to historical data. These considerations represent the essential steps for interpreting the genitive case in the NT.

Challenges and Contributions

In the process of investigating the meaning of adnominal genitive constructions in the Pauline corpus, challenges have been met, facts have been confirmed, and certain achievements have been made.

One serious challenge was the vast area of investigation, which involved hundreds of genitive constructions in the Pauline corpus, whether simple or concatenate. Another important challenge was to scrutinize every genitive, identifying its meaning, and to classify it in the proper category under the main themes of genitive functions.

The positive result of a study like this one is to confirm factuality and to challenge unfounded assertions. The majority of NT Greek scholars at present do not agree with Winer that "the genitive is unquestionably the whence-case,"[6] which some considered *a fact* in the middle of the eighteenth century. When Turner remarks concerning genitives in accumulation, "We can *usually* assume … that the governing gen. will precede the dependent one,"[7] we should be cautious and review the actual usage in the NT. Adjectival genitives, we discovered, appeared in many three-word genitive constructions examined in Paul's letters. Robertson's

---

6   Winer, *Grammar*, 230.
7   MHT$_3$, 218. [emphasis added]

observation that "[t]o go into detail with Paul's writings would be largely to give the grammar of the N. T."[8] is confirmed by identification of about thirty kinds of genitive usage in Paul's letters.

In researching and classifying each of the adnominal genitives according to their main functions fresh contributions have been made in four areas: (1) *categorization*; (2) *confirmation of existing meanings*; (3) *designation of new meanings*; and (4) *investigation of concatenate genitive constructions*. In the area of *categorization*, five main headings were chosen: (1) genitive of definition, (2) adjectival genitive, (3) objective genitive, (4) subjective genitive, and (5) ablatival genitive. All genitive usage in the Pauline corpus may be classified satisfactorily under these headings representing the major syntactic functions of the adnominal genitive.

Confirmation of Existing Meanings

Genitive of Identification

In the area of *confirmation of existing meanings*, a new contribution to understanding the "genitive of identification" has been made. Beekman and Callow observe that the relation of genitive of identification occurs in two ways: one by place-name, the other by the people of that place-name.[9] However, the identifying factor as described by Beekman and Callow could be considered pure definition and accordingly needs adjustment. It is better to relate the identifying factor to a way of distinguishing contrasting ideas, statements, events, or persons. The label *genitive of identification*, related to the idea of distinction and defined as such, has been discussed and located in the category of genitive of definition.

Attributed Genitive

Another meaning that has been researched and confirmed is "the attributed genitive." This kind of usage resembles the adjectival "Hebrew" genitive in function but differs in form. In "Hebrew" genitive constructions *nomen rectum* serves as an adjective describing *nomen regens*, while in the "attributed genitive" the order is reversed, *nomen regens* plays the adjective role describing *nomen rectum*.[10] Blass, Debrunner, and Zerwick have not investigated this adjectival sense deeply. Wallace, however, has observed the need for more research in this topic.[11] In the present work, serious

---

8   Robertson, *Grammar*, 130.
9   Beekman-Callow, 255.
10 For example, "newness of life" (Rom 6:4) for "new life."
11 Wallace, *ExSyn*, 89n50.

investigation has been made to identify such uses of the adjectival headwords, first, in the Hebrew OT, so as to indicate the background of this genitive, and second, in the Pauline corpus.

Genitive of Apposition

Genitive of apposition also has been subjected to a special treatment. Grammarians generally use the term "appositive" and "epexegetic" interchangeably to refer to the same genitive modification. Although the two expressions are similar to each other, they are not identical. The label *appositive genitive* identifies the simple apposition of genitive substantives; the label *epexegetic genitive* indicates an *additional explanation*. According to this proposition the subject has been divided into two usages: *the substitute usage*, and *epexegetic usage*, and has been illustrated as follows: in the phrase κυρίου Ἰησοῦ Χριστοῦ, the noun Ἰησοῦ is placed in *apposition* to κυρίου, similarly is Χριστοῦ to Ἰησοῦ. The following phrases demonstrate the epexegetic genitive: σημεῖον ἔλαβεν περιτομῆς (Rom 4:11), ἐπαγγελίας γὰρ ὁ λόγος (Rom 9:9), τῷ θεμελίῳ τῶν ἀποστόλων καὶ προφητῶν (Eph 2:20), and θώρακα πίστεως καὶ ἀγάπης (1 Thess 5:8). The distinguishing factor between *substitution* and *explanation* in the use of this kind of genitive is a nuance that the interpreter should explore.

Genitive of Association

Concerning the genitive of association, it has been asserted that "association is expressed … only by the substantive with the preposition μετά."[12] Wallace, however, surfaces uses of the genitive of association prefixed with σύν.[13] Further investigation has proved that genitives of association without prepositions appear in the Pauline corpus, such as τὸ ποτήριον τῆς εὐλογίας ὃ εὐλογοῦμεν, referring to the prayers of blessing *associated* with the offering of the cup (1 Cor 10:16), and ἡ ἄμμος τῆς θαλάσσης, "the sand that is *alongside* sea coast" (Rom 9:27). In this category belong Paul's use of the word κοινωνία, which carries the meaning of association (1 Cor 10:18, 20; 2 Cor 1:7).

---

12 Brooks-Winbery, 18.
13 Wallace, *ExSyn*, 128–29.

Designation of New Meanings

In the area of *designation of new meanings*, this study finds fresh ways to grapple with adnominal genitive constructions. These categories are extensions and refinements of previous grammars' understandings.

Plural Genitive as Hebrew Adjective

Using the genitive in plural, as an adjective to describe the headword, is a phenomenon well rooted in LXX renderings of Hebrew texts, and occurs frequently in Paul's letters. Some Bible versions have recognized the usage of genitive in plural as adjectival and have applied it,[14] but NT grammars have largely remained silent about the adjectival plural genitive. Treatment of genitive plural constructions, especially adjectival ones, is an important feature that should appear in every serious study of genitive syntax.

Genitive of Accordance

The sense of the genitive of accordance is well attested, though it occurs in only a few instances in the Pauline corpus. The meaning of accordance in genitive usage has not attracted the attention of grammarians, thus, remained outside genitive categorization. Designating this new sense in the list of genitive meanings constitutes another proposed contribution to adnominal genitive syntax.[15]

Ascription-Recipient Genitive

The value of the *ascription-recipient* category is based on the fact that sometimes the genitive of definition, being *nomen rectum*, does not define attributes as much as it becomes a recipient of attributes. This modification gives fresh insight, resulting from precise examination of genitive definition usage. Though distinguishing between the two is not an easy matter, context is a good guide for determination.[16]

---

14 Examples include: 2 Cor 1:3 "the father of mercies" (KJV NASB NRSV), becomes "all-merciful father" (NJB TEV REB), and Eph 3:11 "the purpose of ages," becomes "the eternal purpose" (KJV).

15 Some illustrations: "the grief *according to* the world" (2 Cor 7:10); "the measure that *agrees with* the limit" (2 Cor 10:13); "for building up *according to* the need" (Eph 4:29); and "grows *according to* God's design" (Col 2:19 REB).

16 There are adequate examples of this meaning in Rom 3:1 Τί οὖν τὸ περισσὸν τοῦ Ἰουδαίου ἢ τίς ἡ ὠφέλεια τῆς περιτομῆς and in 1 Cor 1:25 ὅτι τὸ μωρὸν τοῦ θεοῦ σοφώτερον τῶν ἀνθρώπων ἐστὶν καὶ τὸ ἀσθενὲς τοῦ θεοῦ ἰσχυρότερον τῶν ἀνθρώπων.

Genitive of Manner

The *genitive of manner* has been also designated to refer to some genitive uses that answers questions beginning with *how*. The genitive of manner appears at least three times in the Pauline corpus, a sufficient number for giving recognition. The phrase "the death of the cross" (Phil 2:8) is a good example of the function of this type of genitive. It describes the *way* Jesus died: on a cross (See NIV REB NRSV NET CSB).

Genitive of Resemblance

The genitive of resemblance is designated as an important modification in the meanings of the adnominal genitive. It is strange that traditional NT grammars do not include it in genitive classifications. This aspect of genitive meaning, however, is not neglected in modern commentaries. The proposition of resemblance has been applied to several genitive phrases in this study with very satisfying results. An expression such as "the faith of Abraham" (Rom 4:16), paraphrased as "a faith like Abraham's," could not have been understood properly without applying the *resemblance* aspect of the genitive.[17] Including *resemblance* as an aspect of genitive's syntax here contributes to a better understanding of certain problematic genitive expressions.

Concatenate Genitive Constructions

In the area of *investigation of concatenate genitive constructions*, a thorough investigation has been made on the three- and four-word genitive constructions in Chapters Five to Six. The results of this investigation appear as a pioneering accomplishment in this field of study.

Finally, the two main objectives of this study have been to establish a comprehensive categorized list of the genitive meanings, and to prepare a set of criteria for interpretation of adnominal genitive constructions. These two objectives have, in our opinion, been satisfactorily achieved. With pleasure we present this study with all its implications to readers for further investigation. The growing body of computer aids and databases for NT research will certainly lead to a further refinement and application of these results.

---

17   Likewise, the expressions: "the jealousy of God" (Rom 10:2; 2 Cor 11:2), "the worship of angels" (Col 2:18), "the endurance of Christ" (2 Thess 3:5), "the judgement of the devil" (1 Tim 3:6), and "the work of an evangelist" (2 Tim 4:5).

Bibliography

Black, David Alan. *Linguistics for Students of NT Greek: A Survey of Basic Concepts and Applications.* 2nd ed. Grand Rapids: Baker, 1995.

Cotterell, Peter and Max Turner. *Linguistics and Biblical Interpretation.* Downers Grove: IVP, 1989.

Young, Richard A. *Intermediate NT Greek: A Linguistic and Exegetical Approach.* Nashville: Broadman & Holman, 1994.

Index

A

Abbott, T. K. 164n5
Ablatival genitive 7–8, 39, 40, 47, 71, 123–124, 179, 222
   of comparison 127–128
   of separation 124–125
   partitive genitive 126–127
Ablative function 44
Abrahamic faith 121
Accusative objective genitive 105–106
Adjectival genitive 10–11, 42, 71, 91–92, 146, 147, 172–173, 179, 215, 222, 223, 224
   adjectival head word 146–147, 213
   adjectival middle word 147–148, 149, 150, 213–214
     describing the head word 148–150
     describing the third word 150–151, 214
   headword and third word 223

attributed genitive 101–104
descriptive genitive 92–93
genitive of manner 104–105
Hebrew genitive 94–101, 225
qualitative genitive 93–94
Adnominal four-word genitive constructions
   adjectival genitive 172–173
   cumulative genitive 170–171
   enigmatic four-word adjectival constructions 173–174
   epexegetical genitive 171–172
   five-word genitives 174–177
   meanings 169
   in Paul 166–169, 176
   in the NT 176–177
   six-word genitives 174–177
   structural elements
     four-word genitives connected by καί 161–166
     pronoun 162
     pure nouns 161–162

Adnominal genitive construction 3, 4
  ablative and genitive 6–7
  anarthrous head nouns 189
  basic tools 16–17
  challenges and contributions 224–225
    concatenate genitive
      constructions 228
    confirmation of existing
      meanings 225–226
    designation of new
      meanings 227–228
  concatenate construction 37
  defined 5–12
  exegesis 2
  four-word 59
  genitive interpretation 192
  levels of investigation 15–16, 220–222
    categorization 222
    criteria for genitive
      interpretation 223–224
    four-word genitive 223
    genitives in concatenation 222–223
    level of meaning 222
    three-word genitive 223
  method of investigation 15–16, 220
  nature of the genitive 12–15
  problematic genitive interpretation 219
  semantics 220–221
  statistical survey 22, 23
  structuralism 220–221
  three-word 59
  traditional grammars 220
  transformational grammar 221
  two-word 59
Adnominal genitives *see also* Adnominal
  genitive construction
  interpretation 43
  semantics of *see* Semantics of adnominal
    genitives
Adnominal three-word genitive
  constructions
  adjectival genitive 146
    adjectival head word 146–147
    adjectival third word 151

  adjectival middle-word 147–148
    describing the head word 148–150
    describing the third word 150–151
  cumulative genitive 144–146
  Hebrew genitive 147
  list of three-word genitive
    constructions 153–159
  meanings 144
  multivalent functions of middle
    word 151–153
  semantic aspects
    inter-relational approach 143–144
    sentence approach 142
    subject-predicate approach 142–143
  structural elements
    article-implicit substantives 139–140
    noun-participle 139
    noun-pronoun 138–139
    noun-pronoun-adjective 139
    pure nouns 137–138
  three-word genitives connected by καί
    additional head word 140
    middle-word with an additional
      middle-word 140–141
    third-word with an additional
      third-word 141
Adnominal two-word genitive constructions
  ablatival genitive 123–124
    of comparison 127–128
    of separation 124–125
    partitive genitive 126–127
  adjectival genitive 91–92
    attributed genitive 101–104
    descriptive genitive 92–93
    genitive of manner 104–105
    Hebrew genitive 94–101
    qualitative genitive 93–94
  adnominal genitive meanings 71
  genitive of definition
    appositive (epexegetic)
      genitive 86–91
    ascription-recipient genitive
      (ascribed-to genitive) 85–86
    genitive of accordance 84–85

genitive of association 82–83
genitive of identification 77–79
genitive of location 80–82
genitive of relationship 75–77
possessive genitive 72–75
objective genitive
of advantage 106–108
of derivation 112
of destination 108–109
of reference 110–111
pure (accusative) objective
genitive 105–106
superlative genitive 112–114
subjective genitive 114–115
instrumental genitive 119–120
of authorship 117
of cause 118–119
of origin 116–117
of resemblance 120–123
of source 115–116
Alford, H.
genitive of resemblance 123
Anarthrous substantives 184
Antithetic parallel constructions 201
Apollonius' Canon 32, 138, 188, 211
Appositive (epexegetic) genitive 86–91, 198, 209, 215, 226
Aramaisms 21
Arichea, D. C. 90n85
Ascription-recipient genitive (ascribed-to genitive) 85–86, 102, 102n135, 227
Attributed genitive 10, 44, 101–104, 145, 225–226
Author
different passages 201–202
principles of semantics 64
usage in similar contexts or similar constructions 204–205

B

Babylon 35
Baptismal metaphor 196

Baptismal teaching 97
Barclay, W.
law of Spirit and life 144
Barnett, P. 77n27, 173
Barr, J. 51
Barrett, C. K. 83, 170n24, 172, 173, 198n66
translation of Rom 3: 21–31, 121
Barth, M. 85n57, 90n86, 91, 100n121, 148n20, 207
Beale, G. K. 87
Beekman, J. 3, 5, 22, 44, 163, 225
genitive in concatenation 210
genitive of identification 39
semantics of adnominal genitives 62–64
syntax and semantics 62
Betz, H. D. 201n72
genitive of origin 117n190
Bible translation
linguistics 58
Black, D. A. 57
lexical meaning 220–221
structural meaning 54, 220–221
Black, M. 56
Blanke, H. 207
Blass, F. 11, 36–37, 53, 55, 209, 210, 220
adnominal genitive 1
Concatenation of Genitives with Different Meanings 23
genitive of origin 117n189
Bockmuehl, M. 81
Book of Acts 20
Bratcher, R. G. 77n25, 90n87
Brooks, J. A. 10, 40–41, 126
genitive of association 82
subjective genitive 120
Bruce, F. F. 84, 91, 145, 170, 171n26
Hebrew genitive 96
Büchsel, F. 128
Buttmann, A. 23, 30–31, 55, 137, 191
genitive in clusters 31, 166, 209
genitive substantive 30
Semitic languages 30–31
subjective and the objective genitive 30
Buttmann, P. K. 30

C

Callow, J. 3, 5, 22, 44, 163, 225
  genitive of identification 39, 210
  semantics of adnominal genitives 62–64
  syntax and semantics 62
Caragounis, C. C. 41, 186n26
Carson, D. A. 4, 5n13
Cascadia Syntax Graphs of the NT 17
Cause-effect relationship
  linguistic theories and development of
    theories 52
  obedience and faith 205
Chamberlain, W. D. 7n25, 12, 46
Chomsky, N. 55
  transformational grammar 60, 65,
    195, 196
  transformational-generative theory 221
Christ
  agent of God 203
  as God and Savior 187
  believers' love 45
  circumcision 196
  endurance 123
  preaching 205
  sanctifcation of the church 120
  second coming of 145
Christian community 81n36
Christian hope 165
Christian movement 205
Christians
  grow and rejoice 82
  resurrection 125
  spiritual well-being 112
Christic faith 121
Collins, R. 208
  σκεῦος-wife option 208
Colossians 19
Comparative-historical period 53
Concatenation of genitives 23, 36, 40,
  64, 136, 228 *see also* Genitive in
  concatenation
Confirmation of existing meanings
  attributed genitive 225–226

genitive of apposition 226
genitive of association 226
genitive of identification 225
Conjunctions
  καὶ 140, 175
  in genitive constructions 140, 144,
    186–191
Contemporary texts 206–209
Conzelmann, H. 100n126, 123
Corpus Paulinum 19, 153
Cotterell, P. 65, 221
Cranfield, C. E. B. 171, 172n32, 183n16
Cumulative genitive 25, 170–171, 213, 215
  adnominal three-word genitive
    constructions 144–146

D

Dana, H. E. 10, 11, 34, 35–36
Davis, W. H. 46
de Boer, M. C. 149n21
Debrunner, A. 11, 36–37, 53, 55, 209,
  210, 220
  adnominal genitive 1
  Concatenation of Genitives with
    Different Meanings 23
  genitive of origin 117n189
Deissmann, A. 24
de Saussure, F. 54
Descriptive genitive 71, 92–93, 122
Designation of new meanings 227
de Waard, J. 196
De Witt Burton, E. 56
  objective genitive 109n161
Dibelius, M. 100n126, 123
Divine wrath 180
Dodd, B. J. 184
Downs, D. J. 89n76, 198, 198n64
Dunn, J. D. G. 73n11, 91, 144n14,
  197, 205n78
  sinful passions 99n116
  subjective meaning 122
Dyscolus, A. 188n32

E

Easley, K. H. 46
Edwards, J. R. 20n4
Elgvin, T.
   σκεῦος-wife interpretation 208
Ellingworth, P. 88n73, 123, 123n211
Enigmatic four-word adjectival
   constructions 173–174
Epexegesis 88
Epexegetic genitive 38, 86–91, 128, 171–
   171, 226
Epexegetic usage, appositive genitive 87–91
Ephesians 19
   adnominal genitives 23
Event propositions 63
Exegesis 24–25, 191
Exegetical principles for genitive
   interpretation 43
   authorial usage 204–205
   contemporary texts 206–209
   different passages by the same
      author 201–202
   figures of speech 193–195
   genitive and non-genitive
      expressions 203–204
   immediate context 197–198
   parallel genitive expressions 200–201
   relationships between substantives 192–193
   same wording but different
      meanings 199–200
   septuagintal influence 206
   surface grammatical structures 205–206
   verbal head nouns 195–196
   wider context 199

F

Family/household relationship 75 *see also*
   Physical genitive of relationship
Fee, G. D. 81, 82n43, 145n15
   genitive of location 82
   Hebrew adjectival interpretation 96

Figurative genitive of relationship 62, 75, 77
Figures of speech 64n52, 193–195
Fisk, B. N. 22
Fitzmyer, J. A. 56, 151, 163n2, 171
Five-word genitive constructions 174–177
Four-word genitive constructions 15,
   16, 23, 70, 179, 210, 214, 222, 223 *see*
   also Adnominal four-word genitive
   constructions
   connected by καί 162
      Eph 4:13, 163–164
      Rom 2:5, 163
      Titus 2:13, 164–166
Frame, J. E. 90n84, 93n99, 149n22,
   175, 206n81
Francis, F. O. 207
Fung, R. Y. K. 118n193
Funk, R. W. 36, 54n17
   genitive of definition 97n110
Furnish, V. P. 79n31, 174
   objective genitive 111n172

G

Gamaliel 21
Garlington, D. B. 206n80
   concept of obedience 205
Genitive(s)
   ablatival 179
   adjectival 179
   adnominal constructions 69
   adnominal phrases 196
   and non-genitive expressions 203–204
   clusters 16, 23, 168
   definition 7, 179, 222
   expressions 193
   four-word genitive construction 222
   grammatical uses 57
   in concatenation 222–223
   in NT grammars *see* NT (New
      Testament) grammars
   interpretation, exegetical principles
      for 223–224

authorial usage 204–205
contemporary texts 206–209
different passages by the same
    author 201–202
figures of speech 193–195
genitive and non-genitive
    expressions 203–204
immediate context 197–198
parallel genitive expressions 200–201
relationships between
    substantives 192–193
same wording but different
    meanings 199–200
septuagintal influence 206
surface grammatical
    structures 205–206
verbal head nouns 195–196
wider context 199
objective 179 *see also* Objective genitive
of accordance 84–85, 227
of apposition 80, 226
of association 82–83, 226
of family relationship
    direct relationship 76
    figurative relationship 75, 77
    general relationship 76
    physical relationship 75–76
of identification 39, 77–79
of manner 228
of relationship 40
of resemblance 228
plural constructions 227
state propositions 63
subjective 179
with substantives 1
three-word genitive construction 222
two-word genitive construction 222
Genitive constructions 20
adjectives and participles 215n103
adnominal construction 13
ambiguity 14–15
appurtenance 12–13
concatenation 13
conjunctions in 186–191

figurative expressions 194
figures of speech 224
meanings 24
non-figurative terms 193
nouns, abstract conceptions 193
propagation of meanings 14
relationship between nouns 192
substantives 195
syntactical meanings, investigation 221
verbal-inherent subjective-objective 196
Genitive in concatenation 41
four-word genitive 214–215
    additional categories 215
interpretation
    history 209–210
    principles 211–212
    three-word genitive 212–213
multivalence of the middle word 214
syntactical categories
    adjectival genitive 213–214
    cumulative genitive 213
Genitive of definition 71
appositive (epexegetic) genitive 86–91
ascription-recipient genitive (ascribed-to
    genitive) 85–86
descriptive genitive 92
genitive of accordance 84–85
genitive of association 82–83
genitive of identification 77–79
genitive of location 80–82
genitive of relationship 75–77
human personality 74
possessive genitive 72–75
Geographical genitive of location 80
Gianollo, C. 107, 74n16
Goded Rambaud, M. 51, 52
Grammarians *see also specific persons*
genitive of definition 72
genitive usage 4
Grammatical meaning of words 56
*Grammatik des neutestamentlichen
    Griechisch* 36
Greek genitive 33, 34
Greenlee, J. H. 46

Green, S. G. 31–32, 74n16
  genitive of partition 126
  genitive of separation 32
  genitive usage in context 32
  Handbook to the Grammar of the Greek Testament 31
Green, S. W. 31n7
Griechische Grammatik 30
Griechische Schulgrammatik 30
Guthrie, D. 19n2

H

Hansen, G. W. 104
Harris, M. J. 99, 165n11, 187
Hawthorne, G. F. 185n24, 188n31
Hays, R. B. 202
  Faith of Jesus Christ 205n79
  message of faith/gospel-message 205
Hebraism 100n122
Hebraistic Genitive 12
Hebrew Bible
  plural genitive as pure adjective 99
  four-and five-word genitive constructions 169
  three-word genitive expressions 152
Hebrew genitive 38, 42, 92, 94–97, 145, 147
  adjectival genitive 94–101
    three-word genitive 174
  constructions 225
Hellenistic Greek grammar 52, 53
Hellenized Jew 166
Hermann, G. 53
Holy Spirit 60, 96, 198, 200
Howard, W. F. 39
Hull, S. D. 188, 189n33
Hultgren, A. J. 121n202

I

Immediate constituent analysis 54, 220
Immediate context 197–198, 224

Indefinite pronouns 126
Instrumental genitive 119–120
Interpretive principles of genitives 1
  conjunctions in constructions 186–191
  emphatic position of the *nomen rectum* 182–186
  exegetical principles for genitive interpretation 191–109
  in concatenation 209–215
  syntactical aspects 180–182
Inter-relational approach
  three-word genitive construction 143–144, 212
Interrogative pronouns 126
Investigation of concatenate genitive constructions 228

J

Jewett, R. 76n23, 163, 175, 198, 198n67
  appositive genitive 170
Jewish circumcision 196
Jewish education 22
Johnson, L. T. 121
Joüon, P. 97n113, 98n114

K

Käsemann, E. 110n168
Kernel analysis 61, 65
Khalaf, G. 16
Knight, G. W. 100n125, 111

L

Language *see* Semantics of adnominal genitives
Lenski, R. C. H. 76n21
  concatenation of genitives 175n45
Lexham Syntactic Greek New Testament 9
Lexham Syntactic New Testament Database 17

Lexical meaning of words 55
Lexical semantics 4
Lincoln, A. T. 77n26, 84, 96, 100n122
Linguistics 3, 58
Lock, W. 21
Logos Bible Software 17
Lohse, E. 90, 145
Longenecker, R. N. 194
Louw, J. P. 3, 57, 64
   semantics of adnominal genitives 64–65
Lünemann, G. 28
LXX 21, 167, 168
Lyons, J. 54

Moulton, J. H. 32–33, 39, 46, 53
   genitive of definition 32
   Prolegomena 56
   subjective/objective genitive 33
   syntax of genitive 32
Moulton, W. F. 28
Mounce, W. D.
   subjective genitive 100
Multiple genitives 13, 38, 136
Multivalence of middle word 214
Multi-word genitive constructions 128
Muraoka, T. 97n113, 98n114
Mystic genitive 24

M

MacDonald, W. G. 46
McKnight, S. 200n69
Mantey, J. R. 10, 11, 34, 35–36
Martin, R. P. 173
Melick, R. R., Jr. 4n11, 81, 85
   divine peace 93n98
   faithfulness of Jesus 120
Metaphorical genitive of location 80–82
Metzger, B. M. 170n23
Michaelis, W. 4n10
Middle word, multivalent functions 151–153
Milligan, G. 186
Moo, D. J. 88n74, 89n75, n77, 99, 108, 119
Morphology 58
Morris, L. 76n22, 88n74, 119
Moule, C. F. D. 14, 35, 38–39, 105n142,
   165, 189n34, 194n53, 195
   adjectival genitive 91
   attributed genitive 103n138
   characteristic literary features 20
   epexegetical genitive 86–87
   genitive and accusative 10
   genitive of definition 11, 72
Moulton, H. K. 3, 24, 191, 192n45, 220
   Bible translators 192
   semantics of adnominal genitives 60

N

Nägeli, T. 21
Nida, E. A. 3, 14, 64, 77n25, 90n85
   semantics of adnominal
     genitives 60–62
Nikiforidou, K. 8–9, 74n14
Nomen rectum 2
   emphatic position
     Article \+ Article$_g$ \+ N$_g$ \+ N 183
     Article \+ N$_g$ \+ N 183, 185
     Article \+ Ng (Pronoun) \+
       N 183–184
     Ng (Pronoun) \+ Article \+ N 184
     Ng \+ N 184
     Ng (Pronoun) \+ N 184–185
     prepositions 185–186
Nomen regens 2, 181–183, 188
   genitive of destination 108
Non-genitive expressions 203–204
Noun-pronoun three-word genitives 139
Novum Testamentum Graece 16
NT (New Testament) grammars 15, 220
   genitive clusters 209
   genitive in, survey by
     Blass, F. 36–37
     Brooks, J. A. 40–41
     Buttmann, A. 30–31

Dana, H. E. 35–36
Debrunner, A. 36–37
Green, S. G. 31–32
Mantey, J. R. 35–36
Moule, C. F. D. 38–39
Moulton, J. H. 32–33
Porter, S. E. 42–43
Robertson, A. T. 33–35
Turner, N. 39–40
Wallace, D. B. 44–46
Winbery, C. L. 40–41
Winer, G. B. 28–30
Young, R. A. 43–44
Zerwick, M. 37–38
Greek grammars 52
semantics *see* Semantics of adnominal
genitives
Numerals 126

O

Obedience and faith
cause-effect relationship 205
Objective genitive 71, 179, 222
of advantage 106–108
of derivation 112
of destination 108–109
of reference 110–111
pure (accusative) objective
genitive 105–106
superlative genitive 112–114
O'Connor, M.
plural Hebrew genitive as adjective 97
superlative genitive 112n177
O'Donnell, M. B. 51
OpenText.org 17
Order in genitive constructions 207
OT (Old Testament)
adjectival Hebrew genitive 94–95, 148
attributed genitive 101–102
parallelism 20
plural Hebrew genitive as adjective 98–99

P

Palmer, F. R. 51n1
Parallel genitives 144, 200–201, 224
three-word genitives 148
Parallelism 149, 150
genitive of association 82
Partitive adjectives 126
Partitive genitives 80, 126–127
Pastorals 19
Pauline Hebraisms 21
Peirce, C. 54
Perschbacher, W. J. 7n22, 46
five-case system 7
Personifications of abstract expressions 193
Phoebe 81
Phonetics 58
Phonology 58
Phrase structure trees 58
Physical genitive of relationship 75–76
Plenary genitive 45
Plural genitive
Hebrew adjective 97–98, 227
in the NT 99–101
in the OT 98–99
Porter, S. E. 3, 6, 7, 10, 42–43, 51, 52, 55n21,
182n11, 203
Possessive genitive 8–10, 40, 72–75, 209
Pragmatics 51, 52, 58
Predicate nominative and adjective 195
Prepositions
genitive constructions, uses 185
Principle of compositionality 58
Problematic genitive interpretation 219
Prolegomena 56
Pronoun 162
Pure nouns 161–162
Pure (accusative) objective genitive 105–106

Q

Qualitative genitive 93–94

R

Rationalist philology period 53
Rengstorf, K. H. 73n10
Restrictive genitive 10
Richardson, N.
   Paul's Language About God 193n48
Ridderbos, H. N. 109n162
Robertson, A. T. 2, 19n1, 20, 33–35, 46, 47,
   53, 56, 87, 165, 220, 224
   ablative with adjectives 35
   adnominal genitive 34
   *A Grammar of the Greek New Testament in
      the Light of Historical Research* 33
   concatenation of genitives 166
   genitive
      case of appurtenance 13
      investigation 44
      meaning 10–11, 72
      of relationship 75
      with substantives 1
   history as an interpretive tool 207
   interpreting genitives in
      concatenation 210
   predicate genitive 34
Robinson, A. 85
   spiritual principle of the mind 60
Ross, A. P. 113n178
Ross, L. R. 58n34
   modern linguistics 58
Rydbeck, L. 5

S

Sacrifice and service 194
Same wordings, in genitive constructions
   with different meanings 199–200
Satan 125
Schmidt, D. D. 52
   comparative-historical period 53–54
   rationalistic period 53
   structuralist period 54
   transformational-generative theory 55

Schmiedel, P. 28
Schweizer, E.
   subjective genitive 122n207
Self-abasement 208
Semantics of adnominal genitives 42, 45,
   142, 203, 220–221
   Beekman, J. 62–64
   Callow, J. 62–64
   grammatical meaning of words 56
   history of linguistic theory 52–53
      comparative-historical 53–54
      rationalistic period 53
      structuralist 54
      transformational-generative 55
   lexical meaning of words 55
   Louw, J. P. 64–65
   Moulton, H. K. 60
   Nida, E. A. 60–62
   semantic meaning of words 57–58
   syntactical meaning of words 57
   Taber, C. R. 60–62
   three-word genitive constructions
      inter-relational approach 143–144
      sentence approach 142
      subject-predicate approach 142–143
   Wonderly, W. L. 59
Semantics of New Testament Greek 64
Semitisms 21
Sentence approach
   three-word genitive approach 142, 212
Septuagintal influence 206
Shakespeare 20
Sharp, G. 164n6
   Christological implications 164
   constructions with dependent
      genitives 187
   TSKS construction 141
Six-word adnominal genitive 174
Slavery and sonship 149
Spirit of wisdom 193
Stanley, C. 21
State propositions 63
Stevens, G.
   subjective and objective genitive 191

Stolk, J. V. 107–108
Strachan, R. H. 77n24
Structuralism 54, 220–221
Structuralist period 53
Structured polysemy 8
Subjective genitive 9, 39, 71, 114–115, 179,
   181, 197, 198, 210, 222
   instrumental genitive 119–120
   of authorship 117
   of cause 118–119
   of origin 116–117
   of resemblance 120–123
   of source 115–116
Subject-predicate approach 142–143, 212
Substantives
   article-headed phrases 181
   internal relations 224
   relationships between 192–193
Substitute usage, appositive genitive 87
Sumney, J. L. 122
Superlative genitive 112–114, 126
Surface grammatical structures 205–206
Syntactical aspects of genitive 179–180
   as substantive 180–182
Syntactical meaning of words 57
Syntax and semantics 57

T

Taber, C. R. 3
   semantics of adnominal genitives 60–62
Textual mechanisms 58
Thayer, J. H. 30
The Semantics of Biblical Language 51
Third-word genitive construction 164
Thiselton, A. C. 54, 79n30, 111
   genitive of association 83
Thomas, D. W. 194n52
Thomson, I. H.
   Chiasmus in the Pauline Letters 196n59
Thrall, M. E. 4
   immediate and wider contexts 199
   Spirit of the Lord 199

Three-word genitive constructions 15,
   16, 23, 70, 179, 202, 210, 222 *see
   also* Adnominal three-word genitive
   constructions
   additional third word(s) 141
   adjectival features 213, 214
   adjectival genitive 206
   adnominal genitive 23
   grammatical and semantic aspects 213
   Hebrew adjectival genitives 174
   interpretation 212–213
   inter-relational 212
   levels of investigation 223
   meanings 144
   sentence approach 212
   subject-predicate approach 212
Torrey, C. C. 56
Towner, P. H. 100
Traditional Greek grammars 4, 220
Transformational-generative
   theory 55, 221
Transformational grammar approach 43, 60,
   62, 65, 142, 221
Translators 30, 59, 106, 192
True genitive 39, 47
TSKS personal constructions 140, 141, 164,
   165, 188
Turner, M. 65, 221
Turner, N. 20, 21, 22, 24, 25, 38n23, 39–40,
   47, 56, 142, 171, 191, 210, 224
   characteristic literary features 20
   genitives with adjectives and adverbs 40
   subjective genitive 81
   treatment of genitive 40
Two-word genitive constructions
   adnominal genitives 2, 4, 15, 23, 70, 179,
   210, 212, 222
   semantics 128

V

Verbal genitive 43, 45, 114n180
Verbal head nouns 195–196

W

Wallace, D. B. 2, 3, 11, 44–46, 165, 182, 211, 222n3, 225
  ablatival genitive 124
  adjectival genitive 91
  affected and unaffected meaning 52
  descriptive genitive 40
  genitive in concatenation 46
  genitive of apposition 87n67, 88n68
  genitive of association 82, 226
  genitive of definition 71
  genitive of sphere/place 80
  Greek Grammar Beyond the Basics: An Exegetical Syntax of the New Testament 44
  partitive genitive 126
  semantic situation 52
  subject-complement and object-complement constructions 189
  taxonomy 70
  TSKS construction 140, 164
  verbal genitive 45, 63
Waltke, B. K.
  plural Hebrew genitive as adjective 97
  superlative genitive 112n177
Wanamaker, C. A. 122, 123n210, 145n17
Waterman, G. H. 195–196
  The Greek "Verbal Genitive" 196n57
Weima, J. A. D. 200, 200n71
Wider context 199, 224
Winbery, C. L. 10, 40–41, 126

genitive of association 82
subjective genitive 120
Winer, G. B. 28–30, 32, 46, 55, 220, 224
  adjectival genitive 146
  genitive cluster 166
  genitive in concatenation 209
  genitive nouns 137
  genitive of kindred 75, 206–207
  Grammatik des neutestamentlichen Sprachidioms 28
  meaning of genitive 7
  parallel passages 30
  physical relationship 75
  rationalistic period 53
  simple genitive of dependence 29
  subjective and objective genitive 191
  transformational grammar 30
Wonderly, W. L.
  semantics of adnominal genitives 59
Word order and meaning 58
Worship of angels 208

Y

Young, R. A. 43–44, 64, 110, 222n3
  genitive of disassociation 125

Z

Zerwick, M. 12, 37–38, 42, 45

Studies in Biblical Greek

D. A. Carson
General Editor

This series of monographs is designed to promote and publish the latest research into biblical Greek (Old and New Testaments). The series does not assume that biblical Greek is a distinct dialect within the larger world of *koine*, but focuses on these corpora because it recognizes the particular interest they generate. Research into the broader evidence of the period, including epigraphical and inscriptional materials, is welcome in the series, provided the results are cast in terms of their bearing on biblical Greek. Primarily, however, the series is devoted to fresh philological, syntactical, text-critical, and linguistic study of the Greek of the biblical books, with the subsidiary aim of displaying the contribution of such study to accurate exegesis.

For additional information about this series or for the submission of manuscripts, please contact:

editorial@peterlang.com

To order books, please contact our Customer Service Department at:

peterlang@presswarehouse.com (within the U.S.)
orders@peterlang.com (outside the U.S.)

Or browse online at WWW.PETERLANG.COM